Changing Times

Changing Times

Work and Leisure in Postindustrial Society

JONATHAN GERSHUNY

OXFORD
UNIVERSITY PRESS

OXFORD
UNIVERSITY PRESS

Great Clarendon Street, Oxford OX2 6DP

Oxford University Press is a department of the University of Oxford.
It furthers the University's objective of excellence in research, scholarship,
and education by publishing worldwide in

Oxford New York

Athens Auckland Bangkok Bogotá Bombay Buenos Aires
Calcutta Cape Town Dar es Salaam Delhi Florence Hong Kong Istanbul
Karachi Kuala Lumpur Madras Madrid Melbourne Mexico City Mumbai
Nairobi Paris São Paulo Shanghai Singapore Taipei Tokyo Toronto Warsaw

with associated companies in Berlin Ibadan

Oxford is a registered trade mark of Oxford University Press
in the UK and in certain other countries

Published in the United States
by Oxford University Press Inc., New York

© Jonathan Gershuny, 2000

British Library Cataloguing in Publication Data
Data available

Library of Congress Cataloging-in-Publication Data
Gershuny, Jonathan.
Changing times : work and leisure in postindustrial society / Jonathan Gershuny.
p. cm.
Includes bibliographical references and index.
1. Economics—Sociological aspects.   2. Work—Sociological aspects.
3. Leisure—Sociological aspects.   4. Time—Sociological aspecs.   I. Title
HM548 .G47 2000 306.3′6—dc21 00–032362

ISBN 0–19–828787–9

10 9 8 7 6 5 4 3 2 1

Typeset by Kolam Information Services Pvt, Ltd, Pondicherry, India
Printed in Great Britain
on acid-free paper by
T.J. International Ltd.,
Padstow, Cornwall

Acknowledgements

I must express my thanks to the three sponsors who have financed this work over a very extended period. First to the Joseph Rowntree Foundation, for whom what follows constituted just *one part* of the projected work that they supported in the mid-1980s; I have now returned to work on social innovation and the impact of IT, which also formed part of that even more over-ambitious project. Then to the European Foundation for the Improvement of Living and Working Conditions, which funded much of the early part of the international time diary-data collection, and also the preparation of the previous draft of this book in 1991. And then to the ESRC for supporting work on the Time-Use Diary Archive during 1992, and for providing me with occasional opportunities for continuing this work inside the Institute for Social and Economic Research at Essex University.

Thanks also go to many friends and colleagues: to Graham Thomas, Sally Jones, and Patrick Baert, who at various points acted as research assistants; to Ian Miles, Anthony Heath, Duncan Gallie, Ray Pahl, Oriel Sullivan, Nick Buck, with whom I have discussed much of what follows, to my great benefit; and to Kimberly Fisher and Anne Gauthier, both currently working on the data, who warned me of pitfalls in the latest version of the time-use dataset. Sally Jones, Anne Gauthier, and Kimberly Fisher are also joint authors of Appendix 2.

I have been tempted to blame the enormous delay since the 1992 draft of this text, on my (then, new) VC at Essex, Ron Johnston, who told me in spring of 1993, that if I spent the summer in Oxford working on this book I'd have no Research Centre to come to in Essex in the autumn. But in retrospect I realize that while the draft I was working on then undoubtedly contained, somewhere within a rather cluttered text, some new thoughts and findings, I was at that time not quite so sure exactly what or which these were; my work in revising the text over the last few months has been a search within that mostly unexcavated block of rather intractable stone to discover at least the general shape of the hidden statue. What precipitated the production of this draft were some increasingly insistent questions, from friends (and others less kindly inclined) about what exactly it was I had been doing about time, for all these years, and also a very welcome though all too brief study leave in the early summer months of 1999 (authorized by my new new VC Ivor Crewe—to whom, my thanks, as well as to my old one for delaying me until I knew at least approximately what it was that I wanted to write).

But there have also been two distinct institutional developments that meant that this work had to be completed during 1999. The first is the imminent arrival of a tranche of new datasets, including the new Eurostat cross-national comparative time-use study, in the field during 1999 and 2000, which will provide new material on more than twenty countries, and, in addition to the British contribution to the Eurostat study (jointly financed by the UK Office of National Statistics and the ESRC), also a new British time-use diary-based household panel study, financed by British Telecom. The discussions in the text that follows are intended to contribute to the study of this unprecedented wealth of new time-diary materials.

The second new development, rather more parochial, is a broadening of the responsibility for the continuation of the special time-use data collection on which this book is based. The Multinational Time-Use Data Archive has acquired two additional joint Directors, Andrew Harvey, of St Mary's University, Newfoundland, Canada, and Duncan Ironmonger of the University of Sydney, Australia, who will collaborate in a Multinational Time-Use Study based jointly at their two institutions as well as at the Institute for Social and Economic Research at Essex University: a collaborative project with bases in three continents!

Times are changing for time-use research. I remember in the mid-1980s, discussing the future of cross-national comparative time-use research with John Robinson, the originator of much of the US material used in this book, and the person who introduced me to time-diary research. Our view at that time was that the expense, and the rather esoteric nature of the work, meant that never again would there be a research opportunity like that afforded by the UNESCO multinational comparative time-use research project Alexander Szalai in the 1960s. Now, with so many of the countries of the developed world collecting new time-diary studies at the end of the 1990s, many of them to a standardized design (a process overseen, if often rather reluctantly, by Eurostat in Luxembourg), which will become available in the first few years of the new century, *and* the very considerable heritage of older studies discussed in what follows, that time seems to have come again.

Finally, amidst these colleagues and institutions, I must give pride of place to Sarah and Asher Gershuny, who tolerated my absence from home, and to Esther Gershuny who also cared for them while I was gone, in both cases on the condition that I finally and actually got this *written* while I was away.

Jonathan Gershuny

Iraklion, Crete and Opatje, Croatia
May–July 1999

Contents

1. **An Introduction, and a First Summary**   I
   1. *Accounting for change in social and economic structure*   I
   2. *The three convergences*   4
   3. *Why the regularities?*   8
   4. *Time-use theory and time-use evidence*   II
   5. *A cross-national comparative time-use dataset*   13

2. **Work and Leisure: Historical Change in the Conditions
   of Life**   16
   1. *Bloomsday: the extraordinary significance of the mundane*   16
   2. *Time and development*   19
   3. *The interdependence of production and consumption time*   21
   4. *The logic of progress*   28
   5. *High- and low-value services, production, and consumption*   33

3. **Are We Running Out of Time?**   46
   1. *Two views of leisure and development*   46
   2. *A current thesis: the end of leisure*   50
   3. *Antithesis: growth and leisure*   58
   4. *Synthesis: a changing class distribution of leisure time?*   69

4. **The Individual's and the Society's Day: Micro- and
   Macro-Theories of Time Use**   76
   1. *Preliminary remarks*   76
   2. *Determining daily events: microsequential theory*   84
   3. *Allocating time: micro-aggregate theory*   93
   4. *Balancing time: macro-theory*   97
   5. *A summary*   100

5. **The History and Future of Time Use: Empirical Evidence**   105
   1. *A multinational longitudinal time-diary data collection*   105
   2. *Economic development and change in work and leisure time*   110
   3. *Behavioural vs. structural change*   117
   4. *The work–leisure balance*   131

6. **Explaining Time Use**   137
    1. *National differences and historical change*   137
    2. *The elements of the models*   141
    3. *Decomposing variance*   150
    4. *Conclusions*   157

7. **A Concise Atlas of Time Use: Twenty Countries,
   Thirty-three Years' Change**   160
    1. *The principle of the conservation of the day*   160
    2. *Four sorts of time use*   171
    3. *A whole-world summary: the virtuous triangle revisited*   219

8. **Time-Use Models of Economic Development**   222
    1. *Three final models*   222
    2. *An empirical estimation*   223
    3. *Welfare and change in time allocation: the UK case*   229
    4. *Time use and welfare: the nature of social improvement*   231
    5. *Technological innovation and change in a society's time budget: a
       two-class, two-good demonstration*   236

9. **Humane Modernization**   242
    1. *Time use and 'progress'*   242
    2. *Public policy for humane modernization*   243
    3. *Liberty, equality—or fraternity*   247

Appendix 1. **Telling the Time: Some Reflections on Time-Diary
Methodology**   249
    1. *Estimating time use: two experiments*   249
    2. *Narratives: telling the day*   253
    3. *Constructing the diary*   255

Appendix 2. **A Longitudinal, Multinational Collection of
Time-Use Data—the MTUS**
(by Jonathan Gershuny, Kimberly Fisher, Anne Gauthier,
Sally Jones, and Patrick Baert)   270
    1. *The MTUS project*   270
    2. *Methodological choices in time-budget research*   272
    3. *A summary codebook for WORLD 5.5*   287

References   289

Index   295

1 An Introduction, and a First Summary

1. Accounting for change in social and economic structure

This book is about what we all do for a living, and for other people's livings. Our work is more than just what we do in our jobs, it is also what we do without pay, in our households, for our families, and for members of the wider community. And what we do for other people's livings is, that we use *our* non-work time, to consume the products of *their* work.

Each of these activities—the paid work, the unpaid work, and the consumption—is a distinct category of time use. So if we can measure how the members of a society spend their time, we have the elements of a certain sort of account of how that society works. And if we can make these sorts of measurements repeatedly, at different stages in the history of a society, then we will have the basis for a developmental account of social and economic change.

Social scientists have been attempting to construct social and economic developmental accounts for several centuries at least. This is a challenging research field. It is particularly difficult to do because the categories for such accounts do not—in principle cannot—exist prior to the first formulations of the accounts themselves, so there is no prior evidence of the size or extent of these categories. An example is found in an essay by the nineteenth-century British civil servant Robert Giffen (1904). The rates of growth of the farms and the mines and the manufacturing staples were falling, and yet the income tax receipts were buoyant, and people generally felt good about the economy: what could be going on? One of the possible answers, he told the annual meeting of the British Association for the Advancement of Science in 1887, was perhaps hinted at in the returns to the decennial census, which had since 1851 given a description of the occupations of all household members. If one looked at this evidence very carefully and in the right way, one could just dimly make out a regular increase in the numbers of people engaged in what he called 'incorporeal functions'—people who did not produce material objects, but immaterial 'services' (though Giffen himself did not employ this particular word, he had in effect discovered the 'service sector').

Perhaps, he speculated, it was because the nation's production took ever more largely this incorporeal form, that it continued to boom despite the failure of the industrial staples. Services did not impinge on economists' consciousness as a matter of national economic importance at this time, which was of course the point of Giffen's lecture (indeed Adam Smith had asserted more than a century before that these were 'unproductive'); there were no measures of service consumption, and there was certainly no established notion of a 'service sector'. Nevertheless, the category was needed, it had to be invented. And once a category exists, the statistics are collected and routinely organized by it, the world becomes to a degree a less puzzling place.

This was the sort of challenge faced in the middle of this century by the pioneers of the systems of National Accounts. Clark and Fourastie had to invent the categories, and then amass and rearrange the available statistics, so as to put some substance into their accounts of the development of modern economies. Rostow's account of 'stages' of economic growth, which seems so obvious to us now, had its impact then precisely because nobody had previously thought to put together the statistics of industrial production in that particular way.

We now have, as a descendant of this pioneering activity, the System of National Accounts. We have standard classifications for industries and for occupations, and ways of classifying national expenditure, and means of tying these all together neatly into comprehensive accounts of how our economies operate, and how they develop. Done and dusted.

And yet, and yet it is only tidy if we shut our minds to what does not fit. Take all that work we do that is *not in* the national accounts. This problem, and the economic category, was dismissed years ago as the 'housekeeper paradox'. *So* the widowed clergyman marries his house-keeper, and what was waged labour and inside the national accounts, now becomes unpaid labour and the National Product is diminished. We can live with that, said our National Income accountant colleagues, and so indeed we could. But if we do ignore, in our accounts of economic activity, what is going on outside 'the production boundary', then we are likely to miss what is changing, perhaps changing fastest, perhaps providing the dynamism (or the intolerable pressures) that leads to economic and social change . . . just as Giffen claimed when his colleagues excluded the 'unpro-ductive' service sector from their accounts of the Victorian economy.

Take the transport industry: half a million people, in mid-twentieth-century Britain, working on trains and buses to move 50 million people across the landscape. In little more than a quarter of a century, nine-tenths of that work disappeared. Where did it go to? Did we stop moving? What happened, of course, was that the technology changed, and instead of buying 'final transport services'—and employing all those transport work-ers—we now buy goods (cars), and materials (petrol), and intermediate services (running repairs and 'services'), and then we produce the transport services ourselves, by driving the cars. So while that particular activity, the provision of final transport services, may have disappeared from the national accounts, it has gone somewhere else: into the time budgets of private households. We *can* live with that but it is nevertheless an important fact that looms large, for example, in the lives of those busy people who, in the absence of a substantial public transport system must devote a substantial part of their weekends to transporting children and elderly relatives across the landscape.

Or take an example, not from the past but from the future. Roughly one-third of us now have computers in our homes. We may not yet be quite sure what to do with them, but each year, as this new domestic technology gets tied into a global communications technology, new uses emerge. This year: shopping. I buy a subscription to the service, I connect with my local supermarket, and in ten minutes I've made my order, which is delivered later in the day. In this case, half an hour of shopping time has been taken *out of my own time budget*, and, instead of the mysterious mid-century disappearance of transport jobs, we have a mysterious end-of-century *appearance of new sorts of service jobs*—computer programmers, delivery drivers—in the retail sector.

Or, to take another tack entirely, our economies may be booming but we're all feeling more miserable. And when we latter-day Giffens search through the evidence for an explanation, we come up ultimately with the proposition that it is to do with time pressure, not just from our jobs but from all the other things we now have to do to get by—in fact quite often, things that 'mysteriously disappeared' out of the activities included in the national product, and just as mysteriously reappeared in the time budgets of private households. We can live with that.

Or, consider the distributional implications: who is it, exactly, that does these new things that appear in the household's time budget? When the laundry service disappeared, and we bought a washing machine, who had to work that machine at home? We will discuss, later in this book, why this should be, but for the moment let us accept what we do not really need high quality time-use research to tell us: that it is likely to have been the woman of the household and not the man. And yet (as a result of changes not unconnected with what we have already said) she is now also more likely to have a job than she was in mid-century, when she could have called on the laundry service. So the jobs, paid and unpaid, cumulate on women. And yet only the paid jobs appear in the National Accounts.

Of course ultimately we *can't* live with that. If what is changing in our economic life, if what causes stress and unhappiness, and increases inequality (not just, as we shall see, by gender, but also between different social groups), is simply absent from the official accounts of the economy, so there must be pressures for new and more inclusive sorts of socio-economic accounts that give proper names and shapes and sizes to the things that trouble us but are officially and statistically invisible. And these pressures are now producing positive consequences. Committees of various international bodies are now drafting guidelines for extensions to the National Accounts 'production boundary' to include some sorts of unpaid work, and to define and account for 'the informal economy'. Most nations of the world (following the 1995 Peking Declaration of the World Congress of Women) have bound themselves to produce such extended national accounts. And as virtually the sole evidential basis for constructing these extended accounts is the sort of time-use evidence that is discussed at length in this book, so, each year, more national statistical agencies are commissioning new time-diary studies.

My intention in what follows, however, is distinct from (though parallel to) the goal of an 'extended' national income account, including various sorts of unpaid work but denominated in money terms. My objective is at once more general and more limited (in so far as I am less concerned with the business of placing money values on unpaid work): to piece together, for developed countries, a comprehensive account that covers all daily activities, paid work, unpaid work, leisure or consumption time, and sleep. The reason for doing this is a line of sociological and economic argument, pursued through the book (and summarized very briefly later in this chapter), that draws attention to the importance of the interdependencies among the paid work time and the unpaid work time and the consumption time, in establishing the social-structural balance, and indeed the level of economic activity in the society as a whole. In short (holding international trade as a constant, and thinking of 'social groups' as constituted by occupational categories): *it is the consumption activities of the social groups in aggregate—the set of particular things we spend our consumption time doing—that provide the demand for the employment of each of the social groups*.

I aim to produce a historical account of how time-use patterns have changed, in the developed world, over the last third of a century, and to relate these changes in the pattern of daily life as a whole, to the development of that restricted part of our economic life that is conventionally described as 'the economy'.

2. The three convergences

What follows is not a description of 'stages' of time use in the Rostow sense, since what I describe is not a *necessary* sequence. And though, as we will see, *some* aspects of what happens *are* best described in terms of a developmental sequence, there is also some basis for thinking that there are some effects of choices of national policy, as well as some strictly historical effects, in the sense of things that seem to happen simultaneously across countries, as a reflection of the era and not of the particular country's state of development.

I start, in this section, by setting out rather baldly what seems to have been happening to time-use patterns in the developed world in the last third of the twentieth century, and then turn, in the next section, to provide a preliminary version of an explanation of this.

What we will see are *three convergences* in time-use patterns: by nation, gender, and 'class' (though strictly, what we will be discussing is not class at all but merely the position of individuals, or their households, in a system of social stratification or differentiation).

As an expositional device, consider the triangle graph, which allows us to plot three categories simultaneously. We are considering three different sorts of time use: paid work, unpaid work, and leisure or consumption time. There is a fourth, from this point of view a residual category, sleep, which we shall see is, for any social group, to within very few minutes per day a constant over historical time. So without any loss of information, we can express the first three categories in terms of proportions of the waking day, and then plot change in time-use patterns within the triangle. The three apexes of the triangle represent respectively, time spent entirely in unpaid work (bottom left), time spent entirely in paid work (top), and time spent entirely in unpaid work activities (bottom right). Within the triangle, a historical sequence of points that shifts upwards, denotes an increase in leisure time over the period (and since sleep is effectively a constant, this means an *absolute* increase); a shift to the left denotes a proportional increase in unpaid work relative to paid (if this is parallel or downwards-pointing then there is also an increase in absolute terms); and a shift to the right means that an increasing proportion of the work is paid work.

The cross-national longitudinal time-use data (described briefly in Section 4 of this chapter, and at greater length at various points in the book, and particularly in the appendices) displays three distinct historical trends.

The first (illustrated in a somewhat exaggerated form in Figure 1.1; less schematic versions of this and the following two figures will be found at the ends of Chapter 5 and 7) is the *national convergence*. We find over the developed countries in the latter half of the twentieth century there appears to be an approximately constant balance between the totals of paid and unpaid work in a society (generally around 55 per cent paid, 45 per cent). The twenty countries we shall be discussing in this book show overall a general increase in leisure (i.e. a decline in the total of paid plus unpaid work), though some of the richer countries, towards the end of the century, show a small decline in leisure time (we will return in a moment to consider whether it is in fact their wealth, or something else, that leads this to happen). Overall, however, this means convergence towards somewhere just to the right of the centre of the triangle.

We also see, without exception in every country for which we have the evidence, a *gender convergence*. Women, in each country, and throughout the period, do on average much more domestic work and much less paid work,

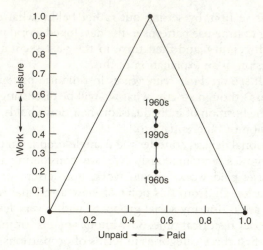

Figure 1.1. Convergence by nation

than men, and the majority of men's work is certainly paid work, so the women's plots will always be found to the left-hand side of the triangle, the men's, to the right. And generally the total balances of work versus leisure, for men and women, in any country and at any point in history, are approximately the same. But over time the balances change. The women come to do absolutely more paid, and absolutely less unpaid work. The men do generally less paid and increase their unpaid. So the trends, for the sexes, are clearly convergent, as in Figure 1.2

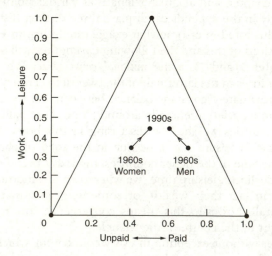

Figure 1.2. Convergence by gender

And slightly more complex, for each sex, over this historical period, we see something like a *convergence* in time use across the different *status groups*. In the 1960s, the higher status (in this example, better-educated) women had substantially more paid work than the lower status; they also had a lot less unpaid work, so overall they had more leisure time. As we move towards the end of the century, we find that for both groups, unpaid work declines substantially—but the decline is larger for the lower status women. Both groups increase their paid work by about the same amount. The consequence is, that by the end of the period, the lower-status women have less work in total, more leisure time than the higher. At the beginning of the period the higher-status men had less of both paid and unpaid work. Paid work time over the second half of the century declined for both groups of men, but more so for the low status than for the high. And unpaid work increased for both, but again, more of an increase for the high status than the low: the overall result is that while higher-status men had less work in total, more leisure, than those with lower social status at the start of the period, by the end of it, higher-status men, like higher-status women, had less leisure time. There is thus an overall convergence in time use between the groups, with more leisure time overall. But an alternative summary of the changes is: *a reversal of the previous status–leisure gradient.* Those of higher status previously had more leisure, and subsequently had less of it, than those of lower social status.

These are the general facts, somewhat though not excessively simplified, which this book establishes, discusses, and speculates upon. Why do these things happen?

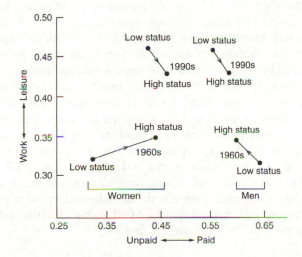

Figure 1.3. Convergence by status group

3. Why the regularities?

These summary trends, as they are stated here, should raise, in the minds of readers, more questions than they answer. There are questions about the composition of the changes. Is, for example, the increase in women's paid work a result of a growth in working hours for those in employment, or is it just a result of an increase in rates of women's employment? Is the decline in men's paid work hours just a result of general increases in male unemployment rates through the last third of the century? There are questions about the detail of the time-use activity categories. Do men *really* do more domestic work, is the growth in their contribution to unpaid work, so-called, really just messing about with their cars or in their gardens? And, equivalently, do women *really* do less cooking and cleaning? There are questions about the evidence: how can we *really* establish how much work and leisure really goes on? Each of these sorts of questions, and more, are discussed at some length in the chapters that follow.

But for the moment let us put these sorts of issue aside, and instead, take the trends as stated at their simplest face value, and consider why they might occur.

(i) *A leisure preference?*   Just about the simplest approach to understanding the general decline in work time is the assertion of a diminishing marginal utility of income: that each increment of real benefit we gain from getting richer, gets smaller. Perhaps our wants are saturated, so that the growing productivity of societies means that we need to work less. However as we will see in later chapters, it is difficult to maintain this view in any strong form, because there are so many alternative ways of taking free time. In particular it might be rational for high-wage earners to work longer hours in order to buy more intensely pleasurable consumption experiences. A radical alternative explanation, advanced at some length in the next chapter, is that there might not be an individual microlevel explanation, but instead a macrolevel answer. Perhaps it is not so much a leisure preference as a consumption-time requirement: a society may *need* more leisure time to consume its growing product in—or indeed *use* more leisure time, in a manner that sounds paradoxical but is not, to stimulate the consumption that provides more jobs. (This particular view has some connections also with the political points made at the end of this section.) As for why, in some countries, we may find leisure time decreasing: this may reflect a change in the relationship between work time and social status (see (iii) below) and it may also have something to do with alternative national styles for the regulation of time use (see (iv) below).

(ii) *A pressure for gender equality?*   There is a strong feminist position which holds that the patriarchal nature of Western societies means that gender inequity will be endemic, and that this will show up in working hours as in much else: it must straight away be said that this is simply not borne out in terms of work- and leisure-time totals which really do seem generally similar between men and women in each country. However: (a) we will encounter evidence of the 'dual burden' phenomenon in which full-time employed women with heavy family responsibilities have a substantially greater total of paid and unpaid work than their equivalently employed partners; and (b) the general phenomenon of women's proportional special-ization in unpaid work (that is, they have the same work totals as their partners but do less paid work) may still leave women disadvantaged, since as a result they gain less work experience, they form less 'employment-related human capital'. So why do we still find the evidence of convergence? It may be that there is, in open societies, which are the great majority of the cases we discuss in this book, a *strain to fairness*. The dual burden *is* unfair, and wives placed in this position will say this to their husbands, and perhaps as a result the husbands will change their behaviour—or perhaps they won't, and as a result the wives will leave their husbands. But, as we shall see, the convergence, such as it is, is still very incomplete: these sorts of time-use change processes take time, on the scale of generations rather than decades.

(iii) *The end of the leisure class?*   We have already suggested one possible answer to the question of why we see the status–leisure convergence or reversal: high earners may choose intensively enjoyable activities and work longer to pay for them. I must say I find this line of explanation implausible as a general answer (though a possible explanation for particular cases). A quite different sociological argument is that we are now seeing a reversal of the 'leisure class' phenomenon: once leisure signified high status, but no longer, now the most important people are the busiest, so, runs the argument, we now demonstrate our status by our lack of leisure. This is surely however more of a description than an explanation; but suppose that the higher-status jobs are also the most demanding, and interesting—often these jobs are now pretty much identical in content to what the leisure class used to do *as* their leisure (not just well-paid legislators and sportsmen, but also the not-so-well-paid social workers and academics)—might we then not choose to work hard at them, and for relatively long hours, precisely because they provide an alternative source of the sorts of intrinsic benefits that might otherwise come from leisure activities?

(iv) *A global model of time allocation?*   All three of the trends may have some relation to 'globalization'—but this means at least three distinct things in this context. First, there is a *technological globalization* in the narrow sense of a worldwide diffusion of particular technical solutions to particular pro-blems of daily life. Global markets mean that the same products are available everywhere, and there must be, to some extent, a standard way of using a walkman or a car or a refrigerator. And even if there is no strictly technological determinism, the *second* meaning of globalization, the *global cultural diffusion* of a common model of consumption, might serve as an alternative. Global media penetration means that there is everywhere a standard (i.e. mostly US) picture of how these technologies might be used, and by whom. The evidence—to get somewhat ahead of the discussion in this chapter—used throughout this book comes from diaries of daily life kept by people from across the developed world. It is striking how similar, from country to country, these documents prove to be. This observation might support either the first or second of these globalization arguments, since not just the television programmes, but also much of the technology itself, came first from the USA. The third sense of the term is *economic globalization*. The fact of a world economy, with free trade and unrestricted capital movements, places ever-increasing restrictions on the range of social and economic policies available to national governments. In fact, during the middle of the period—the late 1970s and early 1980s—covered by this book, there were some real cross-national differences within the developed world, at the least between the sorts of economic policies followed by Thatcher and Reagan, and those of the core members of the European Union, with strongly contrasting impacts for social policy, and implications for time use. We might think of relatively long free-market Thatcherite work hours, as a contrast to the short 'Social Charter' European ones. But now, the growing influence of 'Chicago' economic policies even in Europe, paradoxically emerging as a consequence of the euro, may mean more convergence— and less leisure—in the future.

And here we may step for a moment well beyond the evidence, and go back to the arguments in the previous section. The point of trying to understand what is troubling about the world, is to change it. There are, among the resources available to modern States, what we might think of as 'time-use policies': not just the short-term provision of maximum working hours and statutory holiday entitlements, the provision of ungendered parental leave and gender-blind tax and benefit policies, but also longer-term policies, for the provision of cultural and sporting and other leisure infrastructures, and the focusing of educational systems on the formation of the skills necessary for varied and enjoyable leisure as well as productive work. There is a political agenda that underlies everything that is written here, something positive to set against the excesses of unconstrained Wild-West capitalism. The appropriate deployment of these time-use policies, which would at the margin provide some sort of steer to future trends of the sort described in the previous section (and indeed has to some extent in the past successfully done so within the core of the European Union), might both support future economic growth (by promoting the sorts of leisure consumption that also provides good jobs), and lead to less time-stressed and pressured, less unequal, and happier societies.

4. Time-use theory and time-use evidence

The first part of the book sets out some theory, and discusses some aspects of the social science literature on the use of time. Chapter 2 lays out in a rather general way the elements of the political economy of time use. It presents two key ideas:

(1) *Chains of provision.*   We can think of society's time as organized into a number of systematically linked sets of paid work, unpaid work, and leisure or consumption time, each of which go together to satisfy some particular category of *want*. Some social time goes into growing the oats (and all the preceding agricultural investment and other preliminaries, and the subsequent related manufacturing and retail activity), some more of the society's time goes in the shopping and the cooking, and finally, yet more of the society's time is spent eating the porridge; all to satisfy the 'want' for breakfast. These chains of associated categories of time use might be constructed at varying levels of detail (e.g. 'all recreational activities' vs. 'musical consumption') and any particular want may be associated with alternative 'modes of provision' (e.g. going to a symphony concert vs. watching a music video at home). But in general the concept of 'chains of provision' is a means of organizing a comprehensive account of a society's use of time over a period (just as, on a more restricted scale, categories of final demand may be used as a means of organizing a comprehensive 'input–output' account of a society's economic production).

(2) *Alternative time-use regimes.*   Different societies organize themselves to provide for wants in differing proportions, and through different combinations of modes of provision. Poorer or 'less developed' societies may concentrate proportionately more of their time on providing for basic wants, food and shelter, while richer societies concentrate a larger proportion on more luxurious recreational wants. And at any given level of development, and constrained by the current technology and availability of capital, and the society's culture and traditions, there may be different balances in the manner of provision for these wants (so some societies may tip the 'modal split' in provision for transport wants towards public transport services, others, towards the private car). The political systems influence these balances through the particular mix of particular regulations and subsidies (the 'time-use regime') they place on, and offer to, those who engage in the various activities. The regime thus ultimately determines the patterns of stratification and differentiation in the society, through its

influence on the numbers of paid jobs and the proportions of these that require different levels of skill (and hence earn different wage rates), on how much unpaid work there is and who does it (this is affected by working-time and other family-policy regulation), and on who gets how much leisure time, involving which sorts of consumption (which is affected by both the paid work and the unpaid work distributions).

Chapter 2 therefore concludes with a discussion of two 'ideal types' of time-use regime, which lead in turn to two distinct alternative forms of service economy: the liberal market regime, which operates according to the 'trickle down' principle in which 'the rich get richer and employ the poor', characterized by high levels of social stratification and differentiation, and a social democratic regime in which different groups, each with high levels of specific sorts of 'human capital', purchase different sorts of service from each other (and provide those residual unautomated services that require low levels of human capital for themselves, through their own unpaid work).

Chapter 3 looks in particular at the debate on the relationship between time-scarcity and economic development. It presents the two contrary theses, that, in one view, work diminishes with economic development, leading ultimately to a 'leisure society', or that, in the directly contrasting view, work progressively increases, and indeed leisure time itself becomes less leisurely. I suggest that the reversal of the historic relationship between social status and work time (noted in the previous section) means that those who read and those who write about these matters misinterpret what has happened in their particular professions as a change in society as a whole. (And of course the issue is confused further, by the sorts of 'life-stage effect' in which individuals personally get progressively busier throughout their working lives, and also by the fact that the sorts of jobs done by the busiest people often have some leisure-like quality.)

And then Chapter 4 brings together various lines of micro- and macro-time-use theory from the economic and sociological literatures. The two key ideas here are the two constraints, 'micro' and 'macro' on the aggregate time balance.

The micro constraint is in fact no more than that commonplace of microeconomics, that individuals have a choice between working longer hours, earning more money—but then as a consequence they have less time to spend it in, and must therefore find intensively enjoyable consumption patterns—or working shorter hours, earning less money in total, but with more time to spend it, and can thus opt for more extensively enjoyable leisure activities.

What is rather less familiar is the vitally important macroimplication of this: the goods and services that each individual combines with his or her consumption and unpaid work time *embody the paid work time of other people*. A given pattern of time use outside the economy implies a given pattern of paid work time use within the economy. So alongside the individuals' microbalances, is another, collective, macrosocial time balance. Particular patterns of consumption and domestic work are inextricably associated with particular distributions of high and low human-capital paid work. This allows us to derive a simple-sounding theorem, to the effect that, with *n* commodities, and *n* groups of workers producing these, then knowing just the time devoted to the *consumption* of *n*−1 of these commodities, *the entire pattern of time use, leisure, and work, of the society is determined.*

And then there are three empirical chapters organized so as to deal with the question about the dataset that I find most worrying: given the rather disparate nature of the sample of national samples that it consists of, is it appropriate to treat the dataset as *a* dataset, rather than as *a set of* datasets? I deal with the problem straightforwardly by doing both of these things, and comparing the answers. First, in Chapter 5, I look, country by country, at the trends that emerge, and attempt to establish a first picture of the patterns of change in the broad aggregated time-use categories. Then in Chapter 6, I look rather tentatively at the dataset as a whole, with the aim of discovering how much difference there really is between the countries, and between the historical trends within each of them (answer: not very much). Chapter 7 looks, comprehensively and at some length, at a more detailed activity classification, moving backwards and forwards between the aggregated dataset and the individual country data, with the aim of ensuring that the big picture that emerges from the aggregated evidence remains consistent with that from the individual countries. The very brief summary of trends set out earlier in this chapter is one outcome of this process.

Finally Chapter 8 discusses the valuation of time, and moves forward from the development of accounts of change in time use to the development of a system of social time-use accounts which, denominated in time units, works as a more general parallel to the money-based National Accounts. It returns to the simple theorem proposed in Chapter 4, and proposes a powerful if obvious lemma: *the richest sort of society must be that whose pattern of consumption time implies the maximum proportion of high human-capital paid work*—a proposition with obvious implications for the choice among alternative time-use regimes.

5. A cross-national comparative time-use dataset

There is a brief, but somewhat more technical description of how the dataset was put together at the beginning of Chapter 5, and a fuller description in Appendix 2. But just to get us going consider Table 1.1, which shows the component surveys of the multinational longitudinal dataset used here. There are thirty-five separate surveys, from twenty different countries, and 120,000 respondents in all.

What these surveys have in common is the use of a 'diary' methodology. They consist of sequential accounts of all the activities of a day—or in the case of the Netherlands and the first three UK studies, seven consecutive days (so these countries contribute more than 50,000 days of evidence to the total—giving more than 175,000 days in all). For the analysis in this book I have taken just respondents of 'core working age' (20–59), and the days have been reweighted to make the samples representative of the national population and of the days of the week. And the surveys have been further reweighted to ensure that each country or each survey (as appropriate to the particular analysis), only contributes one-twentieth, or one thirty-fifth, of the evidence for any particular result. The activity classifications have been recoded for comparability, and there is also a small number of common classificatory variables (age, sex, family and employment status, educational attainment, and some others).

It certainly cannot be said to be a random sample of surveys, though it is a haphazard one. I started with some of the surveys collected by Alexander Szalai and his colleagues in the first ever comparative cross-sectional time-diary study carried out for UNESCO in the mid-1960s, added a 1961 sample of UK diaries discovered in the basement of the BBC Audience Research

Table 1.1. The cross-national longitudinal time-use dataset

	1961–70	1971–7	1978–82	1983–90	1990–
Canada	1,828	1,845	8,138	6,351	
Denmark	2,365			2,389	
France	2,898	4,633			
Netherlands		960	2,161	2,348	
Norway		4,309	3,410		
UK	1,702	1,901		1,996	1,211
USA	1,790	1,753		2,268	
Hungary	1,989	4,663			
West Germany	2,137				
Poland	2,863				
Belgium	1,938				
Bulgaria	14,834				
Czechoslovakia	1,668				
East Germany	1,550				
Yugoslavia	2,227				
Finland			8,309	10,277	
Italy (Turin)			2,116		
Australia		1,276			
Israel				3,126	
Sweden				6,178	
Total no. of cases				121,407	

Department in London, and further surveys were joined, one by one, as I persuaded friends and colleagues from across the world to release them to me. There are already a number of newer 1990s surveys (Austria, Italy, Germany, the Netherlands) that have been made available and are in process of preparation. And the whole of the still growing collection will be available to researchers who follow. It is undoubtedly, as yet, thin evidence on which to base a picture of the way the world is changing. But, as was said at the beginning of this chapter, we have to start somewhere.

2 Work and Leisure: Historical Change in the Conditions of Life

1. Bloomsday: the extraordinary significance of the mundane

He gets up early in the morning, buys kidneys for his wife's breakfast at a nearby butcher's shop, and cooks them. He sets off across Dublin, calling first at his office (he sells advertising space), and then on various of his customers. He attends the funeral of an old friend, has an argument in a pub, makes a hospital visit, takes a walk to the seaside, later in the evening rescues an admired younger acquaintance from a potentially embarrassing situation. Then home and, rather late, to bed; his wife is already there though not asleep (she is thinking).

This is one very particular day for one man in a real city. Yet each day for each woman and man on this planet has the same essential structure. We wake up, we do some things, out of habit or duty or choice, for ourselves or for other people, for money or for pleasure or as an obligation. Then we go to bed.

If there is anything concrete in the social world, it is here, in our day-to-day activity. Indeed, in the sum of everybody's daily activity we have all of the objective part of social reality. There are grander abstractions that we use to simplify the great complexity of the world: economic structure, class, culture, exchange. But the reality of these is no more than various sorts of aggregates of the physical and mental events of the daily round.

Leopold Bloom's day (described in rather more detail in Joyce's *Ulysses*) is a good example of one of the ways that accounts of time use can be organized. Everybody's day has the same essential characteristics: a sequence of activities mixed in various proportions—so much paid work, so much domestic work or childcare, so much leisure. The particular order of things we do makes a certain sort of sense to us: these are the things we do to get through our day. We arrived at this particular pattern of activities today, in part through habit (this is what we usually do on this sort of day), and in part through calculation (this or that should somehow get squeezed in somewhere). These calculations reflect feelings of necessity or responsibility or obligation or preference, which may in turn and in part derive from how we think other people would act in our circumstances. There are also constraints and opportunities of time and space: the butcher's shop is open at particular times and is just so far away; we must arrive at our office at one given point in the day and not leave it before another. We are in general aware of how we have coped with the constraints and opportunities of our immediate environment, and our accounts of this constitute one sort of explanation of time use.

Molly Bloom's breakfast: chains of provision for human wants

Explanations of behaviour within this entirely personal and subjective frame are the normal province of microeconomics and microsociology. But they are not really sufficient explanations of either the causes or the consequences of behaviour. Leopold Bloom tells us in a subjective fashion how he as a separate being has coped with the given facts that surround him. Yet these given facts themselves have explanations. That Bloom is able to buy the kidneys just as St George's church clock strikes eight reflects the fact that the butcher arrived at his shop just before seven that June morning in 1904. Bloom's opportunity is the butcher's constraint. Or to make the point more generally, the butcher has a shop in that particular quarter of Dublin, so that people like Bloom can buy the constituents of their breakfasts and dinners, just as Bloom's job in the newspaper office may help to inform or persuade people of what food to buy and where to buy it.

An account of the individual's day, whether in the form of an activity sequence or of an overall distribution of time between activities, has the shortcoming that it ignores the consequential relationships between that individual's activities and those of other individuals. The society's use of time is explained by more than just the sum of individuals' accounts of their own use of time. We need also accounts which make connections between the various activities of different individuals. Consider, for example, Molly Bloom's breakfast.

Molly eats the kidneys, which Bloom shopped for, and then cooked and carried upstairs to the bedroom, which the pork-butcher had previously cleaned and prepared after with a knife that was originally manufactured, and so on. Molly's eating time, and Bloom's shopping and cooking time, and the work time of the pig-keeper and the butcher and the manufacturers of his steel knife, and a range of other activities all come together to constitute a particular small meal. These various consumption and production activities of various men and women are all connected in what we might call the 'chain of provision' for one woman's breakfast.

We need not for the moment be concerned with how to work out exactly how much of which sorts of whose time fits together into chains like this. (Later in this book we shall see how the money we spend on the things we use in our various activities may be translated via input–output matrices into their ultimate constituents of different sorts of labour.) All we need for the moment is to recognize that 'chains of provision'—linked sets of production and consumption activities denominated in terms of time—are an unfamiliar, but very powerful, way of organizing social accounts.

Two hundred thousand days

One day for one man. In this day we see a range of different sorts of economic activities. We see Bloom working for his wages, and we see a little of the substance of the work he is paid for. We see what he buys, and what he does with the things he buys. The detailed narrative description of Bloom's day reveals a fragment of an economy; every economy consists of an aggregation of days like Bloom's.

At the heart of the argument of this book are, as we have seen, records of nearly 200,000 such days, collected over nearly forty years in various developed countries. The book advances the proposition that a large part of the explanation for change in what we think of as economic and social structure emerges as we come to understand how people spend their time and why they do so. This is 'the significance of the mundane'.

Economic structure, in the sense of the grand aggregates of economic accounting, appears very distant from everyday life. The division of employment into the headings of the Standard Industrial Classification or the categories of the International Standard Classification of Occupations, the value-added by branches of industry, the national rate of unemployment: these all seem, and are treated by social science, as if they inhabit a different set of spatial and temporal dimensions from those in which we get up in the morning, cook breakfast, and go to work. And yet it is these very mundane activities that shape (and in turn are shaped by) economic structure. The butcher's meat, the frying pan, the hospital, the shops—the goods and services that we use in our daily lives—constitute in aggregate the society's final demand. The work that we set off to in the morning and return from at night is the labour that adds the value-added that constitutes the national product.

Diaries (and in particular the specially structured diaries used in time-budget surveys) are particularly good ways of establishing exactly how people live their lives. We ask individuals (or in the best surveys, whole households) to give their own narrative accounts of the sequences of activities which make up their days or weeks; from these accounts we can estimate the amounts of time spent in various consumption, domestic production, and waged labour activities (and also, though none of this will be found in what follows, we can use these materials to look at interdependencies, simultaneity, co-presence and absence, to gain a clear picture of how households function). Changes in these aggregates of time use can be used at the societal level to explain changes in economic structure (thus, for example, more free time out of waged work means more time spent in restaurants means more value-added in the catering sector and more employment for cooks and waiters). And as we come to understand the processes by which individuals' and households' time-use sequences are determined (and the ways that governments and firms and other corporate bodies influence these sequences), we then have a line of explanation that relates economic structural transformation to change in patterns of daily life.

The arguments that follow will show that change in the conventional economic structural variables may be accounted for in terms of lifestyle change—and, conversely, that patterns of daily life may be explained in terms of economic structure. They will outline the essential characteristics of a model of the interaction between change in lifestyle and change in economic structure.

All this may sound very academic, and far removed from matters of day-to-day economic management. But it has, on the contrary, the most practical of implications. It provides the necessary basis for understanding the process of the emergence of post-industrial societies, a picture of socio-economic change which is in some respects quite different from that found in the conventional social science literature.

2. Time and development

Change in time-use patterns is not a mere *indicator* of social change; it is itself part of the *essence* of socio-economic development. A 'poor' society is one which must devote the bulk of its time to low-value-added activities which go to satisfy 'basic' wants or needs. The work of such a society is largely concerned with the provision of food and energy supplies; its consumption is accordingly limited for the most part to eating and taking shelter from the elements. Economic development is the process in which the growing technical efficiency of provision for basic wants allows the society to shift its time progressively towards production and consumption activities relating to more sophisticated wants.

This is perhaps rather obvious in the case of technologically 'undeveloped' social groups (though there are somewhat contrary arguments, discussed in a later chapter, to the effect that economic development leads to a progressive loss of leisure). A similar description also holds for the further progress of already developed societies (see Chapter 8). Development means that, over a historical period, a given range of human wants may be satisfied through a smaller proportion of the society's total of time, in turn freeing time which may be devoted (in the form of work or leisure) to the satisfaction of new sorts of wants.

It is a commonplace observation that there is a regular pattern of structural change in the workforce throughout the developed world. We see, in every country without exception, an increase in the proportion of workers in jobs that require relatively high levels of professional or technical training, or of general literacy and numeracy; the 'service class' is increasing everywhere. And, a somewhat related phenomenon, the 'service sector' (i.e. that part of the economy which produces intangible commodities for other producers or for consumers) is also regularly increasing as a proportion of every national economy.

These cross-national regularities are well known. In the chapters that follow, we shall add some further multinational constancies that come along with these developments of the occupational and industrial structure—the 'three convergences' summarized briefly in the previous chapter—changes in patterns of work and consumption time which are intimately related, particularly (but not solely) to the growth of service sectors and occupations in developed societies, but which are much less familiar, and indeed have in the past been quite invisible, because of the absence of the data needed to expose them.

These time-use regularities are in fact, as should already have become clear, not *excessively* regular. There are variations and reversals in the trends (particularly in relation to the work–leisure balance), by country and by historical period, which may reflect differences in national regulatory patterns, and changes in international ones. So, going beyond the current evidence, we may foresee in the future, not one single type of service economy, but rather the emergence of a new sort of *multinational diversity* at the more detailed level of classification of time use, which might be conceptualized as a range of *alternative sorts of service or leisure economy*. These are distinguished by different distributions of paid employment (and hence different patterns of status differentiation), different sorts and distributions of unpaid work, and different characteristic leisure patterns. There is of course a great range of possible characteristics; in what follows we summarize this range through just two contrasting 'ideal types'—'social democratic' and 'liberal market' societies.

These various sorts of change in economic structure and time use all fit together systematically: the growth of the service class and the service sector, the (general but not invariable) growth of 'leisure' time, and the decline of status and gender differentiation by time use, are (as the following arguments will establish) all part of the same process, all part of the same logic of what might, unfashionably, in certain sociological quarters, be considered as economic and social *development*.

We will see cross-national constancies in the development process, but also some not-inconsiderable variations. For example, rather different patterns of evolution of leisure time emerge among the various countries, some increasing their time devoted to television, others with a decline in passive leisure at home, coupled with a growth of out-of-home leisure activities. These differences are as important as the similarities. Though there does seem to be a certain natural trajectory of development shared in all countries, there are no grounds for suggesting that there is any sort of 'hidden hand' pointing us to any single, inevitable, and optimal development path. The nature of the cross-national differences points both to the significance of historical and cultural differences, and to the importance of public policy in influencing the pattern of daily activities, patterns of consumption and production.

This final element in the picture that emerges from the time-based perspective is also part of the same logic. The argument derives quite straightforwardly from the notion of the 'chain of provision'. The consumption of advanced, industrialized societies is by value largely and increasingly services (even though the production of these services may involve more manufactured goods and industrial-type division of labour). The defining characteristic of service consumption is that it requires time from its consumers. And different sorts of service consumption are linked to different sorts of service work (including both employment and unpaid service production). If Molly Bloom took her breakfast at a café there would be more paid service production and employment, and Leopold Bloom would spend less time cooking at home (and have more time free to devote to other activities). It is here that the intimate and mundane facts of the quotidian merge with the grand aggregates of social structure: what we ourselves do in our non-work time, what we consume, is directly related to the quantity and the nature of work both for ourselves and for others. The various sorts of post-industrial service economies may be differentiated by the varying mixes of services they produce and consume.

The process discussed here is commonly referred to as 'economic' development. But this is a misleadingly limited term. Cultural change, change in habits and beliefs and values, is an integral part of the process. The developing society does not just engage in new forms of production, but also in new sorts of consumption. Its members do new things with their time, different sorts of leisure emerge (and also new sorts of activity which share some characteristics of leisure and some of work). New wants satisfied must mean new consumption habits, new beliefs about the propriety of particular courses of action, new scales of value against which to set the new commodities and the new patterns of behaviour.

3. The interdependence of production and consumption time

It may be helpful to readers to provide at this point a brief and simplified first view of the sort of picture of socio-economic development that emerges from our time-use accounts. Most of this book is devoted to the rather painstaking analysis of recent historical evidence of time use. But to dramatize—we start with an invented (or to be more precise, half-invented) example of development of time allocation in the imaginary island (i.e. non-trading) State of Arcadia between the 1480s and the 1980s.

Let us consider first the chain of activities associated with the provision of food in a period preceding the onset of major industrialization (Figure 2.1). In this mostly unmechanized era, we have a very large amount of human physical labour devoted to the business of preparing soil, planting, and harvesting. In this labour, a few implements are used—mostly of wood, a few with metal edges. So as part of the same chain of provision we have some carpenters (who cut and drag their own wood from the forests to their workshops) and some ironworkers who make the edged tools for the farmers and the carpenters. And we have some traders to carry the edged tools from the ironworkers to sell to the carpenters and the farmers (the traders use carts made by other ironworkers and carpenters), and other traders who buy a proportion of the farmers' food to store and sell to people in towns.

The food is preserved and prepared and cooked by the farmers' wives and townswomen (agricultural labour is not in general entirely sex-segregated but food preparation almost invariably is). They use wooden, clay, or iron implements (so we have in addition potters and yet more ironworkers and carpenters in this chain of provision). And finally the food is eaten.

Altogether the most natural way of summarizing this complex chain of activities is as different sorts of time use. We can say how much time, in the society as a whole, is spent in agricultural labour, and by carpenters and ironworkers and potters in the production of the implements used in the provision of food (of course these implements, though they are used, are not entirely *used up*, so we must only count that fraction of the embodied labour time representing the depreciation of the tools), and time spent by women (typically, in societies of this type) in the preservation and final

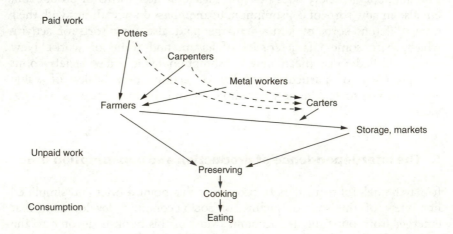

Figure 2.1. The chain of provision of food: pre-industrial activities

preparation of the food. And finally we can include the time spent eating. These are the various activities which lead to the satisfaction of nutritional needs in the society.

We do not have any good general statistics on time use in pre-industrial societies (we shall return briefly to this issue in a later chapter), but for the illustrative purposes of this preliminary discussion, we can invent some plausible numbers (Figure 2.2). Let us say that in this society, 70 per cent of the male adults in the population worked on the land for ten hours per day, six days per week, for nine months of the year. Say that a further 10 per cent of the male population worked similar hours in manufacturing and service activities associated with the provision for nutritional needs. Say 85 per cent of the female population worked four hours per day, seven days per week, throughout the year, on food preparation and cooking. Finally let us guess that adults devoted one and a half hours per day to eating and associated activities.

Consider the average day of the average adult in this society. Of its 1,440 minutes, and according to our guesses, 135 were devoted to agricultural labour, 20 to manufacturing and service activities ancillary to the provision of food, 100 to food preservation and preparation and cooking, 90 to food consumption. A total of 350 minutes, just under six hours, devoted to the satisfaction of nutritional needs; 25 per cent of the day, and assuming 500 minutes sleep, 37 per cent of the waking day.

We do not need to guess about the equivalent numbers for a modern society: in a later chapter, we shall see how to combine data from time-budget surveys with conventional economic statistics to produce reasonably precise estimates. We will see, for example, that in the mid-1980s in the UK, the equivalent total was about two hours and thirty-five minutes, made up of only 15 minutes agricultural and manufacturing labour, 65 minutes food preparation time, and 65 minutes consumption—15 per cent of the waking day. Let us take this as a model for time-use patterns in modern Arcadia.

		1780s	1980s
Paid work		(Minutes per ave. adult day)	
	Agriculture and menial services	138	8
	Manufacturing and sophisticated services	26	8
Unpaid work			
	Food preparation	100	65
Consumption			
	Eating	91	65

Figure 2.2. The chain of provision of food

We can divide the various activities involved in these chains of provision into three groups. First are the various work activities which take place in a more or less public (or 'formal') sphere—paid work activities in the money economy in the modern chain of provision, and in the pre-industrial chain, perhaps work for money wages, or perhaps wholly or partly or at least potentially, subject to some other explicit contract of exchange (e.g. share-cropping)—the agricultural, manufacturing, and service activities. Second are the final food preparation activities, unpaid in both chains, located more privately in households, the 'informal' sphere of production. Third is the activity of final consumption, eating.

Compare the modern chain of provision for food with the older one. The distribution of time between the three spheres has changed markedly. Time in the formal sphere related to food provision has been reduced by the mid-1980s to just about 10 per cent of its pre-industrial total; food-related informal work time is about 63 per cent of the pre-industrial level; food consumption time about 72 per cent of the pre-industrial. In this area of provision there is a proportional shift of time out of the formal economy and towards consumption; but as we shall see in a later chapter, quite different shifts emerge when we look at other chains of provision. What is most important is the change in total time devoted to this purpose.

The reduction of time necessarily devoted to the satisfaction of particular categories of human wants (in the case of nutrition, from more than a third of society's total waking time to less than one-sixth) is at the heart of what we mean by economic development. We are not worse nourished now than formerly. On the contrary, the quantity of food has increased considerably, and now most of the society eats more food than it needs to stay healthy. It is rather that 'productivity' in this chain (i.e. time required for a given level of food provision—the society's efficiency in satisfying its members' wants or needs for nutrition) has increased even faster than the demand. The more we eat, the less we want food; the more efficiently we provide for nutritional needs, the more time we have for other less 'basic' purposes.

Economic development means, in terms of time use, that we need to spend a smaller proportion of the society's time in achieving 'basic' purposes; this in turn means that more time can be devoted to more sophis-ticated or 'luxury' purposes. Satisfying needs for basic purposes such as nutrition with fewer minutes of the society's time means that more of the society's time can be devoted to other sorts of domestic services that were not previously provided for, and to leisure activities.

A simple picture of time use in the development process

There is a very simple graphical representation of this change in the society's allocation of its time resources. It takes the form of the box in Figure 2.3, which represents the division of the society's 'great day', the

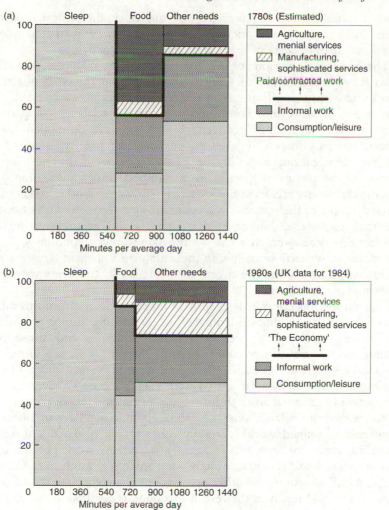

Figure 2.3. Adult time use over two centuries

total (adult, for convenience) time of the population, expressed as 1,440 'great minutes'. The box is divided horizontally into a series of columns, in proportion to the total time the society devotes to various activities. Let us group the activities of the members of the society into just three categories: sleep, nutrition-related and other activities. The width of the middle column in the box represents the aggregate of the formal and informal work and consumption time associated with nutrition. We can divide the columns vertically in proportion to the time spent in the different sorts of food-related activities. The top part of the food-related column represents formal work, the middle section represents informal work, the bottom, consumption. These three vertical sections themselves can be further divided to represent different sorts of work and consumption activities.

The horizontal divisions of the box represent the purposes of activities (the sorts of human wants they relate to), the vertical, the types of activities (work and leisure classifications). Each column represents a chain of provision, a set of work and consumption activities, related to a particular purpose. The very much reduced version we have developed for this chapter has only three categories of 'purpose' and five 'types of activity', but the classification can easily be made more detailed. The simplified version of the picture it gives is in one respect misleading: some of the work in the society relates to the satisfaction of wants in other societies, and similarly, some of the society's wants are satisfied through work elsewhere. We shall see later (Chapter 8) that imports and exports can be quite satisfactorily dealt with in terms of the same time accountancy. But for the moment, we shall remain with the simplified Robinson Crusoe society within which each human want means some work, and every moment of work meets some want.

The nature of economic development emerges clearly from this picture. Through history, we find horizontal shifts, in which columns representing the more 'basic' wants become relatively thinner, and those representing more 'sophisticated' wants become thicker (as we see in the comparison of Figures 2.3(a) and 2.3(b)). And we find vertical shifts, in which the mixture of activities associated with each purpose changes—a larger proportion of informal work to formal (or a smaller—unlike the shift from 'basic' wants, the balance does not seem to shift regularly or necessarily from paid to unpaid work); certainly more skilled paid work relative to unskilled; more (or less: this is again less certain) work per minute of consumption time. Of course, exactly what are 'basic' wants in this context, and in which directions the other proportions change in, are the subject of some doubt, and much of the rest of this book is devoted to the investigation of these questions. For the moment, we need only note that this accounting system, consisting of the division of the society's day by the purpose (i.e. the kind of want that is satisfied) and the type of activity (paid work, unpaid work, consumption, and the degree of skill—or in the language of Chapter 4, 'human capital') that is involved, is a particularly helpful framework for the consideration of the processes of social change.

It gives an aggregate picture of the society. But if we choose our system of classification with care, it also carries a weight of distributional information. In modern societies, the main mechanisms for the distribution of income, and for the allocation of status, are related principally to employment. The sector of the economy, and the occupational category of employment, largely determine the extent of the individual's command over the society's resources. So, if we adopt an appropriate occupational (or industrial-occupational) classification for the 'type of activity' dimension, the time-accounting system also shows some approximation to the proportions of the members of the society falling into the various status categories. From the aggregate number of minutes per day the society devotes to the various paid occupations (combined with information about normal hours of work), we know (approximately, depending on the relative hours of work of members of the various occupational sectors) what proportions of the society are professional workers, skilled, unskilled, and unemployed. Comparing the two simple day pictures, for example, we see immediately the substantial declines in the relative size of the agricultural labouring and menial service classes, and the growth of manufacturing and sophisticated services.

It shows the variety of ways that technical change (in the broadest sense) may influence the society. The society may reduce the amount of paid labour necessary to produce commodities, through innovations in production processes. Or it may reduce the amount of unpaid work necessary to convert purchased commodities into useful services, through the development and diffusion of domestic labour-saving machinery. Or indeed the consumers may, as a result of other sorts of innovations, spend less time in consuming these final services without reducing the level of satisfaction they achieve (the example I have in mind is the reduction of the length of meal times; gourmet readers may of course question whether this can be consistent with a maintenance of the level of satisfaction). Any of these changes—'innovations in chains of provision'—may serve to free part of the society's great day, which may henceforth be devoted to the satisfaction of new wants.

And, most important, this sort of accountancy shows the interdependence between various sorts of production and consumption activities. It shows how particular amounts of particular sorts of paid work are associated with particular amounts of specific sorts of unpaid work or consumption time.

Socio-economic development means new sorts of production position, and new sorts of consumption, and new relationships between them. There are two sorts of balance, two sorts of time-budget constraint, that must be set against each other. Each individual has both paid work and consumption activities; the paid work time must earn enough to buy goods and services, yet leave enough time to consume them. This is the micro time budgeting constraint, familiar to economists. And there is a second, less familiar, macro time budget constraint: the outcome of all the microprocesses must leave the society with enough of the various sorts of paid labour to provide for all the consumption wants. The macrotime budgeting process balances the total of consumption activities with the total of production activities. (These two time-budgeting processes are discussed in detail in Chapter 4.)

Arriving at a society's overall time budget requires a solution which satisfies these two constraints. With any given level of technical knowledge, there are alternative possible societies. But any given society, at any historical point, only has access to a constrained subset of these. The range of accessible forms of organization is limited by the productive capacities of the society, and limited also by the society's culture of consumption.

4. The logic of progress

Balancing production and consumption

These, then, are the characteristics of modern (and modernizing) industrial societies: growth in the numbers of skilled workers as a proportion of all employment; growth of time allocated to the production and consumption of sophisticated services (and more leisure/consumption time overall); and reduced time-use differentiation by class and gradually by gender. The coincidence of these characteristics across the developed world is not a randomly occurring empirical accident; they all fit together into what we might call the *logic of progress* or *modernization*.

Economic development means increasing the efficiency of production, increasing the real value-added of an hour's work. But society's time is in fact made up of the time of individuals. Moving from low- to high-value-added work time in a society means having more high-value-added people, more people with high levels of productive skills. New work-skill categories—loosely, new high skill 'classes'—are a prerequisite for development. But to complement the new sorts of work of these new 'classes', there must be new sorts of demand, new sorts of consumption.

The distinction between work and consumption is not always obvious to us in the course of our daily life. The given meaning of 'work' contains the implication of arduousness and personal constraint, and perhaps also that it is undertaken for some instrumental purpose distant from the activity itself. Our own experience of our jobs may be nevertheless of enjoyment, we may find them relaxing and interesting; we may even believe that we might continue to do them even if we were not paid to do so. Much of our leisure activity by contrast may actually be more strenuous and constrained, and less pleasant than our work. For these reasons we may be tempted to regard the conventional distinction between the two activities as arbitrary or even meaningless. But even if the distinction is not apparent to us as we live from day to day, it is still very real and important: paid work and consumption are distinct and symbiotic categories at the macro level.

Our paid work both enables and is enabled by other people's consumption. What we consume determines what others produce (and vice versa). There are no grounds for assuming a causal priority among the two sorts of activity. But at any historical point of time there is a balance: such and such a consumption pattern matches just such a pattern of paid employment. (Of course 'balance' here does not preclude the sort of imbalance in which a particular national pattern of consumption is only consistent with a substantial level of unemployment.) Growth in the employment of particular sorts of work skills entails growth in particular sorts of consumption activity. So socio-economic development means change in both the distribution of jobs, and in the distribution of non-work time, among various sorts of people, and among various types of activities.

We can, in short, only get to be doctors, teachers, engineers, if other people want medical and educational and technical services and can pay for them. People doing low-value-added jobs cannot afford to pay for many high-value-added services. The more high-value-added producers and consumers, the fewer people available to provide low-value-added 'face-to-face' services. So a diminishing proportion of the population can purchase menial household services, and hence a growing part of the society must engage in these on an unpaid basis (at least in so far as these tasks cannot be automated). Similarly women who possess salient economic skills but nevertheless remain as domestic producers outside paid employment are in effect purchasing overpriced menial services—and are thus increasingly likely to take paid jobs.

As we move from a low-value-added to a high-value-added society, we must find new forms of high-value-added consumption. We cannot *all* be doctors, teachers, and engineers, since few of us want to spend all our time consuming medical, educational, and engineering services. The high-value-added society must collectively develop new high-value-added occupational specialities and matching new high-value-added consumption habits. Development requires an increasingly varied range of sophisticated services, and as the range of services increases, consumption patterns necessarily become more diverse, there is more scope for individual choice, and the old clear-cut class pattern of social differentiation by time allocation necessarily decreases.

Stratification and differentiation

New forms of production mean new sorts of jobs. Production processes become more complex, and the component tasks in production for a particular category of want become more various and specialized, so new sorts of social position emerge. (These changes show up in time-use evidence in the form of the growth in work time deriving from skilled or technically qualified workers and people in other sorts of administrative professions.) The nature of the relations between people also changes: more complex production requires new lines of authority, so new patterns of subordination and superordination must emerge. These sorts of changes in the social relations of production are very familiar to us. But the time accounts also draw our attention to other sorts of social relations which are often missing from traditional sociological arguments: *social relations of consumption.*

There are relations of sub- and super-ordination between producers and consumers. The characteristic class relations in a less developed society (such as Europe only a century ago) were those of master and servant. In such a society, members of the subordinate classes were subject to a double (or multiple) derogation. The lower classes were badly paid, and consumed rather limited services which were different in kind from those consumed by the upper classes (i.e. the servants do not have servants). And they were engaged in face-to-face interactions in which the employer was dominant in something more than is implicit in any hierarchical and purposive organization: servants were considered as belonging to an inferior order, whose personal wants have a lower moral status than those of their masters and mistresses. This double derogation was reflected in the distribution of time. There were sharp class differences in time spent in work in such societies. Men and women of the superordinate class had relatively short hours of paid work (if any), and work within their households was carried out, on a paid basis, by servants. Members of the subordinate classes by contrast had long hours of work, with men (and some women) in paid employment, and other women in un-mechanized domestic drudgery (non-employed wives in their own homes, other women and some men in the households of the superordinate class).

But later stages of development involve the mass substitution of consumer durables for some of the simpler sorts of face-to-face services. We see the phenomenon of 'self-servicing' in which domestic equipment, operated by unpaid members of private households, is used to provide household services in relatively efficient ways. Paid labour producing the domestic equipment in factories and elsewhere substitutes for paid labour in private households. This provides two sorts of improvement for the once-subordinate classes: they have more access to services, and the nature of these services is less socially divisive. In the time-use evidence, the convergence of modes of provision for various basic services translates directly into the allocation of time to domestic work. There is a move from the state of society in which some are servants and others masters to the state in which virtually all adults are simultaneously domestic producers of services and consumers of them. This translates into a convergence in time-use patterns between what were previously distinct social groups. Most of the time-use data we have collected refer to a rather more recent historical period, so the process of change does not show up clearly in what follows. But the outcome, the consequences of this historic process, are very plain in our material: there are surprisingly small differences between social strata, social status indicators such as income and education explain much less of the variation in time use than do family or employment status.

This convergence in time-use patterns among the social classes is a fairly dramatic feature of the middle part of the twentieth century; it took place for the most part just outside the historical range of our data collection, though as we shall see, it does still register in the evidence that takes us from the 1960s to the 1990s. With quite as dramatic a potential is the change in the pattern of differentiation of time use between the sexes. The great majority of unpaid domestic production continues to be carried out by women within households. But the progressive movement of women into the workplace, from the later 1950s, challenges this gender segregation. The 'dual burden' that results from taking a job *and* doing all the housework produces pressures for change in the distribution of housework. Our data collection, with its earliest evidence coming from the 1960s, is very well situated to document the early stages of the process through which the contradiction between the ungendered workplace and gendered domestic work is resolved. We have already seen an, as yet very incomplete, convergence between the men's and women's unpaid work which is somewhat analogous to that between the status groups.

In a developed society, there are other and more important sorts of face-to-face relationship between consumer and producer than those between master and servant (e.g. patient and doctor, claimant and welfare worker). In the master–servant pairings the consumer predominates over the producer of the service, in the latter two cases the dominance is more symmetrical or even reversed. As new technologies and new forms of organization for the delivery of services (new 'modes of provision') emerge, and the balance between modes changes, we often find a shift to producer dominance (perhaps because of the higher-skill requirements of these positions in the new modes), and sometimes to something more ambiguous (as between diner in a smart restaurant and the waiter). But the single predominant cleavage has disappeared. In a modern society, people have a mix of statuses, some deriving from their work, some from their activities outside work. Their pattern of consumption time use itself is no longer a source of social differentiation (though some special attributes of it may be used for this purpose: for example social position is asserted, not merely by going to the opera, but also by where you sit in the opera house). A modern society has multiple and cross-cutting consumption differences instead of a single and comprehensive cleavage (the processes through which these emerge are discussed in Chapter 8).

This is not to say that there is now less social differentiation based on consumption than formerly. But it emerges in other ways. Differences that were once expressed in terms of time allocation are perhaps now expressed in spatial terms, and particularly in terms of the possession or use of special commodities or services whose particular function is to denote wealth. What emerge are multiple consumption fractions rather than simple and comprehensive consumption classes.

Certainly the consciousness of occupation-related social status survives; and this is more than just a fossil of old injuries and loyalties. Some aspects of class reproductive advantages are maintained or even enhanced in modern societies. The fungibility of financial capital into human capital, and human capital back into financial, which allows the intergenerational transmission of class position through the educational system, persists and is indeed made more reliable as a result of the modern society's need for skilled and certificated labour. And some sorts of class behaviour persist (e.g. voting), partly as a function of childhood socialization, partly as a reflection of the operation of the perceptual field (i.e. geographical separation of occupational groups plus a tendency of members of similar occupational strata to socialize with each other). But the process of modernization we have outlined means that the stark contrast between the classes in their day-to-day mundane time-use patterns, which was a central feature of earlier stages of development, now disappears. And indeed, as we shall make clear in a moment, the socio-economic 'logic of development' in fact *depends* on the disappearance of this sort of class differentiation. To put it at its simplest: as the number of high-value-added workers increases, the market for their products must continually widen. A modern high-value-added society must provide for mass consumption not élite consumption.

Pre-modern societies

Time For the majority, long hours of subsistence work
Status Small élite 'leisure class', remainder undifferentiated by time use
Gender Strong differentiation by task

Industrializing societies

Time Long hours of work for subordinate classes
Status Single cleavage, multiple derogation of subordinate classes (hence strong differentiation)
Gender Strong differentiation by task

Modern industrial (or 'post-industrial') societies

Time Declining work time, providing opportunities for increasing consumption
Status Converging work-time patterns, multiple cross-cutting cleavages in leisure (i.e. weak differentiation)
Gender Gradually diminishing differentiation

Figure 2.4. A developmental typology of time use

5. High- and low-value services, production, and consumption

The convergence in patterns of daily life both across status groups and sexes, and amongst the developed societies, is the most striking finding emerging from the empirical materials described in this book. But nevertheless, coming particularly from the theoretical arguments that follow, is a rather different theme: of *alternative* patterns of development within the general scheme outlined above. The discussion of the systematic interconnection of patterns of consumption and production, the interdependence of daily life and employment structure, which is at the heart of the theoretical discussions that follow, as well as of its more empirical reflection in the changing nature of the work–leisure balance in developed societies, suggests the potential for some really rather substantial divergences between States. There are different possible mixes of consumption and production leading to quite distinct patterns of social differentiation, resulting from different views of the appropriate role of state intervention in the development process. These differences are perhaps most appropriately understood in terms of different patterns of time use: the investigation of these, indeed, is one of the most promising prospective applications of time-budget research. So the final part of this chapter is devoted to the implications of the more theoretical arguments of this book for the patterns of time use that may be expected in different sorts of developed societies.

As a preliminary, we must consider the different employment implications of different sorts of service consumption. Modern societies are dominated by service industries and occupations. We of course recognize that, whatever the significance of services, manufacturing activities are also a vital part of the modern society. There are two somewhat connected reasons for this. Self-servicing relies on durable goods, these are internationally traded and the society must have the means to purchase them. And a significant part of the 'service' workforce produces intermediate services for manufacturing (including research, design, software and production engineering, marketing, and distribution services); maintaining at least the most profitable of these probably requires the existence of an indigenous manufacturing base. But let us nevertheless concentrate first on that core of service activities related directly to provision of services to consumers.

Clearly there is no one necessary pattern of development. We might define 'modernization' (within the 'chains of provision' perspective) as 'the process of reducing the proportion of the society's great day required to provide a given level and quality of services'. There is evidence, in the following chapters, which may be interpreted as the emergence of a common worldwide technology reducing the time requirements for provision of a range of simple wants or needs. But what then? What do we do, as a society, with the time freed by the modernization process?

There is an important choice: between high- and low-value-added final services. (By high-value-added service activities, I mean chains of provision which involve the combination of substantial amounts of skilled labour with consumers' time.)

The easiest examples are in traditional services. Consider traditional 'grand' opera: the opera house seats an audience of say 3000, the orchestra, principals, and chorus total 150 people, and the same number again provide ancillary services. Let us say that an hour's performance takes ten of rehearsal and other preparation, then each hour's consumption time by an opera-goer calls for an hour of someone's production time. Contrast this arithmetic with that of a TV soap opera. There is a cast of fifteen, the labour of fifty others—perhaps 1,500 person hours of production time per hour of prime soap; there are, say, 15 million (or 150 million hours) viewers—here the ratio could be 1,000 or 10,000 or more hours of consumption time for every hour of production time.

Or take fast-food as against fine-food services. In our local French restaurant, the proprietor and chef markets for fresh produce, supervises purchases, and tastes the food, his apprentices chop and stir, the waiter advises us what to eat and drink. Contrast this with the fast-food establishment: the food is mass produced in a remote factory, transported frozen, and the major unmechanized labour is shared between essentially untrained cooks and checkout operators, and customers are self-trained to select and carry disposable food containers. To judge by the prices, high-value eating-out might easily involve a ratio of paid labour to consumption time which is five or ten times that of the low-value-added equivalent.

The particular examples of high-value-added services may seem somewhat élitist and rather old-fashioned. But consider: sports, adult and continuing education, fine arts and crafts, counselling services and so on, all fall into same category. All of these involve the paid work of skilled workers in combination with the consumption time of people who are able to pay for them. And in addition to these are those services which may act as substitutes or supplements for unpaid caring activities in the home, child-care services, care of the chronically sick and elderly; all these again require trained, often highly trained, workers. Plainly, which sorts of leisure services people spend their time consuming is of very great importance for the evolution of the wealth and welfare of the society. The society may devote its production and consumption time to low-value or to high-value services. Prospects for 'progress' depend on what sort of service economy develops.

Simplifications should not significantly mislead, and in one respect our terminology is misleading. We have used 'low-value' services to mean services with high consumption time combined with a small amount of paid work time. But in fact the particular sorts of paid work involved in such services are themselves often very high-wage and highly skilled (e.g. television). As more leisure time is taken in the form of television and other electronic screen-based forms there may be, in absolute terms, a growth in related high-value employment—yet, the amount and the value of the paid work *per minute of consumption time* both fall. There are in fact two different notions involved in high-value services (i) concerning the amount of paid labour and (ii) concerning the value of that labour. As we have described it, the 'improvement' that comes with the development process does rely precisely on the substitution of a smaller quantity of higher-value-added labour for a larger quantity of lower-value-added labour. Yet still, on average, the value of paid work associated with each minute of consumption time increases with economic development.

So 'high-value-added services' is used in what follows to describe chains of production which involve a high value of embodied labour per minute of consumption time. (The concept is also sometimes used here *relatively*, as in the contrast between meals prepared by a master chef as opposed to a short-order cook.) Development, modernization, involves an increase in the overall value of the work in the society; if work time does not increase, as a proportion of the society's great day, it must also therefore involve a growth in the value of the work associated with each minute of consumption. Hence (and as long as there is no shift in the balance of time from leisure to work), development means increasing high-value service consumption. But of course this increasing value might either be associated with a general increase in the value of all paid labour, or with a growing polarization, with one part of the labour force remaining at a relatively low level of value-added, and the other with a continuously increasing level of value-added. We must therefore now turn to a discussion of the *distribution* of production and consumption within the society.

Alternative service economies

This distinction between high- and low-value-added services finds a reflection at the level of the State. Different mixes of the different sorts of service provision are associated with different sorts of society. There is, as we shall see, a wide range of possible patterns of leisure service consumption. But, to concentrate our minds on the implications of the choice of the consumption mix, let us just consider the two polar alternatives: one a type of society whose pattern of consumption is skewed towards high-value leisure services, the other, skewed towards low-value services. Let us, for the sake of a clear discussion (and without, for the moment, any strong expectation that we will necessarily be able to associate the empirical evidence for any particular country with these) draw a binary ideal-type distinction, between social democratic and liberal market states (I have in mind here something analogous to the sorts of ideal-type welfare regimes asserted by Esping Anderson in his *Three Worlds of Welfare Capitalism*). The 'chains-of-provision' argument suggests that there should be a correspondence between the nature of the State's regulatory activities and its pattern of leisure consumption: social democratic States tending towards high-value service consumption, liberal market States towards the low-value pattern. Let us look first at the patterns of production and consumption that characterize these two ideal types, and then at the differing systems of social and economic regulation that may be presumed to lead in one or the other direction.

The high-value service-consuming *social democratic State* benefits (and also as we shall see, suffers what some might consider ill-effects) from a (mostly) virtuous circle of income flow. The more high-value service producers, the more potential consumers of high-value services; the more doctors and members of other skilled caring professions in the society—the more potential restaurant customers and opera-goers. This is in part a matter of disposable income, and also a result of education and other factors which give people the capacity to enjoy consumption (the process of accumulation of human capital as an input to consumption is discussed in Chapter 4). And in turn the highly trained, well-paid, professional providers of leisure and other similar services, themselves constitute further demand for medical and other caring services.

We cannot, to repeat the earlier point, all be doctors (though there is no effective ceiling for time devoted to medical services, since, for example, the society may evolve a quasi-therapeutic model of leisure, as in the Central European culture of spas and 'cures'). If the paid work in the society is to consist increasingly of high-value-added production *and* grow in volume, the society must develop new sorts of high-value-added consumption. The society as it develops needs more sophisticated tastes, more sophisticated skills in consumption. We must as a society (and to continue our élite example), go sufficiently often to the opera that we can afford to pay opera singers well enough to motivate their lengthy training. And this in turn presumably requires that we provide appropriate educational patterns for children and adults, so as to recruit future opera patrons as well as opera singers. Or if not (or as well as) opera, then (also) other forms of consumption, music, sports, crafts. And presumably, as part of this high-value package, there must be a recognition that some members of the society, who are simply not able to be high-value producers, must nevertheless receive sufficient transfer payments to allow them to live decently and make a social contribution appropriate to their abilities.

The adjustment of gender roles plays an important part in the emergence of this sort of virtuous society. As women cease to provide unpaid caring services (or from another perspective, domestic services at what are in effect subsistence wage levels paid in kind), some of these are substituted for by professional or semi-professional workers. *Some*, but not *all*; just as full-time domestic servants virtually disappeared from developed societies two generations ago, the large numbers of professionally trained workers and the generally high real wages in the high-value-added society, mean that it may be difficult to arrange for domestic cleaning, *ad hoc* household maintenance, irregular or informal childcare, and similar services. The pressures that come from this labour market constraint lead to a thoroughgoing change in the patterns of men's and women's activities.

Men in such societies are forced to change, not merely their household activities, but also their attitudes to paid work. In a high-value-added society there are no longer respectable ways of avoiding their household responsibilities; their wives also have high-value jobs and there is insufficient low-wage labour available to substitute for them (there may also be legislation providing job and other security on the basis of parental rather than just maternal responsibilities). So they find no excuse for doing other than sharing the unpaid domestic work, alternating with their wives in taking days off work to care for temporarily sick children, to visit schools, to wait for the arrival of household service engineers, and so on. (My model for this sort of society is modern Finland. When, surprised by the extent of the gender convergence apparent in the Finnish data, I questioned my colleagues at the Finnish Central Statistical Office, they reassured us that we had correctly interpreted the data: 'the women think it is the Garden of Eden' the senior (woman) social statistician told me, though her junior (male) colleague added that 'the men are not so certain'.)

The opposite pole is not simply a low-value-added society, but rather, the dualistic *liberal market society*. This will contain some high-value-added, skilled occupations, doctors, lawyers, engineers, and a limited number of the sorts of skilled cultural and recreational workers we have discussed previously. But a growing proportion of the workforce in this sort of society is progressively deskilled, often operating the sorts of automated parodies of traditional services represented by the fast-food establishment. This sort of society will specialize in low-value-added services for low-income consumers, together with some cheap(ish) services for the minority of rich consumers. In this dual society there are no very intense pressures for substantial adjustments in gender roles. Only a minority of women, those with particularly high-value skills, find their place in the core workforce, while the others remain specialized in more peripheral, low-paid menial service work.

The liberal market society is likely to be poorer than the social democratic society. The wealth of any society is the sum of wealth generated by its members. A society that engages on average in the production and consumption of low-value-added services, must (*ceteris paribus*) have a lower GNP than societies which specialize in higher-value services (so the dualistic society is less likely than the other to find resources for transfers to the least well-off). It is of course possible to oversimplify and exaggerate the contrast between these two sorts of society. There is a continuum of service jobs from the lowest-wage and lowest-skill levels to the highest, and there is an infinite range of possible mixes among them. And both sorts of society have in common the basic gain from modernization, the shift of time away from provision for the more basic wants; all that differs is the range and quality of those services above the subsistence level.

Taking in each other's washing

I have asserted the existence of a systematic connection between the mix of consumption activities, the mix of occupations in the society, and the overall level of wealth in the society. Is the association between type of State and type of consumption mix simply a matter of accident? The connection depends on the State's attitude taken to intervention in the economy. It turns on the view, in the society's dominant political ideology, of how the consumption mix in a developed society evolves. Does it do so naturally, with no intervention from the State, or, in part through some process of guidance or regulation?

There is a 'trickle down' model of economic development, which asserts that a society can best care for its worse-off members by making the best off yet better off. The best-off then spend their money providing jobs for the rest of the society. In this view, *the rich employ the poor.* But what do the rich buy from the poor? Plainly not high-value services, because if the poor produced high-value services they would not be poor. This model is plainly consistent only with a stratified society with great disparities in the distribution of productive skills. It requires a mass of low-value-added workers. The 'trickle down' assumption is, following these arguments, not necessarily an appropriate basis for public policy in advanced economies. It implies the development of a relatively low-value-added society, and inhibits the development of a modern high-productivity service sector.

The arguments of the preceding pages are to the effect that economic development implies a declining proportion of the population in the low-value-added worker category (with no associated decrease in the size of the employed population). More high-value service workers require more high-value service consumption to keep them in employment; and the growth of high-value-added employment provides the effective demand for high-value-added services. Following this model, everyone, in a developed society, buys high-value services from everyone else. The (relatively) wealthier parts of the societies are, and become progressively more, dependent for the maintenance of their positions on the consumption patterns of the mass of the society; so, we might say, *the (relatively) poor* come literally to *employ the rich.* Socioeconomic development, in this argument, is inextricably bound up with the development of 'human capital', skills for both production and consumption (we shall discuss the broad sociological meaning of this term in Chapter 4). And simply making the rich richer has no impact on the level of human capital in the society.

The alternative to 'trickle down', as a view of the development process, is a particular pattern of social and economic regulation. In this view the conditions of society within which economic activities take place are not 'natural', but result from the interaction of human activities with the regulatory actions of the State. The State effectively determines the balance between supply and demand, and hence the level and nature of economic activity, not merely (or even principally) through its economic policy, but also through social policy (in its broadest sense, including the labour market, education, transport, and other issues). It intervenes so as to promote the development of human capital (and thus actively increases the number of higher-value-added workers; as we shall see in Chaper 4, the educational system also influences the development of categories of human capital employed in consumption). It also takes on responsibility for the stimulation of investment, and the direct provision of infrastructure; what follows however stresses in particular the importance of social policy as an influence on time allocation and hence consumption patterns in the management of economic development.

The proposition that 'the poor employ the rich' has obvious connections with Keynes's use of the relatively low 'marginal propensity to consume' of richer households in the *General Theory*: but what follows from it is a rather more physiocratic discussion, concerned not so much with *whether* the poor spend their income (as in Keynes) as with *what the money is spent on*, or alternatively, in terms of what follows here *how their time is spent* and hence which particular sorts of jobs are created. The regulation approach has at its centre the State's role of establishing an appropriate balance between production and consumption (as in Aglietta's *Theory of Capitalist Regulation*). It sees the regular progress of development of the capitalist system as best promoted by establishment of appropriate regulatory 'regimes' in both spheres.

The *regulation of production* involves such activities as the development of productive infrastructure (institutional, including the legal framework for corporate activity, as well as physical); the development of systems of industrial relations and employment protection appropriate for the current 'best practice' in the physical organization of production (e.g. maximum working hours, parental leave, holiday entitlement); provisions for the maintenance and development of skills suitable for current technology and management practices (i.e. systems for continuous retraining); the provision of incentives for investment within a general policy on taxation of profits; and the development of a system of publicly coordinated research and development activity.

The *regulation of consumption* involves, to a considerable degree, parallel activities to these: the development of an appropriate infrastructure for consumption (not just, as in Keynes's time, domestic electricity and water supplies, but also cultural, sports, and social care facilities); institutional regulation (which may include direct regulation of activity, e.g. the length of the workday or school-leaving and retirement ages); provisions for formation, through the educational system and other media, of consumption skills and tastes (in informal production, and most important, in leisure and cultural pursuits, thus forming the basis for demand for cultural and other recreational services); as well as policy for income redistribution through the personal tax and social security systems so as to prevent the social exclusion of those with the fewest skills.

Regulation is quite distinct from central planning. Planning involves direction of production, fixing of prices and wages, quotas and rationing, and inevitably results in progressive distortions of the operation of the economy. Regulation, by contrast, involves at a minimum no more than the recognition that the framework of rules enforced by the State (or the absence of them) is not neutral, but has economic consequences. Given that the government of the day must perforce operate some set of rules concerning a very wide range of human activities (education, health, transport, family, international relations, defence), then even a principled refusal to establish such rules must be, in a world economy in which at least *some* governments normally do establish *some* such rules, itself clearly a form of regulation.

The particular significance of regulation in this sense is (to state the very obvious) that it influences the structure of economic activity; it influences (though it does not determine) the distribution of time across the society's great day. An older minimum school-leaving age, for example, means less paid work in total but more employees in educational jobs. Sunday opening of shops means (probably) more retail workers and more shopping time than would otherwise be the case. Less government spending on roads means (if public transport provisions are constant) fewer construction workers and longer travel times. Tax relief on expenditures on pre-school childcare means more employment for nursery nurses and more women overall seeking jobs. And so on. Given that governments must perforce regulate, a refusal to consider the economic consequences of the broad range of government regulation may be considered somewhat perverse.

'Trickle down' may admittedly be indispensable at some early stages or states of development. With low levels of agricultural and manufacturing output, the majority of a population must of necessity be engaged full time in producing subsistence commodities. In these circumstances economic growth may certainly be best promoted by the 'trickle-down' process of purchase of goods and services by the rich from the poor. A (small) proportion of the population may be supported by taking in the rich folks' dirty washing, and an even smaller group could be supported by, for example, supplying medical and legal services to the rich and engineering services to the State. It is certainly not the case that in a near-subsistence economy the poor could support themselves by taking in other poor people's washing.

But in an advanced industrial society a version of 'taking in each other's washing' is pretty much what does occur. Indeed this is just what we mean by the term 'service economy'. Basic material requirements (e.g. for food and shelter) may be provided by a small minority of society's productive effort: the majority of all economic activity is in the provision of services which are ultimately consumed by other service providers. Now suppose that, among the richest members of society are those (broadly 'the service class' in its current sociological sense) who use their skills in employment which contributes to production of sophisticated services for the population as a whole. Then, statistically speaking, the poor *do* employ the rich. (Or, to put it less picturesquely, the employment of professional and technically or artistically trained workers, and of people in administrative professions ancillary to these, is dependent on the consumption activities of the whole of the population.)

The 'service class' successor to the small group of lawyers and doctors and engineers and other professionals and technical specialists and artists who once provided their services to a limited class of the pre-industrial rich, has now grown to include a substantial proportion of the population; it is indeed of such a size that it can only be supported by providing services to the whole spectrum of the society. Certainly some significant social groups are left out of this analysis: *rentiers* with inherited wealth (and less well-heeled pensioners) who demand services are not in general involved in their production. But the proposition that as we move towards a service economy, the richer members of the society are increasingly involved in providing services for the poorer is still broadly accurate.

The trickle-down model leads to the dualistic liberal market economy, with a population polarized into two classes, respectively low-wage, low-skill, low-value-added service workers (the 'servant proletarians'), and high-wage, high-skill, high-value-added workers (the 'service aristocracy'). But the more closely we specify this society the more clearly we see its inherent limitations. A significant proportion of the population may be employed as low-wage workers providing menial services to members of the high-wage sector, and another substantial part might be engaged in providing low-wage 'Macdonald's' services to other low-wage workers. But where, in such an economy, is the demand that supports the specialist high-wage service workers? A large low-wage sector can presumably only support a very small high-wage sector: this variant of the service economy has many proletarians for each member of the service aristocracy.

To contrast with the servant economy, we have our alternative caricature picture of a Nordic-type high-value-added social democratic service economy. Taken beyond its limits this brings us to an absurd science fiction image (e.g. Asimov's *I Robot*), quite as filled with internal inconsistencies as the servant economy (e.g. the impossibility of motivating human capital formation). But the contrast is sufficient to demonstrate the central point.

Making rich people richer may certainly encourage them to spend more money and thus employ poorer people. But the types of jobs generated by the trickle-down mechanism would be likely to tend towards the low skilled, the low waged, the relatively menial. If this mechanism is the only basis for public policy choice, the society would, to say the very least, certainly miss opportunities for steering itself towards the high-value-added end of the continuum: it would maximize neither the size of the service class, nor the value of services provided.

The politics of progress

It is sometimes asserted that we have reached the end of 'progress'. But the evidence points only to a disjunction in economic development through the later 1970s through to the earlier 1990s (perhaps analogous to the disjunction of the 1920s and 1930s), in what has never anyway been assumed to be a smooth process. What we find is to some extent consistent with writings of the 'post-modernist' school: diversifications of consumption styles, the absence of a 'leading social class' But on one really quite central issue, the argument of this book is quite substantially at variance with the post-modernists: it maintains a clear notion of modernization as a continuing theme in developed societies. This book is a work of historically grounded sociology rather than futurology. Yet the historical outline summarized in this chapter and this book does provide, from the viewpoint of the end of the 1990s, not just a basis for identifying progress (or the lack of it), in the past, but also a picture of the general nature of further progress in the new millennium.

The difference between the two 'ideal types' of alternative service societies ultimately turns on the nature of consumption above the basic provision of food and shelter. The liberal market economy, over time, develops a leisure consumption pattern which might be characterized by lowbrow TV and fast food, providing relatively few good jobs, and many low-value-added unstimulating ones. The social democratic State, by contrast, has diversifying consumption of services which also provide stimulating and well-paid jobs for their producers. Such societies have growth in time spent in music and theatre, visual arts and education, time devoted to consumption of good food and drink, with a growing participation in active sports and games to compensate for these. They will also have growth in the paid 'caring' services to compensate for the lesser availability of unpaid or subsistence-wage production within households. These are caricatures, no doubt, yet they do indicate a meaningful range of alternative possibilities for development. (And they also illustrate how the difference between the alternative development patterns may be understood from contrasts in time-use patterns.)

The choice of these two polar cases does imply a certain sort of political judgement. But it would not be correct to interpret the former as necessarily an outcome of traditional leftist welfare state policies, nor is the latter a necessary outcome of right-wing laissez-faire politics. For example, the UK had, by the mid-1970s, a decade of welfare state policies, yet still showed something quite close to our dual society model. And Germany, which until recently has not had leftist governments for several decades, does seem to correspond to the high-value model.

Let us contrast these two modern service economy caricatures with a third, representing the old Eastern European-type centrally planned economy. To put it picturesquely, we would see, in 1980s East Germany, or Czechoslovakia or Poland, an onion shaped distribution of effective income, with a small class of artists and sportsmen and bureaucrats with foreign currency and benefits-in-kind towards the top, and older retired people towards the bottom; we would see long hours of work, with women in particular carrying a particularly heavy and disproportionate dual burden of work for money and unwaged labour at home. These characteristics all relate more or less directly to the low wage differentials enforced by these states (which mean lack of reward for human accumulation and efficient work, and hence low productivity in the broadest sense) and to the rigid centralized state planning system.

What differentiates our two modern sorts of societies from the old Eastern European type is specifically the larger wage differentials, which in turn mean higher returns to human capital, higher rewards for the development of economically salient skills. By comparison, the income distribution in the liberal market may be represented in terms of some rather longer and thinner vegetable... a carrot perhaps, to convey the image of increased social differentiation. In this dualistic society there are both substantial gender and class differences. Most women have jobs, richer women employ poorer for menial domestic work, so poorer women carry a dual burden of paid and unpaid work. Evidence in the following chapters will suggest that in such societies, those of higher status may have longer hours of paid work than the average, leaving little time for consumption; those of lower status may have, in addition to insecure employment, rather shorter hours of paid work. The dualistic economy may certainly be richer than the centrally planned economy—but it is not necessarily richer than the third type.

The social democratic State may in principle have wider wage-rate differentials, even after tax, than the liberal market, yet still have a smaller dispersion of incomes: distributionally, it is another onion. The apparent paradox is simply resolved: the wage differential between low- and high-value-added producers may be higher, but in the social democratic state there are far fewer low-value-added workers. In such States the combination of wage differentials with appropriate patterns of public regulation (of the education system and other aspects of social and material infrastructure, including the provision of childcare and leisure facilities) serves to motivate human capital formation more effectively than could wage differentials on their own. In such States, patterns of employment of men and women tend to converge, and hours of paid work of both high- and low-status workers are limited by, among other things, the requirement to provide their own domestic services on an unpaid basis.

A trend towards a high-value-added social democratic State is of course inconsistent with high and rising levels of income dispersion, but the implication of the model I have set out is that any attempt to reduce income dispersion by any means other than by raising the general level of productive human capital, is doomed to failure. We do not get 'all to employ each other's services' by taxing the rich and skilled and subsidizing the poor and unskilled. And with this exception, the politics implicit in the model do not really correspond to a general position on the traditional Left–Right dimensions, but to much more specific positions on some particular areas of public policy which were touched upon in the previous section. The model thus contributes, in a rather specific manner, to what has come to be known as 'The Third Way' but this is way beyond the scope of the present discussion.

The time-accounting approach that forms the substance of this book allows us to show some quite unequivocal historical evidence of social

	Distributive characteristics (by class and sex)	Wage differentials	Income dispersion	National income	Sources of domestic service work
Centrally planned e.g. pre-1990 E. Europe					
	Relatively egalitarian	Small	Low	Low	Mainly women's unpaid domestic work
Liberal market e.g. UK					
	Relatively inegalitarian	Large	High	Medium	Low wage paid, mainly women's unpaid
Social democratic e.g. Finland					
	Relatively egalitarian	Large	Low	High	Both sexes' unpaid domestic work

Figure 2.5. Three alternative service economies

progress through the second half of the twentieth century. There has been a decline in status–group differentiation (though we may suspect that most of this lies outside the period covered by our data); there has been a shift (detectable even over the last thirty years, as we shall see in Chapter 8) of the society's time away from the provisions for basic needs; and there has been reduction, relatively small as yet but continuing, in inequalities associated with gender. And most important, we can see possibilities for more of such improvements in the future. It would appear that, on the basis of our arguments, and from the new evidence which we present on the evolution of living and working conditions in the developed world, progress is still possible.

Readers might wish to remember that we arrive at this rather global summary of social change having started by thinking about the characteristics of a narrative description of a single day. In Chapter 4, we present in a more systematic way the theoretical basis for connecting diary accounts of the day with national accounts of social and economic structure. For now however we should note merely the prophetic nature both of James Joyce's account of Bloomsday and of its central characters: Leopold Bloom is (in Dublin in 1904) perhaps the first of his sex to proclaim himself 'the new womanly man'; while Molly Bloom, her daughter grown, has re-entered the labour market, by returning to her old profession in the service sector (she is a singer). Joyce, throughout the book, explains the events of Bloomsday as the outcome of Bloom's interior monologue which relates his current activities to fragments of information and memories of previous events from Bloom's life; this recursive relationship, in which past experiences provide the basis for current activity, is central to the microsociological model provided in the following theoretical arguments. But, before we turn to the theory, let us consider some of the received and current views of the association of time-use patterns with economic development.

3   Are We Running Out of Time?

1. Two views of leisure and development

At the heart of the current discussions of the relationship between economic development and the distribution of time lies the question of whether leisure increases or decreases as societies get richer.

There are two views of the historical evolution of the balance between work and leisure in societies. Some people believe in the possibility of progress through the development of new techniques for manipulating the physical environment so as to satisfy human wants, and for organizing the human efforts involved in the satisfaction of these wants. We move, through history, from unremitting effort to wrest our subsistence from a hostile world, to an increasingly leisurely existence. For those who hold this view 'progress' has been, and continues to be, if not an unproblematic fact, still the central fact, of social life. And at the centre of 'progress' is the growth of leisure time and the differentiation of leisure activities.

But there is a contrary view that contends that as we get richer we get busier. The benefits of economic development are problematical; there may have been progress of a sort in the past, but even this brought costs. Manipulating the natural environment to extract advantage from it means polluting it. Changing traditional patterns of work and of consumption means destroying previous cultures. In this second view, increasing the sophistication of the techniques we use for meeting our wants also raises our expectations, so we work harder and longer as we get richer. Even when our paid work time reduces, the pressures and disciplines of the workplace make our work more stressful. Outside our paid work, we find more worklike tasks to do for ourselves and our families. And even our leisure becomes less leisurely, as we try to cram more and more consumption into our day. In this view, 'progress' increases work, and reduces the quality of our leisure time.

This chapter discusses these two contrasting views, it attempts to explain how they arise, and proposes, in effect, that the question of the future prospects for the work–leisure balance has no single and simple answer. We must disaggregate the question, to ask: 'Work or leisure *for whom?*' And this in turn raises questions about the effect of the alternative policy regimes that influence work hours. But before we consider the two contrasting views of the prospects for a leisure society, we should start by placing them both in the context of the work of the first (and today largely unread) social scientist to discuss these issues in an extended way: Thorsten Veblen prefigured elements of both of these lines of argument—and indeed may, with hindsight, be understood as foreseeing an important aspect of the late twentieth century evolution of work time patterns.

The leisure class and the end of leisure

Veblen's *Theory of the Leisure Class* is a discussion of the processes through which societies construct the concepts of leisure and work. At the heart of his book is the idea that consumption activities are a means, indeed the *principal* means, of social differentiation. Veblen sees the distinction between work and leisure as deriving ultimately from what (following Adam Ferguson's social developmental typology) may be viewed as the first step in social development, that from 'primitive savagery' to 'barbarism'. The former of these states is marked by poverty, either the absence of any concept of ownership of goods, or else communal ownership, and by the unremitting nature of subsistence labour. In such a society, social differentiation exists only in relation to gender. 'In nearly all these tribes the women are, by prescriptive custom, held to those employments out of which the industrial occupations proper develop at the next advance. The men are exempt from these vulgar employments and are reserved for war, hunting, sports and devout observances.' Of course, in terms of their contribution to the 'chains of provision' of welfare of the primitive group, these men's activities may in reality be *nearly* as important as the women's. But 'primitive man', according to Veblen, does not see things in this light:

In his own eyes he is not a labourer, and he is not to be classed with the women in this respect; nor is his effort to be classed with the woman's drudgery, as labour or industry... his work may conduce to the maintenance of the group but... cannot without derogation be compared with the uneventful diligence of the women. (Veblen 1925: 5)

The argument relies in part on an assumption of the influence of primary sexual characteristics on the selection of gender roles: 'The habitual pursuit of large game requires more of the manly qualities of massiveness, agility, and ferocity, and it can therefore scarcely fail to hasten and widen the differentiation of functions between the sexes.' Men develop 'prowess' in combat with animate beings, women, 'diligence' in the manipulation of the inanimate vegetable world. So we arrive at a first distinction among different categories of activity, that between men's and women's activities: women's occupations are those out of which the 'industrial occupations' will develop, men's, leisure activities. We have, at first, a leisure *sex*.

Veblen gives us two conditions for the subsequent emergence of a leisure class:

(1) the community must be of a predatory habit (war or the hunting of large game or both); that is to say the men, who constitute the inchoate leisure class in these cases, must be habituated to the infliction of injury by force and stratagem; (2) subsistence must be obtainable on sufficiently easy terms to admit of the exemption of a considerable proportion of the community from steady application to a routine of labour.... Under this common-sense barbarian appreciation of worth or honour, the taking of life...is honourable in the highest degree....Arms are honourable, and the use of them, even in seeking the life of the meanest creatures of the fields, becomes an honorific employment. At the same time employment in industry becomes correspondingly odious, and in the common-sense apprehension, the handling of the tools and implements of industry falls beneath the dignity of able-bodied men. Labour becomes irksome. (Ibid. 7)

The effective use of force in war brings control over services, in the form of slaves, and pecuniary gain, booty; and these in turn give rise to a distinct pattern of life. The original distinction between men's exploits and women's industry is transferred to, respectively, the dominant class (i.e. the group of individuals who successfully assert themselves over others through aggressive or warlike activities) and the subordinate. In Veblen's account, the first dominant social class originally defined itself through 'non-productive use of time. Time is used non-productively (1) from the sense of the unworthiness of productive work, and (2) as an evidence of pecuniary ability to afford a life of idleness' (ibid. 43). Leisure, 'conspicuous abstention from labour' (ibid. 38) thus comes to be identified as the basic index of social status.

Of course, changed conditions of life lead to changed meanings. But old symbols persist. Conspicuous idleness becomes detached from its original implication of prowess at arms, yet still continues to carry the symbolic implication of high social status. Following from Veblen's argument come various consequences, from the emergence of a specifically idle servant class as a particularly effective marker of status (since it serves to demonstrate on behalf of the employers of servants, over and above honourable idleness in person, the ability to pay someone else to be idle) to the bored wives of the 1890s American middle classes (by just the same argument). And since the mark of the social élite is leisure, so leisure itself becomes desirable by association, and is striven for even by those who are not members of the leisure class:

The vicarious consumption practised by the households of the middle and lower classes cannot be counted as a direct expression of the leisure class scheme of life.... it is rather that the leisure-class scheme of life here comes to an expression at the second remove. The leisure class stands at the head of the social structure in point of reputability; and its manner of life and its standards of worth affect the norms of reputability for the community. (Ibid. 83)

An integral part of Veblen's argument is an explicit behavioural model, a theory of consumption:

[E]ach class envies and emulates the class next above it in the social scale, while it rarely compares itself with those below or with those who are considerably in advance . . . the standard of expenditure which commonly guides our efforts is . . . an ideal of consumption that lies just outside our reach . . . all standards of consumption, are traced back by insensible gradations to the usages and habits of the highest social and pecuniary class—the wealthy leisure class. It is for this class to determine, in general outline, what scheme of life the community shall accept as decent or honorific. (Ibid. 103–4)

'Work' and 'leisure', in Veblen's theory, are social constructs. We may, in everyday life, use these words as if they were unproblematical: but their meanings derive from a rather distant historical context (we may however remain only incompletely convinced of Veblen's argument that they descend from the honorific system of a barbarian age). There is no discussion of any intrinsic worth or desirability or purpose of leisure. Veblen (unlike some more modern leisure theorists) does not suggest any natural hierarchy of preference for leisure over work, or assert that it has any specific recuperative or compensatory function. On the contrary: the 'subjective value of leisure . . . is no doubt in great part secondary and derivative.' It reflects the usefulness of leisure ' . . . as a means of gaining the respect of others' (ibid. 38). The 'performance of labour has been accepted as a conventional evidence of inferior force *and hence inferior social status*; therefore it comes itself, by a mental short-cut, to be regarded as intrinsically base' (ibid. 38; my italics).

Even if we reject the specific argument that the high status of leisure derives ultimately from the primitive division of activities between the sexes, we can still accept the more general sociological point, which is the very distant historical origin of the invidious comparison between leisure and work that is embodied in our normal unconsidered use of language: access to leisure was perhaps the prime means through which the superordinate class differentiated itself from the subordinate.

This account of Veblen's text might suggest that he inclines towards the 'historic growth of leisure time' view. But in fact his description of the move from pre-industrial to industrializing societies introduces a second mechanism for social differentiation. In addition to the conspicuous waste of time, there is also the reputation-enhancing conspicuous waste of money. 'Both are methods of demonstrating the possession of wealth, and the two are conventionally accepted as equivalents. The choice between them is a question of advertising expediency' (ibid. 85).

They may be equivalents. But they are not equally accessible to all members of the society. To be effective as an assertion of status, it is not sufficient simply to use time wastefully: it must be wasted according to strict codes and canons of behaviour. 'The growth of punctilious discrimination as to qualitative excellence in eating, drinking . . . affects not only the manner of life but also the training and intellectual activity of the gentleman of leisure.' Those members of the lower classes who seek upward mobility do not have the life-long training in these codes which is necessary for their successful application (in this view Veblen anticipates Bourdieu's discussion of cultural capital, discussed in Chapter 4). So the upwardly mobile might be better equipped to deploy conspicuous possessions to assert their new social positions than to mimic unsuccessfully the upper-class conspicuous deployment of leisure time.

Besides, there is the late-nineteenth-century leisure paradox: 'entry to the leisure class lies through the pecuniary employments' (ibid. 229). The main mechanism for social mobility is through hard work, 'productive efficiency and thrift' (ibid. 35–6), which might tend to encourage industrious habits which persist even when a degree of wealth has been achieved. As 'increased industrial efficiency makes it possible to procure the means of livelihood with less labour, the energies of the industrious members of the community are bent to the compassing of a higher result in conspicuous expenditure. . . . the increment of output is turned to use to meet this want, which is infinitely expansible.' So, we may infer, even some of those who are paid enough to be able to use their time wastefully (in Veblen's terms) choose instead to continue to work hard, and waste their money instead.

And finally, leisure as it becomes less scarce, becomes less useful as a means of social differentiation. Leisure time is strictly limited by the length of the day. People of even the most exalted status cannot occupy the day with more than 24 hours of leisure. Leisure time's usefulness for the assertion of social position is diminished by a process of inflation similar to that described by Fred Hirsch in *The Social Limits to Growth*. The wasteful use of money, by contrast, has no such upper bound. So, as the dominant class is constituted increasingly from those who deploy their superior skill to earn superior salaries, their social position may well be demonstrated, not through leisure, but by deploying their limited time to amassing additional pecuniary advantages. This is by no means a necessary outcome of Veblen's theory, but we certainly cannot conclude from his arguments that his view was that the lives of those of superior social status will necessarily remain leisurely throughout the whole course of socioeconomic development, let alone that he would predict the emergence of a leisure society.

2. A current thesis: the end of leisure

There are three ways in which it has been recently argued that the richer a society becomes, the less its members have the opportunity to relax and, in the now unfashionable 1960s' phrase, 'do their own thing'. These arguments are to do with, respectively, paid work, unpaid domestic work, and the nature of leisure time itself.

- The first is that, through history, work time increases: time spent working for money in 'the economy' grows (according to this argument) with economic development.
- The second refers particularly to women. It has two parts: first, it suggests, domestic work (broadly defined) does not reduce, and may even increase over historical time despite improvements in domestic technology; second, women do most of it, and as they move into paid work they continue to have the main responsibility for it.
- The third is that what leisure we have is increasingly congested with more and more consumption activities. There is a nice paradox here: each year we have to work harder in our free time to consume all those things that we have been working harder to produce in our work time.

More paid work over time?

There are various strands of evidence about 'market' and similar work time. There is, first of all, evidence from anthropologists. A small number of what might from some viewpoints be considered 'primitive' economies survived intact long enough to be subjected to studies by modern anthropologists. Looking at these studies, it does rather surprisingly appear that those cultures with the least sophisticated agriculture have the shortest working day. Figure 3.1, for example, plots the average minutes of daily work in a representative range of different cultures (adapted from Minge-Klevanna 1980, who also provides a strikingly clear empirical confirmation of Veblen's

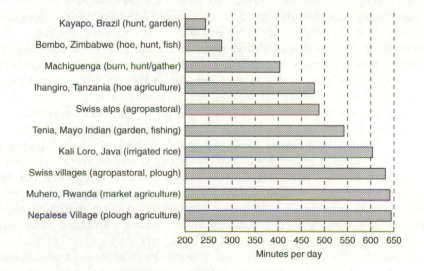

Figure 3.1. Work time in ten villages

assertions about gender divisions in less developed societies). We see that hunter-gatherers, or those with rather low-technology agriculture, have very short work times, hardly more than four hours per day in some cases. As more sophisticated techniques such as irrigation and ploughing emerge, and particularly as patterns of consumption become more complex, and the societies move from subsistence to market production, so hours of work rise. The most economically sophisticated of these groups are also the most closely tied into a market system, and have around eleven hours work per day.

The evidence for this view is summarized most entertainingly in Marshall Sahlins's classic text *Stone Age Economics*. The argument is neatly captured in his description of an African culture:

The Hadza, tutored by life and not by anthropology, reject the Neolithic revolution in order to keep their leisure. Although surrounded by cultivators, they have until recently refused to take up agriculture themselves 'mainly on the ground that this would involve too much hard work'. In this they are like the Bushmen, who respond to the Neolithic question with another: 'Why should we plant, when there are so many mongomongo nuts in the world.' (Sahlins 1970: 27)

Historians of economic development in the developed world echo this same argument. In pre-industrial societies there may have been twelve hours or more of work on work days. But the very large number of public holidays and religious feast days, together with low levels of activity during the winter, mean that for both artisans and agriculturalists, work time averaged across the year could have been as low as 2,100 hours, considerably less than in a modern economy (Wilensky 1961). From the Reformation onwards, the numbers of public holidays declined, the amount of off-season agricultural work increased, and work discipline in manufacturing industry intensified, so that by the mid-nineteenth century in Europe yearly work hours had risen to 3,500 or more (Thompson 1967).

Modern economics, as we have seen, explains this sort of increase in work time in terms of individualistic rational choice. Avoiding the technical details, the argument comes down to a proposition that by working longer hours we can earn more money, which we can spend to make our leisure time more intensely enjoyable. We work more and have less leisure, but the shorter leisure time, when combined with the extra money we can spend on it, could provide us with more satisfaction in total than we might alternatively have gained by taking more leisure combined with less money (e.g. Becker 1965; Juster and Stafford 1991).

It *may* be, for this sort of reason, rational for higher-wage workers to work longer hours, though there is nothing in the theory that suggests that they *must* do so—it depends on the shape of their preferences. However, the

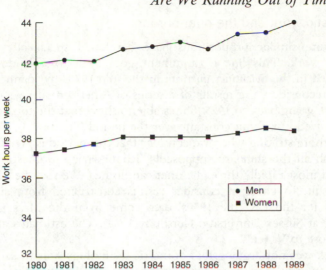

Figure 3.2. Actual working hours, adult men and women

empirical evidence from time-use data over recent decades has shown quite regularly that some better-qualified and hence higher-earning workers, tend to work considerably longer hours than less well-qualified and lower-earning workers; Wilensky claimed some evidence for this in the USA in the late 1950s, as did Young and Willmott in their *Symmetrical Family* study of the London region in 1970 (1973). This is of course cross-sectional evidence, but some might wish to infer from this that over time, as the working population gets on average more highly qualified, and earnings rise, so will hours of paid work.

And overall the cross-time evidence of change in hours of work, over the last decade or two, in the UK and in the USA, is not inconsistent with this view. Figure 3.2 charts the working hours of full-time manual workers in UK manufacturing industry from the 1970s to the 1990s. For both men and women, hours of work have been rising pretty steadily. More general data from the British New Earnings Survey suggest that white-collar work time may have been rising similarly. And a number of books and articles in the USA over the last decade have argued that the working hours of US men have not fallen for at least forty years (e.g. Owen, 1988; also see Owen 1989; Schor 1993).

So, economic and sociological theory, historical and anthropological evidence, and modern working-time statistics, all apparently converge on the proposition that work may increase rather than decline over historical time.

Domestic work and the dual burden

And quite similar propositions have developed specifically concerning unpaid work. This line of argument goes back to a landmark article published in the *Scientific American* in the mid-1970s by Joanne Vanek. Dr Vanek reconsiders the results of a series of American surveys of women's time use going back to 1925. She is able to show that the total of domestic work stayed just about constant over the period (Figure 3.3). This result is all the more striking when we consider that this period is precisely the one in which all the standard supposedly 'labour-saving' domestic equipment diffused most rapidly through American homes. We may be suspicious of this result: to check it consider results constructed from similar early surveys for the UK (the 1930s' data come from the Mass Observation Archive at Sussex University: Gershuny 1983). The estimates are astonishingly close to Vanek's.

Vanek was not arguing that domestic technology fails to save labour in any given task. Her argument is, rather, that the increased productivity of domestic labour encourages an increase in the range and quality of domestic production. So, though labour per task declines as new domestic technologies spread to more and more households, more tasks are carried out—clothes are changed more often, standards of cleanliness or cooking are raised. If the number of tasks increases at a faster rate than the rate at which labour per task decreases, then overall there is more work time.

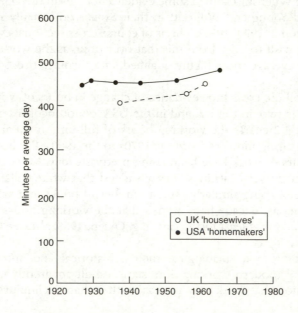

Figure 3.3. All unpaid work

Hence we have the apparent paradox (which in fact has a perfectly straight-forward explanation): domestic labour-saving devices may mean more domestic work.

We have to consider this argument together with the issue of who actually does the domestic work. Time-use studies arrive at a very clear conclusion on this: domestic work, and particularly core domestic tasks (such as cooking and cleaning), are quite strongly gender segregated. Domestic work, empirically, *is* women's work. But women's work is more than *just* domestic work. A very general phenomenon, throughout the First World, is that more women are seeking and getting paid jobs. Do women, as a result, do less domestic work?

Michael Young and Peter Willmott's *The Symmetrical Family* was the first of a series of studies which show that this growth in women's employment leads to a rather lopsided sort of symmetry (see also Meissner *et al.* 1975). Women become more like men within the workplace but not in the home, according to these and subsequent studies. Men hardly increase their domestic work when their wives go out to work; women do reduce their unpaid work, but not proportionately to their increase in paid work. The clearest way to demonstrate this is to adapt the jargon of conventional economics, through the 'elasticity' of time spent in domestic work with respect to paid work—that is, to look at how much domestic work time reduces as a result of each unit of increase in paid work time. Figure 3.4 plots these sorts of elasticity for women's 'core domestic work' (cooking and cleaning) in Britain in 1961. Two things emerge from this figure. First

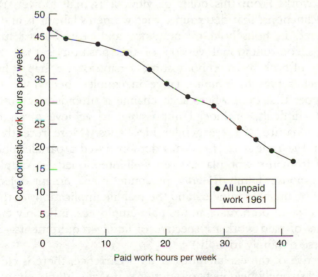

Figure 3.4. Elasticity of UK women's unpaid work with respect to paid work-hours

there is some elasticity: the more paid work, the less domestic work. But second, if we look closely at the scales, we realize that the change in domestic work is much smaller than the change in paid work: in Britain a shift from no paid work to 35 hours per week, brings with it a reduction from about 45 hours to 22 hours of domestic work per week. In other words, for each hour of extra paid work, these women did around half an hour less of unpaid work. So getting a job meant a substantial increase in their total (i.e. paid plus unpaid) work time.

The equivalent figures for men show very little change: irrespective of their hours in employment, they did around 30 minutes of domestic work per day. Why (assuming this evidence is correct) is there so little adjustment of the sexual division of labour? Two answers have been suggested.

The first is one that is not spoken any more—but it may be that some men still act on this belief. The clearest statement of it comes in fact from a Japanese discussion of this phenomenon:

Housewives by nature enjoy doing housework. They are happy to prepare delicious meals and provide fine clothes for the family. . . . For housewives, it is difficult to distinguish between housework and leisure. For this reason it is questionable to think that all time used for housework is work. (NHK 1971: 66)

This is not a line that we hear very often nowadays. What we do hear however is the female reflection of this male attitude: that the image of women as encapsulated in the Japanese quotation, combined with men's coercive power in marital relations, is what determines the pattern of women's work. From this point of view, it is male power, rather than female inclinations, that determines that women's labour is and should be concentrated in household maintenance and reproductive functions. A rather less confrontational version of this position is that the 'gender ideologies' of both sexes embody some version of the 'happy housewives' view, which serves to inhibit change in couples' behaviour. Hochschild (1989) argues that even where such change is intended by both partners, it may be difficult, or indeed impossible, to achieve given the deeply entrenched nature of these gender ideologies. (More recently the same author, in *The Time Bind* (1997) has demonstrated a parallel phenomenon operating from the workplace. Even well-intentioned US employers who explicitly espouse 'family friendly' personnel management objectives, may in practice be unable to understand the real-life implications of these for the work patterns of both male and female employees, inflexibly encouraging long hours of paid work irrespective of family requirements—in fact the very reverse of family friendly.)

Irrespective of the explanation for its occurrence, there is clearly a very widely and strongly held view of women's growing 'double burden' of paid and unpaid work. And one implication of this view is that there has been a recent historical decline in women's leisure time: if more women are getting jobs, and women don't reduce housework proportionately when they get jobs, then women in particular must have had an increase in their total of work over recent historical time.

Congested leisure?

We have considered change in paid and unpaid work time. Let us assume (as indeed we will see from the evidence in Chapters 5, 6, and 7) that not much happens to sleep time with economic development: so we must now turn to 'free' time. Much of the literature here is similarly pessimistic. Indeed, it is (as arithmetically speaking it must be) simply the mirror of argument about paid work. The first element in the thesis was that better-paid people, or people higher in the occupational scale, work longer hours for money. Better-paid people who work longer hours have more money to spend but less time to spend it in. Thus they have to cram *more* spending into this time. The richer we become, the more our 'free' time is crowded with consumption activities.

The original source for this line of argument is Steffan Linder's witty riposte to Veblen, *The Harried Leisure Class* (1970). His central message is of a social developmental *sequence*. He starts with the sorts of anthropological data that we have already touched on, and draws from these the general conclusion that 'traditional' societies have a surplus of free time. Linder claims that there is an intermediate stage, which he terms 'time affluence', exemplified by early twentieth-century Sweden, or Japan in the 1950s. And finally, economic development leads to 'time-famine' cultures, exemplified by the USA.

Linder provides us with a series of vignettes of harried Americans trying, with diminishing success, to cope simultaneously with all the mechanical and gustatory fruits of their affluence. Here is the ultimate harassed consumer: 'after dinner he may find himself drinking Brazilian coffee, smoking a Dutch cigar, sipping a French cognac, reading the *New York Times*, and entertaining his Swedish wife, all at the same time, and with varying degrees of success' (Linder 1970: 79).

The Harried Leisure Class is a very funny book. But the central question that Linder poses is a very serious one: is leisure still leisure when it ceases to be leisurely? Though it is now more than a quarter of a century old, Linder's book prophetically outlines the whole of the modern 'running-out-of-time' argument. We pay for economic growth, he tells us, by losing the essential characteristics of leisure. And the argument he makes is both explicitly Veblenian (in so far as he adopts Veblen's 'trickle-down' theory of consumption, in which each class in a hierarchical class system seeks to emulate the pattern of life of the class placed immediately above it), and also looks forward to the pessimism of Fred Hirsch's *Social Limits to Growth* (1977), which explains the collective irrationality that emerges from this: if members of *each* class succeed in emulating the previous consumption patterns of the immediately superior class, then *everyone* acquires more consumption—and there is no change whatsoever in the status-ordering, since each class has increased its consumption *in step*. This is the mechanism at the heart of Linder's account: an inflationary increase in the intensity of leisure activities, such that over time any given level of leisure activity denotes a declining level of social status.

Readers might wish to pause for a moment to consider whether they find these arguments convincing. Is it in fact their observation or experience that, as time passes, work time increases and that they also have to work harder at their leisure?

3. Antithesis: growth *and* leisure

The alternative view is that leisure is scarce at early stages of economic development, and becomes more plentiful through development.

The leisure problem

J. M. Keynes's essay 'The Future Possibilities for our Grandchildren', first published in 1928, is remembered now as an example of optimism in the midst of a great economic Depression. What may easily be forgotten is that the essay's optimistic message about the temporary nature of the developed world's short-term economic problem contains a paradoxical pessimistic long-term fear that 'the economic problem' (in the more general sense of how scarce resources can be made to meet the vast extent of the world's total wants) would eventually be *solved*.

Keynes's starting point is the remarkable rate of economic growth over the previous two centuries. On average, he estimates something of the order of 2 or 3 per cent growth per year, a seven- or ten-fold increase in a century. This leads him to assert that the then-current pessimism about the economic future is

wildly mistaken. We are suffering, not from the rheumatics of old age, but from the growing-pains of over-rapid changes, from the painfulness of readjustment between one economic period and another. The increase of technical efficiency has been taking place faster than we can deal with the problem of labour absorption; the improvement in the standard of life has been a little too quick. (1928: 322–8)

Taking the broad view, Keynes tells us, the economic problems of 1930 are just transitional, a brief frictional incident in the long historical progress of exponential economic growth. Divide human needs into two categories, he tells us (in an argument repeated forty years later almost word for word by

Hirsch): those which are 'absolute in the sense that we feel them whatever the situation of our fellow human beings may be'; and those which are 'relative in the sense that we feel them only if their satisfaction lifts us above, makes us feel superior to, our fellows'. The second class of needs are inherently insatiable. But the first class, the 'absolute' (or in the context of more recent discussions, we might say 'basic') needs, are, Keynes claimed in 1930, close (in historical time) to being satisfied. He suggests that eventually, say by the year 2030, the 'economic problem'—that is, the problem of satisfying the absolute or basic needs—may well be solved. (And, we might add, competitive consumption of the Linder–Hirsch sort is environmentally costly—and is so obviously a poor means of resolving positional rivalries that it clearly cannot drive a growth in consumption indefinitely.) 'This means that the economic problem is not, if we look into the future, the permanent problem of the human race.'

What, Keynes asks us, is so startling about this? Simply, the struggle for subsistence has always previously been the primary and most pressing problem for the human race—and indeed that 'of the whole of the biological kingdom from the beginnings of life in its most primitive forms.... If the economic problem is solved, mankind will be deprived of its traditional purpose':

Will this be a benefit? If one believes in the real values of life, the prospect at least opens up the possibility of benefit. Yet I think with dread of the readjustment of the habits and instincts of the ordinary man, bred into him for countless generations, which he may be asked to discard within a few decades.

The permanent problem for the human race, as Keynes constructs it, is simply finding enough things to occupy the day with. He points to the acute psychological problems of those who have been deprived of their traditional tasks and occupations. 'To those who sweat for their daily bread leisure is a longed-for sweet—until they get it.' Keynes quotes from what he claims to be an epitaph written for herself by an old charwoman:

> Don't mourn for me friends, don't weep for me never,
> For I'm going to do nothing for ever and ever.
> With psalms and sweet music the heavens'll be ringing,
> But I shall have nothing to do with the singing.

Doing nothing except listening to the singing: Keynes's temporal equivalent of the heavenly choir is the radio. His image of the leisure society is of an indefinite extension of (1930s) passive leisure activities. He suggests (perhaps having in mind the contemporaneous evidence on the psychological consequences of unemployment from Jahoda, Lazarsfeld, and Zeisel 1972) that it will only be for those who have to do with the singing that life will be tolerable. Keynes's leisure problem is filling the space left by the decline of work.

We have, Keynes tells us, solved the problem of providing for basic needs. We may choose, out of greed or stupidity, to allow the marginal pensioner to die of cold, the marginal child grow up with crooked bones because of malnutrition. But even in relatively poor rich countries, we could certainly prevent such occurrences if we wanted to. No doubt a few years of economic growth would not come amiss. But having made up for current shortages, it is, (he suggests to us, in 1930) rather difficult to imagine just exactly what future growth might consist *of*. New technologies mean less labour is needed to produce the goods and services we know we want. What we should fear, Keynes tells us, is that we may abolish work.

The leisure society

Veblen, from a sociological perspective, sees leisure time as the currency of social differentiation: as societies become more complex and highly differentiated, so leisure time becomes more widely diffused across the society (and hence devalued as a currency of status). Keynes gives us a simpler economist's view, that leisure time grows as a result of that progressive advance in techniques of production that allows the satiation of economic needs. The French sociologist Joffre Dumazadier in *Towards a Society of Leisure* added a basically political explanation: he sees leisure as an aspect of human liberty, and he accordingly views the historical growth of leisure time as a part of the process of *political* modernization.

By adopting this developmental view he is, in part, following Veblen. In a quite direct sense, the 'democratization' of leisure constitutes relief from the consequences of political tyranny for work time. The reduction of the working hours of manual workers, the emergence of new 'proletarian' leisure activities which have not 'trickled down' from upper-class practices, and the increasingly even spread of traditional leisure activities across the social classes—all these must represent some sort of escape from the temporal consequences of feudal power and the oppressive tendencies of industrial capital. And he is also, in part, following Keynes, in so far as the growth of leisure time means an escape from the metaphorical tyranny of economic want.

And there is yet another idealistic element: the connection between leisure and citizenship. Reducing the proportion of the day that must be devoted to work, frees time for education and self-improvement, for political participation, and for cultural activities. And, less idealistic, there is the intrinsic attraction of new leisure technologies. Dumazadier echoes the Lynds' 1937 respondents in *Middletown*, who celebrate the radio and the motor car as family toys, new sorts of focus for play with other members of their own households.

In this last sense Dumazadier's book plays spring to the high summer of American futurology in which the essence of leisure is high-technology play. From Huizinga's *homo ludens* we advance to Kahn, Brown, and Martell (1976) whose view of progress (only slightly exaggerated) is the helicopter in every garage. From leisure as an attribute of the active citizen, we slide, even in Dumazadier's relatively sober text, towards leisure as escape from responsibilities, a reversion to an infantile state in which *we just don't have to work*.

One central strand of modern notions of the leisure society sees leisure activities as the residue, simply what is left behind when we take away work. We solve the economic problem, and what is left is leisure. There are connections with the concept of the diminishing marginal utility of income, which reaches its end point in the notion of a post-materialist society, the society in which there is nothing left to work *for*.

Economic growth and the leisure preference

Let us go right back to the beginning of the 'running-out-of-time' argument to the anthropological evidence of very short work times in very 'primitive' cultures. The most important question we have to ask is: why did these particular cultures survive to be studied? Presumably these particular groups found particularly cosy ecological niches. We might suspect that the reason there were so many mongomongo nuts in the world was that no one, other than the Bushmen, was particularly keen on eating them. If there were competition for them, they would become more difficult to find, work time would rise. And then, perhaps, their answer to the Neolithic question would be different. It is only when gathering becomes difficult that we must start to garden.

In other words, the *surviving* Palaeolithic cultures, those that lasted long enough to be studied by twentieth-century anthropologists, may well be very unrepresentative of Palaeolithic cultures in general. Similarly the medieval historical evidence of rather short yearly average hours of work comes from the surviving records of relatively rich and successful towns, where the profits on artisanal work are sufficient to support frequent holidays. Can we be sure that the evidence that we do not have, of struggling towns and of the ultimately unsuccessful guilds whose records have not come down to us, would not tell us a very different story? Again, it may be that the conditions for the survival of the evidence are also conditions which select those cases with shorter than average work years. Again, a problem of selection.

And the modern data on work-time discussed earlier in this chapter were similarly selective: they were, simply, too modern (and too focused on Anglophone countries). Remember, the evidence in Figure 3.2 covered just the 1970s to the 1990s. Figure 3.5 shows the same UK data series, but going back to the 1940s. The regular five-year oscillation we see from the late 1950s to the late 1970s is simply the business cycle. At the low point in the

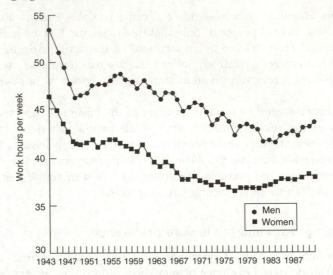

Figure 3.5. Actual working hours, adult men and women

business cycle, there is less overtime, and unions are successful in negotiating shorter basic hours, since the employers are happier with this than with higher pay rises. After the upturn, hours at first rise, but then as the business cycle approaches its peak and profitability increases, unions succeed in lowering basic hours further. The cycle of increase and decrease in hours is repeated, but each time at a lower level. There is in effect a ratchet, to the beginning of the 1980s: a slow, regular, step-by-step reduction of work hours.

Viewed in this longer-term perspective the work time increase of the 1980s and the 1990s looks rather an exception to the general pattern. And the longer our perspective becomes, the more exceptional the 1980s seem to be. The evidence for the earlier part of the century is rather less reliable, and covers manual workers in the whole of the economy rather than just manufacturing, but confirms the generally downwards trend. And Figure 3.6 gives us an even longer view. These very long-term data are for London alone, and only for men in some particular trades. But there is similar evidence for a dozen other cities, which show just the same trends and levels (Dept. of Employment 1971). And though the comparison with our more recent manufacturing data suggests that the 'normal' hours of the early data series understate the 'actual' hours of work, it would nevertheless seem that the conclusion we have to draw is that the long-term historical trend of paid work hours, at least for men in manual occupations, has been really quite strongly downwards for something like a century and a half, and that the reversal of this trend, at least for the UK, from the start of the 1980s,

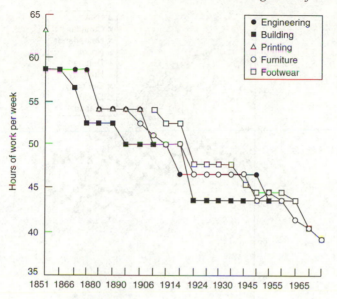

Figure 3.6. Normal hours of manual work in various industries: London men

may be quite misleading as a guide to the longer term. But, of course, on this evidence one might still argue that 1980 marks the point at which the downwards trend of the last century and a quarter is finally reversed, and that in future the trend will continue upwards. Here we must turn to some more general international evidence.

Figure 3.7 charts normal work hours for ten developed economies from the 1960s (for both sexes together, since in five of the cases the evidence is not available separately by sex); of these, the USA stands out most clearly as exceptional in maintaining its work time apparently constant for the three decades from 1960. The UK and Canada fit the more general pattern until the 1980s, and then show an increase in work hours. The other seven show declines in work hours continuing through the 1980s.

Of course, this is the period of the maximum rate of entry of women into the paid workforce; it could be that the apparent reduction of work hours is an artefact of the 'dilution' of the mean for men with long hours of paid work, by increasing numbers of women with shorter hours of work. So Figure 3.8 charts paid work time for the sexes separately just for the five European economies for which we have appropriate data; we see that a general downwards trend shows separately both for men and for women in the Netherlands, Germany, and Spain, Norway shows a generally level pattern, and that the 1980s trend of increasing work hours in the UK is

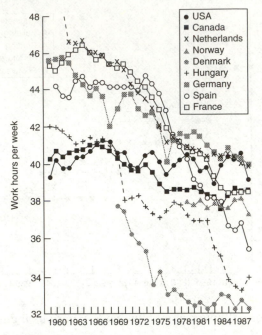

Work hours per week

	USA
●	USA
■	Canada
x	Netherlands
▲	Norway
✹	Denmark
+	Hungary
▥	Germany
○	Spain
□	France

1960 1963 1966 1969 1972 1975 1978 1981 1984 1987

Figure 3.7. Normal work hours, men and women, manual occupations in manufacturing

still the exception. Plainly, if the continental European countries behaved in quite a different manner, we cannot conclude that the 1980s increases in paid work time in the Anglophone countries was any sort of historical inevitability. Presumably what we see here is the reflection of a difference in the natures of the economic and other policy regimes in the two groups of countries.

The multinational statistics quoted here (which come from various ILO *Yearbooks*) rely on a very varied collection of methodologies. So the evidence of these last figures is in itself no more than suggestive as to change in the workforce as a whole. And this evidence does cover only manual workers in manufacturing industry. These workers are declining as a proportion of the total workforce, and the manufacturing sector in many developed economies has become much smaller. There may be quite different patterns for other occupations and industries—but there are no extant historical statistics for these. Indeed, the conclusion to the 'time-squeeze' debate that I suggest at the end of this chapter, and which is supported by the time-diary-based evidence for the second half of the twentieth century, is that the question of what happens to work time only becomes a meaningful one once we differentiate by social status.

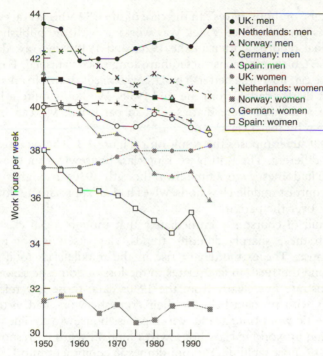

Figure 3.8. Work hours in manufacturing, manual occupations

Unpaid work time

What then of unpaid work? The pessimistic view had two elements: the historical constancy of domestic work time, and the tendency for women to maintain their domestic work burden when they take on new paid work responsibilities.

We started with Vanek's startling finding that domestic work time showed, if anything, a slight upward movement throughout the period of diffusion of 'labour-saving' equipment to households. This must count as one of the more successful sociological papers; its influence has been pervasive and survives to this day. We still, after nearly thirty years, find it quoted approvingly in academic articles, and the finding now has become one of those free-floating social science 'factoids', routinely accepted by non-specialists who may have never seen or even heard of the original text (for example, the science fiction writer Michael Crichton gave an extended though unattributed summary of Vanek's original *Scientific American* article in his novelization of the film *Jurassic Park*).

But Vanek's picture does not tell quite the whole story. Figure 3.3 estimates the average domestic work time for the whole population of 'homemakers' or 'housewives'. In the case of the USA, this average estimate is all that is possible, since Vanek was working with the published tables from original reports written in the 1920s and 1930s; the raw data from which these tables were constructed have long since vanished. For the UK however we can do a little better. The UK evidence is drawn from a cache of manuscript diaries dating from the mid-1930s. We know quite a lot about the people who kept these diaries, and in particular, we can break the sample down by social class.

Figure 3.9 superimposes the result onto Figure 3.3. The picture we now get is very different. The British working-class housewives show a continuous decline in domestic work time from the early 1950s through to the mid-1970s. By contrast middle-class housewives had an approximate doubling of housework over the period.

We should of course say immediately that though social class is associated with these sharply differing trends, class itself is not really the effective cause. The extraordinary rise in the middle-class total between the 1930s and the 1960s in fact relates to the loss of domestic servants. (We can demonstrate this clearly from the 1930s data: those few middle-class housewives with no paid help for their domestic work had virtually the same domestic work time as the working-class housewives.) The period of rapid decline in working-class housewives' unpaid work corresponds with the period of most rapid diffusion of domestic equipment into UK homes,

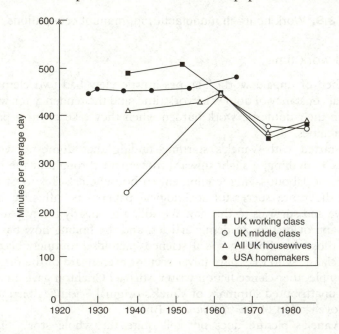

Figure 3.9. All unpaid work

and is presumably to be explained in part at least by the influence of this new domestic technology. By the 1960s the totals for the two classes have converged, and the declining trend continues, with further diffusion of domestic equipment. The overall trend turns upwards again as we move into the 1980s: this reflects an increase in shopping and childcare. If we look just at the core housework tasks of cooking and cleaning, we find a continuous decline in housework time from the early 1950s.

The apparent constancy in the total, in the UK at least, is thus an artefact produced by the conflation of the downwards effect of the new domestic technologies for working-class women, and the substantial increase in work caused by the loss of paid domestic service in middle-class households. Vanek (1978), in her more academic writings on this subject, does in fact also make clear that her early data include a large number of middle-class urban women with paid domestic help (much of the American data for the early period comes from a survey of women college graduates). But the careful qualification in the original articles is lost in subsequent use of Vanek's materials by others, and only the dramatic and slightly misleading central finding survives.

It is only a surmise that this pattern of events holds also for the USA, but the surmise is supported by the fact of the strong middle-class bias of the early US material. And there is certainly strong US evidence both for the early impact of domestic technology: the Lynds, interviewing women in Middletown, asked how their housework time compared with their mothers' at a similar period. Table 3.1 shows, for example, very substantial reductions in working-class women's clothes-washing time between the 1890s and the 1920s, which were explained by the Lynds' respondents in terms of the newly acquired washing machine; the 'business' (i.e. middle-) class women show little change presumably because the availability of private domestic services had if anything increased over this period. (Note however that the estimates of time use here derive from questionnaires, and indeed substantially retrospective questionnaires for the mothers' time. So

Table 3.1. Change in women's domestic work, Middletown

	Working class		Business class	
	1924	1890	1924	1890
Washing, ironing time/week (column %)				
none	0	5	60	50
0–2 hours	2	1	0	3
2–4 hours	20	3	15	10
5–8 hours	54	30	20	15
>9 hours	24	61	5	23
No. of households	*120*	*94*	*40*	*40*

really the strongest claim that can properly be made for this evidence is that it records how women who had themselves lived through the first and rapid diffusion of domestic technology, themselves *thought of* the effect of that technology.)

The second element in the pessimistic view is the relative inelasticity of unpaid work with respect to paid which results in women's 'dual burden' of paid and domestic work. In this case all the evidence, from all the time-use surveys without exception, supports the proposition that women bear on average a disproportionate burden of housework when they enter paid work. (And, similarly, the evidence is consistent with the view that in general husbands fail to increase their contributions to housework so as to reduce the burden on their wives.)

But the evidence usually employed to demonstrate this tends to be cross-sectional (i.e. using evidence from a single time-use survey to compare people in different employment situations at a particular point in time); the longitudinal evidence, though it is still quite worrying, does suggest a slightly less pessimistic conclusion.

Let us reconsider the 'elasticity' curve in Figure 3.4. Recall that in the UK in 1961, the cross-sectional rate of substitution was something of 25 minutes reduction of domestic work for each extra hour of paid work. By the mid-1980s, as we see from Figure 3.10, the cross-sectional rate of substitution is not much changed. But the total of domestic work is considerably lower throughout the full range of paid work times: the elasticity curve as a whole has shifted quite dramatically downwards. Women doing a 35 hour per week

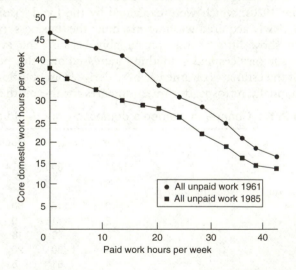

Figure 3.10. Elasticity of UK women's unpaid work with respect to paid work-hours

job in the mid-1980s had had about 17 hours of unpaid work, something like three-quarters of an hour per day less core domestic work than their equivalents in 1961—despite the fact that those in the 1980s are much more likely to have husbands and families. They are still not losing this unpaid work on an hour-for-hour basis with paid work, but the dual burden effect is diminishing. (These elasticity estimates and their shifts over time are, as we shall see in Chapter 7, mirrored in the time-use estimates from other countries.)

Many more women have jobs now than thirty years ago. But, never-theless, on the basis of the UK 1961 cross-sectional evidence we would have predicted much higher levels of domestic work for the 1980s than was actually the case. Plainly, as is often the case, the cross-section elasticity curves are not a sound basis for historical predictions: many more women now have jobs than previously, but employed women in general do less unpaid work now than they did. (And men's domestic work time, according to the evidence we shall be discussing in later chapters, increases substan-tially, albeit from a very low base.)

4. Synthesis: a changing class distribution of leisure time?

Neither the theoretical arguments we have discussed so far, nor the empiri-cal evidence we have considered, are entirely convincing answers to the question of the nature of the work–leisure balance. In the following chap-ters, we shall try to establish some more adequate theory and more extensive empirical evidence. But we can now go at least some way towards explaining the widespread perception that modernizing societies are 'run-ning out of time'. The explanation rests on differences among social classes and between the sexes in the evolution of the balance between work and leisure.

Time use and social differentiation

Veblen argues that, in pre- and early industrial societies, class divisions of society, though based on material possessions and inherited positions, are expressed most fundamentally in time: he suggests that access to free time is the primary means of social differentiation. Those with possessions and positions use these to annex leisure. They constitute a leisure class which relies for its extensive consumption on the labour of a 'working class' which by definition has scarce leisure, and has much lower levels of consumption.

The class division is accentuated by the nature of the consumption activities of the leisure class, which itself serves (and indeed is intended) to demonstrate the subordinate position of the labour class. The degree of division will necessarily vary between societies. In part, this intersocietal variation will reflect the size of the surplus above the level of subsistence. Let us say that the surplus is the amount of unallocated time left in the society once its members' subsistence needs have been satisfied. If there is no surplus, then obviously there can be no leisure class. The surplus in turn reflects the natural productive endowments of the physical environment, and also the organization and technology employed to satisfy the wants of the members of the society.

Different forms of social organization have impact both on the size of the surplus and on its distribution. Veblen concentrated to a large degree on the European feudal model of development, in which the development of military organization enables a rather extreme division of the surplus, and allows its reproduction and intensification through conquest and oppression. The accumulated surplus is exchanged for stores of weapons, and for contracts of military fealty, and these in turn permit further accumulation. The possession of this accumulated surplus, as well as its origin as spoil gained through warfare, is (Veblen tells us) symbolized in the engagement of the males of the upper class in games and pastimes that mimic military prowess (and also by the idleness of the women of this class which, in Veblen's extended and very serious joke, may be taken as symbolizing their status as booty from successful raids).

This pattern may continue into succeeding stages of development. The feudal division between the aristocratic leisure class and the common labouring class, reproducing itself through inherited real property and inherited arsenals and associated personal fealties, and expressed as conspicuous (if strenuous) idleness, can to some degree be matched or imitated by merchants who use accumulated financial capital, or by the children of the factory masters of the early Industrial Revolution using material capital. Leisure is made honourable by association with the class that is able to idle.

Alternative ways of distributing leisure

But there are alternatives to Veblen's sort of pre-industrial division between the labour and the leisure class. There is a wide range of possible methods through which the society might allocate or distribute its surplus. At one extreme the surplus can just be left to rot (as the unpicked fruits in the territory of a group of hunter-gatherers will simply wither on the bough); the European feudal model is the opposite extreme in which the surplus is efficiently transformed into social structure through a hierarchical structure of fealties (via the exchange of military services for intermediate positions in the hierarchy). One alternative to the feudal solution is the potlatch, in which redistribution and stability of social structure is maintained by 'blowing' the entire surplus in an occasional cathartic and egalitarian orgy of consumption. Here what is honorific is not leisure itself, but the individual's responsibility for allowing others to enjoy it; rather than aiming for personal leisure, people in such cultures might work long hours in order to be members of the party-throwing class.

Another example—this not envisaged in Veblen's account—which serves to avoid the accumulation of a surplus (and the social instability that results from it), is the temporally structured dissipation of the surplus. The ancient Jewish leisure practices, the sabbath, the one- or two-day holiday at each new moon, the yearly cycle of holy-day pilgrimages to Jerusalem, the sabbatical year (one year in seven in which no agricultural labour was undertaken and all slaves were freed), and the Jubilee (occurring every fifty years, in which all real property reverted to its original owners) combined to provide extensive leisure without a leisure class, leisure distributed across the society (or at least across all the men of the society).

The other important factor is technology. For any given social structure or pattern of organization, the technology determines the surplus. The more useful knowledge, the larger the surplus. Knowledge ('human capital') is productive when it is embodied in individuals. Human capital may be reserved (in the sense that individuals or members of particular social groups can be prevented from acquiring it), but if it is to be used it must be possessed by someone. Other things being equal, the more knowledge a society wishes to deploy in its productive activities, the more people must be knowledgeable, the larger is 'the knowledge class'.

Of course, in such matters, other things never are equal, and the variation in the distribution of knowledge (for consumption as well as for production) is the main source of the difference between the various sorts of service society discussed in Chapter 2. But holding these variations on one side for the moment, let us first consider what is common across all societies in the course of development. We can certainly say that the process of economic development is dependent on the growth in the total quantity of knowledge, and hence on the growth in the size of those classes consisting of people who use special knowledge in production.

This growth leads inevitably to changes in the distribution of leisure. Those who develop their own skill will wish to extract a 'rent' for it and will be able to do so. As economically salient skills diffuse more widely across a population, fewer people are willing to engage in menial low value-added face-to-face servant-type production. And, indeed, in modern societies the new production that results from technological advance is often precisely of goods that can be used to substitute for servants—and for some of the unpaid labour that was previously contributed almost exclusively by women. Thus, 'self-servicing' (Gershuny 1978): those who previously consumed menial services produced by others, now both produce and consume their own.

We can put this concretely as a view which corresponds to Veblen's own speculations about the end of the leisure class. As the general technological level of the society rises, there emerge requirements for very high levels of

skill or productive competence, whose possessors can extract a 'rent' that
rivals or exceeds that of the possessors of material capital or the inheritors
of the feudal class, and positions towards the top of productive organizational hierarchies increasingly become sources of honour. And as production processes become more complex, more paid jobs may require skills
which command such rents. So a growing proportion of the richest and
most honoured members of the society have paid work in productive
institutions; and the specifically idle rich become a diminishing minority
in industrializing societies.

Previously, as we might say in Veblenian language, some members of the
labour class (mostly single women) produced low-value services for consumption by the leisure class in exchange for low wages, while other
members of the labour class (mostly married women) produced services
on an unwaged and unmechanized basis, for their own households. Long
hours of paid work for labour-class men, long hours of unpaid for labour-
class women; short hours (if any) of both sorts of work for the leisure class.
But with the later stages of industrialization, this sort of class differentiation, at least in terms of the broad aggregates of time use, may largely and
rapidly disappear. Those of superior social status increasingly achieve this
through their paid work, and some at least of these may compete for that
status by working longer hours. And as increasing numbers of women enter
this competition through the educational system, they will seek to remain
within it through their participation in the paid workforce, and will increasingly refuse to accept the traditional exclusion from these positions of
honour in the wider society as a result of their differential responsibility
for unpaid work within the household.

Changing patterns of class and gender difference

We can use the foregoing arguments and evidence to piece together a
somewhat conjectural long-term historical summary of the changing
work–leisure balance and its class and gender distribution. There is little
doubt that the very simplest social groups for which we have any sort of
evidence show a very considerable gender differentiation along the lines of
Veblen's contrast between men's exploits and women's industry. Minge-
Klevana (1980) shows how this categorical distinction corresponds to a
substantial difference in work time (greatly to the advantage of the men).
It is not implausible that the technical change and growth in productivity
during the 'neolithic revolution' may have led to some increase in work
time, and similarly there may be some grounds for asserting that there was
an intensification of work effort and work time through the first stages of
the Industrial Revolution.

But it is clear that paid work time, at least for manual workers in
industrial societies, has been reduced substantially since the middle of the

nineteenth century. What we have to establish in the following chapters is the theoretical basis for, and evidence of, what happens next, to paid work, and to unpaid work, and how these are distributed.

So far we have established three distinct sets of hypotheses.

As regards the overall total of *leisure relative to work*, we have the propositions (from Chapter 2) that as the society becomes more productive, and shifts its time proportionately from the satisfaction of basic to luxury wants, there may be at least the weak presumption that leisure time increases so as to provide an increased opportunity for members of the society to consume what they are increasingly effective at producing. It was also argued that societies can influence this balance through their choice of production and consumption 'regimes'.

As regards *differentiation between social classes*, we have discussed in this chapter a number of reasons for expecting a convergence, or even a reversal, of the previous patterns of distribution of work and leisure. We have the Veblen observations that (i) in advanced societies the possession of knowledge salient to productive activities is the major source of positions of high social status; (ii) while there is a maximum of 24 hours per day to be leisurely in, there is no upper bound to the extent of (and hence honour to be gained from) getting and spending the money gained from expenditure of similarly limited work time—so those with knowledge will be increasingly tempted to deploy their time in work; (iii) there is also the Becker proposition that short bursts of time devoted to intensely expensive but enormously pleasurable activities, paid for by long hours of work, may be more rational for those with the most production-salient knowledge than longer hours of less expensive and less intensely pleasurable leisure (though, with the exception of consciousness-altering substances with various degrees of legality it is quite difficult to imagine what these activities actually are); and (iv) we also note that the work activity of these 'knowledge workers' may itself be intrinsically enjoyable (and in part corresponds to the previous leisure activities of the erstwhile leisure class). So, just as (generally low-status) manual work time undoubtedly declined from the middle of the nineteenth century, so the work time of higher-status 'knowledge workers' may have increased, relative to manual, or maybe even absolutely, during the second half of the twentieth.

We also have some clear reasons to expect a (slow) *gender convergence* in the balance of the different sorts of work. If (whether for honorific or other reasons) women increasingly enter into and intend to remain in the paid workforce on at least equal terms with men, it is simply unfair that they should be expected to maintain a differential responsibility for unpaid work within traditional 'family' households. So they may be expected (i) to reduce the household total of unpaid work, where they remain responsible for it, and (ii) to seek to convince the male co-residents of their households to make appropriate contributions to the remaining unpaid work, or (iii) eventually leave, or observing these difficulties never enter, households where the first two strategies fail to redress the unfairness.

And I cannot resist adding a somewhat *ad hominem* (or in one respect, more specifically *ad feminam*) speculation here. I suspect that the vehemence and wide visibility of the current 'running-out-of-time' argument may relate to the specific life-circumstances of the writers on this subject (and perhaps also to some degree to their readers').

Consider: they, we, tend to be in the middle course of life (as most writers are). They are successful at their jobs (evidence: they're getting prominently published) and as a result are probably heavily in demand to write more, and speak and visit more. They probably have partners and children (since most middle-aged successful people do). So their own subjective life-experience will have been of a monotonic movement from the freedom from time pressure of graduate school and the single life into the increasing harried states of multiple-job coupledom and parenthood. The 'time-bind' argument, that life is getting tighter all the time, thus corresponds closely to their observations of their own lives.

Yet this correspondence is no real evidence at all. The 'running-out-of-time' argument is in fact about historical change, not about the personal experience of change through the lifecourse. It might, for example, be true that life always gets more hectic between young adulthood and middle age—and yet *also* true that over historical time life at any given life-stage gets *less* hectic. The gradient of time pressures through the first half of adulthood might be unchanged, while still the absolute level of time pressure at any life-stage decreases over time. (Indeed this corresponds to the evidence discussed in the later chapters of this book.)

It is not really possible to distinguish between historical change and life-stage effects through our own personal experience, because we live through these both simultaneously. Pretty much the only way we can make sense of this distinction in our own lives is to compare ourselves with our parents. And we are particularly likely to be misled as a result of the specifics of our own social situation. As writers (and hence members of the middle classes) we are quite likely to have had middle-class parents. If there has indeed been a reversal of the class–work-time gradient, then certainly our fathers will tell us we're working more than they did at the equivalent stage of their careers. But this only tells us about what has been happening to the (minority) middle-class part of the society. We know that something rather different has been happening to the rest of the society—it could as well be that the *average* change between father and same-class son, across the society as a whole, is in fact a *reduction* of paid work.

And the same problem is doubled and redoubled if we (middle-class British or American writers) happen also to be women. Our mothers will then also probably have been middle-class women. When they were our age (and we were children, and formed our expectations of middle-aged, middle-class lifestyles) they are likely to have been non-employed, and to have had a considerable amount of paid domestic help at home. We, by contrast, have jobs, and can't afford a nanny. And we're now doing the sort of job our fathers used to do, but (see previous paragraph) having to work longer hours at it. No wonder they tell us we're working too hard. No wonder we believe them.

4 The Individual's and the Society's Day: Micro- and Macro-Theories of Time Use

1. Preliminary remarks

Recursiveness and the first tongs

The Talmud lists ten unnatural objects that God created at the end of the sixth day, immediately before the first sabbath; these were the mechanisms necessary to His grand design, which were however not well integrated with the rest of creation. Among these ten was, according to one authority, that particularly unnatural object, the tongs that made the first tongs. Tongs were a crucial tool for workers in bronze in classical antiquity. But they were made of bronze.

The problem here is one of 'recursiveness'. Tongs are needed to make swords, that is easy to understand. Tongs are needed to make tongs: so how was the first pair made? Rather than asserting their extraordinary creation, we could say that the first, very crude near-tongs were made by pulling at a mass of molten bronze with a pointed stick, and then the near-tongs were used to make simple tongs, and the simple pair to make a more sophisticated one, and so on.

This is a recursive explanation, an explanation of a phenomenon which involves the phenomenon itself. This notion will be unfamiliar to many readers. Most common-sense explanations of day-to-day phenomena work non-recursively, that is why 'the first tongs' present a conceptual problem. Recursiveness is nevertheless a most important mode of explanation in many branches of science; some phenomena (notably but by no means exclusively in biology) can only be explained recursively. What follows is a sociological argument that works in a recursive mode.

From Bloomsday to Molly's breakfast

The conjectural history of the balance between work and leisure outlined in the previous chapter fits both the available evidence and the new comparative material presented in the following chapters. But the discussion lacks an adequate theoretical basis. Veblen's framework is insightful, it covers the necessary combination of micro- and macro-sociological issues, but modern readers may well feel it is not entirely plausible. This chapter, starting from (for the most part) more recent theoretical approaches, will construct a rather more general sociological theory of time allocation.

The major problem to be addressed is making a connection among three distinct levels of time accounts. To understand behaviour or action at each of these levels we need three corresponding lines of theory. These levels each involve distinct sorts of behavioural constraint, and have as we shall see different sorts of freedom of action. Yet they fit together hierarchically, and the accounts at each level must balance with the accounts at each other contiguous level. So, in order to adjust these three levels of action with each other, we will also need two intermediate processes of articulation (Figure 4.1).

The first level of time account deals with the development of the day in the form of the sequence of activities as they are actually experienced by individuals. We get up, we dress, wash, eat breakfast, take the children to school, clock on at the factory, and so on. We are aware, if not always in a conscious manner, of the constituents of this sequence, and any deliberations we may make on maintaining or changing our patterns of activity are located, for the most part, within this sequential awareness. (We will refer to this level of discussion as microsequential theory.)

This first is a particular sort of microsocial time account. At this level social facts are comprehensively accounted as, literally, a story, a narrative. This is the level of awareness described in Joyce's account of Bloom's day. This is the level at which we experience time and make decisions about our activities. At this level the model is very straightforward, we have habits, our days and weeks are for the most part habitual sequences of activities; behavioural change is the piecemeal modification of these habitual sequences. There are options for alternative activities at particular places and times of day; the accessibility of these are determined by the individual's position (or the household's position) in the social structure. In turn, the individual's location in the social structure is a consequence of his or her previous actions (i.e. education, job and marital history, leisure patterns). What we have done determines who we are; who we are determines what we do; what we do determines who we become. This is a recursive model at the micro level.

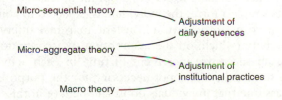

Figure 4.1. Three levels of theory, two forms of articulation

To differentiate this level of account from the next, the reader is asked to participate in a brief thought experiment. Consider: how much time, during the week ending last Sunday, did you devote to your job? To washing dishes? To watching television? Most people, in all but rather special circumstances, will be unable to answer these questions straightforwardly. (The exceptions are those who are paid on an hourly basis or are constrained to keep an hour-by-hour log of their work, and those who do not engage at all in the particular activity.) The point is that the answers to these questions are not normal types of self-knowledge. We do not know, for the most part, how much time we devote to the things we do (some empirical evidence of this lack of self-knowledge is given in Appendix 1). Nevertheless, we can give a quite detailed narrative of the events of our day, from which aggregate time balances can be calculated. This is, incidentally, the reason that we collect and analyse diary evidence, rather than asking respondents for direct time estimates. This is also what distinguishes the first level of account, the level of sequential, narrative, temporal awareness within which all conscious action takes place, from the next level of account, which still concerns the individual, but which concerns aggregate facts about the individual of which that individual is in general not aware.

The second level deals with the aggregate arithmetic of this experience for the individual. The durations of the various activities in the daily sequences which make up our consciousness may be added up to produce, for each of us, aggregate totals of the time we have devoted to the various categories of activity—so much sleep, so much work, so many minutes of childcare, and so on. This is the 'micro-aggregate' level of discussion. Even though we are for the most part unaware of what these aggregate totals are, there are nevertheless certain constraints on the aggregate distributions of our days amongst the various activities. (And as we shall discuss in a following section, these aggregate totals of experience accumulate through our lives to form 'human capital' relevant to both consumption and pro-duction.)

Conventional economic theory, and some approaches to sociological theory (e.g. Coleman 1990) would seek to understand the individual's day as the outcome of a rational process of allocation of aggregate totals of time. The 'rational choice' model of time allocation sets a time budget against a preference schedule to select an optimum feasible combination of activities. In its simplest form, the individual is expected to adjust his or her activity pattern so as to achieve a constant marginal utility across each category of activity (which, on the assumption of a continuous decline in utility from each successive increment of time in each activity, serves to maximize the total utility). It is not necessary, for the purposes of this sort of theory, to assume that individuals do in fact behave in this way, but only that groups in aggregate behave *as if* individuals do so.

For our purposes, however, it is perfectly sufficient, and rather more helpful, to construct a model in which 'comprehensive rationality' is just one among a range of behaviours that may precede the events of the day. Indeed, it is one extreme of the range, where the other extreme is simply repetition of previous behaviour (i.e. 'habit'). We might also add, in the light of the previous discussion of the individual's general ignorance of his or her own aggregate time balance, that intentional, comprehensive rational choice leading to marginal adjustment of the time totals (as opposed to piecemeal adjustment of the activity sequence, which we shall discuss in a moment) will be rare to the point of complete absence from any sample of real people.

But if what follows rejects the overall 'marginalist' approach to the explanation of time-use patterns, it still relies heavily on one specific and very important aspect of the marginalist theory, that concerned with the 'time-budget constraint'. Becker's major contribution (1965) to the following discussion comes from his identification of a time-budget constraint in the form of necessary mixes of paid work and consumption time. Holding unearned income on one side for a moment, we all need to spend time earning money to buy goods and services, which we then need to spend time consuming. The more time we spend earning money, the less time we have to spend on the commodities we spend our money on.

There are two sorts of variation in time-requirement characteristics of commodities: first, at any given individual income level, the more expensive a commodity is, the more paid work time is required to buy it; and second, some commodities require a lot of time to yield satisfaction (e.g. a country walk) whereas others (e.g. a glass of whisky) yield satisfaction quickly. People with different social structural characteristics (i.e. wage rates, consumption skills) will therefore tend to engage in different mixes of work and the various consumption activities. Without assuming any particular process of maximization of satisfaction, it is clear that some particular combinations of consumption are simply inaccessible to some people; in particular people with a lower rate of pay cannot consume those more expensive services which require longer consumption time—they simply do not have enough hours in the day. We can achieve some at least of the conclusions of the Becker-type approach, without having to make any sort of assumption about procedures for choice among the range of options defined by these sorts of budget constraint.

There is also a third level of account, symbolized in these discussions by the set of connected activities concerned in Molly Bloom's breakfast. This deals at the level of the society with the relationships among the aggregate amounts of time in various categories of activity spent by the various members of the society. Time spent in some sorts of activities by some people, often requires time to be spent in some other sorts of activities by other members of the society. Molly eats her cooked kidneys, others must fatten the pigs and manufacture the oven. We go to the opera; others must sing in it. (This level of discussion might be thought of as macrosociological.)

The theory must establish at the macro level what the conditions are of association between different sorts of amounts of time devoted to the various production and consumption activities. The society's 'great day' is the aggregate of the narrative sequences of all its members. But the various components of the narrative sequences must add up in some very specific ways. In addition to the individual Becker-type budget constraint, there is another, societal-level budget constraint. The sum total of time devoted to each category of consumption, by members of the society, must be associated with an appropriate sum of times devoted to a particular corresponding set of production activities. A given national audience for opera will support just so many opera singers. (There are also other sorts of macro-interdependency, including those of simultaneity of time and space: for every Bloom who wishes to buy a breakfast kidney at 8 a.m., there must be a butcher's assistant available to sell it.)

The three levels of discussion fit together in an hierarchical manner: the microsequential is summarized within the micro-aggregate, which is in turn encapsulated within the macro. It is clearly possible that the accounts at any one level may fail to 'add up' at another level. In such a case there must be some adjustment.

For example, Leopold Bloom's day consists of a mix of production-related and consumption activities, he spends some time at the newspaper office, and some time at the pub. Of course, on any one day these do not have to balance—but through the whole set of his days, he must spend enough time at the office to earn enough money to buy the amount of beer required by the amount of time he spends in the pub. He may not know either the amount of time he spends at work or at the pub (just as the readers of this chapter are in most cases unaware of how much time they spend in these and other specific activity categories). But an imbalance between his work time and his consumption time as a whole may eventually impinge on his consciousness through the medium of a drain on his financial resources. He will presumably react to the temporal imbalance thus revealed by some sort of behavioural adjustment, some systematic change in the sequence of activities that make up his day. He may perhaps decide to stay in the office at lunchtime rather than going to the pub. In this case he makes an adjustment to his daily temporal sequence without ever knowing, let alone explicitly considering, his aggregate temporal balance. (We might note that there are other sorts of potential imbalances between these levels, as for example an imbalance in the total work time of spouses as revealed by one engaging in a recreational activity at a time of day that the other is at work or cooking, which results in a domestic argument; this may be resolved by adjustments in the distribution of domestic responsibilities, without either spouse ever knowing what the actual work time totals are.)

So the first process of articulation is that individual behavioural adjustment which from time to time intervenes between the micro-sequential and the micro-aggregate time accounts of individuals or small groups.

We have already mentioned an example of the second process of articulation. Suppose Molly Bloom does decide to take her breakfast at a café. There are consequences at the micro-aggregate level: she (or Leopold Bloom) must in principle transfer some time so as to earn enough to pay the margin of extra cost of the café breakfast over the home-cooked one. There are also potential implications at the macrolevel. The café becomes more crowded. An entrepreneur may as a result infer a growing demand for public catering facilities and open a new restaurant, thus increasing employment opportunities and altering, in a small way, the structure of the economy. People see Molly Bloom at the café: observing her adds to the informal statistical collection that constitutes each individual's perception of what is 'normal behaviour'. As such observations are made and are discussed by members of some social group, they may influence a change in what is accepted to be normatively sanctioned for that group.

Molly Bloom's new breakfast habit cannot be said to be a sufficient cause of either the change in economic structure, or of the change in norms, since each requires in addition responsive action by other individuals. The change in individual behaviour also involves action by social groups. The fact that fashionable entertainers now eat out at breakfast time may be noticed in the 'lifestyle' pages of the newspapers. Expansion-minded entrepreneurs see the opportunity to build more cafés, or design larger ones; factory or office managers may arrange that catering facilities are available in the morning as well as midday. Religious leaders decry the further erosion of the home base of family life, and professional nutritionists note the reduction in parental control of their children's food intake, and so a new contrary subgroup norm emerges that decries café breakfast-taking as marginally immoral. Politicians propose new regulations. And so on. Or to put it more generally: structural and normative adjustments intervene between changes in the individual's and the society's aggregate time balance

The first level of account provides a minor example of recursion in the relationship of biography to behaviour. The full system of three levels of account and two processes of articulation constitutes a grand recursion. The first level (sequential accounts) is nested within the second (the aggregate day for the individual), and the second is nested within the third (the balance of time of the great day for the society). The two processes of articulation enable adjustment of balances at the higher levels to changes at lower levels. But there is also a reverse influence, of the highest level on the lowest.

At the highest level, at the level of the balance of activities that make up the great day of the society, we have what determines the size and nature of the material institutions which constitute the structural characteristics of the society (for example the level of availability of jobs, or of service facilities for consumption). And here we also have what determines those immaterial institutions (the shared or negotiated perceptions of statistical regularities, agreed views about the sorts of activities that are, and hence are accepted as proper to be, undertaken by particular sorts of people) which constitute the society's norms. These high-level characteristics of structures and norms influence in turn the pattern of actual opportunities and constraints that we experience from day to day, and within which we evolve our quotidian sequences. This is the grand recursion, in which the pattern of daily life determines social structure, and social structure in turn determines the pattern of daily life. The aggregate of what we all do is what the society does; what the society does both enables and constrains what we can do as individuals.

The physiocratic model of time allocation

The first two of the three levels of social account are, in one way or another, well represented in modern social theory. The microsequential level is covered by elements of the arguments of Hägerstrand (1978; see also Carlstein and Thrift 1978; Giddens 1984; and Bourdieu 1979), while the micro-aggregate level is derived from a well-established economic model due originally to Gary Becker (1965; also Gronau 1977; Kooreman and Kapteyn 1990a, b; 1992). The third level is however less familiar; we should, before going further into the detail of the argument, give a general picture of what is involved in the macrotheory.

It involves a line of argument that has been out of favour in anglophone social science for some two centuries, (though it has survived among French writers of the regulation school: Aglietta 1979). In the 'physiocratic' model the physiological interdependence of the vital organs of a human body is a metaphor for the interdependence of the production and consumption patterns of the various groups or classes in a society. Quesnay (a physician as well as the originator of the physiocratic approach) constructed what is perhaps the first formal economic model (the 'economic table'), which demonstrated the connection between patterns of consumption or styles of life, and economic structural patterns, the sizes of social groups or classes, and the nature of their production activities (Quesnay 1798).

Quesnay's model is described through flows of money among the various social groups (with distinct production and consumption characteristics— peasants and artisans and landowners in Quesnay's case). The later part of this chapter presents a model in which what passes between groups is not money, but time; members of each group in a society spend some of their time in activities which ultimately go to meet the wants of other people, and in exchange receive other people's time as embodied in goods and services which meet their own wants. What follows has a rather wider scope than Quesnay's original argument: he described just the aggregate expenditure balances among the various social groups; what follows starts at the level of the determination of individual behaviour (i.e. time use), and relates this to the broad balance of activities among social groups. Thus, what emerges is a new time-use theory which relates the sizes and activity patterns of social groups to the work–leisure balance in the society.

One detail of the original physiocratic argument does survive, as a footnote to mainstream Anglo-Saxon economics: the operation of the 'economic table' provides an analogy with the operation of the income multiplier in Keynesian models. But our use of Quesnay's concept is considerably broader. We make the general assertion that economic structure may be understood in terms of the balance between the consumption and production activities of various groups or classes in a society. (Quesnay's model is rejected in a famous passage of *The Wealth of Nations*, but for reasons which are not at all relevant to the arguments made here: Smith 1910.) The central proposition of physiocratic models concerns the consumption patterns of social groups (the Estates of France for Quesnay, industrial or occupational categories in what follows: I shall sometimes use the tendentious term 'classes' to describe these). The overall consumption patterns of the classes in aggregate constrains not just the demand for the labour of each particular class but also, in a way that can be very simply explained, the supply of labour by each class.

In the broadest of terms, what I have to say has much in common with the standard account of the development of industrial societies, in which the growth and decline of occupational groupings is a consequence of twin changes, in the relative efficiency of production of various commodities, and in the pattern and distribution of consumption of these commodities. What is distinctive in what follows is the clear theoretical statement of the connection between styles of life (i.e. consumption patterns) and economic structures, which can be straightforwardly estimated from empirical (time- and money-budget) data.

What follows is a model of what might be termed the 'material economy', a model of the actual flows of goods and services among the members of a society, as denominated in terms of labour and consumption time. In doing so, I am not intending to suggest that the material economy is in any sense more real than the money economy; indeed, prices and wages play an important role in this account of the material economy. And undoubtedly, by using time rather than money as the accounting instrument, we do lose some understanding of short-term operation of the system. But to compensate, we gain a rather more general picture of the longer-term processes of socio-economic change. The physiocratic model explicitly includes considerations of what people do with (and hence why they want) the goods and services purchased or otherwise acquired from 'the economy', and reasons why people might wish to supply their labour, rather than treating these as extrinsically determined propensities of the economic system. The account of long-term change in economic structure that follows is perhaps more interesting from a sociological perspective than is the conventional economic explanation. It allows us to contribute a specifically sociological perspective to the understanding of the evolution of economic systems.

2. Determining daily events: microsequential theory

The microsequential theory of time use is essentially recursive. Rather than the single-step solution of a set of simultaneous equations, the sociological explanation of time allocation envisages a multiple iteration: behaviour is explained in terms of a progressive modification of habits and abilities. What we do now is what we did before, with small changes. What we do is constrained by what we can do. What we can do is determined by what we have done. There are two important elements to this part of the microsocial theory: the long-range model of the determination of social location (for which we may adopt a version of the 'human capital' approach related to that of Bourdieu); and the short-range model of how social and geographical location determines the activity sequence (our account is based on Hägerstrand's temporo-spatial modelling but also draws on Giddens's application of this approach).

Human capital

The central concept employed in Bourdieu's model is a metaphor. Just as the behaviour of an enterprise is determined by the nature and location of its physical plant or 'capital', that of the individual is determined by his or her 'human capital'. It is the fixed set of abilities, knowledge, experience, and social (and geographical) position that, in the sociological approach, determines the individual's actions. But, just as in the case of the enterprise, this 'fixed set' is only fixed at one instant in time. The present capital of the enterprise is a consequence of previous behaviour. The research, the marketing, the investment, the sales of the recent past, determine the current state of the firm. That past behaviour was itself the consequence of previous capital endowments and so on, recursively.

And so for the individual. Current skills, experience, qualifications, and social connections, constitute the individual's economically relevant human capital and determine his or her economic activity options. These are themselves the consequences of previous behaviour. Holding this job, passing that examination, gives access to a particular range of new employment opportunities. And the previous behaviour is itself the consequence of previous capital endowments, perhaps economic (a still earlier job), or perhaps 'social capital' (i.e. a personal network of friends and acquaintances), or 'cultural capital' (the general information about cultural artefacts absorbed as a by-product of daily life), or else 'educational capital' acquired through schooling. We might parenthetically note that the use of the term 'capital' here really is no more than a metaphor. There are some crucial differences between the economic and the social economists' use of the term. Among the more important of these are: (i) that financial capital depletes with use, whereas human capital is enhanced; and (ii) investment in human capital may happen simultaneously with consumption, even pleasurable consumption.

In Figure 4.2 we see an account of a life history. Its subject is born into a household, and by this involuntary action acquires a set of personal characteristics and a share of the household's social and material capital. She also acquires a routine, again involuntarily (though it may not seem this way to the rest of the household), a pattern of sleeping and waking, of fluid inflows and outflows. *At* this point, both personal capital and routine are imposed, but *from* this point, both of these characteristics are progressively modified by the individual's own activity patterns. Each distinct action adds particular skills to the individual's repertoire, each repetition of a sequence of activities reinforces habits; habitual sequences involve repetitions of actions which reinforce skills. In a slightly broader sense, the routines are themselves skills, learned procedures for accomplishing the task of getting through the day.

The modification of the routines are subject to three categories of influence: the child's own existing skills and habits; the availability or accessibility of new activities; and the child's projects and fantasies. The toys she plays with are those she knows how to play with, and the more she plays with them the more she knows how to play with them. The toys she plays with are the ones her parents place in her reach. Some of the toys within her reach are played with, because they interest her, others do not, and are ignored. To refer to the skills and habits and projects and fantasies as the child's 'own' is of course misleading, because they result in large part from previous constraints and options provided by the parents. But nevertheless whatever their origin, from the child's point of view they are certainly personal, and from almost the very first they are somewhat distinct from the parents' projects and intentions.

The balance of influence changes. For an older child, it is no longer just the parents who establish options. The local or national State determines when the child must go to school, and what sorts of schools are available (both through direct public provision, and through public regulation of private provision). Television programmes and television advertisements, suggest new sorts of play.

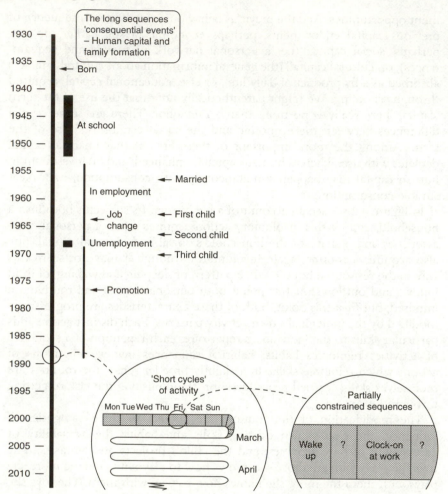

Figure 4.2. The micromodels: the recursive determination of activity patterns

The child's own skills determine her responses to these options. Her socialization within her own home forms the stock of social and cultural 'capital' she carries into her school. These in turn determine how she reacts to the educational process within the school. Those children who have developed educational skills informally outside the school respond well to formal instruction; those who have the same sorts of cultural capital as their teachers are better able than others to understand instruction, and to communicate their own capacities to their teachers. So they are able to exchange or transform their informally derived skills into those of the formal educational system. Their prior endowments of skill and innate abilities determine their subsequent endowments.

Similarly outside school: the activity of reading long stories develops the ability to follow extended narratives, which allows for the enjoyment of long stories, and reinforces the habit of reading. Skills of sociability developed at home or play groups become a resource which determines the child's ability to enjoy collective leisure activities. The cultural and social capitals accumulate.

And as the repertoire of skills develops, so does the grand skill which is constituted by the child's habit of mixing reading and listening and socializing and studying in particular proportions, of doing particular activities at particular times of the day and the week. Encapsulating all the other categories of human capital (but itself a sort of capital in so far as elements of it may from time to time be exchanged for other categories of capital) is 'routine'. Circumstances mean that certain things (e.g. school, eating, cleaning teeth) have to be done; many other things (reading stories, riding a bicycle in the garden) she has learned to do and to enjoy are also fitted into the day. The child develops habitual patterns of activity.

But there is more than just routine. Routine is how we currently live our lives. We fit into our daily lives some of the things we know how to enjoy; other things that we may be able to do, or that we speculate or fantasize about doing, are absent—these are 'projects'. Projects inform choice among alternative activity options. And in turn personal capacities and household resources (i.e. 'human capital') will progressively modify projects.

The interactions of the same triad, of personal abilities, constraints on current activities, and preferences about the future—endowments of 'human capital', the availability of 'activity options', and the development of life 'projects'—dominate behaviour throughout the life course. Throughout, there is the continuing reproduction, enhancement, and exchange of the various categories of cultural, social, and educational capital. Past activities cohere to establish present social position, which in turn establishes expectations and hence future behaviour. And throughout life there remains the same subjective perception of personal autonomy, and the illusion of the internal origin of action.

And there other exchanges of capital. Educational qualifications are transformed into financial resources: the qualifications gained in formal education give access to particular sorts of employment. And the job itself adds to skills, and therefore may give access to other, better paid-jobs. Past leisure habits form 'cultural capital', and when combined with financial resources, enable a pattern of leisure activity, which may in turn contribute to the individual's social connections and add to 'social capital'. (We should remember here the inappropriateness of the 'capital' metaphor. When we listen to a symphony we learn about symphonic structure. We simultaneously enjoy a concert and further develop our abilities to enjoy concerts.)

Time geography

So it is that on a particular Thursday morning in March in her thirty-fourth year, the subject of Figure 4.2 gets up at 7 a.m., makes breakfast for her husband and children, drives him to the station, delivers the elder child to the play group, returns home to wash up. And so on. She has in her thirty-four years done a particular range of things: passed so many examinations, worked at various jobs, married a man with his own particular allocations of the various categories of human capital, settled in a particular sort of house in a particular place, had so many children. These serve to define her as the sort of person who 'ought' now to be doing a particular range of things: so much housework, so much childcare, shopping and cooking. She develops a routine which allows her to meet these expectations and engage in certain other activities related to her own capacities and projects—which is how she comes to spend this Thursday morning the way she does.

And now she is offered a job in a factory. Returning to work is indeed part of her life project. But can she modify her routine so as to meet all her responsibilities and achieve this aspect of her life project? She would have to clock in at 9.00 a.m. And this is a problem. She is responsible for looking after the children. There is a crèche that would take care of the younger child. But the rules of the crèche are that she cannot leave him there before 8.45 a.m. The three dimensions of Figure 4.3 represent North–South, East–West, and Midnight–Midnight respectively. The downward-pointing cone whose apex is the crèche at 8.45, represents the set of times and places that she can reach from the creche starting at 8.45. The shape of the cone reflects the conditions of the transport system. The factory at 9.00 a.m. lies outside this 'cone of possibility'. So given the constraints (her membership of the household, the presence of children and the division of responsibilities for caring for them within the household, the transport system, the geographical location of the household, the crèche and the workplace, and so on) she turns down the job.

The 'time-geographic' model suggests a range of alternatives. The rules governing the time of opening of the crèche, or the timing of work at the workplace, could be made more flexible. The locations of any of the three 'activity stations' (i.e. the geographical setting of the activities) could change (e.g. placing of the crèche at or near the workplace). The public transport system might be improved, or the household might buy a faster car. The 'work strategy' of the household might change (i.e. the husband adjust his hours of employment to take responsibility for delivering the youngest child to the crèche).

We see from this example that labour market behaviour is influenced not just by wage rates, but also by a wide range of public and private regulatory activities, by technological or organizational changes in public and private service provision, by changes in the geographical location of activities, by

'Stations' — conventional locations for particular activities,
e.g. sleeping and eating at home, working at workplace, shopping at supermarket.

Hence

Minimum (travel) time between some pairs of activities.
'Cone of possibility' — the set of points subsequently accessible from an
                         initial location in time and space.
                      — a function of distance, travel time, transport schedules.

A geographer's map

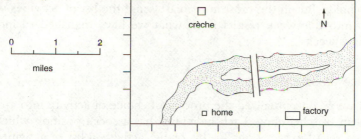

A time-geographer's map

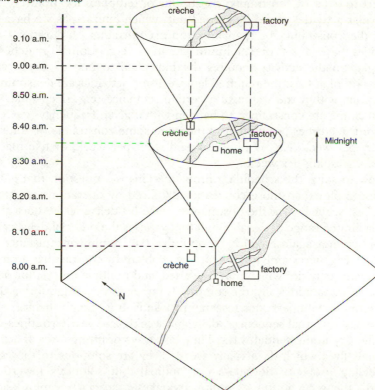

Figure 4.3. Spatial locations

changes in the allocation of responsibilities among members of households, and by changes in the range of other activities that households undertake. As for the labour market, so for each other category of time allocation. We have a range of activities which we hope to fit into our days and weeks. These reflect in part expectations attached to our position in the social structure, in part explicit or implicit agreements with other members of our households. But in the most immediate sense the list of activities we want to fit into this week results from what we have managed to include in previous weeks.

Choice as scheduling

We have reconceptualized the process of choice of activity into a complex problem of scheduling. Each individual has a social position which establishes a set of expectations for his or her activity, a list of activities which have somehow to be 'fitted in' to daily life. And they have to be fitted subject to a set of constraints: constraints of temporal location (i.e. when particular activities are to be carried out) which interact, as we have seen, with the constraints of spatial location; constraints of duration—some activities have a set or minimum duration (e.g. football matches), so engaging in the activity requires the individual to find or free a vacant 'time-slot' of at least the required length. Some activities are constrained to take place within the frame of a certain sequence (e.g. sleep-wake-wash-dress). Some are constrained to happen with a given frequency (e.g. eating two or three times per day). And there are some constraints of volume or density per week (e.g. 35 hours of paid work per week, or five machine-loads of washing per week).

How to solve the scheduling problem? This is a question that is vastly more complex than those conventionally faced by operations researchers. 'The best sequence for the postman to make his deliveries in' does at least have a limited range of variables (all that varies is the order of delivery), and simple criteria against which to optimize (i.e. minimizing distance travelled). The general time-use scheduling problem by contrast has a range of very many activities which may be varied, and multiple criteria for optimization. But, paradoxically, the solution is rather more straightforward than for conventional operations research problems. It is, simply, habit.

We have habitual sequences, daily and weekly and yearly routines which mostly vary in inessential ways. These are ways of fitting a set of activities into our lives which do actually work. They are solutions to the general scheduling problem: doubtless not optimal, but solutions nevertheless. Indeed, the very notion of optimality takes a special meaning, since a consequence of particular routines may be the modification of criteria. Habit may mean that we learn to enjoy the things we do, and to disparage those we do not do. So we carry on doing what we do. (Or alternatively it may mean that we get 'habituated' to the things we habitually do, and discount them relative to things we currently do not do, and accordingly change our patterns of activity.) The solutions, in this sense, progressively redefine the problem.

The daily routine is a local, temporarily stable, solution to the problem of how to fit in all the things we might do. But irrespective of the currently stable patterns of activity, we may nevertheless maintain within our 'life projects' aims which we currently fail to achieve. When we are offered new activity options, we evaluate them in terms of how they might allow us to fit in some of our unachieved aims, by marginal modifications of our habitual sequences, holding as much else constant as we can.

The offer of a new activity option is of course not just a matter of a new option becoming available. We must somehow become conscious of the innovative possibility, and of its implications for the achievement of unsatisfied aims. The relationship between innovations and life objectives is not necessarily straightforward. An application of a new piece of domestic technology, for example, may lead to the rescheduling of one part of the day, thus freeing an 'activity slot' at some quite different part of the day or week. Some individuals are continuously and actively in search of such possibilities, and once they are identified, attempt to incorporate them immediately into their routines: these individuals correspond most nearly to the economists' model of rational behaviour.

But there are other ways that activity patterns are modified than just the active search for new options. The availability of options may be imposed on the individual's consciousness by demonstration or example. Or it may be the result of an accident, perhaps as a result of a trivial departure from routine. Our heroine (to revert to the extended example from the previous section) may perhaps walk down a street she has not previously visited and discover a bus route she was previously unaware of, which would enable her to get from the crèche to the workplace in the required time. As a polar opposite to the economist's rational individual actively searching for new options is the totally serendipitous individual who only ever happens upon alternative options by accident. Real populations are presumably distributed among various points between these two poles.

'Routine' and social change

We have in effect replaced choice by routine. In this account, it might seem that there is not much left to be explained. There is a classic sociological distinction between routinized behaviour and motivated action: the latter is infrequent and marginal to the patterns of everyday life. What we have described will operate so as to produce a population with routines which change (if at all) only very gradually and in random-seeming directions. So far we have not mentioned collective processes, we have not yet given any place to social coordination and interaction. The foregoing is an 'over-socialized' model to replace the 'undersocialized' approach of microeconomics (Wrong 1961). The position we hope to establish, however is parallel to that summarized by Granovetter's (1985) notion of 'imbedded-ness': Granovetter sees firms, we see individuals and households, as imbedded in broader social processes and historical contexts. There is more to social change than the aggregate of individuals' drifting activity patterns. Two further features must be added to our account:

(1) Norms are what is generally accepted to be normal. This is not a mere statistical concept, it involves the individual's perception of what is generally believed (which reflects both direct observations, and discussions with others about their observations). Circumstances may lead to change in individuals' behaviour. Take for example women moving into paid employment: this may in principle happen without changing norms (i.e. the action may still be taken by each individual to be exceptional even when, statistically speaking, it becomes the rule). But this is unlikely to remain the case for long. As the change is observed and commented upon, what is generally accepted to be normal may also change. This is not necessarily a regular or continuous process; publicly agreed perceptions of normality may lag well behind the statistical facts (a decade ago one might still have been told that 'people do not normally sleep together before marriage'). Or alternatively they may advance well ahead of the facts (we may now be told 'men share the housework nowadays'). But nevertheless we may expect a certain association between the behavioural reality and the agreed social percep-tions: as what is generally believed to be done changes, so does 'the done thing'. Statistical rules are transformed, albeit irregularly, into normative rules. And change in norms feeds back into changes in behaviour, perhaps providing sanctions for those who were previously dissuaded from what they assumed was outside the norms, encouraging waverers, and, more generally, modifying individuals' projects. So, what we have described does not necessarily restrict societies to gradual and stochastic change, but also allows rapid monotonic shifts in behaviour, in cases where the public perception of normal behaviour 'switches'. (We shall discuss examples of such rapid changes later in connection with domestic work.)

(2) We must also bear in mind the influence of political and other programmes. Individuals' 'projects' and their perceptions of 'options' may reflect something in the wider societal arena. Interest groups and political parties promote new patterns of public regulation; information about these circulates, and coalitions form to support or oppose them, and as a result new patterns of behaviour emerge. Similarly, entrepreneurial firms with new products or services promote new technical or organizational means for achieving day-to-day objectives, and enable change in activity sequences. In addition to individuals' projects there are entrepreneurial or political

'animal spirits' which promote social innovations. Again, we see the possibility of rapid, unidirectional, and in this case *directed*, social change.

But to get any further, we must move away from the sequential framework to an aggregate level. What follows is moderately complex. It can be stated precisely, if in a somewhat cumbersome manner, in the form of a mathematical model. We will express the central ideas in a rather simpler, somewhat less general, but equivalently precise manner; the main line of the argument can be followed entirely from the text, though readers may also wish to work through the rather straightforward equations in the figures, and some additional text enclosed in square brackets is included to guide this. (Readers who find the following sections difficult to assimilate may wish to turn first to the final section of this chapter, in which the micro- and macro-models are brought together in a simple summary.)

3. Allocating time: micro-aggregate theory

The individual's aggregate time budget—'aggregate' in the sense that to calculate it we must add up the totals of elapsed time in each activity—is the subject of conventional time-budget analysis. There are twenty-four hours in the day, and hours of a given day spent in one activity cannot be spent in another. If we take more leisure, we must do less work. All the sociological and economic theorizing about time allocation hinges on the simple micro-aggregate constraint: for any individual, more time in one activity means less time in another.

Gary Becker (1965) produced a very simple microeconomic model of allocation of time between work and other activities. Consider the time budget in Figure 4.4. The bar chart shows the way an individual divides the average day among paid work, the consumption (or use) of three different categories of purchased commodity, and sleep. To simplify the argument, let us assume that sleep time is a constant; the first step is to build a picture of the relationship among the four remaining time-use categories that make up the day.

All consumption takes time. Let us say that there is a fixed coefficient which gives the amount of time required for the consumption of a unit of each commodity. An average cinema performance, we might find, takes 1 hour and 45 minutes. There is also a second fixed coefficient which gives the amount of paid work time required to buy the commodity. The price of the commodity, divided by the individual's wage rate, gives the amount of time that must be spent in paid employment to purchase a unit of the commodity; if the cinema ticket costs £5, and the individual's wage rate is £10 per hour, then the unit of cinema consumption requires 30 minutes paid work.

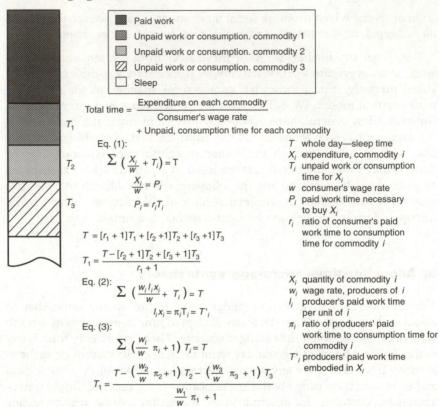

Figure 4.4. A micro-social time-accounting identity

These two coefficients, respectively the ratios of paid work time per unit of a purchased commodity, and of consumption/use time per unit of that commodity, are the core (though slightly simplified) of Becker's time-use model. Once we know these two coefficients for each of the three classes of commodity, then the range of alternative patterns of time use is quite considerably constrained. Our individual has, once sleep is accounted for, say 16.5 hours to dispose of on any day. On any given day any individual may of course 'save' in the special sense that the time devoted to paid work provides more income than is 'spent' by devoting time to consumption, and hence using purchased commodities. Or equally, on some days there may be 'dis-saving' perhaps by devoting all the available time to consumption activities. These different sorts of days must nevertheless over some span of time cancel each other out. It would seem sensible for the purposes of our model to assume that on the average of the individual's days, there is neither saving nor dis-saving. So if we know, for example, how much of the average day the individual devotes to the consumption activities T2 and T3, we can work out by simple algebra, how much time must be devoted to T1, and to paid work T'.

[Consider Equation 1 in Figure 4.4. The individual's total of waking time is constituted by the expenditure on each commodity divided by his or her own wage rate (which gives the paid work time necessary to buy the commodity) plus the time spent using or consuming each commodity. Since we have fixed coefficients of combination between paid work time and expenditure, and consumption/use time and expenditure, we must also have fixed ratios between paid work time and consumption time. And given this fixed ratio (r) between consumption time for each commodity and the consumer's paid work to acquire the commodity, we can derive a simple expression that gives the time spent in any one category of consumption from the time devoted to the other two categories of consumption.]

Becker uses this reasoning (as do subsequent theorists) to produce a micro-behavioural theory of time allocation, in which individuals have a schedule of preferred trade-offs between the various possible combinations of T1, T2, and T3 (a 'utility function'), which may be used to decide on the optimum combination of different sorts of consumption (and hence, on their total of time devoted to paid work).

For the present argument, however, we do not need to subscribe to this particular restricted behavioural model. Individuals *may* act (in this sense) rationally. However Becker himself would not in fact insist that all or indeed any individuals actually carry out a complete rational calculation of the alternatives, but only that the outcomes of any choices look in aggregate *as if* rational choices have been made (e.g. Becker in Lévy-Garboua 1979). For general sociological purposes it would seem sensible to assume that there will be a range of 'choice' behaviours in the population, from the relatively rational and calculating, to the quite strongly habitual; in the latter case time allocation is driven by norms, and any change in consumption of one class of commodity forced by circumstances will have generally random consequences for consumption of the others. As long as any *departures* from randomness are consistent with some conceivable utility function, Becker's *as if* expectation is satisfied.

All that is necessary for the present argument, however, are the pairs of time-use coefficients and the assumption that the average day has neither saving nor dis-saving; these give us, not a behavioural model, but an accounting model. Simply: the day must consist of amounts of paid work and consumption time (T', T1, T2, and T3) mixed in proportions which conform to the requirements of the paired coefficients; the average day, in our simple model, consists of time spent in consumption, and time spent by that same individual at work to pay for the goods used in that consumption.

Thirty- and eighteen-hour days?

And now we can make the crucial further step beyond the Becker micro-model that allows us to consider flows of time between people. The price of a unit of a commodity may be thought of as being made up as the product of two components: an amount of embodied labour, and the wage rate of that embodied labour [which allows us to derive Equation 2 from Equation 1]. This includes, not just the labour embodied in the materials out of which consumption commodities are constructed and the direct labour of assembling them, but also the labour embodied in the plant and equipment used in their production. The labour involved in the cinema performance includes not just the ushers and projectionists, but also the embodied labour of those who supply the electricity, build and maintain the cinema, and so on. This involves a somewhat long-term view of national accounts; rather than the convention of single-year macroeconomic accounts, it summarizes flows of production over a five- or ten-year period. Investment activities such as building cinemas may be treated in the long-term accounts in just the same way as intermediate stages in the production of the final marketed commodities are treated in the more conventional single-year accounts. The 'embodied labour' thus also includes that part of the price of a commodity that might otherwise be attributed to returns on the capital employed in its production. (Chapter 8 explains the accounting system through which the extent of this embodied labour may be calculated.)

So the micro-accounting constraint tells us, not just about the amount of paid labour that the individual must contribute in order to buy commodities, but also about the amount of labour that is required to produce the commodities that are consumed. The consumer's labour time required by a given expenditure on a commodity is the total expenditure divided by the consumer's own wage rate. The actual work time required to produce the commodities that are purchased, the producers' work time, may be calculated as the consumer's paid work time multiplied by the ratio between the producers' and the consumer's wage rates. The fixed ratio between the consumer's work time and consumption time means that the producers' work time may also be expressed in terms of consumption time. Thus, a given level of consumption of a good, implies both a particular supply of labour by the consumer (i.e. the paid work necessary to buy the good), and a particular demand for the labour embodied in the good that is consumed. [This relationship is expressed in Equation 3.]

This is a crucial extension to the micro-aggregate theory, an extension that has a quite paradoxical-sounding implication: the individual's day is in one sense not limited to twenty-four hours. Our own work earns money with which we buy the work of others as embodied in the goods and services we consume. The rich (or rather those with high-wage rates) may in this special sense have substantially more than 24 hours in the day, while the poor have substantially fewer than 24 hours, which leads us to think about the social balance between the time spent consuming goods and the time devoted by others to producing them.

4. Balancing time: macro-theory

Alongside the micro constraint is another, macro constraint, which concerns the balance between various activities of people in different groups in the society. At one level this second sort of balance is not unfamiliar. We readily understand that, for instance, we cannot all be medical doctors, because the society as a whole only wants sufficient medical services to support a relatively small number of people in these sorts of jobs. Or (a similar but not identical argument) we may recognize that only a minority of us could drive cars if cars were individually handmade, whereas we can all have mass-produced cars. These are special statements of a rather less familiar principle which is of great importance in determining a society's overall time budget.

The macro constraint involves the connections between amounts of time allocated to consumption and to production. If members of some groups in a society devote a particular amount of time to the consumption of particular commodities, there is a requirement that some other group devotes its time to producing these commodities. A society that devotes more of its time to some particular sort of leisure consumption will also require an increase of time devoted to some related category of paid work. If (and of course we are simplifying here) the society devotes more of its time to watching ballet, then it must also take more of its time in the form of work for ballet dancers. This is the crucially important sense in which, at the macro level, *more leisure may mean more work*.

The picture is in fact a little more complicated than this. Technical or organizational change alters the coefficients which relate together some people's paid work time with other people's unpaid work and consumption time; so, for example, improved design of theatres might allow an increase in the size of the audience with neither degradation in quality or growth in employment. But the point of the example stands: though work time may compete with personal consumption in the individual's time budget, yet still production time and consumption time are complementary in the society's time budget.

In Figure 4.4 we considered just the individual. Let us now consider a society, made up of a set of groups, or loosely 'classes', each of which specializes in the production of one particular commodity. So the three commodities of Figure 4.4 correspond to the three classes in Figure 4.5. Let us simplify, by representing each class by a single person.

Define a 'production class' as the set of all those members of a society involved in producing a given range of commodities. The total of paid work time supplied by a class equals the total of paid work time required by the society's consumption of the commodities produced by that class.

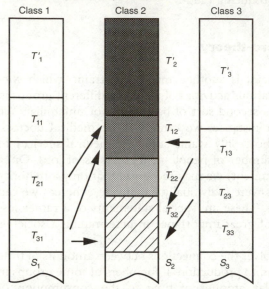

T_j' paid work time from class *I*

T_{ij} unpaid work or consumption time devoted to commodity by members of class$_j$

S_1 sleep time class$_j$

S_j hence a theorem:

The aggregate time allocation of a class is determined by the consumption patterns of the other classes in the society

Where P_j is the proportion of the population in class *j* and π_i is the ratio of paid work time to consumption for commodity *i*, we can derive:

$$P_1\pi_3 T_{31} + P_2\pi_3 T_{32} + P_3\pi_3 T_{33} = P_3 \frac{w^1}{w_3} \pi_1 T_{13} + P_3 \frac{w^2}{w_3} \pi_2 T_{23} + P_3\pi_3 T_{33}$$

Which gives Eq. (4):

$$T_{32} = \frac{P_3 \dfrac{w_1}{w_3} \pi_1 T_{13} + P_3 \dfrac{w_2}{w_3} \pi_2 T_{23} - P_1\pi_3 T_{31}}{P_2\pi_3}$$

T_{12} can be derived similarly, and T_{22} and T'_2 from Eq. (3)

Figure 4.5. A microsocial time-accounting identity

Each person, in this very simple society, produces one commodity: person 1 produces commodity 1 and so on. So the total supply of labour from person 1 is determined by the amounts of consumption of the three goods by class 1. And the total of time spent consuming commodity 1 by all three people determines (via the consumption–production time coefficient) the total demand for labour from person 1. At any real historical point demand and supply of labour will be equated. This equation—the requirement that the total of paid work time supplied by a class equals the total of paid work time implied by the society's consumption of the commodities produced by that class—constitutes a second time-budget constraint, a macrosocial accounting constraint. [This relationship is expressed formally by Equation 4 in Figure 4.5.]

These macro relationships, between consumption patterns and demand for specific sorts of labour, when combined with the microtime-budget constraint, lead to a rather remarkable result. We can demonstrate, as in Figure 4.4, that elements of the consumption time of each person are in effect determined by other elements of the consumption time of the other people. Figure 4.5 contains a worked example. We start with the equation of the labour demand deriving from the society's consumption of commodity 3 with the total of labour supply from person/class 3 [i.e. Equation 4]. Straightforward manipulation of this equation demonstrates that the time devoted by person/class 2 to the consumption of commodity 3 is determined by how much time person 3 devotes to consuming commodities 1 and 2, and how much person 1 devotes to commodity 3. And similarly the time devoted by person 2 to consuming commodity 1 is determined by person 1's time spent in consumption of commodities 2 and 3, and person 3's time spent in consumption of good 1.

We have already seen that, for an individual in a three-good world, if we know how much time is devoted to the consumption of two goods, the time devoted to the consumption of the third is determined. Now, if we know the consumption patterns of persons 1 and 3, we can derive the time devoted by class 2 to the consumption of goods 1 and 3; and knowing person/class 2's time devoted to the consumption of goods 1 and 3, we can derive its time devoted to the consumption of good 2. In short, the consumption/time-use patterns of two of them completely determine the consumption pattern of the third.

Now relax the assumptions somewhat, thinking now, not of individuals but of groups of people, insisting only that members of each group are only involved in production of the good associated with that group. Within each group, we may now have households, with members sharing purchased commodities, and perhaps specializing so that some spend more time using commodities (e.g. in unpaid housework, thus, gender divisions re-enter the argument) and others spending more time in paid work. The accounting equations will still hold: the aggregate time allocation of one group is still determined by the aggregate time allocation of the other two.

We have discussed the three-class, three-commodity case. But a similar logic will apply more generally: if there are n production groups and n goods, then the time allocation of $n - 1$ groups will determine the time use pattern of the nth. We have, in fact, a rather powerful theorem: the aggregate time allocation of a class is determined by the consumption patterns of the other classes in a society. We have discussed propositions which are no more than accounting identities. But accounting relationships can have behavioural implications. The theorem establishes the relationship of mutual constraint between the society's aggregate of specific acts of consumption and its aggregate of specific acts of production.

(This line of argument is taken a little further in Chapter 8, which (with some additional assumptions) demonstrates formally how welfare benefits accrue from technical change, and shows how the sizes of social classes must change as a result of technological progress.)

5. A summary

This chapter has developed what are in effect two distinct perspectives: a micro model, representing the processes through which individuals arrive at their daily activity patterns; and a macro model, covering the essentially arithmetic constraints that tie together the time-allocation patterns of individuals in a society.

The micro model is summarized by Figure 4.6. At its heart is the image of the 'long sequence', the extended series of millions of events or activities which make up an individual's life history. Of these events, some are 'consequential' in the sense of having influence on subsequent events. The events of schooling, employment, and household formation (together with the 'events' of birth and the characteristics of the household of origin) determine in various ways the individual's responsibilities, preferences, and aspirations. And the 'consequential' events, together with the time-geographical constraints, also determine the options available for meeting these responsibilities, preferences, and aspirations.

The consequential events serve to establish the individual's position in the social structure. The position interacts with the established programme of activity, and the individual's projects and preferences, and spatio-temporal constraints, and material resources, to determine new patterns of activity. And the new patterns of activity may include some consequential events, which serve in turn partially to redefine the individual's social position. Technological advances may modify the effects of the spatio-temporal constraints; a new piece of household equipment, for example, may reduce the amount of time required for a particular domestic task, enabling a change in the established sequence of activities. And public regulatory activity (or private enterprise)—leading perhaps to the development of a new bus service, or the development of a new local leisure facility—may have a similar effect.

The micro model works on the assumption that the whole of the social context is a given, that the social and economic structure is unaffected by the individual's actions. This is of course true for any one individual, but untrue for the set of individuals, since they *constitute* society. The macro model explores a set of constraints, quite as real as those of geography or personal resources, which are nevertheless invisible at the micro level.

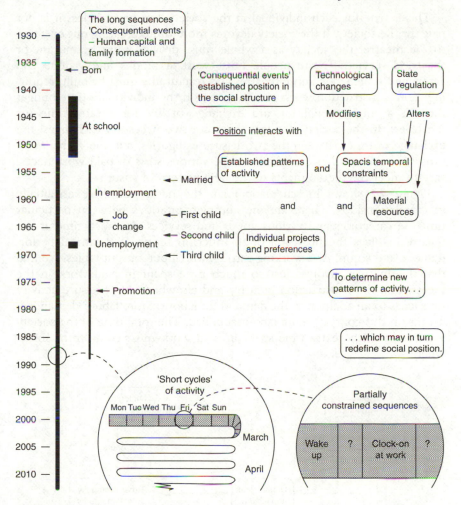

Figure 4.6. The micromodels: the recursive determination of activity patterns

When an individual chooses, for example, to spend a block of time that had previously been passed watching television or eating a meal at home, at a theatre or a restaurant (and in the associated travel), the decision has no other necessary implications for his or her *own* time allocation. Two hours, or whatever, of the individual's time is transferred from one leisure or consumption category to another; all of the other activities could remain exactly as they previously were. No matter how many individuals make this transfer of time between leisure categories, no one individual is in any way constrained to make any other change in activities.

This is true for each individual in the society, but nevertheless it is not true for the society. If the society devotes more time to eating out or going to the theatre, the society as a whole must provide more restaurant or theatrical services—more people must work as cooks and waiters and actors and stagehands, more theatres and restaurants must be built, requiring more construction workers, and so on. In the individual's time budget there is a single straightforward exchange of TV for theatre time (or whatever). In the society's budget there are two necessary exchanges: the exchange of time between the two leisure categories, and the exchange of time from some other category into the various sorts of paid work necessary to meet the requirements of the new pattern of leisure.

Figure 4.7 shows in schematic form the nature of these essentially macrorelationships. There are the complementarities between particular time-use categories and various goods and services: so much time at the theatre involves the provision of so much in terms of theatrical performances, and so on. And working through the input–output tables, we find that this in turn involves just so much time spent in paid work in the theatre and the construction industry and elsewhere. New leisure activity thus leads to an addition to the demand for labour. More labour demanded, means (in this context) more labour supplied. The total time of the society is a constant; the extra time spent in paid work must come from somewhere.

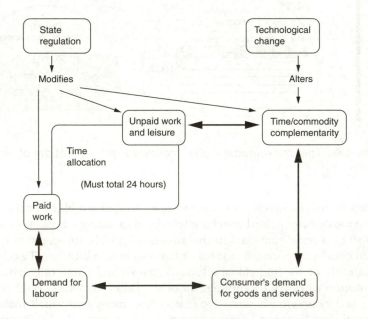

Figure 4.7. The micromodel: final demand and work–leisure balance

In short, the macro model, which relates all of the various sorts of work in the society to all of the consumption activities, adds a higher-level constraint to the obvious micro constraints of location in time and space. Spending time using goods and services requires that further time be spent producing goods and services. One person's leisure is another's work. The more leisure, the more work.

At any point in time there is a particular balance in the society: just so much leisure and consumption time, associated with just so much work; so much time devoted to the satisfaction of basic needs, so much to sophist-icated. Over historical time this balance alters; the coefficients of comple-mentarity between, on one hand, time spent in leisure consumption and domestic work activities outside the economy, and on the other, goods and services produced by the economy, change through history.

These two, the micro and the macro, imply a third perspective: a process of social innovation, which leads to systematic shifts in time-allocation patterns over historical time. We may divide the society's time according to the various sorts of purpose or want; over time we see a change in the mix of activities that goes to satisfy each class of want.

At one historical point, meeting a particular want involves various sorts of paid work, unpaid work, and leisure. At that point in time, different sorts of people in the society will meet the same class of need in different ways. Some (high income—to revert to the example of housework in the 1930s) will use a lot of (other people's) paid work (i.e. domestic servants) and a small amount of (their own) unpaid labour, leaving a lot of time for consumption and leisure. Others (low income) will have to use a lot of their own unpaid labour, leaving little leisure. The society's mix of activities related to 'shelter' is constituted by (i) the mix of activities in each of the two alternative (i.e. high- and low-income) 'modes of provision' and by (ii) the distribution of the members of the society between the two modes (or the two income classes).

Technological change is manifested in the evolution of new modes of provision for human wants, which involve new mixes of activities and different patterns of cost. Over historical time we find shifts in the distribu-tion of the members of the society between the various available modes of provision. We find (to continue the domestic services example) by the 1960s a much smaller proportion of the households in the society satisfying their wants through the old high-income (domestic servant) mode, and a very much smaller proportion through the old low-income (unmechanized domestic labour) mode. The majority of the population turn to the new mechanized self-servicing pattern, as a result of the rising cost of purchased domestic services, and the falling cost of domestic equipment. The change in the mix of paid and unpaid work and leisure activities associated with 'shelter' over time reflects a historical shift in the distribution of the population among the various modes of provision. And this historical shift in turn reflects, in part at least, technical innovation in the design of consumer goods, and in the processes of production of those goods—technical innovation means new products and new price patterns.

There is however more to change than just technology. It also results from the various actions (or the inaction) of the State. Public authorities influence income distribution through the tax and benefit systems, they influence the relative cost and performance of alternative modes of provision for needs through the provision and regulation of infrastructure, and they influence time allocation directly both through the provision of final services (education, medicine, social) to consumers, and through the direct regulation of time (working hours, holiday and retirement requirements).

Private enterprises, and individual entrepreneurs, of course have a major role to play in the emergence of new modes of provision. Private institutions responding directly to individual needs (as manifested and sanctioned through direct payments for goods and services) are undoubtedly better placed to manage and direct the development of new products than are public institutions (which are dependent on opinion surveys and occasional elections for the same sorts of information). Nevertheless the environment of costs and taxes and infrastructural services within which enterprises operate is determined by the State. And the overall level of final demand on which private enterprises depend (and the distribution of demand among the various groups with different patterns of marginal spending) relates to state activity. Thus the combination of state 'regulation' (in the broad sense) and innovative entrepreneurial activity leads to the development of the new consumption and production regimes which lead in turn to new patterns of time allocation in the society.

5   The History and Future of Time Use:
Empirical Evidence

1. A multinational longitudinal time-diary data collection

Time use and time budgets

Economists collect a great deal of information about what goes on in the realm of work (using the term in its narrowest sense of 'paid employment'). We know how many jobs there are, of what sorts, in which industries. We know in great detail which goods and services are produced in the economy, and to whom they are sold. And we know how these characteristics have changed over the recent past. Using this knowledge, we can construct generalizations about the way paid work is changing—knowing the distribution of employment between branches of production, for example, we might be expected to have firm grounds for asserting that we are at present becoming post-industrialized (or perhaps de-industrialized, or post-materialist, or a service society, or a leisure society, or information-based or globalized or whatever). We can certainly find evidence that, for instance, an increasing proportion of those who want jobs cannot find them, or that more women have jobs now than previously, or that there are more non-manual workers than there were.

But outside this very narrow span of human activity, we are surprisingly short of empirical evidence about activity patterns. This is true even of paid work *time*. If we look, for example, in the International Labour Organization *Yearbook*, which is the bible of employment data, we find just one data series, which for many countries until recently included only full-time employed men in manufacturing (ILO 1987). The data from this source are hedged about with qualifications: each country has different methods for estimation, different definitions of what is meant by work. The explanatory notes to this data source make it clear that it cannot be considered a particularly reliable source of information. We simply do not know, from official sources, how much paid work is done in most societies. And what is true for paid work is all the more true for unpaid work. After all what *is* unpaid work? Clearly cooking and household cleaning; but how about shopping, gardening, domestic travel? Until the 1980s no Central Statistical Offices anywhere in the developed world published official estimates of unpaid or domestic work. We now find some official estimates from just a few countries (e.g. the Netherlands, Finland). There are now some emerging standard definitions (Hawrylyshn 1976,1977; Goldschmidt-Clermont 1982; Goldschmidt-Clermont and Pagnossin-Aligisakis 1995; OECD 1997). But there are no proper international reporting standards comparable to those for national income statistics, and certainly no time series.

So we have no firm basis in official statistics for generalizing about such issues as the extent and distribution of unpaid work, or the total amount of work (in the broader sense which includes unpaid production) done in the society, or about the composition of leisure activities, or about how these are changing. This is the reason for setting up a special collection of what is really the only general source of evidence of what people do with their time—time-diary or 'time-budget' surveys.

Time-diary research includes a wide range of different approaches, undertaken for a number of different purposes: common to all of them is the collection and analysis of people's accounts of their own activities. The field has a very long history: it is usual to trace its ancestry back to the Russia of the 1920s (this work is described extensively in Zuzanek 1980), entering Western sociology as a result of the work done by Lundberg and the Russian émigré Pitrim Sorokin in the USA during the 1930s (Sorokin and Berger 1939; Lundberg, Komarovsky, and McInerny 1934). But in fact time-diary techniques had been used as a device for mapping the pattern of daily life in Britain during the first decades of this century (Pember-Reeves 1913), and a larger (though by modern standards, still very small) time-budget exercise was carried out as part of the 1930 Social Survey of Merseyside (Jones 1934). And the technique has been very widely used. There have been more than sixty national-level studies from at least thirty countries—and there are many more special-purpose studies of subsections of the population.

This is a rather large body of empirical work, and considering the fundamental and comprehensive nature of the data it yields, it ought to have had a substantial effect on social science: in fact its impact has been less than impressive. With a few honourable exceptions, the publications that emerge as a result of time-budget research are somewhat disappointing.

Why is this? One reason is a scepticism about the quality of time-diary data. Casual conversation with researchers who have not worked in the field yields somewhat negative views of the reliability of time budgets. But the substantive research literature generally affirms that the research technique is reasonably reliable (a review is contained in Juster and Stafford 1991). Certainly it is possible to demonstrate that individuals sometimes slant their accounts, as for example husbands exaggerating, or wives minimizing, accounts of male domestic work in surveys concerned with the domestic division of labour. But there is no basis for dismissing time-budget data as generally and in principle less acceptable than any other form of questionnaire data (indeed the arguments and evidence provided by Appendix 1 suggest that it is much better than the alternative questionnaire approach to estimating time-use patterns). So the explanation for the limited impact of the data must be sought elsewhere—in failures in performance, rather than inherent defects in the data collection.

It may come, in part at least, from the practical complications of time-budget analysis. The data are enormously difficult to collect and analyse. The great diversity of life circumstances and of individual lifestyles means that very large sample sizes are needed for even the most straightforward of analyses. If the raw information is collected in the form of manuscript diaries, the natural language descriptions must be translated into a closed activity coding frame. The data must then be reorganized, perhaps transforming the initial sequential form of the diary ('7 a.m., got up, washed; 7.15 had breakfast') into an aggregated form (thirty minutes per day spent washing and dressing, seventy minutes eating, and so on). And then, as we shall see in the later part of this chapter, the behaviour that is described by the data is very complex; very careful model specification is necessary before any clear patterns begin to emerge. The analysis of time budgets is in fact anything but straightforward. These practical difficulties may explain why literature in the field often gives the impression that researchers have been exhausted by the rigours of data collection and preparation, and have only very meagre residuals of intellectual energy to devote to analysis.

A time-budget data collection

At the heart of this book are a number of empirical questions. How do people spend their time? How has the pattern of daily life changed over the last decades? How is changing lifestyle connected to change in economic structure? Time-diary data are obviously key material evidence for this line of enquiry.

But we cannot answer the two latter questions simply by going out and collecting time diaries. A single time-budget survey, conducted at a distinct moment in history, can only give equivocal answers, if any at all, to these sorts of questions. Any one set of diaries may illustrate the current pattern of daily activity, but it cannot provide many clues as to how the pattern is *changing*. Such material can tell us, for example, about the current disposition of work and leisure between men and women, but it will not show the *historical trend*. There are sociological tricks we can play: for instance, by identifying a 'leading class' and assuming that activity patterns diffuse from it into the mass of society (this approach, derived from Veblen's theory of consumption, is the technique used by Young and Willmott in *The Symmetrical Family*). But the results this technique yields are no better than the theory that underlies it, and the theory can only be confirmed by the empirical evidence of *changes* in activity patterns over historical time.

Many of the most interesting questions involve historical change in some form or other; and yet the time-budget research instrument is essentially unsuited to long-term retrospection. Few people if any can recall detailed sequences of activity from ten or twenty years ago. How then are we to use time-budget evidence to answer questions of social change, other than by waiting for history to happen? The obvious solution is: the *secondary* analysis or reanalysis of *existing* historical time-budget material.

The empirical part of this book thus relies on an attempt to synthesize a historical time-use data series out of a very varied collection of disparate materials collected for a wide range of original purposes (the Multinational Longitudinal Time-Use study (MTUS) is described in some more detail in Appendix 2).

Intertemporal time-use comparisons (i.e. studies of change in time alloca-tion over historical periods) have previously been carried out in single countries; in Denmark (Schmidt *et al.* 1989), Norway (Norway Statistisk Sentralbyra), Japan (NHK 1971, 1991), the UK (Gershuny and Jones 1987), and most notably in the USA (Robinson and Converse 1972; Robinson and Godbey 1997); and there are cross-time comparisons of change in two countries (e.g. Canada-Norway: Harvey and Gronmo 1984; USA-Russia: Robinson, Andreyenkov, and Patrushov 1989; and a recent series involving Finland and a number of Eastern European countries (Niemi 1983; Andorka *et al.* 1983). There has also been one major multinational comparison of time-use patterns at one historical juncture, the UNESCO-sponsored 1965 study involving twelve countries (the 'Szalai' Multinational Comparative Time-Budget Research Project: Szalai 1972.). And at present (indeed this is part of the motivation for writing this book) Eurostat is organizing a new harmonized time-use data collection exercise, involving at least seven EU States, and many more from Central and Eastern Europe, whose results will become available in the early years of this millennium. The data described in this book however constitute the only extant large-scale multinational and intertemporal data collection.

A major problem in intertemporal and international comparisons of time-use patterns is inconsistency amongst the data collected. A wide variety of classificatory data and non-diary time-use data accompanies diaries from different surveys, but the most acute dilemmas occur among the activity classifications; and of course, the less detail that is provided in the original code frame, the greater the area of uncertainty. For example, all respectable time-budget surveys will include at the least a specific code for general housework, but just what does 'housework' involve—washing up? clothes washing? painting a wall? gardening? Or (to choose a particular problem that preoccupied the Eurostat 'committee of experts' for a number of years, and may still not have been adequately resolved) how can we ensure that we are distinguishing adequately between gardening for pleas-ure and subsistence agricultural production? (Readers may perhaps need to be reminded that the latter activity is currently of considerable importance in some parts of Europe.) Or (at the point that the World Wide Web becomes a routine fact in households across the developed world) how can we adequately allow for the still-developing range of computer-related activities? Most modern surveys provide separate codes for many of these activities, but the historical materials vary considerably in their coverage.

Another troubling issue is of the nature of the samples. For many of the original datasets, full information about the original samples has disappeared, or has not been made available by the original collectors. In some cases there was a restricted age range, so, in the current version of the current datafile we have included only respondents between the ages of 19 and 60. This restriction has however yielded one incidental advantage: we have been able to obtain some (just about) tolerably consistent population estimates of distributions by sex, age group, and employment status, for each country and year for which we have a survey, from the ILO *Yearbooks*. Each of the samples has been reweighted *ex post*, to correspond to these distributions, and also to give (as we *know* to be the case!) an equal number of days of the week for each sex/age/employment status group. As for seasonal variation, which we suspect to be of not inconsiderable importance in the determination of time-use patterns, we have for the moment ignored this (though the original collectors of the data have in some cases helped us by ensuring that successive surveys in particular countries have been collected over similar times of the year.).

The data file currently employs a forty-category activity classification, and a less detailed twenty-activity categorization. Both are designed to be consistent with the detailed activity list from the Szalai survey, which has greatly influenced subsequent research. Consequently, in most cases recategorization from the original codes to the Archive codes has been straightforward. The forty-category classification is not fully compatible with some surveys. (The earliest Danish surveys, for example, where the original survey instruments coded activities into very broad categories, make for problems.) But even so, it has generally proved possible to create activity categories comparable at, at least, the twenty-activity level.

In short, many heroic assumptions have been piled on top of each other in order to allow us to compile this comparative dataset. Are they, in the end, justified? Readers will have to form their own conclusions.

Work on the data file is ongoing, differentiating the 'sample of samples' to allow fewer restrictions (wider age range, more detailed activity codings, some representation of the original sequential and multiple simultaneous 'time-use event' evidence from the diary files where these are still available, obtaining more ancillary 'personal characteristic' variables from the associated questionnaire materials—but for a subset of the surveys) without losing the possibility for the more comprehensive but basic analysis of the whole data collection.

The plan of the empirical discussion that follows is straightforward. The remaining part of this chapter sets out an initial sketch of the overall patterns of cross-national difference and historical change that emerges from the dataset. Chapter 6 explores the nature of the patterns of international and intertemporal variation, so as to provide grounds for a more detailed scheme of summary and description of the time-use evidence. Then Chapter 7 provides a more comprehensive picture of the developing activity patterns of 'the world' as it emerges from the evidence that we now have to hand.

2. Economic development and change in work and leisure time

Let us now return to the straightforward question we opened in Chapter 2: what has happened to time use in the developed world over the last thirty years? What is the empirical evidence about change in the work–leisure balance?

What follows in this chapter is an attempt to provide a simple preliminary answer to the straightforward question of how work and leisure time changes with economic development. More detailed discussion of the multinational time-budget data archive from which the evidence used in this chapter is drawn, and of the rather complex techniques involved in moving from time-budget survey data to national estimates of time use is delayed until later in the book; for the moment we press ahead to discuss the overall trends.

The general argument concerns the connection of the work–leisure balance to economic development. So, to give a first crude picture of change, we simply plot the various societies' aggregate time allocations against their national incomes at the time of the survey. (Cross-national comparative estimates of national incomes are themselves by no means unproblematic: what follows is based on estimates from the database published by Summers and Heston (1988). We have also, for reasons which will immediately become apparent, broken down the national estimates by sex.

Figure 5.1 shows paid work for men. On the horizontal axis are minutes of paid work per average day for each survey (that is, minutes per day averaged across the seven days of the week). On the vertical axis are estimates of GNP per capita in the equivalent of 1980 US dollars. So what is plotted is a particular view of the association of men's paid work time with economic development. Or to be more precise, it is a combination of two different sorts of views. The individual points, for the (sometime) two Germanies, Yugoslavia, for the 1960s, Sweden, Israel in the 1990s, and so on, represent a sort of comparative cross-section: the comparison of different societies (with their different national incomes and paid work times) at particular historical instants. The lines connect successive

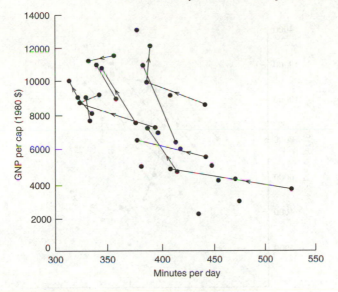

Figure 5.1. Men's paid work time

Note: Arrows indicate successive observations from the same country, hence, historical change

historical points for the same country; so, for a subset of the countries, we can also compare the longitudinal evolution of income and work time. We have restricted the population base to ages 20 to 60, so the result does not reflect the growth in the size of the retired population (though there is a small influence from the increase in participation in higher education which slightly reduces the paid work time of people in their early twenties). The two views give the same message: men's paid work reduces with economic growth.

The correlation between national income and men's paid work time is not that strong: there is, as we see from the figure, quite some variation in the level of paid work time at any given level of GNP (though some of this variation may be due simply to the particular procedure for moving national GNP to the common dollar base). But the trends are plainly quite strikingly similar across countries.

The equivalent picture for women (Figure 5.2a) may at first seem rather more confused. But we can interpret this as two separate trends. There is the comparative cross-section. For the (then) communist countries in this group, virtually all women had paid jobs, from before the mid-1950s. For these countries, the evolution of women's paid work time has the same pattern as that for men: as the society gets richer they do less paid work. And there is the trend for 'First World' countries. Here the overall hours of work for the society as a whole are subject to conflicting processes. In fact,

(a)

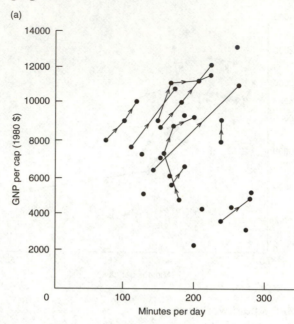

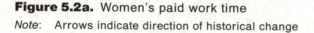

Figure 5.2a. Women's paid work time

Note: Arrows indicate direction of historical change

as we shall see a little further into this chapter, women with paid jobs in these countries do about the same amount, or perhaps a little less paid work as their countries get richer; but in these countries during the early post-war years, relatively few women had paid jobs, and subsequently (i.e. with economic growth) women's rate of participation in paid work has increased. The combination of these two trends produces a small but regular increase in the total of women's paid work time in the First World countries. So Figure 5.2b, which is simplified by excluding those ex-communist countries for which we have no longitudinal evidence, looks no more complicated than Figure 5.1. It represents quite regular and explicable cross-national trends.

What of unpaid work? Figure 5.3 and Figure 5.4 adopt a very broad view of this, including not just housework and cooking, but also shopping, childcare, non-routine jobs, and gardening. First consider women (Figure 5.3). Once more we have a very clear cross-sectional and longitudinal trend. Women's unpaid work time declines over historical time and with economic development.

This plot shows really very substantial reductions in unpaid work time of, in some cases, more than an hour and a half per day. Women's unpaid work time reduces with economic development. However, we will see, here and

(b)

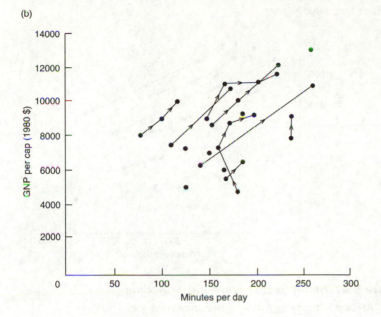

Figure 5.2b. Women's paid work time (excluding ex-communist coun-tries)

Note: Arrows indicate direction of historical change

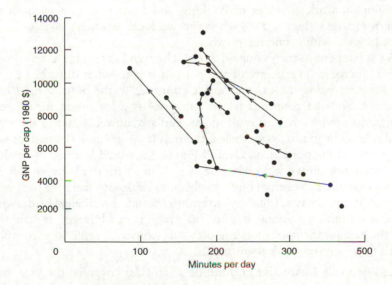

Figure 5.3. Women's unpaid work time

Note: Arrows indicate direction of historical change

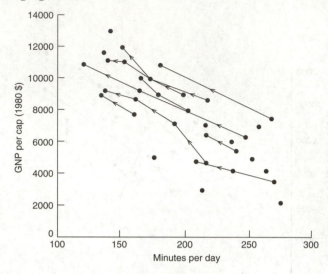

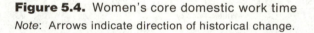

Figure 5.4. Women's core domestic work time

Note: Arrows indicate direction of historical change.

in later chapters, that within this set of unpaid work activities there is really some considerable variation. Time spent with children, for example, has increased substantially. If we take a narrower definition and include just the core unpaid work activities of cooking and housework, an even clearer pattern emerges (Figure 5.4): wherever we look, women's core domestic work reduces with economic growth.

What happens to men's unpaid work? The trend data (Figure 5.5) show a general increase. The clarity of the pattern is somewhat disturbed by the points representing the ex-communist countries in the bottom right-hand quadrant, and the countries which can give us a longitudinal picture of change do not by any means all move regularly upwards and to the right-hand side of the graph. Nevertheless the trends are generally consistent with the scatter of the point data. Overall Figure 5.5 would lead us to conclude that men's unpaid work time has been growing with the increase in GNP, and this growth has been of quite a substantial absolute size over the period covered by this dataset. (Readers' attention should nevertheless be drawn to the fact that the horizontal axis on this graph is much larger in scale than was the case for the corresponding previous women's graph; women still do much more unpaid work than men.)

And (we will discuss this in more detail in later chapters) the increase is not concentrated, as some feminist critics of this result have suggested, in non-routine jobs. Altogether the largest proportional growth lies in the routine cooking and cleaning activities. Figure 5.6 is again somewhat

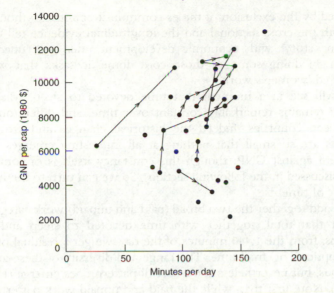

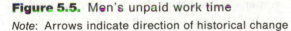

Figure 5.5. Men's unpaid work time

Note: Arrows indicate direction of historical change

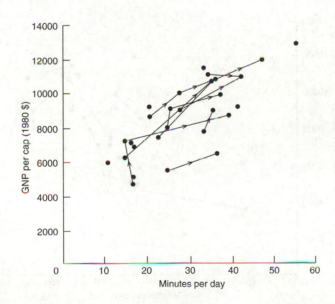
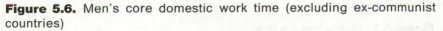

Figure 5.6. Men's core domestic work time (excluding ex-communist countries)

Note: Arrows indicate direction of historical change

simplified by the exclusion of the ex-communist countries—though in this case both the cross-sectional and the longitudinal evidence tell essentially the same story: with economic development, men are, unequivocally, increasingly doing some of those core domestic tasks that were once considered 'women's work'.

We will see in a moment that time devoted to sleep, washing, and dressing remains remarkably constant over time, and differs only a little as between countries. Indeed the historical changes and cross-national contrasts are so small that nothing at all interesting emerges when we plot them against GNP (though this constancy itself is of some interest and is discussed in the following section). So we can turn to the final broad category of time use.

If we add together the two broad (paid and unpaid) work categories, and subtract that total, together with time devoted to sleep and personal ablutions, from the 1,440 minutes of the day, we get a residual of 'leisure', 'consumption', or 'free' time. The range and diversity of these activities is enormous, but nevertheless some sort of pattern does emerge (Figures 5.7 and 5.8). Note first that, while the paid and unpaid work patterns differed sharply between men and women—indeed they showed directly contrary tends—the leisure patterns are, both in trend and indeed point for point in

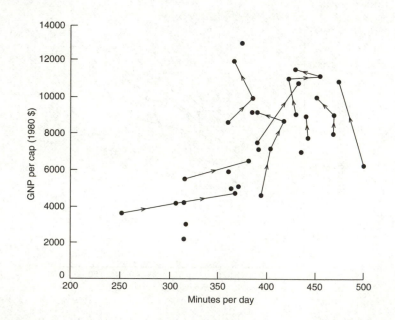

Figure 5.7. Men's leisure time

Note: Arrows indicate direction of historical change

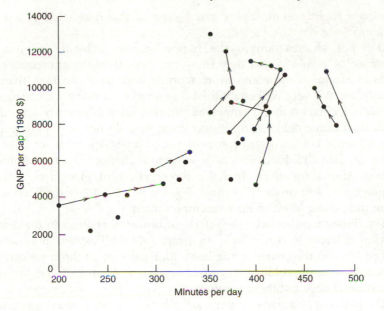

Figure 5.8. Women's leisure time

Note: Arrows indicate direction of historical change

each country, very similar for men and women. And the trends are in both cases reasonably clear, a movement, with economic growth, from the bottom left-hand quadrant to the top right-hand. A trumpet, perhaps, a traditional ram's-horn *shophar*. Can we not however detect a bending backwards of the trend line for some of the richer countries? Clearly the empirical evidence, now we get to put it together, suggests something more complex than the simple monotonic tendencies set out in the literature discussed in Chapter 3.

3. Behavioural vs. structural change

We can now take a very preliminary step towards the consideration of what it is that is actually *changing* in these graphs. Let us start by making a simple distinction between two different sorts of historical shifts in time use. There are changes which may be best understood as consequences of shifts in economic and sociodemographic *structure*. And there are others which can be understood as change in the *behaviour* patterns specific to people in particular locations in the sociodemographic structure. (We will develop a slightly more sophisticated view of this distinction in the next chapter.)

One possible reaction to the major changes exhibited in this first sequence of graphs is that they show no more than the consequences of shifts in economic structure. More women have paid jobs now than previously, and it is very well established that (even controlling for variations in household circumstances) employed women do substantially less housework than non-employed. And more men now do not have jobs: perhaps they do more housework in compensation. So perhaps what we have seen so far are just the direct effects of structural change. Figures 5.3 and 5.4 perhaps shows no more than the direct effect of growth in women's employment, and similarly, perhaps Figures 5.1 and 5.2 perhaps reflect no more than rising levels of male unemployment.

The distinctions between the effects of historical changes in the distributions of different sorts of people (in a sense we shall explain in a moment) and changes in the characteristic behaviour patterns of those various sorts of people is an important part of our argument. In this chapter we try to apportion change in time-use patterns between these two categories.

The patterns of activity on any particular day must, as was argued in the previous chapter, be explained in terms of a very much longer-term perspective. The long sequence of activities that makes each individual's life history interacts with the constraints and opportunities of the current circumstances to produce the daily patterns. This history serves in various ways to direct, and constrain, and motivate interactions with the material world. The long sequence of the life dominates the short cycle of the day.

Our consciousness, as individuals, is the outcome of this extended historical string of events, past activities, or experiences. There are many millions of individual events that make up a life. We get up, we wash and clean our teeth, make breakfast—every day of the year, every year of our lives. Of these millions of activities, some disappear without trace from the consciousness, inconsequential as shouts in the street. Others, for example the events of our formal education, become aggregated with large numbers of similar events, and jointly influence our current behaviour. (We do not, for the most part, remember individual lessons, but we nevertheless read and write and do our jobs as a result of the sum of our lessons.) Yet other singular events also influence subsequent activities in quite pervasive ways. Some at least of the earlier events in the long sequence influence later ones.

And we have already established in the course of the more theoretical discussion in the previous chapter, what at least some of these 'influential' or 'consequential' events are (and we shall demonstrate and quantify the importance of some of these particular categories empirically in the next chapter). There are the 'events' of birth which establish our gender and other genetic characteristics, and the resources and capabilities of our 'household of origin'. There are the activities of childhood: the formal and informal education and socialization that add to our stock of human capital. There are more adult events of household formation and dissolution: leaving the parental home, marriage, divorce, having children. There are events in the labour market: taking jobs, leaving or losing them. There are the regular physiological processes of maturation and ageing. And there are more irregularly occurring events, such as those which lead to the development of a physical disability. The occurrence of such events can be viewed as *the process of formation of social structural characteristics*. People who have experienced these particular sorts of events acquire particular statuses, become particular sorts of people. Married women, employed graduates, mothers of small children, have acquired peculiar characteristics as a result of certain particular events or experiences, and may be expected to behave in particular ways by virtue of these experiences.

There is obviously a difference between the 'consequential' events and the inconsequential ones. And there are different sorts of consequentiality. Hearing a shout in the street, or a symphony in a concert hall, cleaning the house and cooking lunch, getting a job and doing it, finding a husband and doing the emotional work necessary to stay married, conceiving a child and bringing her up, all are events that take place on the same temporal scale, they each occupy just so many minutes, they all form part of the 'long sequence'. Yet they differ in the scale of their consequences. The shout in the street may have none. (Yet the chaotic nature of our existence means that it may occasionally—a racial taunt, perhaps—change it utterly.) Hearing the concert adds to that stock of knowledge we call cultural capital, which may in turn allow us to enjoy the music more, and hence encourage us to attend concerts more frequently. Cleaning and cooking—these may *seem* inconsequential, but if we do these regularly and frequently and our colleagues do not, then we have less time and energy for our jobs than they do, and our careers may suffer. As our time-theorizing becomes more thoroughgoing, and its focus extends to encompass more of the life-course than just the day or the week, more of these events can be treated as consequential ones in discussions such as this. Yet for the moment we focus just on the impacts of two sorts of such events: those that form our family circumstances (particularly responsibility for young children), and those that have consequences for our employment status.

This is the basis on which we distinguish the two sorts of social change which can take place over historical periods. People belonging to particular structural categories behave in certain characteristic ways: so, change the proportions of the population falling into these various categories over a historical period—provide more jobs, have fewer children, for example—and the overall pattern of daily activity of the society as a whole must change. And the characteristic behaviours associated with particular categories—the nature of the influence of the 'consequential' events on subsequent activity patterns—may change over historical time.

One traditional view of empirical research is that descriptions run prior to explanations; time-budget evidence requires exactly the opposite treatment. Simply listing the results of time-budget surveys as overall averages of amounts of time spent in particular activities produces quite meaningless pictures, since these averages are across different sorts of people with quite different life circumstances. Survey or population average estimates of amounts of time spent in childcare or outdoor sport compound the activities of young mothers with those of widowers living on their own, young athletes with disabled pensioners. To make sense of time-use data it is necessary to disaggregate the sample by those social-structural categories which 'explain' the variance in the activity averages—we need to look separately at the mothers and the widowers. Of course these 'explanations' are often rather tautologous or teleological: we do childcare 'because' we have children, we do paid work 'because' we fall into the category of the full-time employed. In these cases our survey data serve just to freeze an arbitrary instant of an ongoing recursive process. In other cases they are not explanations in any sense at all: we do not keep house 'because' we are women, but because of a norm attached to that gender category (or from a different perspective, because of our gender ideology). The explanation is the norm (or the ideology), not the sex. But, nevertheless, we have to arrive at 'explanations' (in the variance-explaining sense) as a prerequisite for giving sensible descriptions.

At a given historical juncture we have a set of cross-cutting explanatory classifications, some of them determined wholly externally or exogenously to the individual (sex, age), some of them endogenously determined in part at least by the individual (employment status, stage in the family/life cycle)—all of which relate to earlier 'consequential events' in the long sequence of activities which is the individual's life history. And associated with each of the categories defined by these cross-cutting classifications is a particular pattern of behaviour.

Shift-share analysis: reweighting cases

So there are 'type 1' changes, in the structural composition of the population. And there are 'type 2' changes, in the behavioural consequences of belonging to one or another social-structural category. 'Shift-share analysis' is a procedure for distinguishing between them. It can be done through a multiple regression procedure, but for reasons set out immediately below, what is done here involves merely reweighting survey cases so as to dispose of the effect of compositional variation. The difference between any pair of surveys can be broken down into two components: with two surveys A and B, the cases in B are reweighted so as to produce a survey B' which has the same structural composition as A. Now the differences between A and B' will all be behavioural in origin, and the differences between B' and B will all be structural; any A−B will equal the sum of A−B′ and B′−B.

In Chapter 6 we shall go through the formal process of identifying the main classificatory categories which are associated with variation in time use. What emerges from this is pretty much what we have already suggested on a priori grounds: of the micro variables, sex, family status, and employment status are of major importance. In this chapter will use a simple graphical analogy to shift-share analysis to separate out those aspects of change due to shifts in these particular demographic and employment categories, from 'behavioural' changes.

The regression-based methodology for examining change in time-use patterns is well developed and straightforward (see Jenkins and O'Leary 1997). It involves, for any pair of historical observation points, obtaining a regression on time use for each point, as well as the mean values or frequencies of each of the regressor variables for each observation. With this information it is no more than simple arithmetic to 'decompose' historical change into its structural and behavioural components. But the problem we face in this and the following chapter is of a somewhat different order: thirty-five historical time points, twenty countries, nine countries having two or more observations, means a very large number of potential pairwise comparisons. So instead of the formal regression procedure, we will adopt a rather more informal graphical approach (and a more formal approach to the decomposition of the variation in time use is postponed to the following chapter).

Ours is a multinational *and* longitudinal survey collection, which means that we have two different sorts of differences to consider. We must think about *changes over historical time*, in some cases with multiple observation points, and also about *contrasts among countries*. So for our purposes, we need to do, not one, but two different sorts of reweighting. In what follows we will not in fact go through the whole shift-share process of apportioning change to the four components (i.e. structure/behaviour for country combined with structure behaviour for period). Instead, we present the material in the form of charts illustrating three different situations.

In the *first*, we see uncorrected means of time spent in various activities for each country, sex, and survey. These show the actual changes in time allocation over the historical period, and the actual differences between countries.

In the *second*, means are reweighted so that, for each country and sex, the distributions of people in each combined employment and family-status group are exactly the same in the subsequent surveys as in the first survey for that country (these are referred to as 'base-year composition-weighted' or simply 'base-weighted' estimates). These show that part of the historical change in each country that is specifically behavioural and not related to compositional changes. The national differences shown in this second category of charts reflect both behavioural differences between the countries, and those due to differences in the structures of the various national populations at the date of the first survey in each country.

In the *third* sort of chart all the surveys are reweighted so that their composition (in terms of sex employment and age/family status) are identical (in fact we reweight all the surveys to resemble the structure of the earliest survey in our collection, that for the UK in 1961; for this reason these charts are referred to as being 'UK-base-year weighted'). They show just the behavioural components of both the historical changes and the national differences.

We should add that this procedure involves a logical short-cut. A behavioural change, as we have described it, is a historical change in the time allocation of a particular structural category or sort of person; yet, strictly speaking, all that emerges from our shift-share approach is a change in the appropriately weighted averages of a set of structural categories. It would be logically possible that a set of contrasting behavioural changes among the various structural categories could cancel each other out, to give a false impression of behavioural constancy over historical time. So (in very special circumstances) the procedure we outline can give false negatives: it may give us the impression of no change where there is change. But it cannot give a false positive: if a behavioural change is registered by this procedure it must really be present.

We will see, in Chapter 6, that the effects of employment and family status are in general much smaller for men than for women. One concomitant of this finding is that compositional differences in the sample structures tend to have less effect on estimates of men's time-use patterns than on women's. So what follows will often provide just the unweighted chart for men, even though we may show all three sorts of chart for women. Since a large part of the concern is with historical change, this analysis includes only those countries for which we have two or more historical observations.

Paid work

Figure 5.9 plots men's unweighted paid work time (in which we also include travel and job-search activities) not against GNP (as in Figures 5.1 to 5.8) but against the date of the survey. A reasonably straightforward trend emerges: the total of paid work time declines through the first part of the period (with just one apparent exception, the USA). Britain and Canada show small increases as they enter the 1990s. Hungary has altogether the fastest decline in paid work time, starting from the highest initial level. The countries are quite tightly bunched together, and have a relatively constant rate of change. Where the samples are reweighted to give a constant structure over time, the patterns are substantially unchanged; we are entitled to

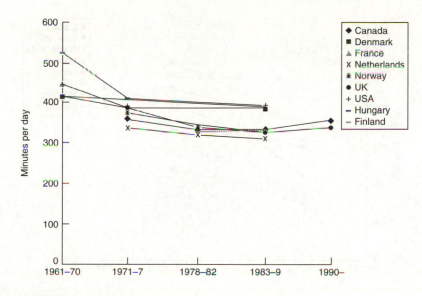

Figure 5.9. Men's paid work time

conclude from this that the historical change in men's work time is behavioural rather than structural (in particular it is not a consequence of a growth of unemployment). Though in the case of the USA, once we correct for rising un- and non-employment for men from the 1960s to the 1980s, we see a very much smaller fall in paid work time over the first part of the period, and a small rise over the second half, which suggests a predominance of structural change just in this particular case. By contrast the UK base-year-weighted results show the countries more closely bunched together, indicating that much of the cross-national variation relates to structural differences, particularly in male participation and unemployment rates.

Women (Figure 5.10a) show the contrary historical trend. The countries have relatively similar rates of increase in paid work time, but we see much more national variation in the absolute levels than in the case of men. The UK, pretty much the middle case in terms of absolute level, actually shows a small decline in women's work time from the 1960s to the mid-1970s (which is explained in a moment). We see large changes over time. The general trend, at least for the 1970s onwards, is for an increase in women's paid work of thirty or forty minutes per day per decade. We see large absolute differences between countries: the extreme cases are Hungary, approaching 300 minutes paid work per day, while the Netherlands just breaks above 100 minutes.

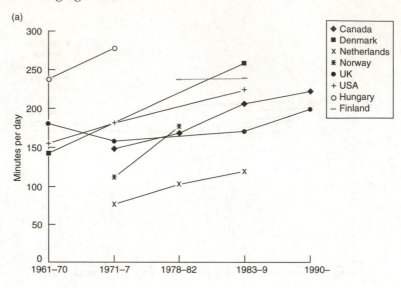

Figure 5.10a. Women's paid work time

The reweighting process allows us to explain away quite a large part of the longitudinal and cross-national difference. Remember that the number of minutes per day devoted to an activity is the product of two different factors: the rate of participation in the activity, and the time spent doing it by participants in it. In the case of paid work, the first of these is changing very quickly; the reason for the decline in UK women's paid work time in the 1960s, for example, was the very rapid rise in the number of part-time workers, combined with a small decline in both the numbers and the hours of work of part-time workers.

Participation in paid work is captured clearly as one of our structural characteristics: so a base-year reweighting of the cases shows how the historical change in paid work time would have looked, for each country, if the composition (particularly important in this case, split between women employed full-time, part-time, and not at all) had remained unchanged within each country. The base-weighted chart for women's paid work (Figure 5.10b) presents a really very considerable contrast to the unweighted picture. A very large part of the upwards trend has disappeared; in some countries it is converted to a decline.

This demonstrates very clearly that most of the historical change can be put down to the structural shift of women into part- and full-time work. Once we remove the effects of the structural shifts, women's paid work time shows, in each country, relatively little historical change. There are small declines in some countries (e.g. UK, Norway) and increases in others

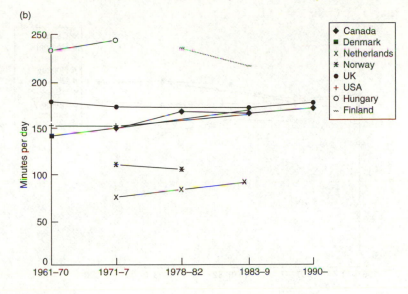

Figure 5.10b. Women's paid work: base-year weighted

(Netherlands, Finland). In this case—and quite unlike the men's equivalent—we conclude that virtually all the historical changes are in the structural composition, with only rather small changes in the behaviour associated with the structural categories. Women in any given combination of family and employment circumstances spend an almost unchanged amount of time in paid work throughout the period. Differences across history within countries relate very largely to historical changes in the attachment of women to paid work. We cannot say that this particular finding is in itself very startling; but the very fact that the result corresponds so closely with our expectations does serve to demonstrate the effectiveness of the technique.

And the second step in the decomposition of difference produces a rather less unsurprising result. The base-weighting serves to lose the historical trend observable in the unweighted picture, but it nevertheless leaves some rather substantial differences among the absolute levels of women's paid work in the various countries. Figure 5.10c, which reweights all the samples to resemble the employment and household-compositional structure of the UK in 1961, makes it plain that the cross-national differences are also largely structural. Once we reweight all the samples to simulate a cross-time and cross-national constancy in the structural composition of the sample, a major part of the cross-national difference disappears. Hungary as the sole East-bloc country in this part of the time-budget archive remains as

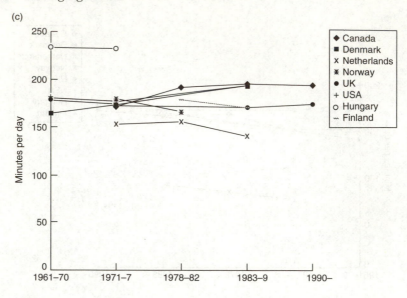

Figure 5.10c. Women's paid work: UK base-year weighted

an outlier. But with this exception, the countries generally fall into a quite narrow band within 150 to 200 minutes of paid work per day.

Unpaid work

Figure 5.11a shows the unweighted average of women's daily core work. This shows very substantial historical changes: we see reductions in unpaid work time of the order of an hour or more *per decade*. (If we were to look at the broader category, in which we include shopping, childcare, and odd jobs as well as household cooking and cleaning, we would find a rather slower rate of decline, and there would be a small upwards turn as we move into the 1990s, a development associated, as we shall see in Chapter 7, with the growth in shopping and childcare.) Of course, a large part of the very substantial decline may relate to the increase in women's paid work time that we have already noted. So we must control for structural change. The base-year weighted changes in women's routine unpaid work are shown in Figure 5.11b. As a result of the reweighting, the downwards slope is considerably less steep, and indeed we find small increases from the 1970s onwards. We conclude that a not insubstantial part of the reduction in women's unpaid work is structural (i.e. relates to the increasing attachment to paid work). Nevertheless the trend is still one of substantial reduction. The broader category of unpaid work (not exhibited here) shows small overall increases from the 1970s onwards once we control for structural

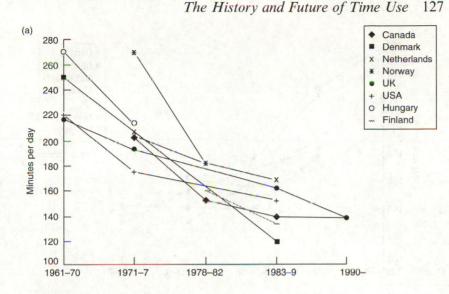

Figure 5.11a. Women's core domestic work time

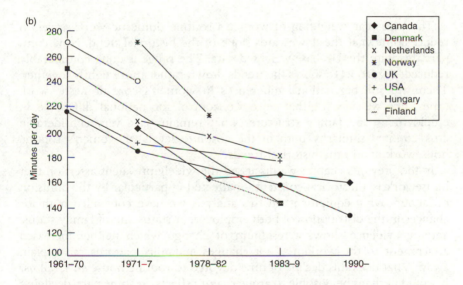

Figure 5.11b. Women's core domestic work time: base-year weighted

change. But given the magnitude of the changes shown in Figure 5.11b it would be reasonable to conclude that the largest part of the reduction is not structural but behavioural (i.e. the reduction in housework applies to women in each structural category).

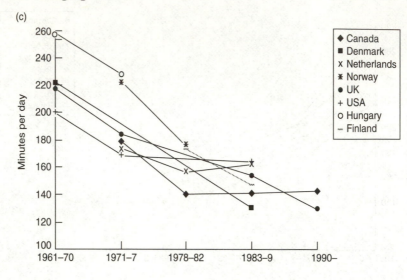

Figure 5.11c. Women's core domestic work time: UK base-year weighted

The base-year weighting of women's routine domestic work serves to reduce somewhat the downwards slope of the historical trend. Now compare this with the UK-base-weighted data. The range is quite considerably reduced: Figure 5.11c shows the trends drawn rather more tightly together. There are still big national differences in women's core domestic work times, but we can see that once we control for national difference in employment and family structure, what remains is a very considerable cross-country similarity both in the absolute levels of women's routine housework and in the historical trends.

In the previous chapter we discussed the widely prevalent assertion that housework is a historical constant, unaffected in particular by the diffusion of labour-saving equipment. In this analysis we have controlled both for changes in the distribution of both employment status and of family status. Yet the evidence shows a residuum of change which neither increased attachment to the workforce nor changes in family patterns can explain away. What does this decline of time devoted to routine housework tell us? It would perhaps be possible to argue that it reflects, in some part, declining standards of housekeeping. But, given that the historical period we are considering is precisely the period which saw the mass diffusion of household durables, it would surely be perverse to argue that this reduction was not in substantial part due to the spread of labour-saving technology.

Figure 5.12 shows the unweighted trend in men's daily allocation of time to core domestic work. The totals are very small relative to the women's

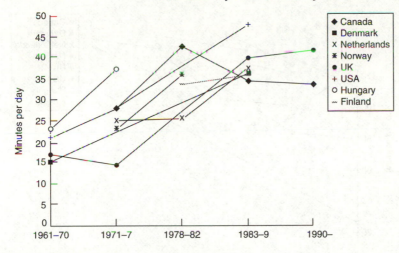

Figure 5.12. Men's core domestic work time

equivalent. But there is the very clearest of upwards trends, most marked from the mid-1970s onwards. This pattern is hardly changed by base-weighting (though arguably we should be using for this analysis some quite different structural categories, concerning the work-sharing behaviour of the households; we might well then see that the small average growth in men's routine domestic work corresponds to a 'structural' growth in the proportion of the sample falling into a 'two-job couple' category—but unfortunately only a small proportion of the surveys provide us with the data this analysis would require.) We should particularly note the historical phasing of the change: most of the increase is found in the later part of the period. Does this suggest the influence of the women's movement on men's daily practices?

So far we have just looked at core domestic work. But the best grounded arguments for the constancy of women's domestic responsibilities are in fact about other aspects of unpaid work: childcare, shopping, DIY, gardening, etc. There is some question as to whether growth in time devoted to these activities compensates for loss of time spent in core domestic work. It is certainly true, as we shall see in Chapter 7, that these have increased in many (though not all) countries. Figures 5.13 and 5.14 show that even when we add these into the evidence, we still see the same broad pattern. Figure 5.13 (unweighted men's data: the weighting makes little difference here) shows the previous general pattern of increase in men's domestic work; the single exception is Hungary, where liberalization of the economy, leading to more efficient retail services, meant that less time was spent in that most characteristically East-bloc activity, queuing. Men in Denmark

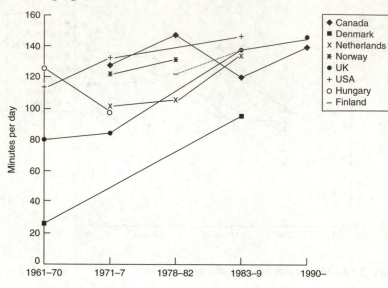

Figure 5.13. Men's unpaid work

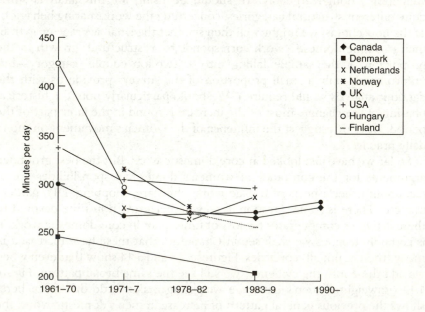

Figure 5.14. Women's unpaid work: UK base-year weighted

show a particularly low total because (as a result of shortcomings in the original data collection) domestic travel and shopping are not included in these estimates. Again Figure 5.14 (UK-base-weighted women's data) shows generally the same pattern of decrease in women's unpaid work as did the core domestic category, though, once we control for structure, some small increases are apparent in the recent period for the UK and Canada; but nevertheless, considering the period overall (i.e. counting change from the 1960s onwards), the downwards trend is maintained even in these two countries. And again, comparison of the unweighted with the UK-base-year-weighted pictures suggests that some part of the cross-national differences relates to structural factors.

We should also add that it is not, in fact, all that clear that these non-routine domestic activities are best regarded as work. The Hawrylyshn criterion, that any activity that may be substituted by some purchased service without loss of utility may be considered to be work, raises a problem: shopping, childcare, DIY, gardening, all have some intrinsic satisfaction so, though we can certainly purchase these services, they still lie on the contested borderline between work and non-work (Hawrylyshn 1977). In our discussions we will keep an open mind on this issue. But it certainly remains true that core domestic work is still the great bulk of the unpaid work-related activities, and includes the most onerous of them; so we will take this as the central indicator for unpaid work.

4. The work–leisure balance

There are some substantial differences in the sizes of these changes in the various countries. But the general direction of the trends is constant across countries. Even when we control for the major structural changes over the last decades, we find evidence of reduction in work time. Men do less paid work and more unpaid, even once we have controlled for the effect of growing unemployment. Women do less unpaid work, even controlling for the effect on housework of their growth in participation in paid work over the period.

Let us move now away from the consideration of behavioural change to the broader question of how the overall social balance has shifted between work and leisure time. The triangular graph in Figure 5.15 (Figure 5.16 is simply an enlarged version of the central portion) summarizes both the overall change in time use for the nine countries with cross-time data, and also the pattern of time use in those countries for which we have only a single historical point of observation. It does so without controlling for shifts in the various structural variables we have discussed so far: it provides an initial, simple, summary answer to the essentially empirical question posed by Chapter 2.

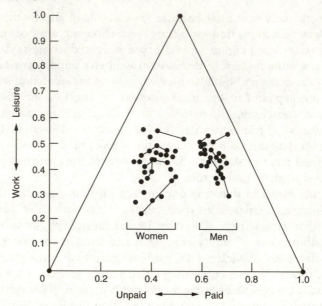

Figure 5.15. The virtuous triangle: work and leisure in the second half of the twentieth century

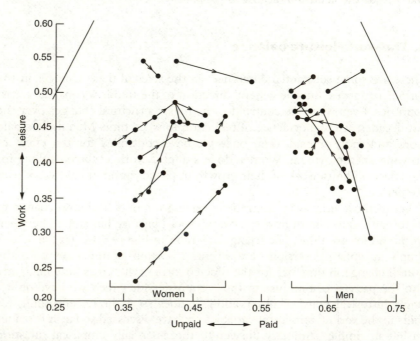

Figure 5.16. The changing work–leisure balance, 1960s–1990s

To draw this triangle graph, we have added, separately for men and women (aged 20 to 60) in each of the thirty-five surveys, paid work, unpaid work, and leisure time, and then expressed each of these three broad categories of activity as a proportion of the resulting total (so that the three proportions represent the division of all time other than that devoted to sleep). The triangle summarizes the disposition of all waking time. Someone who devoted all his or her time (other than personal care) to paid work would be located at the bottom right-hand apex of the triangle graph; someone with no leisure whatsoever who divided time equally between paid and unpaid work would be located at the middle of the base of the triangle; and someone who divided time equally among the three activities would be placed at the centre of the triangle.

The arrow on each line shows the historical sequence, pointing from the earlier to the later survey. The group of plots on the right of the graph are for men from each country, those to the left side of the graph refer to the women.

We might note a number of features of this graph. First, we see national convergence, in the sense that for each sex, the later points are less scattered than the earlier. This phenomenon is particularly marked for men: the distribution of overall time among the broad aggregates that make up daily life have become, by the 1980s, really very similar indeed, especially considering the range of different sorts of society—the group includes, after all, the USA and Hungary. We might perhaps wish on general grounds to argue with the sociologists' convergence thesis as regards the grand aggregates of economic structure and economic performance, but at the broad but more (literally) mundane level we are considering, life-styles have clearly converged.

Second, we see a gender role convergence. If gender work roles conformed to the 'traditional' pattern with men engaged exclusively in paid work and women exclusively in unpaid work, then the men's and women's points would all lie respectively on the right-hand and the left-hand sides of the triangle. If the *proportional* gender segregation were to remain unchanged over time, then the lines in the graph would all be extensible to converge at the apex of the triangle. In fact, all the lines point further inwards than this, the women's lines all pointing somewhere to the right of the apex, and all the men's lines pointing somewhere to the left of the apex. So while there is still quite evident gender work role segregation, it is, without exception in this data, decreasing.

Third, and most obviously of all, the countries mostly move away from the base of the triangle over the period covered by our data. The closer a point is to the base of the triangle, the larger the proportion of work (paid plus unpaid) in the waking day; the further from the base, the smaller. So, for all the countries covered in the figure, the balance of waking time has shifted in general away from work, towards leisure. In each case, national product per capita increased through the period covered by the surveys. On this evidence, we can say that the balance between work and leisure has shifted decisively towards leisure with the economic growth of the 1960s to the 1980s. And the trend shows sufficient cross-national regularity that we should perhaps suspect some common underlying sociological explanation.

Time and economic growth

Sometimes the things that are most obvious are also the least apparent. For any individual or any society, there is a balance: the more work, the less leisure. But, as we saw in Chapter 3, there is also a sense in which, for a society as a whole, there is a rather different balance: the more leisure time, the more work. This is a paradox, and like most paradoxes, its explanation is very simple (work time is required to produce leisure services). But its implications are rather important. It suggests an alternative future that is not envisaged in the standard literature on the development of developed societies: a leisure society, but a profoundly materialist one, in which the increase in leisure time plays a central role in maintaining and promoting economic growth.

There is the economists' notion of the 'diminishing marginal utility of income' that as societies get richer and their labour productivity rises, so the desirability of each increment of money income decreases, and people wish to deploy the increasing productive potential of their economies, not to produce more material goods, but to provide the opportunities for more leisure. The idea of diminishing marginal utility underlies the arguments of those sociologists who identify an imminent post-materialist economy.

But it may be that the causal arrow points, not from economic growth to leisure, but in the opposite direction, from leisure to economic growth. The argument goes like this. Consider the notion of 'productivity growth'. Increase in productivity means that over historical time an hour of paid work gives rise to an increasing quantity of goods or services. If a society wishes to maintain its level of employment, it must increase its consumption of goods and services at the same rate as the growth in output of goods and services. But consumption of goods, and particularly consumption of services, itself requires time: if more commodities are produced by the society, then somehow time must be made available for consumption of these.

There are really two different ways of coping with this. The *first* is the scenario outlined by Linder in *The Harried Leisure Class* (Linder 1970). The society maintains its hours of paid work at a constant level, which means that an increasing level of consumption must be crammed into constant leisure time. Leisure itself becomes as a result increasingly unleisurely—and we get Linder's ever more heavily burdened consumers. The *second* way of coping with the consumption consequences of productivity growth is simply to reduce work hours so as to increase the time available for consumption activities. And this is the interpretation that we would place on the evidence of increasing leisure time in the multinational data.

The second of these possibilities tells us that, far from being an indicator of a post-materialist society, increasing leisure time may well be the mechanism for maintaining the stability of an ever more materialist society. Growth in leisure time promotes, enables, in part causes, stable economic growth. More leisure time provides the extra time for consumption, which allows the number of jobs to be maintained despite labour productivity growth. More leisure means more work. (And we must be concerned, not just with how much leisure, but also with the nature of the leisure activities. More high-value-added leisure consumption means more high-value-added jobs.)

Long-term prospects for leisure societies

We have a picture of a long-term declining trend in work. There is less work in the broadest sense. On the basis of the best available evidence, we can say that we are plainly not 'running out of time'. Is this so surprising? Reconsider the 'full wallets, full diaries' view of work set out in Chapter 2. In fact there is nothing in the economic theory that requires people to respond to higher wages by working longer hours. The argument in the mainstream theory in fact arrives at the conclusion that higher wages can either lead to more work (through an 'income effect') or to less work (through a 'substitution effect').

Jobs are created by leisure. On the one hand, are the jobs producing goods which enable the reduction of time spent in undesired unpaid work activities. On the other, are the jobs in the production of the leisure services used during the extra uncommitted time thus liberated. More paid jobs (coupled with a reduction in average working hours) making the equipment that enables a reduction in undesired unpaid work. And the time thus liberated is spent in leisure (or other sophisticated service) consumption that leads to other new jobs in the service sector. The intensity of consumption increases to match the growth in productivity—with no saturation of demand and no necessary overcrowding of time. This is a line of economic growth that clearly improves living conditions.

What emerges, both from the theoretical argument and from the empirical evidence, is a picture of economic progress that is by no means exhausted. What we have seen in the previous chapter, and will see in some more detail in what follows, suggests a line of opportunity for the future, a prospect that combines aspects of what are elsewhere described as 'information societies' and 'leisure societies'. Just as the electromechanical technologies did in the 1950s and 1960s, the information and communications technologies may allow us in the future to spend less time in isolated and undesirable unpaid work to provide for basic needs, freeing time which we may devote to satisfying more sophisticated and luxurious tastes in a relaxed and sociable manner.

This pleasant social prospect is not however a necessary future. Some may argue that the benign working-out of a hidden logic of progress will bring it about. But the evidence from the last major 'wave' of economic development suggests that some state intervention will be necessary. And (following the arguments in Chapter 2) there are plainly different sorts of possible leisure societies, some more pleasant, richer, less status- and gender-divided than others. Last time round (during the 1950s and 1960s) the growth was promoted by combinations of Keynesian demand management (essentially income redistribution) and (in some countries) state planning to stimulate particular sectors. We would suggest that the emergence of the humane and leisurely line of socio-economic development foreshadowed in these pages requires some analogous forms of state intervention. We will return to consider what these interventions might consist of at the end of the book.

6   Explaining Time Use

1. National differences and historical change

How do nations differ?

We know that national time-use patterns do differ. One of the most
entertaining chapters of the description of the previous multinational
time-budget study, *The Use of Time* (Szalai 1972) was provided by Philip
Converse, who developed a spatial model of the national differentiation of
time allocation. He started with an index of similarity of time-use
patterns for each pair of countries (essentially the weighted sum of mean
differences between each pair of countries for each time-use category; see
Harvey *et al.* (1984) for a discussion of such indicators). He then used
smallest space analysis (Guttman 1968) to represent this matrix of differences in a two-dimensional form (rather as one might construct a crude
map from the matrix of distances between pairs of towns in a road atlas).
What emerged was a 'spatial' representation of the differences among the
dozen countries in the study that did in fact resemble a Mercator projection
of the northern hemisphere. And, finally, in what is almost an excess
of statistical versatility, he proceeded to use factor analysis to 'explain' the
east–west and north–south dimensions of his time-use map in terms
of two groups of socio-economic variables—the east–west dimension,
furthermore, being interpretable as primarily related to ideological differences.

Sadly there are no such firework displays in what follows. But our
question is somewhat related. We need to know how to model national
differences in time use. There are really two possibilities: either there is a
common multinational pattern of influence of social demographic and
economic variables such as sex or employment status, and national differences, if they exist at all, are restricted to across-the-board increments or
decrements to time-use categories (i.e. irrespective of sex or employment
status, people in each country do more of some sorts of activities and less of
others); or, alternatively, the influence of the social and demographic and
economic variables may differ substantially between countries, so that there
is no common cross-national model.

What is at issue, in this chapter, is the nature of the model that we will
have to use in order to get an adequate picture of the national differences
and historical changes in time use that are buried in our big dataset. Can

we, for each aggregate time-use category, simply estimate a single straightforward linear regression, with country, period, age, sex, employment status, family circumstances, and so on, as variates? Or is it the case that the effects of the variates all interact, so that such a model would be grossly misleading, and that to understand our data we have to go to the opposite extreme, and look separately at each of the cross-cutting groups?

An extension of the Przeworski–Teune programme

The Przeworski–Teune programme for the conduct of multinational comparative research has its origins in a very simple sort of causal modelling, first described by Herbert Simon in *Models of Man* (1957). Simon's approach relies on the notion of a 'spurious correlation': this is a correlation between variables A and B which is in fact a result of the influence of some variable C, which has a real causal effect on B, and which is also correlated with A. In such a case, the apparent effect of A on B will disappear once we control for the effect of C on B. Przeworski and Teune's (1970) multi-national comparative research programme was designed for the analysis of datasets with a number of cases, regions, perhaps, or historical periods, representing each country. Some part of the variation in the characteristics of these cases could be associated with the country variable. But, they ask, is it really something intrinsically and irreducibly *national* about national differences that leads to this association between the country and the characteristics of the individual cases? Or, alternatively, is it some other identifiable social, economic, or political characteristic of the cases? The P–T programme is the attempt to show that the country association is spurious in the sense that it disappears once other independent variables are controlled for. It tries to replace the proper names of countries, in accounts of social phenomena, with more general sociological variables.

But this programme (or at least the straightforward literal implementation of it) really only makes sense in the analysis of multinational datasets in which the country variable explains a large part of the variation in the characteristics of the cases (which is of course less likely where the units of analysis are individuals rather than, say, regions). If the effect of country is not initially apparent, it cannot be made to *dis*appear. And sometimes there may be national differences which are initially not apparent, but are, in a manner quite contrary to the P–T programme, *revealed* by the introduction of other variables

There are in fact three quite distinct sorts of *national difference*.

The first has to do with gross differences in the *composition* of the population in each country. Let us suppose that, in the language developed in the previous chapter, there are individual level social-structural characteristics that determine time allocation. Then, if the frequency of occurrence of the salient characteristics varies across countries, the country variable will initially appear to explain a good part of the variation in time use, but once we extract that part of the variability in time use associated with the structural characteristics, that associated with country disappears.

The second is the previously mentioned, quite straightforward, situation in which country has a simply *additive* effect on behaviour patterns. It may be that, at least partially independent of any particular personal characteristics people in some countries do more of some particular sorts of activities (and hence remembering the necessarily conservative nature of time use, less of some others). Any residual national difference that remains after controlling for the relevant structural characteristics may fall into this additive category.

These two together constitute the sort of national difference envisaged by the simple Simon version of the Przeworski and Teune model of comparative research.

The third has to do with *interactions* between the country variable and other variables. It may be that the coefficients that relate membership of particular structural categories to particular patterns of time use, vary systematically across countries. In this case, no amount of controlling for compositional differences will have any revelatory effect, since the real differences that exist between countries are averaged out in the calculation of compromised cross-national coefficients. In such a case, the difference is not in the composition of the population, or in general national dispositions to engage in particular activities, but in the disparate natures of the distinct national models that determine behaviour.

We shall indeed find some (undramatic) examples of this sort of difference. In general, in the data we shall be discussing, apparent national differences in time-use patterns are often very much smaller than those associated with such variables as sex and employment status. Our efforts are, therefore, not bent on abolishing national differences, in our statistical models, since a straightforward view of the data in fact gives a (perhaps misleadingly) small impression of national differences. Rather, we will find ourselves introducing extra 'interactive' variables into our statistical models—or in practice introducing specific national models—in an attempt to make apparent the otherwise hidden national differences.

So the variance reduction approach advocated by Przeworski and Teune does not quite meet our needs. We can in principle envisage four distinct possibilities, in a multinational comparison of micro survey data. There may be (i) a considerable variation in some dependent variable associated with country (due either to an additive or to a compositional effect); and this association may (ii) be substantially *reduced* by the *addition* of other independent variables into the equation; these are the situations envisaged by Przeworski and Teune. Or (iii) there may be only a small raw correlation between country and the dependent variable, which (iv) may be *increased* once we take account of its *interactions* with other independent variables. (Or indeed there may be no association whatsoever between country and the dependent variable.) What follows is in part an attempt to distinguish between these four cases (which thus encapsulates the Przeworski–Teune approach).

And then there is the additional complication of *historical change*. Just the same considerations apply. There may be population compositional changes between successive observations. There may be genuine additive effects of 'period'. And there may be interactive effects, such that the coefficients that relate membership of structural categories to behaviour change over time. So the remaining part of the research programme, the comparative-longitudinal part, has a parallel set of questions to the comparative cross-national part. Do we *reduce* variation explained by period by *adding* other variables? Do we *increase* the variation explained by period by *interacting* it with other variables?

This chapter is devoted to a programme of variance decomposition to explore these and related issues. It may be that a more technically soph-isticated statistical approach, of multilevel modelling (Goldstein 1987), will in the end prove more appropriate for the overall purpose of exposing cross-national longitudinal variation in time use. But what follows does at least have the virtue of simplicity, and the technique, if computationally cumber-some, does do the rather simple job that I have set out in a valid and informative manner.

This programme is not undertaken for a merely formal purpose; raising the level of variance explanation by adding interaction terms, or failing to do so, has severely practical implications. 'Explaining' variance—or in other words, reducing the sum of squared distances from each observation to the value predicted for it by the explanatory model—indicates the existence of systematic differences in behaviour of subgroups within the dataset. There is a complex mass of empirical material to discuss. We have time-use data from many different countries and dates. From these data, we have to construct a summary of historical change. Do we have to present separate descriptions of each country's time-use patterns, or is there a common multinational model of time allocation which can be used to simplify the discussion? The more important the interaction terms, the less we can rely on single, simple cross-national and intertemporal models. The results that emerge from this chapter are in fact a necessary element of the central discussion of the book. The formal programme of investigation of alter-native models of variance explanation is what allows us to make sense of the alternative sorts of summary of historical change in time-use patterns which are found in the surrounding chapters.

2. The elements of the models

The time-allocation behaviour we have to explain comes in a neat metric in the form of minutes per day devoted to the various sorts of activity. Virtually all the prospective explanatory variables, by contrast, come in the form of nominal categories: country, sex, employment status, and so on (the only exception is national GNP at the survey date, which hardly figures in what follows). So we have the possibility of a very simple mode of analysis: variance decomposition. This corresponds very closely to the procedure envisaged in the Przeworski–Teune programme: new category variables (and new interactions among them) are progressively added in to the explanatory model; as, at each stage, the new variables and new interactions are introduced, the residual explanatory power of country (i.e. the extra explanatory power when country is added to the other independent variables—its part correlation with the dependent variable) may or may not diminish.

In order to carry out the decomposition we have had to impose some further restrictions on the dataset. We wish to use the survey period as a potential explanatory variate. But some countries in the dataset have at present only a single survey; in these circumstances it would be impossible in principle to distinguish the effect of the survey period from that of the country. So for the analyses in this chapter we have simply excluded the single-survey countries, leaving us with the evidence from the nine countries with cross-time data.

This exclusion leaves us still with some 80,000 cases, representing (since some of the surveys cover a full week while others cover single days) about 150,000 diary days. The total of cases in the various countries varies quite substantially, from hardly more than 5,000 to more than three times this number. Clearly this variation in the sizes of the national sample has at least the potential to distort an analysis in which the central concern is the influence of the country variable. A single country with a large number of cases and a pattern of time use substantially different from that of the other eight could give us a quite misleading impression of the importance of the country variable. So I have adopted a (severely conservative) procedure of down-weighting the number of cases in each country to give a total of 2,000, giving approximately 1,000 respondents of each sex in each country (in fact, this procedure was carried out in parallel with the processes of reweighting for socio-economic structure and day-of-week to produce national representativeness, using techniques described in Appendix 2). As a consequence, the analysis which follows has an apparent N of exactly 18,000. This down-weighted N is however still sufficiently large that with very few exceptions each of the associations between variates and dependent variables reported in what follows are significant at the 0.001 level. And in any case, our concern in this chapter is not at all with questions of statistical significance, but exclusively with the appropriate apportioning of variability within the sample.

Four components of the day

One particular complication is that we have not one, but indefinitely many potential dependent variables. In the multinational dataset, as candidate categories for comparison, we have forty distinct and comparable time-use categories for most of the surveys, and twenty that work across the whole dataset (and if we were prepared to lose some more of the earlier less detailed surveys so as to permit a more detailed common classification, we could have anything up to 100 potential dependent variables). Plainly, our programme of variance decomposition would become quite unmanageable if we were to try to operate on a large number of these categories. We must somehow summarize.

In Chapter 5 our preliminary analysis was carried out for the most part using four time-use activity aggregates. In this we are following the suggestions of Dagfinn Ås (1978), Robinson and Converse (1972), and Robinson *et al.* (1989): paid work time ('contracted time' in the Robinson and Ås formulations), including travel to work, job-search activities, and full-time education; unpaid work time ('obligatory time') including cooking, cleaning, shopping, and childcare; personal care ('necessary time') including sleep, personal toilet, and consumption of medical services; and a residual category of leisure consumption. Each of our individual respondents' minutes devoted to these four classes of activity must sum to the proper total of 1,440 minutes per day.

These correspond to some degree to the analytical requirements that emerge from the discussions in Chapter 2 and 3. We will need progressively more detailed categories as we develop the time-use 'mapping' in Chapter 7. But the variance decomposition in this chapter will focus on the four broad aggregates.

The variability of the time-use aggregates

Sociologists have a professional disposition to seek to over-explain behaviour. Our trade involves explaining individual behaviour in terms of attributes of, or relationships to, collectivities; we are not satisfied if we fail to do this. But individuals differ. Tastes vary (even among sociologists with similar patterns of education and training and material environment), and the exigencies and opportunities of each day lead to variation in routines that cannot be traced to any general or systematic characteristics, either of the individual or of the environment. Much of the variation of an individual's behaviour is necessarily irreducible by sociological variables. So we should always start an analysis by asking ourselves how much individual variation we actually hope or expect to explain.

And the logical starting point for this is the empirical matter of how much individual behaviour actually varies. A simple way of summarizing this is the 'coefficient of variation' (the standard deviation of a variable expressed as a proportion of the mean). Table 6.1 sets out the coefficients of variation of each of the four time-use aggregates, for each of the nine countries, together with grand ('world') mean of minutes per day devoted to each.

We should start by noticing that there are two different groups of countries, with some considerable similarities in the coefficients of variation in each group. The first group contains just the Netherlands and the UK, the second, the other seven countries. The Netherlands–UK group has generally lower coefficients of variation than the other countries. Why?

The explanation is that the subject of study, the 'case', in a time-budget survey is not, in fact, the individual, but rather the individual's activities during the time-period of the survey. Time-diary surveys yield information on only a very small segment of an individual's life. We may all spend an hour doing the weekly wash on one particular day in the week, but since, in a single-day survey, sampling is randomly distributed across the week, the result looks as if six-sevenths of us devote no time whatsoever to washing clothes. Much of what appears as interpersonal variation in time-use patterns may in fact be intrapersonal variation. All of the Netherlands surveys, and three of the four UK surveys, are however collected on a whole-week, seven-sequential-day basis. There will still be some intrapersonal variability represented in the weekly surveys (since some activities happen on a more-than-weekly cycle and some occur randomly through the year), but nevertheless the weekly diaries would be expected to contain less intrapersonal variation than the daily. So the coefficients of variation are accordingly

Table 6.1. Means and coefficients of variation

	Paid	Unpaid	Personal	Leisure
Mean mins/day	278	211	547	403
CoV, all	0.95	0.88	0.20	0.47
Netherlands	0.89	0.71	0.13	0.24
UK	0.82	0.82	0.13	0.36
Canada	1.05	0.90	0.23	0.49
Denmark	0.93	1.12	0.22	0.46
France	0.97	0.85	0.18	0.53
Norway	1.08	0.86	0.20	0.47
USA	0.98	0.87	0.23	0.54
Hungary	0.78	0.91	0.22	0.60
Finland	0.92	0.86	0.19	0.46

generally lower in the seven-day-diary countries. (And for just the same reason, at the end of this chapter we will find that levels of variance *explanation* will be substantially *higher* in these countries.)

But having accounted for this systematic difference, we should notice that the coefficients of variation for each of the broad time-use categories are otherwise really quite similar across countries. This provides us with a first clue about the influence of country on time use. (It also provides, in a somewhat circular manner, some supporting evidence of the validity of the comparison of the various materials out of which the multinational archive is constructed.)

Consider first the coefficients of variation for paid work. The daily surveys show a range from 0.92 to 1.08 (excluding Hungary, for the reason given immediately below), the Dutch and British are 0.89 and 0.82 respectively. These rather high values reflect the bimodal distribution of the variable; one-third or so of the cases in each sample spend no time in this activity, because they represent people who are non-employed or have been sampled on a non-work day; and Hungary (with surveys dating from 1965 and 1977) falls out of this particular example because of its (then) very high (East-bloc) rate of women's employment, which reduces the bimodality of the variable. We might on the basis of our *a priori* knowledge of how paid work is distributed, expect quite a large part of this large variation to be explainable—by sex and family status (since we know that both factors bear on employment status), and also by employment status itself (since we might suspect that hours of paid work are relatively similar across occupations).

The coefficients of variation for unpaid work are rather high, and for similar reasons. And here the range of the coefficients among the single-day surveys is rather larger (from Finland at 0.85 to Denmark at 1.12) which may provide us with a hint of possible national differences. As in the case of paid work, we know that there are a number of systematic and substantial influences on unpaid work time (most specifically sex). So again, we might well expect that a large part of this large variation might be explainable.

By contrast, the final two categories show rather less variability. Personal care consists mainly of sleep, plainly a physiological need, though not necessarily constant over time; so it is not surprising that, for the week surveys the coefficient of variation is hardly more than 0.12 (which tells us, since personal care time is pretty normally distributed about the mean, that around two-thirds of adults sleep between 481 (i.e. 547–(0.12*547)) minutes and 613 (547+66) minutes). In this case, we do not have any *a priori* expectations of how to explain variation; for example, having a job might either increase sleep because it is tiring, or reduce it because there are so many other things to do apart from work. And we do know that other people very similarly placed to us (siblings, spouses, friends, colleagues) often have very different sleep patterns from our own. So we would not expect to be able to explain very much of the small variation in this category. We might well be surprised at the big difference between the coefficients for the single-day and the seven-day surveys; this may be explained by the fact that time-budget surveys show quite substantial variations in sleep time between work and non-work days.

The most difficult of the four aggregates to call ahead of analysis is the leisure category. The large difference between the one-day and seven-day groups is just as we would expect, since leisure time varies substantially across the days of the week (mostly but by no means entirely between the weekdays and the weekend). But do we expect to be able to explain a large part of the variation? There is a certain body of social theory that would lead us to expect leisure and other consumption patterns to be quite strongly affected by education and income, as indicators of human and material 'capital' (e.g. Bourdieu 1979). But as in the case of personal care, casual observation gives us an impression of considerable variation within sociological categories. And while unemployment might mean enforced leisure, employment might give the ability to, in effect, buy leisure by paying others to do our domestic work. Altogether, just as the overall level of variation in this fourth category is intermediate between the personal care and work groups, so we might expect to explain rather more of the variation of leisure than of sleep, but rather less than of the 'contracted and obligated' activities.

Potential explanatory variables

We have two essentially different sorts of variables in our grand aggregated nine-country dataset: the first consists of microlevel evidence, characteristics of the individual cases (age, sex, and so on) which derive from the results of the individual surveys out of which the dataset is collected; the second are macro-characteristics of those surveys themselves (e.g. the survey date, the country, the per capita GNP of the country at the survey data). We treat these two sorts of variable in just the same way in our analyses: there are undoubtedly some potential problems in mixing these different levels of observation, but we will proceed cautiously in our analysis, comparing individual surveys with each other to ensure that the aggregate effects are more than just artefacts of differences in the structure of the component samples. As a preliminary, we provide an overall picture of the variation explained by each of the potential explanatory variables.

The central pivot of our analysis is the country variable. Table 6.2 shows, for each time-use category, the overall mean, the national variations, and the proportions of variance explained by this variable. There are large apparent national differences. For paid work, the Netherlands show a particularly low total and Hungary, a particularly high one. We have already seen, in Chapter 5, that this reflects very largely compositional differences, particularly related to employment status, and the apparent variation in

Table 6.2. Country effects

	Paid	Unpaid	Personal	Leisure
Grand mean	282	211	547	399
Canada	−17	2	−10	24
Denmark	19	−64	−45	90
France	12	31	25	−68
Netherlands	−68	−4	3	69
Norway	−28	20	1	7
UK	−11	−10	19	2
USA	12	18	−0	−30
Hungary	77	30	11	−119
Finland	4	−23	−5	24
R-squared	*0.019*	*0.023*	*0.030*	*0.101*

national behaviour is much smaller once this compositional difference is controlled for. (We should also remember that the surveys cover different dates for different countries: e.g. French and Hungarian data for 1980s, while promised to the Archive, have not yet been supplied.) But though there is quite considerable variation in the national paid work totals, country explains only 2 per cent of the variance; there are large amounts of variance from other sources. The gross national differences in unpaid work are hardly smaller, and again we find low levels of explained variance. Personal care also has substantial aggregate differences in national totals, and 3 per cent of variance is explained. And 10 per cent of all variance in leisure time is explained by the country variable alone.

We have seen (Chapter 5) an illustration of the relationship of GNP to time-use totals. Table 6.3 shows this relationship in terms of raw regression coefficients. It tells us that, for every 1,000 US dollars (1980) per capita of extra national income, our data show some twelve minutes less work (paid and unpaid), three minutes less personal care (though in later chapters we shall see that sleep is hardly affected), and sixteen minutes of extra leisure. The regression coefficients are extremely significant (p 0.001) but nevertheless the proportion of total variance explained by GNP is, for the work categories at least, negligible).

The period variable (Table 6.4) shows some substantial differences over historical time, which all correspond to the plots we examined in Chapter 5, but again a rather small proportion of overall variance is explained. Paid

Table 6.3. GNP effects

	Paid	Unpaid	Personal	Leisure
Raw reg* 100	−0.754	−0.502	−0.334	1.590
R-squared	*0.004*	*0.004*	*0.005*	*0.037*

Table 6.4. Period effects

	Paid	Unpaid	Personal	Leisure
Mean	282	211	547	399
61–70	30	20	−4	−46
71–77	−8	7	13	−12
78–82	−23	−9	−4	36
83–89	−1	−22	−10	34
90–	−4	4	2	−2
R-squared	0.005	0.007	0.007	0.028

work shows a ragged and irregular decline over time, again largely a matter of compositional changes (the Chapter 5 analysis suggested that this irregularity disguises two contrasting historical processes, men having a historical decline in their rate of participation in paid work, while women show a historical growth in their participation rate). Unpaid work time shows a regular decline until the small increase in the 1990s, while leisure shows an irregular increase. Yet again we find a small proportion of variance explained by period: less than 1 per cent of variance in paid and unpaid work and personal care, 3 per cent of leisure time.

The macro variables do not appear to have very much explanatory power (at this preliminary stage of analysis); the micro variables do however explain rather more. It appears (Table 6.5) that employment status is one of the most important factors for explaining time-use patterns. Unsurprisingly, 33 per cent of the variation in paid work time is explained by our respondents' own description of their position in the labour market. Note that non-employed people here appear to do fifty-one minutes of paid work per day: this reflects in part that time spent in full-time education is included in this aggregate category (since the total of the four aggregate activities must sum to the population's 1,440-minute day). The final 'just job', column therefore extracts the educational time; there remains 30 minutes per day of 'paid work' for the non-employed, which includes both job-search activities, and activity in 'the hidden economy' (this last category can be separately distinguished in most though not all of the surveys). Unpaid work also

Table 6.5. Employment status effects

	Paid	Unpaid	Personal	Leisure	Just Job
Mean	282	211	547	399	271
Full time	112	−70	−12	−30	117
Part time	−81	52	10	20	−84
Other, non-emp.	−231	145	24	62	−241
R-squared	0.329	0.263	0.022	0.045	0.363

Table 6.6. Gender Effects

	Paid	Unpaid	Personal	Leisure
Mean	282	211	547	399
Man	97	−97	−10	10
Woman	−96	96	9	−9
R-squared	*0.130*	*0.263*	*0.008*	*0.002*

shows the expected relationship to employment status: the stronger the attachment to paid work, the less the unpaid work time. And very nearly as much of the variance in unpaid work time (26 per cent) is explained by employment status. Employment shows the expected weak relationship with personal care and leisure (though when in Chapter 6 we look at the time-use categories in more detail we will see that certain sorts of leisure time *increase* when people have full-time jobs).

Sex is also of some considerable importance (Table 6.6). Men do, on average, more paid work than women: they also do less unpaid work—and indeed the variations in the two categories balance *exactly* (which again means, because of the constancy of the day, that the other pair must also do so). The apparent gender symmetry is to some degree an appropriate corrective to the impression of general gender inequality that derives from the 'dual burden' literature. (There is however a suspicion that diary data may exhibit a systematic tendency to overestimate paid work time, though to a minor degree, relative to unpaid, as a result of the observed fact that diarists tend to summarize the whole period at the workplace as time 'at work', while those doing unpaid work at home are likely to record brief breaks— e.g. 'stopped for a cigarette'. The consequence is probably that the men's total is slightly overestimated relative to women.) As we might also have expected, sex explains less of the variation in paid work than employment status (since employment status is to some extent 'intervening'); sex however explains more of the variation in unpaid work than of paid work (since women participate in unpaid work irrespective of their employment status).

Age and family status (by which we mean principally the number and age of co-resident children) are closely interrelated. For this reason we have manipulated them into a single life- or family-cycle variable, with four values (below 40 years with no children, youngest child 5 years or younger, youngest child older than 5, and 40 or above with no co-resident children). Those with children (Table 6.7) do less paid work, have less leisure, and a little less sleep, and do considerably more unpaid work (in which category we have of course included childcare). This variable shows surprisingly low levels of variance explanation except in the case of unpaid work (though this reflects an interaction with sex: family status is much more important for women than for men).

Table 6.7. Age and family status effects

	Paid	Unpaid	Personal	Leisure
Mean	283	212	547	399
Yng, no yng. kids	53	−89	4	32
Child under 5	−27	62	−7	−29
Child under 15	−2	25	−4	−20
Oldr, no yng. kids	−23	−5	7	21
R-squared	*0.013*	*0.082*	*0.003*	*0.017*

Education is very difficult to code in a cross-nationally comparable manner. And where we must rely on data that have not been collected for a comparative purpose the problem is doubly difficult. In the multinational dataset as a whole we have developed a three-way split, contrasting 'incomplete secondary' with 'complete secondary' (i.e. full high-school graduation) and 'higher than secondary' (by which we intend at least some higher-level diploma or degree). We can however arrive at something reasonably plausible for only the following surveys: Australia 1984; Belgium 1965; Bulgaria 1989; Canada 1971, 1981, 1986, and 1992; Czechoslovakia 1965; Finland 1979, 1987; France 1965 and 1974; Hungary 1965; Israel 1992; Italy 1980; the Netherlands 1975, 1980, and 1985; Norway 1981; Poland 1965; Sweden 1991; UK 1985 and 1995; USA 1965, 1975, and 1985; Yugoslavia 1965.

We have experimented with various other approaches. But for the purposes of the comprehensive analysis of variance in this chapter, we report the results of an even simpler approach, with a binary split between respondents with a less than completed secondary education, contrasted with those with more education. This allows us to report some results for all the datasets in the collection. The better-educated have (Table 6.8) more paid work, less unpaid work, less personal care time and less leisure (though we shall see in Chapter 7, where we use the slightly more refined categorization for a subset of the surveys, that the trends for paid work are more highly differentiated, and the specific leisure categories vary in quite different directions). The differences are all significant but, for each of the four broad categories, less than 0.5 per cent of variance is explained by

Table 6.8. Education effects

	Paid	Unpaid	Personal	Leisure
Mean	282	211	547	399
Uncompleted secondary	−14	8	−1	7
Complete secondary or more	23	−10	−6	−7
Don't know	−18	3	16	−1
R-squared	*0.005*	*0.002*	*0.005*	*0.001*

Table 6.9. Income effects

	Paid	Unpaid	Personal	Leisure
Mean	282	212	547	399
Lowest 25%	−58	0	7	51
Middle 50%	2	1	−8	5
Highest 25%	19	−18	−14	13
Don't know	7	3	6	−17
R-squared	*0.006*	*0.001*	*0.006*	*0.012*

education, and this level does not appear to increase substantially in inter-action with other variables. This fact, together with the considerable varia-tion in the coding between countries and indeed between surveys within countries, means that education has been dropped from all analysis in this chapter beyond Table 6.10 (but it does reappear when we come to discuss some of the more detailed activity categories in subsequent chapters).

'Income' has two possible meanings in a multinational study. It may be an indicator of the individual's absolute command over goods and services; or it may be a stratification indicator. We have used it here in the second way, indicating the relative position of the respondents' household in the national income distribution (though we have drawn on individual income data where household data was not available). We have tried in each country to break down the income distribution into a three-way classifica-tion, distinguishing (approximately) the bottom quarter of the distribution, the middle 50 per cent , and the top 25 per cent . Overall (as we see in Table 6.9), for each of the time-use categories, this variable explains a very small proportion of the variation, and this proportion does not increase in inter-action with other variables. However, the underlying data available to us at the moment is really only adequate in the case of the following surveys: Australia 1974; Bulgaria 1988; Canada 1971, 1986, and 1992; Denmark 1964 and 1987; France 1974; the Netherlands 1985; Sweden 1991; UK 1985 and 1995; USA 1965, 1975, and 1985. So the income variable is not used in this chapter beyond Table 6.10 (though, again, it is used in the next chapter where we deal in detail with particular countries and more detailed activity categories).

3. Decomposing variance

Przeworski and Teune effects

We have seen that different variables have substantial effects for different activity categories. An optimally parsimonious modelling approach would therefore use a different set of independent variables for explaining the variance in each of the activity categories. But one attractive characteristic of the regression approach to modelling time use (and hence of the Multiple Classification Analysis approach which we often employ in this text) is that if the same independent variables are used for each of a comprehensive set of time-use categories, the intercepts and means of each category sum to 1,440 minutes and the regression (and hence MCA) coefficients sum to 0. This allows us to produce tidy lifestyle summaries, accounts which preserve the time-budgeting constraint that each individual has exactly 1,440 minutes to spend each day which have this form: 'such and such group spends more time than the population average in these activities, which is compensated for by spending less time in those other activities.' For this reason, we have been concerned to produce a common model for the four time-use categories.

The analysis therefore uses a single set of independent variables: sex, employment status, age, and child status (these are summarized in the life-stage variable already described), country, and period. We already have the starting position for the variance decomposition in the shape of the final line of Table 6.2, which summarized the proportions of variance explained in the four broad activities by the country variable alone. As we saw, country on its own explains 2 per cent of the variance in paid and in unpaid work, 3 per cent of the variation in personal care, and 10 per cent of the variance in leisure.

We start the variance decomposition by asking the Przeworski–Teune question: how much of this can be explained away in terms of the influence of other socio-economic variables (and effects of 'national compositional' variability)? To answer we need to find the 'part-correlation' of the country variable, with the time-use variables, controlling for all the other variables. A part-correlation is simply the increment of explanatory power gained by adding an additional independent variable. We can calculate this quite straightforwardly by subtracting the correlation of each time-use category with all the independent variables *excluding country* (i.e. line 2 of Table 6.10)

Table 6.10. Przeworski and Teune effects: first version

$R^{**}2$		Paid	Unpaid	Personal	Leisure
line 1	effect of country alone	0.019	0.023	0.030	0.101
line 2	country+period+sex +emp+fam+ed +income+gnp	0.358	0.445	0.059	0.189
line 3	period+sex+emp+fam +ed+income+gnp	0.353	0.428	0.041	0.128
line 4	*effect of country minus other variates*	*0.005*	*0.017*	*0.018*	*0.061*

from its correlation with all the independent variables *including country* (line 3).

This has the effect of reducing somewhat the variance explained by country in the four aggregate time-use categories. Line 1 gives the original estimate of the effect of country alone, line 4 gives the residual once the effects of other variables are accounted for (i.e. line 2 minus line 3). The level of explanation of paid work is reduced from 2 per cent to half of one per cent, unpaid work is also reduced from just over 2 per cent to just under 2 per cent, it reduces personal care time from 3 to 2 per cent, and reduces the effect of country on leisure from 10 per cent to about 6 per cent. The additive effects of the other variables do clearly 'explain away' some part of the variation initially associated with country; these leave country accounting for a very small (but still statistically significant) part of the (large total) variation in the two work categories, and a rather more substantial part of the (much smaller total) variation in personal care and leisure time. We might refer to these as the Przeworski and Teune effects.

Interactive effects: alternative regression models

These P–T effects are estimates of the explanatory power of the country variable independently of the effects of the other variables. What if there are also interactive country effects, what if the effects of other independent variables differ systematically between countries? What if (this is the broader question of the appropriate sort of models) other variables show important patterns of variation? Do we need to take interactions seriously?

The test is quite straightforward. It depends on the distinction between two different sorts of linear regression models, the additive and the interactive. The additive is the straightforward case, in which we might estimate unpaid work, for example, as:

$$\text{unpaid} = sex + country(1) + country(2) + \ldots \, country(n-1) \tag{1}$$

where *sex* and *country* are (0,1) dummy variables, and the value for *country(n)* is the default case where the other country variables are all set to zero. An example of a model, in which sex interacts with the other variables, might be written as:

$$\text{unpaid} = sex + country(1) + country(2) + \ldots \, country(n-1),$$
$$+ sex^*country(1) + sex^*country(2) + \ldots sex^*country(n-1). \tag{2}$$

An alternative, and exactly equivalent way of achieving the same estimates, and the same level of variance explanation, is to estimate two entirely separate regression models with the same form as equation 1, once for men and once for women.

In equation 2 (and the equivalent 'once-for-each-sex' version of equation 1), all the variables (i.e. both sex and country) are interacting with each other, it is a 'fully saturated' interactive model. But it may be that some of the variables do not interact with each other. So that, for example, *within each country-and-sex* grouping, family status does not interact with employment status (i.e. for any woman in any particular country, having small children has an effect that does not vary whether she is employed or non-employed). This 'partially saturated' model could be estimated as:

$$
\begin{aligned}
unpaid = {} & sex + country(1) + country(2) + \ldots + country(n-1) \\
& + emp(1) + \ldots + emp(n-1) + fam(1) + \ldots + fam(n-1) \\
& + sex^*country(1) + sex^*country(2) + \ldots + sex^*country(n-1) \\
& + sex^*country(1)^*emp(1) + sex^*country(2)^*emp(1) + \ldots \\
& + sex^*country(n-1)^*emp(n-1) + sex^*country(1)^*fam(1) \\
& + \ldots sex^*country(n-1)^*fam(n-1).
\end{aligned}
$$

$$(3)$$

Equation 3 has a lot of terms, which makes it very difficult to interpret. And the numbers of such terms increase as the product of (1 minus) the numbers of categories in each of interacting variable. Again, exactly equivalent to equation 3 in terms of variance explanation and estimates of subgroup means, it would also be possible to estimate equation 4 on multiple subsets of the data, once for each 'sex-and-country' group.

$$
unpaid = emp(1) + \ldots + emp(n-1) + fam(1) + \ldots + fam(n-1). \qquad (4)
$$

The coefficients from equation 4 will themselves be a little more directly and intuitively interpretable than those from equation 3, but on the other hand there will now be an awful lot of equations to deal with. (The equation (4) approach has the incidental advantage that it avoids the error-prone business of constructing multiple interaction terms, of which there would be many hundreds by the time we get to the more saturated models discussed below.)

All in all, it will be helpful to reduce the numbers of interacting variates as far as is possible. If, to come to the point, it does turn out that country really does have to be treated as an interaction term, then, for the full dataset, the number of equations we have to estimate and the number of tables we have to assimilate in order to understand cross-national differences in time use, is increased twentyfold. If the historical period of the survey has an interactive, as opposed to an additive, effect, the numbers of equations increase fivefold.

So let us adopt a straightforward and compact notation in which:

$$
sex^*country^*(emp + fam)
$$

corresponds to the model described in equation 3. Readers may now be spared the somewhat time-consuming process of examining the detail of each of the alternative models for each of the time-use aggregates, and instead turn directly to Table 6.11, which summarizes them in terms of their performance in explaining variance.

Interactive effects: levels of variance explained

The empirical discussion of the book is centred on the twin issues of historical change and cross-national difference. Necessarily, then, we must investigate the possibility that the two macrocountry and macroperiod variables have interactive effects. We also know, from previous research, and also from the findings in Chapter 5, that men and women have quite different patterns of time allocation, and we might expect the sex variable also to show important interactive effects. These are the three variables whose effects we investigate in this section.

Let us consider first the Przeworski and Teune question. Line 4 of Table 6.11 recalculates the first, purely additive, version of the P–T effects (line 3 minus line 2): the numbers here are slightly different from those in Table 6.10, reflecting the fact that we have excluded the educational level, household income level, and GNP at survey date from this second set of models. But it gives, nevertheless, essentially the same answers as the previous analysis. There is some reduction in the country effects as we control for the other variates, leaving country with a very small-scale effect relative

Table 6.11. Przeworski and Teune effects: second version

$R^{**}2$	Paid	Unpaid	Personal	Leisure
line 1: effect of country alone	*0.019*	*0.023*	*0.030*	*0.101*
line 2: sex+period+ employment+family	0.353	0.425	0.034	0.117
line 3: country+sex+period+ employment+family	0.358	0.444	0.059	0.188
line 4: country minus all other effects	*0.005*	*0.019*	*0.025*	*0.071*
line 5: period*sex* (employment+family)	0.360	0.467	0.041	0.130
line 6: country*period*sex* (employment +family)	0.375	0.503	0.076	0.216
line 7: country minus other effects, interactions	*0.015*	*0.036*	*0.035*	*0.086*

to the other variates in relation to the *paid work* category (unsurprising since one of these variates is employment status—the additive model is in effect reducing variance by controlling for cross-national and intertemporal variations in labour market *participation*). Country provides intermediate levels of variance explanation in the *unpaid work* and *personal care* categories. And it contributes a larger part of the explained variance in the *leisure* category (though the overall level of variance explanation, in the last two categories, 6 per cent and 19 per cent respectively, is not very high).

However, in the second part of the story told by Table 6.11, country has a little more to say. It does clearly have an interactive effect with the other variates—and particularly when we construct higher-order, two- or three-way interactions involving country with sex and period, we see some more substantial effects. The appropriate way to think of the country effects here is to contrast the model that includes interactions involving the country variable (line 6 of Table 6.11) with the otherwise equivalent interactive models that exclude the country variable (line 5). Country is now seen (line 7) to explain 1.5 per cent of the variance in *paid work*, implying there are not merely national differences in the distributions of employment and family status, but also differences in the regression coefficients relating these to work time for the different countries (and, to get a little ahead of the argument, that we gain some predictive advantage by crossing these with survey period and gender). It contributes 3.6 per cent to the explanation of *unpaid work* (though this is still less than one-tenth of the overall variance explained in this category). It contributes a similar amount to the explanation of *personal care*, though in this case it constitutes about half of all variance explained. And it contributes nearly 9 per cent, out of the 22 per cent of explained variance in *leisure*.

Now for the more general question of which sorts of models are appropriate for understanding the dataset as a whole: Table 6.12 sets out a summary of the variance-reduction performance of a range of alternative modelling approaches, starting (line 1) with the purely additive model we have already seen, then working through various semi-saturated models, to the fully saturated model whose performance is summarized in line 9.

The first group of lightly saturated models (lines 2 to 4) each show improvements in variance explanation over the purely additive model. The only really substantial first-order interactions, unsurprisingly, are with sex in relation to unpaid work, adding nearly 4 per cent to the variance explained, and country and period adding 1.7 per cent and 1.3 per cent respectively, to the explained variance in leisure time.

The second-order interactions (lines 5–7) are slightly larger. Each adds around 1 per cent to the explanation of paid work, around 2 per cent to leisure, and around 1 per cent to personal care. But it is the two second-order interactions involving the sex variable that have substantially the largest effects, again on unpaid work, increasing the variance explained by

Table 6.12. Performance of additive vs. interactive models

R**2		Paid	Unpaid	Personal	Leisure
line 1:	country+period+sex+ employment+family	0.358	0.444	0.059	0.188
line 2:	country*(period+sex+ employment+family)	0.364	0.466	0.066	0.205
line 3:	period*(country+sex+ employment+family)	0.364	0.472	0.062	0.201
line 4:	sex*(country+period+ employment+family)	0.361	0.480	0.062	0.194
line 5:	country*sex*(period+ employment+family)	0.368	0.494	0.072	0.211
line 6:	period*sex*(country+ employment+family)	0.366	0.494	0.067	0.207
line 7:	country*period*(sex+ employment+family)	0.370	0.482	0.069	0.210
line 8:	country*period*sex* (employment +family)	0.375	0.503	0.076	0.216
line 9:	country*period*sex* employment*family	0.382	0.511	0.085	0.223
line 10:	*line 8 − line 1*	*0.025*	*0.067*	*0.026*	*0.035*

5 per cent (the effect of the country/period effect here, though smaller, is still substantial relative to the second-order effects on the other categories.

And the third-order interaction involving all three of the variables we are investigating also adds a further increment of explanation above the second-order models, 0.5–1.0 per cent to each of paid work, personal care, and leisure, and again a little more, 1 to 2 per cent to unpaid work. Line 9, to complete the picture, shows the results for the fully saturated models: there is yet a further increment of explanation, but in each case of less than 1 per cent of total variance. Line 10 summarizes the extra-explanatory power gained by moving from the purely additive model described in line 1 to the third-order partially saturated model in line 8. In each case there is some not-insubstantial improvement. Much the largest gain is in the model for unpaid work.

Further decompositions

We could continue to examine the decomposed variance in the different countries separately; what emerges from this is a striking cross-national similarity in the amounts of variance explained by the independent variables. But rather than giving the entire apparatus, we exhibit just the

Table 6.13. Sex and period interacting with employment and family by country

	Paid	Unpaid	Total variance explained	
			Personal	Leisure
Netherlands	0.794	0.648	0.120	0.319
UK	0.604	0.575	0.125	0.258
Canada	0.300	0.366	0.042	0.124
Denmark	0.274	0.481	0.034	0.070
France	0.414	0.610	0.055	0.135
Norway	0.310	0.474	0.040	0.101
USA	0.356	0.413	0.051	0.105
Hungary	0.360	0.602	0.076	0.179
Finland	0.205	0.310	0.034	0.141

summary table (Table 6.13). We see here three groups: the week-survey countries (UK and the Netherlands), six of the seven one-day survey countries (Canada, Denmark, France, Norway, USA, and Hungary), and, somewhat out of line in terms of levels of variance explanation, Finland.

The first group shows substantially higher levels of explanation than the others, presumably reflecting the previously explained smaller intrapersonal variance in these two countries. We can see high levels of explanation for the work categories, low levels of explanation for personal care, and levels intermediate between the first two for leisure. The second group shows similar patterns of explanation, but in each case lower than the first group, as a consequence of the higher intrapersonal variability. And finally Finland, which shows (in the three aggregate activity categories other than leisure) very much the lowest levels of explanation of any country. Discussions with our Finnish colleagues confirm this result: their explanations are that this stems from the success of Finnish social policy, in particular in reducing gender differentiation in paid and unpaid work. Given the general tendency for reduction in gender differentiation observed in Chapter 5, we might wish to see Finland as in this respect the most 'advanced' of the countries in our sample.

4. Conclusions

The one dominating conclusion from Table 6.12 that has not yet been stated explicitly is that for three of the aggregate time-use categories, the purely additive model does work really rather well. It provides, for paid work, unpaid work, and leisure, respectively 95, 87, and 85 per cent of the overall variance explanation. And still three-quarters of the total explained variance in personal care emerges from the simplest form of model. Three clear implications emerge from the discussions here:

(1) There does seem to be a standard international model. For the two work categories, the great majority of all variation stems from the social or demographic variables, and there is only a small difference between countries. For leisure time overall there is a quite substantial free-standing additive effect of country, which is not substantially reduced when we control for the influence of the sociodemographic variables. But as we saw in Table 6.1, there is very much *less variation to be explained* in the personal care and leisure categories than in the work categories. So the lack of national differences in work time, which varies a great deal across the members of our sample, might be considered a rather more important conclusion than the somewhat stronger national differences in personal care time, which varies rather less. On the basis of these results, we may have a certain degree of confidence in a grand multinational model of time allocation, which estimates a single set of coefficients for the effects of such variables as sex, age, family, and employment status across the various countries.

(2) However, particularly in the area of unpaid domestic work, we see some substantial interactions particularly between the sex variable and the others, which may be interpreted to imply that family and employment status have some different sorts of effects for men and women. So, in addition to the 'whole world' model, we will also certainly have to derive and compare specific coefficients separately for men and for women.

(3) There are some apparent smaller interaction effects from country and period (particularly in relation to leisure, and to a lesser degree to paid work) so we will have, on occasion, to make estimates separately for these categories.

Of course, the main point of carrying out this variance decomposition was to gain some guidance in the construction of the models in Chapter 7, and from this point of view these conclusions must be viewed with the utmost caution. How big an increment of variance explanation from an interactive model is sufficient to allow us to conclude that the coefficients from a purely additive model will be misleading? As far as I am aware, there is no answer to this question. Of course if the increment is zero, then we know for certain that the coefficients of the regression models are identical across the interacted groups. But beyond this the most that can be said is, the larger the increments, the more careful we must be in the implications we draw from the simple models.

Nevertheless, the first of the three conclusions is the most important. Clearly the multinational model, with coefficients estimated across the whole dataset, and with simple additive coefficients for the effects of country and for historical period, is a reasonably good representation of reality. We should certainly not lose sight of the fact, established in the earlier part of this chapter, that, for the two activity categories that do most substantially vary, the overall effects of the two macro variables, country and period, however estimated, are very much smaller than that of other micro variables such as sex and employment status. As a consequence, we might say a Dutch woman's daily pattern of life has, arguably, more in common with that of a North American woman than of a Dutch man; an employed Norwegian's time use is more similar to an employed Hungarian's than to a non-employed Norwegian's; and the time allocation pattern of an employed Canadian woman in the 1960s still looks more like that of a British woman employee in the 1990s than a non-employed Canadian woman in the 1960s. There are, to return to the question with which we opened this chapter, observable in the time-diary dataset, certain national differences and historical changes. But we can say, on the basis of our variance decomposition, that these are in general less important than the cross-national similarities and the longitudinal stability.

7 A Concise Atlas of Time Use: Twenty Countries, Thirty-three Years' Change

'What do you consider the largest map that would be really useful?.... We actually made a map of the country on the scale of a mile to a mile!'
  'Have you used it much?' I enquired.
  'The farmers objected: they said it would cover the whole country and shut out the sunlight.'

Lewis Carroll, *Sylvie and Bruno Concluded*, ch. 11

1. The principle of the conservation of the day

We can now settle to the discussion of some more of the detail of the time-use information in the multinational dataset. There is a mass of this detail to be summarized, and the analogy with the atlas is instructive: map makers must identify the most salient features of the landscape and simplify them. In this chapter we shall employ various different techniques to reduce the scale and simplify the dimensionality of our data. What follows should be viewed, as a concise atlas is, as no more than a partial guide to the real terrain. The tables and figures will also serve as an entry point for those who intend to make use of the survey data files.

The major part of the discussion of this chapter relies on an unfashionable statistical technique, multiple classification analysis (MCA: Andrews, Morgan, and Songquist 1967). This *is* just a matter of fashion. MCA is in fact no more than a simple reorganization of (dummy variable) linear regression output, calculating 'grand means' and 'effect parameters', which have, as we shall see, independent, direct, and common-sense meanings, from the more familiar, and yet less directly and intuitively meaningful regression intercepts and regression coefficients. In all other respects the analyses are exactly equivalent. Since, in the MCA formulation, there is no omitted category for the analysis of categorical variables, conventional MCA output does not give the estimates of the statistical significance of the individual effect parameters. But it is a simple matter to attach the categorical significance statistics derived from the underlying regression to the standard MCA effect parameters; Table 7.5 provides an example of this. (The prejudice against MCA is difficult to fathom, particularly since it serves to bring into the statistical mainstream a specifically sociological approach to under-standing empirical reality, as exemplified by the 'effect parameter analysis' expanded by James Coleman in his *Introduction to Mathematical Sociology* (1964). Or perhaps this sociological pedigree is precisely what has served to taint it. Certainly, some reviewers have been so misled by its conventional placement as an accompaniment to an analysis of variance, as to forget its real identity as a method of presenting ordinary least squares regression results.)

A rather more pertinent objection to what follows is that the normal regression requirements for well-behaved dependent variables is often con-sidered to be violated by time-diary data.

We tend to do only a limited range of different things on any given day, so the time-use estimates from those of our surveys (the majority) which rely on a single day of observations have a lot of zero scores. Day-diary-based evidence of time devoted to a particular type of activity is typically bimodal, with one mode around the mean duration of events of that particular type, and a second mode at zero. We might be tempted to conclude that a Heckman-type (1979) estimation (which looks separately at the processes of selection to participate in the activity, and the determina-tion of the duration of the activity for those who participate in it) is appropriate. I have not, in fact, followed this route, for a practical reason: a dataset derived from approaching forty different source surveys has a distinct dearth of common predictor variables. The requirement of the Heckman procedure that there be *at least one* variable that can be used as an effective instrument to identify likely participants in the activity, and then *not reused* in the analysis of duration, cannot be met for the dataset as a whole.

Fortunately, OLS regression is really rather robust and stands up well to violations of its own requirements. And we do in fact have some direct evidence that the typically bimodal distribution is not a seriously disabling problem. The whole-week diaries from the UK and the Netherlands—which of course have substantially fewer zero-scores—produce very similar regression models to those from the rest of the world with single-day surveys. And of course the more aggregated are the time-use categories, the smaller the problem. In the course of even a single day, most people within the 20–60 age-range covered by this dataset sleep, watch some television, do some paid work and some household tasks, and leave their home for some leisure-related purpose. In fact, considering the seven–category classification on which most of this chapter is based, 62 per cent of the whole sample did some paid work, 74 per cent core domestic, 79 per cent other domestic, 69 per cent out-of-home leisure, 76 per cent watched television, 98 per cent had some other activity in the home such as talking, and just about 100 per cent—all except twenty-two of our 120,000 respond-ents—slept; OLS can certainly handle this sort of data.

MCA is used here (following a suggestion from Harvey and Gronmo 1984; see also Manchester and Stapleton 1991) to display both historical trends and international differences in time allocation. Table 7.1 derives from a series of MCA calculations; it sets out just about the most highly summarized account of historical change that can be derived from the Archive materials. Of course, there is a serious question of whether the estimation of time-use models based on a *single* linear regression is appropriate, given the extent and importance of interactions between sex, country, and historical period with the other regressors (Jenkins and O'Leary 1997). And indeed within the next few paragraphs we will discuss a particular example of how an overcompressed (or 'undersaturated') model of this sort can severely mislead us. But full tabulations for approaching forty distinct country–period combinations for each of the sexes, would tend towards the problem posed by Lewis Carroll's cartographers.

Consider the first column in this table (headed paid work). The entry in the first row of the table is 297 minutes per day. This is the grand mean of paid work and related time, averaged across the week, for all those respondents aged 20 to 60 in the twenty countries covered by the table (a total of approximately 120,000 real cases, but reweighted to 40,000 so as to give an equal representation of each country in the analysis). The remaining coefficients in the column represent the effects of possession of each of the various structural characteristics (sex, employment, family, country), controlling for the effects of all the other characteristics. The entry of 44 minutes in the next row of the table tells us that men on average (and controlling for any variation associated with age, family or employment status, and country) do 339 (i.e. 297+44) minutes per day of paid work. (We shall see in a moment however that 'controlling' in this way can be rather misleading.)

Reading on down the column, we find first a set of employment characteristics. We see that (again controlling for the effect of the other independent variables) those with full-time jobs have approximately 96 minutes more than the average of paid work time while those formally non-employed have 224 minutes less than the average. (This time-use category includes some job-search activities, and also time spent in academic work by full-time students.) Next we find a group of age and family status characteristics. People below the age of 40 with no co-resident children do 21 minutes above the grand mean of paid work, while those with one or more co-resident pre-school-age children do on average 13 minutes less than the grand mean. Then we come to the country effects; we see that Finns and Swedish people have rather less than the average of paid work, while Poles and Hungarians have considerably more than the average. So, for example, a full-time employed Bulgarian woman with a pre-school child in the later 1980s would on this basis be estimated to have 320 (i.e. 297 − 42 + 96 − 13 − 12 − 6) minutes of paid work.

Table 7.1. A summary of time use in twenty countries (minutes per day)

Minutes per day	Paid work	Core domestic work	Other domestic work	Out-of-home leisure	TV and radio	Other home leisure	Personal care
Mean	297	122	108	114	93	159	547
Man	44	−72	−9	14	14	80	10
Woman	−42	69	8	−13	−13	−8	−1
Full time	96	−29	−19	−8	−7	−20	−13
Part time	−46	4	7	9	−4	18	12
Other, non-emp.	−224	70	45	17	19	44	29
Yng, no yng. kids	21	−36	−37	45	−8	30	13
Child under 5	−13	9	48	−15	−6	−13	−11
Child under 15	0	12	1	−10	2	−0	−5
Oldr, no yng. kids	−5	3	−19	−8	10	10	8
Canada	−6	−23	3	14	22	6	−15
Denmark	−14	−6	−69	62	38	33	−44
France	−0	5	11	−26	−25	11	24
Netherlands	−32	−14	−7	17	−2	45	−7
Norway	−32	1	1	52	−18	−3	−1
UK	−15	−12	−12	−6	38	−8	15
USA	7	−11	12	−6	28	−28	−2
Hungary	48	17	7	−23	−24	−37	13
West Germany	9	−10	1	15	−21	−13	19
Poland	35	−2	16	−18	−11	−18	−2
Belgium	13	−6	−18	−13	−1	24	2
Bulgaria	−12	7	8	−28	−6	27	4
Czechoslovakia	23	10	22	−27	−8	−19	−1
East Germany	1	33	13	−22	−2	−17	−5
Yugoslavia	11	17	45	−3	−42	−30	2
Finland	−29	−9	−5	2	3	43	−5
Italy (Turin)	−3	22	−20	23	−18	2	−7
Australia	−6	−5	11	6	9	−24	8
Israel	26	−24	−39	4	27	−11	18
Sweden	−25	10	19	−22	14	21	−17
1960–73	12	10	−3	−12	−4	−2	−2
1974–84	−12	−5	−13	7	5	15	3
85–present	−6	−12	17	11	1	−11	−0
R-squared	*0.350*	*0.524*	*0.175*	*0.070*	*0.079*	*0.114*	*0.048*

The columns of the table each give the full set of MCA coefficients for one particular broad class of time use. Reading across, we have first paid work, then unpaid core domestic work (cooking and cleaning), the other domestic work (childcare, shopping, odd jobs, etc.), then out-of-home leisure (including visits to other people's private houses), TV and radio, other sorts of home-based leisure, and finally personal care (sleep and non-sociable eating). All of the time-use categories used in any of the surveys in our data Archive may be allocated to one or other of these six broad groupings.

One particularly attractive feature of this form of presentation—a characteristic of the arithmetic of OLS regression—is that it preserves, in a neat and visible way, the fundamental characteristic of time: its limited supply. To put this a little pompously: there is what we might think of as *the principle of the conservation of the day*—that the length of each individual's own day is the same, preserved irrespective of what he or she does in it. (I put it like this because there is also a sense, mentioned already, but to which I shall return in the next chapter, that each person uses either more or less than this in their average day.) Each individual has precisely 24 hours, or 1,440 minutes, in their own day. If we sum along the row of grand means, in any table constructed in the way Table 7.1 is, we arrive at precisely this total of 1,440 minutes, so this first row shows the overall average division of these developed societies' 'great day' between various activities. And each of the different types of individual within these societies, similarly, has, in sum, the same total of 1,440 minutes. If the members of a societal subgroup spend on average *more* time than the grand mean in one sort of activity, they must similarly spend *less* time than the grand mean in some other activity or activities. And similarly for historical period: if, in a later era we spend more time doing something, we must also spend less time doing something else. Summing along each of the 'effect parameter' rows, we thus arrive at overall totals of zero.

Take for example the effect of employment status. Those people with full-time jobs spend, as we would expect, more than the average of paid work minutes. But they only have 1,440 minutes in total: so, as we read along the row, we see that they spend on average less than the grand mean of time in every one of the other six broad time-use categories. Their extra time in paid work must be compensated for by spending less time in other activities—we shall return, repeatedly throughout the chapter, to this question of the elasticity of the other time-use categories with respect to paid work time. (And, in particular, this explains why employment is used, in this chapter, both as a major time-use category *to be explained*, and also as a major category *in the explanation* of time-use patterns.)

Interactive effects: some gender examples

Table 7.1 employs the very simplest sort of regression model, in which the various structural characteristics are assumed to have a straightforward independent additive effect. But this additive assumption has the effective implication that, for example, there is the same historical trend of time use for both sexes. This is of course *possibly* true. But what if men and women have different patterns of change? What if, as indeed we established to be the case in Chapter 6, there is an interaction between the period and the sex variables? The interaction could be dealt with by using multiplicative variables (i.e. treat each combination of a sex and employment status, and of a sex and a family status as a distinct category). But an altogether simpler approach, and exactly equivalent in terms of its predictions, is to run the MCA calculations separately for each sex. Tables 7.2 and 7.3 are the single-sex equivalents to Table 7.1.

Now compare the men's and women's estimates for the effect of employment status from Tables 7.2 and 7.3 with those from Table 7.1. The first table assumes that employment status has more or less the same effect for men and for women. Take the case of core domestic work. Table 7.1 tells us

Table 7.2.   Men's time use in twenty countries (minutes per day)

Minutes per day	Paid work	Core domestic work	Other domestic work	Out-of-home leisure	TV and radio	Other home leisure	Personal care
Mean	403	29	86	125	102	155	540
Full time	33	−3	−4	−5	−3	−10	−8
Part time	−107	4	20	21	−2	33	31
Other, non-emp.	−272	25	32	42	28	84	61
Yng, no yng. kids	7	−7	−29	45	−14	−5	2
Child under 5	4	1	25	−15	−4	−5	−7
Child under 15	2	1	4	−11	4	0	−0
Oldr, no yng. kids	−15	5	−4	−16	14	10	6
Canada	−23	1	10	5	28	3	−22
Denmark	−15	−3	−53	53	35	29	−45
France	2	5	2	−22	−28	15	26
Netherlands	−35	−6	−2	7	8	38	−9
Norway	−43	4	17	41	−17	0	−2
UK	−21	−5	−5	−11	37	−14	19
USA	13	2	11	−15	30	−33	−9
Hungary	49	6	3	−15	−26	−29	12
West Germany	10	−9	−1	25	−27	−17	19
Poland	35	13	−3	−16	−13	−14	−2
Belgium	26	−3	−25	−15	−11	24	4
Bulgaria	−10	−17	24	−26	−3	22	10
Czechoslovakia	12	18	9	−22	−4	−16	2
East Germany	18	28	3	−15	−9	−14	−11
Yugoslavia	−2	4	35	19	−45	−23	12
Finland	−37	−2	7	−4	7	37	−8
Italy (Turin)	11	−14	−25	27	−12	12	0
Australia	5	−14	9	8	11	−27	8
Israel	43	−22	−40	−1	22	−17	15
Sweden	−27	17	21	−26	17	16	−19
1960–73	21	−9	−4	−12	−1	3	2
1974–84	−21	2	−9	8	2	15	2
85–present	−12	11	14	11	−1	−18	−5
R-squared	*0.130*	*0.064*	*0.070*	*0.064*	*0.066*	*0.110*	*0.053*

that the difference between a non-employed person's and a full-time employee's core domestic work is 99 minutes. But Tables 7.2 and 7.3 reveal that this difference for men alone is just 28 minutes, while for women alone it is 108 minutes; this indicates a really quite substantial interaction effect. We would expect, from the discussion in Chapter 6, that this sort of gender interaction effect would be particularly severe for domestic work; by contrast, the equivalent calculations for leisure have estimates from Tables 7.2 and 7.3 which are similar to within a few minutes, which means in turn that Table 7.1 is not so seriously wrong in this respect.

Table 7.3. Women's time use in twenty countries (minutes per day)

Minutes per day	Paid work	Core domestic work	Other domestic work	Out of home leisure	TV and radio	Other home leisure	Personal care
Mean	196	210	129	103	85	163	554
Full time	152	−53	−33	−7	−12	−29	−18
Part time	11	−0	−3	−2	−7	2	−1
Other, non-emp.	−162	55	35	8	15	30	19
Yng, no yng. kids	41	−68	−45	40	−1	10	24
Child under 5	−29	14	68	−13	−9	−18	−13
Child under 15	−2	20	−3	−9	2	0	−9
Oldr, no yng. kids	3	3	−30	−1	7	10	8
Canada	7	−39	−3	21	16	8	−10
Denmark	−11	−13	−86	72	42	38	−41
France	−2	6	20	−29	−22	6	22
Netherlands	−33	−21	−11	31	−12	52	−6
Norway	−20	−5	−16	65	−19	−6	1
UK	−11	−19	−19	−1	39	−2	13
USA	1	−22	12	3	26	−24	4
Hungary	48	26	11	−32	−22	−45	13
West Germany	7	−9	5	5	−15	−10	18
Poland	36	−13	35	−23	−9	−23	−3
Belgium	−1	−8	−12	−11	9	23	−0
Bulgaria	−11	30	−9	−31	−9	32	−2
Czechoslovakia	35	3	34	−34	−12	−22	−4
East Germany	−10	32	21	−28	4	−18	−1
Yugoslavia	23	29	55	−24	−40	−37	−7
Finland	−21	−13	−15	7	−1	46	−3
Italy (Turin)	−18	58	−14	20	−24	−7	−14
Australia	−16	0	10	7	8	−18	9
Israel	11	−22	−38	8	30	−7	19
Sweden	−19	−4	14	−18	11	28	−12
1960–73	2	26	−3	−9	−7	−5	−4
1974–84	−3	−12	−17	6	8	15	3
85–present	−0	−30	20	9	4	−6	3
R-squared	*0.397*	*0.294*	*0.245*	*0.077*	*0.086*	*0.136*	*0.051*

One consequence of this interaction of sex with other structural variables is that Table 7.1 grossly misleads us as to the sizes of the sex effects themselves. In Table 7.1 it appears for example that the difference between men's and women's paid work is just about 86 minutes per day, as against the 206 (402−196) minutes difference that appears from Tables 7.2 and 7.3. Even if there were the same proportion of part-time employed men as women, the fact that part-time employment has a different effect for women would mean that Table 7.1 would misrepresent the effects of sex on employment. And the compositional difference—the fact that there is a much larger proportion of part-time employed women than men—serves to exaggerate the consequence of the sex–employment status interaction.

Table 7.4 sets out the differences in estimates that emerge from the two modelling methods and the two samples. We have already seen the difference between the estimates for the two samples using method 1, which treats sex as a simple additional variate. If we treat it instead as an interacting, multiplicative predictive variable, and estimate separate models by sex (method 2), there emerge the quite dramatically different results that were discussed in the previous section. Table 7.4 shows the difference between method 1 and method 2 estimates as a percentage of the mean time devoted to each of the activities. Method 1 emerges as underestimating gender differentials by 41 per cent of the two-sex mean for paid work, an underestimate of 33 per cent of the mean for core domestic work, and 24 per cent for other domestic work. The importance of gender interactions in these models, which we inferred from the variance decomposition in Chapter 6, is indeed very marked. For the remaining categories other than out-of-home leisure the differences are somewhat smaller, in proportional terms, but still substantially present, either in absolute terms of minutes per day, or relative to the overall means. Only in the cases of out-of-home leisure and personal care would the determinants of men's and women's time-use patterns be sufficiently similar to allow us to use method 1.

The interaction between sex and the other independent variables provides us with an image of the sort of problem that *could* arise from the use of the additive model to estimate the effects of country (and period). Table 7.1 was clearly misleading about the effect of sex on patterns of time allocation. What if the split-sex tables are similarly misleading? There is the potential for interaction between the country categories and the other structural variables. In particular, will the historical trends (or the lack of them), as estimated in these tables, stand as good cross-country generalizations, or do they mask substantially differing national patterns? In the light of the potential problems with the MCA technique which are discussed in this section, we must plainly move with great caution. In what follows, and despite the reassurance of the relatively small interactive effect of

Table 7.4. Estimates of male–female differences in time use

Minutes per day	Paid work	Core domestic work	Other domestic work	Out-of-home leisure	TV and radio	Other home leisure	Personal care
Method 1 additive gender effects, from Table 7.1	86	−141	−17	27	27	16	2
Method 2 interacting gender effects, from Tables 7.2 and 7.3	207	−181	−43	22	17	−8	−14
Means, Table 7.1	297	122	108	114	93	159	547
Method 1 minus Method 2 as % of Grand Mean	41%	−33%	−24%	−4%	−11%	−15%	−3%

country established in Chapter 5, we will alternate between multi-country and single-country estimates.

But for the moment, and given the evident importance of the interaction between sex and the country, period, and other variates, we will concentrate on the separate-sex method 2 estimates in Tables 7.2 and 7.3.

Men emerge, as we would expect, as disproportionately specialized in paid work, women in unpaid. The two disproportions in aggregate approximately balance each other out. In the whole sample, with each of the thirty-five component surveys equally weighted, including ten of the early surveys from the 1972 Szalai study (and hence a large proportion of unreconstructed male chauvinist East European countries), men's paid plus unpaid work totals 518 minutes (403+29+86), while the equivalent estimate for women is 535 minutes (196+210+129). Overall, the men show rather more out-of-home leisure than the women, and more television viewing, and slightly less time devoted to other sorts of home leisure and personal care.

In both samples it is clear that the extra paid work done by those in full-time employment leads to a reduction in time devoted to every other category of activity. But, reflecting their much lower total of unpaid work, the effect of men's employment states on their unpaid work is very much smaller than the equivalent for women, whereas the impact of employment status on leisure activities shows much more similarity between men and women. (We will return to discuss this question of the 'elasticity' of time devoted to various activities with respect to work time in more detail in a following section.) These tabulations give the impression that family status has much more effect on women's time use than on men. This is at least in part a reflection of a quite strong association between family status and employment status for women (i.e. women with small children are likely to be non- or only part-time employed) which is almost completely absent for men. The general pattern of the effect of having children is quite clear in both the nine and the twenty, and similar for both sexes: more unpaid work, less out-of-home leisure—and less sleep.

We have already seen that the countries show considerable variation in their totals of paid work. As we would expect from previous discussions, paid work time in the ex-East-bloc countries is generally considerably higher than in Western Europe and North America; and approximately the same pattern holds for women's paid work. Unpaid work, however, shows no tendency to compensate for international differences in paid work. It is particularly clear in the case of women that the Eastern European countries, which have the relatively high totals of paid work, also have the highest totals of unpaid work. The 'compensation' (in minutes, if not benefits) for high levels of work in Eastern Europe comes largely from reductions in leisure time. Czechoslovakia and East Germany spend relatively little time in out-of-home leisure, while Yugoslavia has a markedly low average of time devoted to radio and television. And Polish, Czech, and Yugoslavian women have particularly low totals of personal care and other home leisure time.

Finally, consider the historical period variable. In Table 7.1 looking at both sexes together, it appears that paid work time has reduced by around 18 minutes from 309 to 291 minutes per day, over the third of a century covered by our data. But, split by sex, and two quite different patterns emerge (Table 7.5 repeats the period panels of Tables 7.2 and 7.3 with the addition of significance indications). For men we see that (even controlling for change in the distribution of employment status, and particularly for the growth of unemployment) paid work has declined quite substantially over our period: a decrease of about 33 minutes per day, from 424 to 391 minutes in total. The equivalent result for women is of a virtually constant level over the historical period. Here again we can see the consequence of ignoring the interactive effects of gender. The apparent medium-sized decline in paid work for the sample as a whole disguised two clear and quite distinct patterns: respectively, no significant change for women, and a big decline for men.

And we find a similarly dramatic equivalent for core domestic work (cooking and cleaning). Table 7.1 shows a declining pattern. Core domestic work for the sample as a whole seems to decrease during the 1960s and 1970s and to remain unchanged through the 1980s. When we look separately at the men and women, however, we again find that this was made up of two larger and quite contrary changes. For men we see a monotonic increase, from the start to the end of the period covered by our data, of 20 minutes; men's daily cooking and cleaning is estimated in Table 7.2 to amount to just more than 21 minutes in the 1960s, and just about doubles by the time we reach the recent surveys. The women's change is even more substantial, and in the opposite direction, decreasing by a little under an hour per day over the period covered by our data.

Table 7.5. Significance tests for historical change (minutes per day)

Minutes per day	Paid work	Core domestic work	Other domestic work	Out-of-home leisure	TV and radio	Other home leisure	Personal care
Men
1960–73 (ref.)	21	−9	−4	−12	−1	3	2
1974–84	−21**	2**	−9	8**	2	15**	2
85–present	−12**	11**	14**	11**	−1	−18**	−5
Women
1960–73 (ref.)	2	26	−3	−9	−7	−5	−4
1974–84	−3	−12**	-17**	6**	8**	15**	3*
85–present	−0	−30**	20**	9**	4**	−6	3*

* Sig. at 0.05
** Sig. at 0.005

The changes in other unpaid work are less consistent over time, with declines for both sexes in the 1960s and 1970s, and increases in the 1980s–1990s, affecting, as we shall see in a moment, both some national variations and differences among subcategories of the activities. Out-of-home leisure generally increases for both sexes by about 20 minutes per day. Passive leisure (television and radio) hardly changes for men and increases by 10 minutes or so for women. Other home leisure shows an irregular pattern, of increase then decline, for both sexes (again reflecting both national variations and different trends for subcategories). Personal care, of which by far the largest part is sleep, hardly varies over the period.

We might note that the pictures of historical change in time use we get from this multiple regression-based technique are analogous to those we derive from the straightforward reweighting technique used in Chapter 5. Here, as there, we attempt to show the effect of each independent variable, having controlled for shifts in the distribution of the cases across the values of the other independent variables. There is one major potential difference however, concerning the treatment of correlations between the independent variables: the shift-share approach of Chapter 5 is hierarchical in the sense that, for example, if historical period and employment status are themselves correlated, all the effect of employment status is extracted *first*, through the reweighting process, and only any residual association of the two independent variables with the dependent is attributed to historical period. In the regression analysis by contrast that common variation is shared out impartially between them.

The results discussed so far come from 'whole-world' regression equations. As long as these are broken down by sex they are, as we shall see, a not inadequate summary of general patterns of historical change in time use. But there is (as we established in the previous chapter) some intercountry difference that cannot be coped with using the whole-world approach (because of interactions between country and other variables). And we have only considered some really rather broad activity categories. So we must now turn to a more detailed discussion of the time-use evidence, broken down by country where appropriate, and by more detailed activity categories.

2. Four sorts of time use

Paid work time

We can now turn to consider the MCA effect parameters for the individual countries. There is a marked and entirely predictable difference in the effect of the age and family status categories on the two sexes. Table 7.6, and its

Table 7.6. Paid work by sex and country (longitudinal subsample)

	Canada	Denmark	France	Netherlands	Norway	UK	USA	Hungary	Finland
Men									
Mean	348	399	409	325	361	367	406	466	332
Full time	48	15	27	68	26	53	37	12	44
Part time	-5	-37	-42	-122	-40	-186	-126	1	-54
Other, non-emp.	-209	-178	-305	-266	-226	-304	-244	-224	-227
Yng, no yng. kids	23	-5	4	17	30	8	5	4	8
Child under 5	5	3	24	-2	-8	-7	9	-3	9
Child under 15	-7	16	13	9	-9	-7	-7	6	1
Oldr, no yng. kids	-29	-30	-21	-27	-21	-8	-7	-9	-21
1960–73	-3	10	24		17	33	18	50	
1974–84	-20		-24	3	-17	9	-17	-49	5
85–present	13	-10		-5		-21	-1		-5
R-squared	*0.120*	*0.045*	*0.121*	*0.570*	*0.070*	*0.387*	*0.113*	*0.086*	*0.137*
Women									
Mean	189	203	177	94	143	178	187	258	239
Full time	149	120	188	189	150	179	164	141	71
Part time	25	-3	32	67	28	5	25	-57	-64
Other, non-emp.	-127	-159	-166	-76	-104	-158	152	-179	-171
Yng, no yng. kids	58	20	31	36	77	29	24	22	46
Child under 5	-29	-11	-18	-17	-32	-19	-28	-36	-43
Child under 15	-9	-7	-4	-10	-10	-8	8	6	10
Oldr, no yng. kids	-21	2	5	-12	4	-2	-7	7	-10
1960–73	-21	-14	8	-1	3	5	-2	10	10
1974–84	-1		-8		-3	-1	-3	-11	
85–present	10	14		2		-2	6		-10
R-squared	*0.338*	*0.299*	*0.499*	*0.701*	*0.336*	*0.612*	*0.386*	*0.386*	*0.205*

equivalent for the single-observation countries, Table 7.7, show two distinct effects for women. Look first at the two extreme categories, representing women below the age of 40 with no co-resident children, and those aged 40 and above: without exception, older women spend less time in paid work than younger. Now consider the category of women with pre-school-age children: even controlling for employment status, these women do markedly less paid work than any other group. We might also note that while there are obvious national differences, the general shape of the effect of age and family status on work time is pretty much the same in every country. Plainly there is no very strong interaction between country and the demographic variables in this case.

The pattern of effects of the demographic variable for men is much less tidy. There does appear to be an analogous age effect. On average men with co-resident children will tend to be older than men below 40 with no children, and younger than men above 40 with no children. So we can conclude that (controlling for employment status and historical period) work time declines with age. But unlike the women's case, there is no strong cross-national tendency for the fathers of young children to reduce their paid work. Though ageing apparently reduces work time, having children does not appear to do so. Indeed, in some countries the fathers of young children appear to work longer hours than others. Presumably this is explained by a need for extra income (and may also relate to a desire to stay away from home).

The employment status variable (included here really for consistency with subsequent tables in which it will tell us something more interesting) serves in this case to do little more than to establish that the national subsamples do indeed appear to have hours of employment which are generally in line with their declared employment statuses. But the period variable in Table 6.6 gives us an answer to the question about the importance of country interactions in understanding change in paid work time.

The Table 7.2 whole-world summary of historical change in paid work showed for the historical period from the 1960s to the 1990s (and controlling for structural change over the period) a regular decline in men's time devoted to this activity, and an approximately constant total for women. The (Table 7.6) MCA parameters for men calculated for the various countries individually are (with the exception of reversals of the trend in Canada and the USA for the second half of the period) consistent with this picture. In each case except the Canadian there is a reduction from the earliest to the latest survey. The women's picture is much more confused; having controlled for structural shifts, some countries show increases of women's paid work, some show small decreases; so we must conclude that the whole-world summary is rather misleading in this case (though the size of the historical changes shown here is small relative to the total of women's paid work time).

Table 7.7. Paid work by sex and country (cross-sectional subsample)

Men	W.Germany	Poland	Belgium	Bulgaria	Czechoslovakia	E.Germany	Yugoslavia	Italy	Australia	Israel	Sweden
Mean	418	473	449	381	453	471	434	396	398	409	379
Full time	77	23	30	31	18	5	23	30	24	59	17
Part time	-154	-111	-35	-33	-138	-103	-100		-112	-29	-115
Other, non-emp.	-349	-336	-331	-305	-296	-312	-292	-283	-304	-265	-285
Yng, no yng. kids	19	-16	34	-3	-18	-7	0	-2	-20	11	5
Child under 5	-7	12	12	-10	14	0	25	-14	12	4	5
Child under 15	-22	1	9	-12	-2	18	-7	24	-6	4	14
Oldr, no yng. kids	26	-4	-54	14	-1	-44	-20	-10	23	-38	-22
R-squared	*0.174*	*0.112*	*0.126*	*0.106*	*0.065*	*0.015*	*0.110*	*0.101*	*0.090*	*0.158*	*0.055*
Women											
Mean	168	270	123	282	254	210	198	152	126	187	262
Full time	247	149	227	48	131	130	203	155	203	159	50
Part time	29	-53	118	-5	-46	-0	180		42	41	-44
Other, non-emp.	-146	-257	-92	-249	-186	-205	-168	-120	-115	-150	-198
Yng, no yng. kids	22	18	88	23	132	19	72	30	17	60	21
Child under 5	-9	-22	-32	-104	-8	-37	-28	-39	-1	-22	-42
Child under 15	-7	-2	-22	29	-4	17	-0	9	-2	-3	21
Oldr, no yng. kids	-1	15	14	34	-26	26	-9	-1	-6	9	4
R-squared	*0.504*	*0.524*	*0.485*	*0.168*	*0.376*	*0.362*	*0.562*	*0.373*	*0.436*	*0.356*	*0.131*

Paid work and social differentiation. Breaking down countries by gender and period is straightforward, in this dataset. But, as has already been indicated, social stratification and differentiation variables are altogether more difficult to come by. But nevertheless historical change in patterns of difference between social groups is an important part of the story we have to tell. In relation to paid work, the question set out in Chapter 3 was: have the amounts of work done by different social strata changed *relative to each other* over time?

The preparatory remarks in Chapter 5 established that the only two potential sources of information on social differentiation in this sense that are at present available in the dataset are the education variable (which only provides information that is adequate to this purpose for twenty-seven of the surveys, covering seventeen of the twenty countries), and income (which only exists in an appropriate form in fifteen surveys covering nine of the countries). Of these, only education gives even an approximate indication of individual's social stratum (in the sense set out in Chapter 4, of an acquired position relating to personal characteristics, which give advantages in the labour market, and hence provide positive opportunities in other spheres of life). Income (of the individual, or the household) is a *consequence* of human capital, and human capital, in the narrow economists' formulation of those features of education, training, specific and non-specific work experience which serve as determinants of the wage rate, is perhaps the single most important indicator of social position. But very few of the surveys contain either sufficient information to establish a human-capital estimation (which would require a detailed occupational classification together with other life and employment history data) or an actual hourly wage rate, which could be used as a proxy for these. Income is the product of the wage rate and the hours of work, and since the only reasonably standard information we have across even a subset of the surveys is a (very) approximate indication of individuals' positions in the national income distribution, we conclude that the education variable is the best we can do. Still, we start by looking at both of these indicators.

The difference in the overall totals of work in the two estimations in Table 7.8 indicates the shortcomings, in particular, of the very restricted subsample with adequate income data. It represents fewer than half of the countries, and different countries are represented in each of the three periods. The educational panel, however, represents more than four-fifths of the countries, and, as we established in Chapter 6, six of the countries are represented in either two or three of the columns, and the overall levels and patterns of change by sex are approximately representative of those set out in Table 7.1, and indeed in the country-by-country plots in Chapter 5.

The message of the table lies however in the comparisons between the work times of the educational (and the income) groups at the different historical time points. Men with higher levels of education did less work in

Table 7.8. Paid work time in the two subsamples (minutes per day)

	By educational level				By income level		
	1960–73	1974–84	1985–		1960–73	1974–84	1985–
All	318	259	277	All	286	283	289
Men	447	361	353	Men	429	390	357
Uncompleted secondary	457	360	340	lowest 25%	411	328	271
Complete secondary	453	358	348	middle 50%	431	391	366
Above secondary educ.	414	368	377	highest 25%	435	434	395
Women	196	157	204	Women	149	171	221
Uncompleted secondary	169	138	173	lowest 25%	182	159	158
Complete secondary	215	174	202	middle 50%	141	172	233
Above secondary educ.	253	200	247	highest 25%	147	181	271

the 1960s. In the mid-period between 1974 and 1985 the gradient of work time by educational attainment was approximately level. And by the latest period the gradient has reversed, with the highest-educated group of men working the longest hours, precisely (for men at least) the conjecture raised at the end of Chapter 3, a reversal of Veblen's negative social-status-to-work-time relationship.

There are all sorts of objections to this initial tabulation. To start with, the periodization is arbitrary, and the result may simply reflect the choice of dates. In fact, whether the period is divided into three, four, or five segments, just the same historical effect emerges. This robustness, however, does not answer the main point at issue, which is the question of whether the result is an accidental consequence of the particular national surveys that took place at particular points in history. From this tabulation we know no more than that those countries with surveys carried out in the 1960s show that well-educated men do less work than the less well-educated, while in those countries with surveys in the 1990s, they do more work. The table does not tell us whether any particular country shows this pattern of change. We can only answer this by reference to those countries for which we have repeated observations including an appropriate educational attainment variable. Fortunately there are six of these cross-time datasets, five of which show at least some part of this process of reversal, while the sixth, France, represented only by surveys carried out in 1965 and 1974, does show in both cases the initial position in which the better-educated, higher-status men have less paid work.

Table 7.9 sets out this evidence. We see the general comparative cross-sectional point that the surveys in the earlier years tend to show the negative gradient of work hours with educational attainment (the French example already cited) while the later surveys (e.g. the UK) tend to show the positive. But, of course, the main point is that each country moves along this gradient in the appropriate decade: it does appear to be a historical effect. Notice also that the medium educational level takes in

Table 7.9. Men's paid work time by educational level in six countries (minutes per day)

Canada	1971	1981	1986	1992
Uncompleted secondary	395	320	270	310
Complete secondary	367	346	339	369
Above secondary educ.	317	369	363	369
France	1965	1974		
Uncompleted secondary	445	383		
Complete secondary	447	375		
Above secondary educ.	435	365		
Netherlands	1975	1980	1985	
Uncompleted secondary	340	316	300	
Complete secondary	336	354	331	
Above secondary educ.	356	347	327	
Finland	1979	1987		
Uncompleted secondary	333	331		
Complete secondary	358	329		
Above secondary educ.	320	326		
UK	1985	1995		
Uncompleted secondary	324	322		
Complete secondary	341	336		
Above secondary educ.	342	373		
US	1965	1975	1985	
Uncompleted secondary	448	388	383	
Complete secondary	447	334	411	
Above secondary educ.	431	433	385	

general the median course between the two extreme categories of paid work time.

The process of gradient reversal is apparent but by no means invariable. But, certainly, the longer the historical span of the national data, the more clearly the evidence conforms to the 'negative gradient' hypothesis. We can conclude from Table 7.9 that at least for the longitudinal sample (i.e. sixteen out of the twenty-seven surveys represented by Table 7.8), the summary we proposed, of a historical process of reversal of the status–work time gradient, is certainly a valid one. For the remaining surveys, all that can be said is that, while they are not strictly a random sample of countries, they certainly were not selected in order to prove this particular point! This general question, of whether the changing gradients between the cross-country aggregate estimates of the time use of members of different social (educational, in this case) strata really do represent genuine historical change, is ultimately unresolvable, even with the application of more advanced micro-econometric techniques. We will continue, here, and with similar questions as they emerge later in the chapter, with the straightforward exploratory approach of switching backwards and forwards between the simple OLS-based aggregated models and the individual country estimates, showing where these do (or do not) correspond; the accounts that emerge from the aggregated data should be viewed as hypotheses to be tested against new data as they emerge in the future—though, it is to be hoped, well supported by the currently available evidence.

The second quadrant of Table 7.8, for women-by-educational-attainment, does not show any such change in gradient. However, we should note that we have not yet controlled for compositional changes, and we know that compositional changes in women's employment have been very substantial. And indeed this same problem arises with the remaining two quadrants of Table 7.8, which show the hypothesized change in gradient, in this case indicating social status by income level. But in these latter two cases, what may be represented is a compositional change, related to growing unemployment. So in both cases to interpret the table correctly, we need to control, at least, for the changing composition of employment. A simple solution (though we shall model this properly in a moment) might be to recalculate Table 7.8 just for employees.

And in fact when we do this, the expected change in gradient for women does indeed emerge as clearly for women as for men. In the 1960–73 period, low-educated employed women had 380 minutes work per day, while those (relatively few) highly educated women who then had jobs, worked 274 minutes per day; in the latest period after 1985, employed women of low-educational-attainment women had an average of 286 minutes per day of paid work while the highly educated employed women had an average of 317 minutes per day (the full table of employment status-controlled results is not shown here).

The evidence presented in Table 7.10 in fact goes one step further. Rather than looking at employees, it further restricts the focus to *working days*. One clear development of the last third of a century in Europe (though to a lesser extent in North America) has been the growth in the number of paid

Table 7.10. Paid work time on workdays only (minutes per day)

	By educational level				By income level		
	1960–73	1974–84	1985–		1960–73	1974–84	1985–
All	523	486	500	All	485	503	509
Men	554	522	540	Men	525	535	545
Uncompleted secondary	575	537	541	lowest 25%	503	499	515
Complete secondary	558	509	537	middle 50%	533	537	545
Above secondary educ.	509	503	540	highest 25%	516	553	562
Women	466	424	451	Women	400	440	464
Uncompleted secondary	465	422	440	lowest 25%	411	441	431
Complete secondary	474	436	453	middle 50%	411	444	468
Above secondary educ.	448	412	458	highest 25%	348	427	482

holidays. This will have a great deal to do with the perception or subjective experience of time scarcity. Shorter annual paid work hours, as are indicated over the full third of a century covered by the aggregated dataset, might in fact be consistent with a longer working day. This indeed turns out to be the case. We see that over the period, for both men and women, the mean length of the day has decreased for the less well educated, and increased absolutely for the best educated. We also find from Table 7.10 (and more generally for the employed sample as a whole), the gradient reversal in relation to income reflects more than the fact that low-income families are more likely to include unemployed people in the world of the 1990s than in the 1960s. Even controlling for this fact, it is increasingly the case that the members of the richest households are likely to be working considerably longer hours than members of the poorest.

We can now turn to a more complete model that includes the social stratification indicator alongside the other demographic and economic activity indicators used in the earlier tables. Table 7.11 in fact estimates three separate regression models, respectively for the whole subsample of surveys which include an adequate education indicator, and then, following the practice we have established in this chapter, for men and women separately. It includes interaction terms for educational level * period, which are set out for comparative purposes in a manner analogous to the previous 'reversed gradient' tables (the country coefficients are estimated in this and the similar models later in this chapter, but, as a space-saving device, they have been excluded from the tabulation on the grounds that

Table 7.11. Three models of 'the reversed gradient' (minutes per day)

	Whole subsample			Men only			Women only		
Grand mean	284			385			186		
Yng, no yng. kids	24			11			41		
Child under 5	−12			3			−27		
Child under 15	−17			2			−3		
Oldr, no yng. kids	−10			−20			−2		
Full time	100			38			157		
Part time	−38			−79			17		
Other, non-emp	−210			−261			−150		
Country (coeffs suppressed)	—			—			—		
	1960–73	1974–84	1985–	1960–73	1974–84	1985–	1960–73	1974–84	1985
Men uncomp. sec.	67	32	27	24	−11	−12			
Men complete sec.	58	22	27	17	−19	−6			
Men above sec.	40	41	51	−4	−4	14			
Women uncomp. sec.	−55	−43	−42				−15	−1	−4
Women complete sec.	−42	−34	−35				−0	6	−2
Women above sec.	−25	−29	−19				15	12	15
R-squared	0.367			0.162			0.409		

they do not add useful information). The men's gradient reversal comes out very clearly. However, once we control correctly for the other variables, the women's change in fact shows up here as a *reduction* in a previous negative gradient. Well-educated women employees emerge as becoming *less* disadvantaged in work hours relative to less educated women: the interpretation must clearly be that the women's change is essentially a compositional one. Unlike the men's case, the substantial growth in well-educated women's work hours relative to those of less well-educated women, relates to the faster rate of increase in their participation rate over the period.

Unpaid work time

Unpaid work time, in its broadest sense, could be considered to include five distinct groups of activities: *routine housework* (house- and clothes-cleaning, tidying, and organizing); *cooking*, including preparation both for major meals and other snacks; *childcare*, a broad category which encompasses the bodily care of young children, playing with children and escorting them (though, since we focus here entirely on the 'primary activity' diary evidence, overall childcare time is underrepresented, since 'background' childcare, being in a general way responsible for children while yet simultaneously concentrating on other activities, is excluded from the accounting); *shopping* (in which are included travel to and from shops together with other non-recreational travel for domestic purposes which is not included in the childcare category); and finally the group of non-routine *odd jobs* (which range from intermittent but quite obligatory activities such as running repairs to domestic equipment, to pet care and gardening).

In Chapter 3 we set out the main lines of argument about how unpaid work time changes over time. It has been asserted that household work time is not reduced by the introduction of new technologies into the household (e.g. Vanek 1978). It was (and is) quite clear that at any historical instant, heterosexual couples in which the woman is employed have maintained a relatively traditional gendered pattern of domestic responsibilities, with the woman bearing the main responsibility for the first four of these categories. The consequence is that she bears an inequitable dual burden of job and housework (e.g. Young and Willmott 1973). And it is inferred from the cross-sectional evidence of this phenomenon that over a historical period in which women's paid employment has changed from the exception to the norm, the domestic division of labour has failed to adjust to this change in women's work pattern.

The evidence presented here, however, demonstrates that the cross-sectional inference from a single historical time point is partially (though not entirely) misleading. Domestic practices are produced by combinations of individuals' views of what is appropriate domestic behaviour (reflecting their 'gender ideologies' and their knowledge of norms which might apply to them). Employment situations change literally overnight (one day we have no job, the next we have one). But, what follows from the arguments of Chapter 4 is that individuals' views of appropriate domestic behaviour can only change slowly. So, in an era of rapid growth in women's employment, we might expect a *lag* in the adaptation of domestic practices. In these circumstances, the cross-sectional evidence at a given historical point would be *expected* to show an imbalance between men's and women's work—which is nevertheless a *misleading* indication of the historic trend. Instead of the cross-sectional evidence itself, we should look at the historical change in the cross-sectional relationship between husbands' and wives' (or rather, since only a minority of the surveys include 'spouse' time-use data, married men's and women's) time use.

The arguments are difficult to assess, particularly since a number of the changes have happened simultaneously. Women's participation in paid work has increased, as we have seen, during a period in which men have reduced their paid work time and unemployment rates have risen. And during the early part of this same period, the (supposedly) labour-saving technology has diffused most rapidly in Europe. It is very hard to disentangle the various strands of change; what is really needed to validate the various arguments is a social experiment in which the time available for domestic tasks is varied without any other changes in circumstances.

Unpaid work elasticities. Social experiments, and particularly experiments on the sort of scale implied by this problem, are normally beyond the resources of social scientists. But Alexander Szalai was able to report a natural experiment that conforms precisely to this requirement (Szalai 1972). His research was based on a large factory located in the rural plains of Hungary, at a considerable distance from any substantial centres of population. The workforce consisted of young women from farming families; as the settlement pattern was diffuse, the workers were of necessity recruited from a wide geographical area, and some had to travel a great distance to work each day, yet the hours of work in the factory were constant for all employees, so the full length of work time (factory plus work travel time) varied by four to five hours per day. With the single exception of the geographical location of their homes the workforce of the factory formed a homogeneous sample. So by comparing the non-work time allocation of those with long and short work travel times, Szalai was able to study what he called the 'compressibility' of different sorts of time use—the extent to which time devoted to particular activities by people with long working days was curtailed by comparison with people with short work days. He was able to show what was given up as time got short, or, which comes to the same thing, the difference made by extra uncommitted time to the overall pattern of time allocation (his result, incidentally, was that sleep time was the most compressible, followed by leisure at home).

Szalai's particular evidence of time-compressibility in rural Hungary in the late 1950s is not of any great significance for the present discussion, particularly since most of the subjects of his research were single women without heavy family responsibilities. But the methodology is suggestive. For example, household panel data, which contain indications of the sharing of domestic work patterns, can be used to investigate the consequences of changes in partners' employment status for subsequent patterns of sharing of domestic work (e.g. Gershuny *et al.*, 1997).

And we can use the multinational time-use dataset for this purpose. We can look, at any historical period, at how people with different amounts of paid work time vary their domestic work time. We can establish the elasticities of unpaid work time with respect to paid work; and see in particular the extent to which, at any historical point, women's unpaid work varies with increasing participation in paid work (we saw an example of this sort of analysis for the UK in Chapter 3). And then we can compare these elasticities over time—in particular, to see what happens to women's unpaid work elasticity over historical time.

This analysis is not in fact quite as straightforward as it sounds. To calculate the elasticities in a sensible form, we have to set domestic work against some estimate of people's normal or actual hours of paid work. This is no problem for those countries for which we have whole-week data (the Netherlands and the UK); in these cases we can straightforwardly group the respondents according to their hours of paid work during the diary week, and then find the mean of unpaid work for each group. But obviously we cannot do this for the single-day surveys. We have in most cases (the exceptions include Norway, Hungary, Italy, and Israel) a questionnaire-derived variable which gives 'normal hours of paid work'. So rather than using just the diary data, the figures that follow combine the diary data for core domestic work on the Y axis, with the questionnaire data for weekly work hours on the X axis.

Consider first the women's elasticity estimates (Figure 7.1). They exhibit three clear features. First, there is, in each case, some evidence of cross-sectional time-elasticity: women with longer hours of paid work clearly do less unpaid (at least up to the point that their jobs require 45 hours per week). Undoubtedly, part of this effect reflects the fact that those women with longer paid work hours tend on average to have smaller or less demanding households (i.e. fewer or older children). But as other evidence presented here demonstrates, the negative elasticity of housework time with respect to paid work time remains evident even when we control for differences in household structure. Second, the curves shift substantially downwards over time: women with a given level of paid work do less unpaid work at successive historical time points. And third, the majority of the downwards shift of the elasticity curve comes in the earliest period for which we have evidence, from the 1960s to the later 1970s, and the

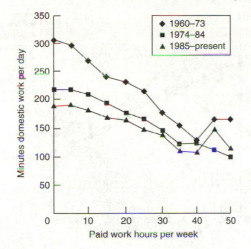

Figure 7.1. Women's elasticity of domestic work with respect to paid work time

changes from the 1970s–80s to the 1980s–90s, though in the same down-wards direction, are rather smaller. What is happening at the right-hand side of the figure is not immediately clear. Women with relatively long hours of paid work do not diminish their domestic work, and over time this appears to have slightly increased: this may reflect a compositional change, more women with demanding families and uncooperative partners—or no part-ners at all—taking full-time jobs. Or it may imply, following, for example the Berk (1985) 'gender factory' suggestion, or similar ideas in Hochschild (1989), that some women with full-time jobs are trying simultaneously to assert more traditional gender ideologies.

The countries do differ from each other. But the Figure 7.1 pattern is no artefact of accumulation. The shifts in the successive surveys for each country show a definite family similarity. The general pattern of the curves, the relative positions of adjacent work-time groupings, varies quite con-siderably between countries, but given the independence of the samples and the quite separate processes for calculating the unpaid work time means for each work-time group (and also given the vagaries of the questionnaire-based evidence of the paid work time) there are quite remarkable similar-ities among the various surveys in the different countries. (These figures thus incidentally provide strong support for the national longitudinal com-parability of the data.) And the overall levels for the countries are not that dissimilar. Figure 7.2 compares just the most recent of the surveys.

The elasticity effects in the mid-range at least are really very similar. Take the sections of these plots between 15 and 40 hours of paid work per week, as the basis for a numerical estimate of the elasticity. The reductions over

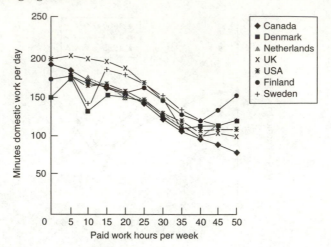

Figure 7.2. Women's elasticity of domestic work with respect to paid work time (late 1980s–1990s)

this range vary from 40 minutes per day in Finland, to 90 minutes in the UK, with an average across the seven surveys of 60 minutes less core domestic work per day with the extra 25 hours per week in paid employment; in round terms, over this range of employment hours, one hour less cooking and cleaning for every 3 extra hours of paid work per day. Now compare this cross-sectional elasticity with the historical shift in the Figure 7.1 curve: the downwards shifts, at each point in the range, are of the order of 50–70 minutes from the earliest to the latest period. Moving from 20 to 40 hours of paid work has quite different implications in the 1990s than it did in the 1960s.

The men's plots also show three different sorts of features (Figure 7.3). They show some evidence of a negative cross-sectional elasticity, though in each case this is weaker than that for equivalently placed women. But in the men's case the historical shifts are for the most part in the opposite direction to the women's. The curves shift upwards over time, men at each level of paid work have increasing amounts of unpaid work in the successive surveys. And there appears to be a difference in the periodization of the shift; while most of the change in the women's elasticity curves seems to have taken place in the 1960s and the 1970s, the whole of shifts in the men's curves happened between the 1970s and the 1980s.

Five of the seven of the more recent men's curves which we see in Figure 7.4 are again really quite similar, particularly in the region between 30 and 50 hours of paid work per week. The exceptions are the USA and Sweden where men who have short hours of paid work do amounts of cooking and cleaning that would almost register on the same scale as women's.

But, of course, the point of this analysis is that the changing distribution of unpaid work between the sexes is determined, not just by the shape of the cross-sectional elasticity curves, but also by the historical shifts, upwards or downwards, in these curves. The argument is closely related to our previous discussion of structural versus behavioural changes: hours of paid work are for most people quite strictly determined by the requirements of

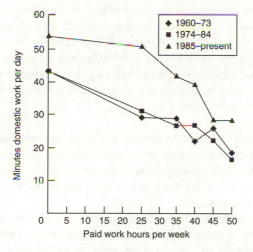

Figure 7.3. Men's elasticity of domestic work with respect to paid work time

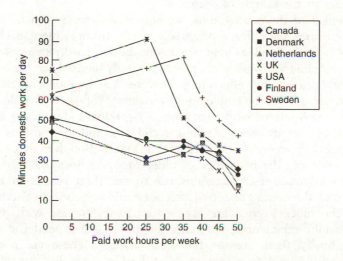

Figure 7.4. Men's elasticity of domestic work with respect to paid work time (late 1980s–1990s)

the job, and so different points on the cross-sectional elasticity curves represent different positions in the socio-economic structure (different 'structural locations' in the language of Chapter 4). The historical shifts in these curves in this sense represent changes in the behaviours specific to these particular positions. We see, in the historical and cross-national comparison of these curves, some quite regular and (and in the case of women, very substantial) changes in behaviour.

But before we attempt to go any further in interpreting these changes, we should consider some more of the detail of the allocation of time to unpaid work in the full set of countries in the datafile. So far in this chapter we have looked at the evidence for just two broad divisions of unpaid work: core domestic activities and others. We can now consider each of these in turn, looking at the countries separately, and in a little more detail at their respective component activities.

Core domestic work. We saw in the earlier cross-national summary tables a reduction of about an hour per day of women's core domestic work, and an increase of about 20 minutes per day in men's contribution to this activity. Table 7.12 shows the patterns of change for each of the countries for which we have cross-time data.

Just as we would expect from the elasticity plots we have been examining, those in full-time employment do less core domestic work, those in part-time employment do an intermediate amount, while those out of employment do more. For men the employment status difference is a small one. For women the difference is a large one. In both case the effect is very regular across the sample of countries.

The effect of the demographic variable is also pretty much consistent across countries, but differs substantially by sex. Younger men do a little less than the (already small) average; their contribution hardly changes with the presence of children, while older men, absolutely regularly across countries, do slightly more (this effect may however partly reflect a correlation between the age and the employment variables). Young women do remarkably less core domestic work than other age-groups, and the work increases progressively, for mothers of younger children, and for mothers of teenagers, and then, in every case, and in contrast to (though perhaps also as a consequence of) the behaviour of older men, declines a little for older women without co-resident minors. (Of course, these results are seriously confused by the concatenation of life-course and age-cohort effects; in each survey the older women are also, *ceteris paribus*, those with the more traditional life experiences, and hence the more distinct gender ideologies.)

And, finally, there are the historical changes. These are remarkably regular, with hardly an exception. Men, having controlled for differences in family and employment status, are seen regularly to increase (slightly) their core domestic work. Women, substantially—by anything from half an

Table 7.12. Core domestic work (longitudinal subsample, minutes per day)

	Canada	Denmark	France	Netherlands	Norway	UK	USA	Hungary	Finland
Men									
Mean	35	26	31	29	29	28	33	31	35
Full time	−4	−1	−3	−6	−2	−5	−5	−2	−3
Part time	5	6	8	2	−5	12	20	−4	9
Other, non-emp.	17	11	29	33	15	30	33	39	16
Yng, no yng. kids	−6	−3	−0	−3	−10	−7	−8	−10	−10
Child under 5	3	1	−1	3	1	−0	−1	−2	3
Child under 15	−2	−2	−6	−4	3	2	4	4	4
Oldr, no yng. kids	7	4	10	7	8	6	7	3	7
1960–73	−6	−11	−5		−7	−10	−10	−7	−1
1974–84	8		5	−4	7	−12	−5	7	
85–present	−1	11		7		11	15		1
R-squared	*0.027*	*0.059*	*0.049*	*0.133*	*0.035*	*0.145*	*0.061*	*0.040*	*0.036*
Women									
Mean	157	186	229	188	226	177	182	241	148
Full time	−46	−58	−66	−73	−53	−59	−53	−51	−18
Part time	−6	2	−17	−25	−6	13	−13	10	26
Other, non-emp.	39	76	59	29	35	44	50	66	41
Yng, no yng. kids	−58	−57	−53	−28	−94	−52	−48	−61	−68
Child under 5	20	40	−3	−4	−1	15	14	9	15
Child under 15	31	20	23	20	32	23	14	13	29
Oldr, no yng. kids	2	−14	1	5	1	8	10	2	18
1960–73	31	40	5	6	28	45	23	15	
1974–84	−9		−5		−29	7	−10	−15	9
85–present	−10	−40		−10		−26	−14		−9
R-squared	*0.226*	*0.363*	*0.306*	*0.324*	*0.290*	*0.397*	*0.218*	*0.240*	*0.191*

Table 7.13. Core domestic work (cross-sectional subsample, minutes per day)

	W.Germany	Poland	Belgium	Bulgaria	Czechoslovakia	E.Germany	Yugoslavia	Italy	Australia	Israel	Sweden
Men											
Mean	11	32	17	24	37	47	23	17	16	21	56
Full time	−3	−3	−6	−1	−2	0	−2	−1	−0	−3	−2
Part time	1	21	−4	0	8	−6	−14		−4	12	28
Other, non-emp.	34	39	76	12	45	−25	34	11	7	10	31
Yng, no yng. kids	−4	−16	−13	−5	5	16	−9	−5	−2	−10	−9
Child under 5	−1	−3	8	−1	0	−0	3	2	−1	1	4
Child under 15	1	4	−0	2	1	1	4	−2	−1	2	2
Oldr, no yng. kids	4	10	6	2	−6	−17	−6	6	8	1	6
R-squared	*0.050*	*0.041*	*0.145*	*0.009*	*0.018*	*0.016*	*0.040*	*0.013*	*0.012*	*0.014*	*0.026*
Women											
Mean	238	215	256	177	240	265	277	260	218	167	143
Full time	−102	−47	−89	−8	−44	−49	−58	−71	−63	−61	−15
Part time	10	−1	−62	−11	24	6	−41	−9		−5	26
Other, non-emp.	53	84	38	44	62	76	48	55	35	52	44
Yng, no yng. kids	−59	−73	−97	−70	−85	−49	−79	−126	−65	−93	−47
Child under 5	10	11	34	16	11	2	14	18	14	23	15
Child under 15	29	14	26	11	13	−1	12	31	19	8	9
Oldr, no yng. kids	0	−5	−17	4	−14	14	−2	38	−12	2	10
R-squared	*0.326*	*0.285*	*0.282*	*0.065*	*0.172*	*0.215*	*0.190*	*0.327*	*0.212*	*0.176*	*0.122*

Table 7.14. Cooking and cleaning (minutes per day)

	Men		Women	
	Housework	Cooking	Housework	Cooking
Grand mean	13	16	102	108
Empstat				
1. Full time	−1	−2	−26	−28
2. Part time	2	2	0	−1
3. Other, non-emp.	11	13	27	29
Famstat				
0. Yng, no yng. kids	−3	−3	−33	−34
1. Child under 5	1	−0	10	−0
2. Child under 15	1	1	9	12
3. Oldr, no yng. kids	2	3	−1	4
Country				
(coefficients suppressed)				
Historical stage				
1. 1960–73	−4	−5	25	1
2. 1974–84	3	−1	−7	−4
3. 85–present	3	8	−33	3
R-squared	0.033	0.069	0.187	0.301

hour to an hour and a half per day—reduce it. If ever there were scope for a scientific generalization about a social regularity tied to a historic period, this must be it.

Table 7.13 (in a pattern of exposition that will be repeated for each of the broad activity categories in turn) shows the equivalent evidence for those surveys for which we have evidence only from single historical time-points. The patterns appearing in the cross-sectional subsample are so nearly the same as those in the longitudinal that the same paragraphs of description will stand for both. And indeed the very considerable cross-national similarity in these regression models is the main evidential plank in the argument for the use of the aggregate whole-world summaries which appear from time to time in this chapter. (It also explains the obsessive, and to readers perhaps tedious, repetition of this pair of tables in the next few sections of this chapter.)

Table 7.14 gives a summary of a more detailed breakdown of the various domestic work categories calculated from the country version of the whole world. Housework and cooking show somewhat similar demographic effects. For women the summary gives substantial effects of age and family status: younger women with no children do substantially less of both cooking and routine housework than those with co-resident children. For housework, the age of the family seems not to make a great deal of difference, but in the case of cooking, there is a very clear peak for older families. In both categories of activity, older women with co-resident children have less housework than those without children. The effects of age and family status on cooking and housework are less marked for men. But in both cases, there appears to be a pretty continuous rise through the life stages, with older men in each country spending more time in these routine unpaid work activities than do younger men.

What is notable, in this table, and particularly given what is a rather similar pattern of social structural effects, is the contrast between the historical evolution of women's time devoted to these two activities. Virtually all the previously noted reduction in core domestic work time is concentrated in cleaning and general housework. Women's time devoted to cooking remains generally unchanged. There may be some technological aspect to this: improvements in materials (both for furnishings and in the means for cleaning them), and the more general diffusion of mechanical cleaning equipment (which, through Europe at least, happened over the first part of the period covered by our data), and indeed improvements in housing design (notably the virtual disappearance of external combustion open-fire heating technology) will certainly have had an impact. But there have been analogous improvements in cooking-related materials and technologies (e.g. the availability of ready-prepared fast foods and deep-freezers to store them), and a similar period for their diffusion. So why has women's cooking time not reduced?

The obvious inference from the data is strong support for the Berk–Hochschild gender ideology arguments. The household is where we 'manufacture' our identity. The traditional female ideology of creative care and nurturing is best expressed through cooking. House cleaning is mere maintenance, and the better it is accomplished, the less overt and noticeable it becomes. Cooking, however, is an expressive activity, it is overtly productive, in terms of the 'chains of provision' argument in Chapter 2 (it was the desire to evade the unhelpful Marxist production–reproduction dichotomy that explains my use of the term 'provision' in this context)—indeed, for the great majority of us, employed or not, cooking for our own households often seems the only genuinely productive thing we get to do in the course of a normal week. Clearly, women who wish to spend less time in domestic tasks, but still maintain their traditional creatively nurturing role *as* women, and indeed men who seek a new creatively nurturing role as men, will dump the housework, and cook.

Support for this view comes from the education level–historical trend evidence in Table 7.15. Once we control for the structural variates, we see that the better-educated women—who we may expect to have the resources to buy labour-saving equipment, and additionally to buy in external labour to carry out the housework—reduce their housework time if anything slightly faster than the less well-educated women, certainly maintaining

Table 7.15. Cooking and cleaning by historical period and educational level

	Housework			Cooking		
Men						
Mean	12			18		
Yng, no yng. kids	−3			−4		
Child under 5	1			−0		
Child under 15	1			0		
Oldr, no yng. kids	2			4		
Full time	−1			−2		
Part time	3			3		
Other, non-emp.	12			15		
Country (coefficients suppressed)						
	1960–73	1974–84	1985–	1960–73	1974–84	1985–
Incomplete secondary	−3	1	2	−3	1	5
Complete secondary	−3	2	1	−5	−0	4
Higher than secondary	−5	1	5	−6	−1	7
R-squared	*0.036*			*0.064*		
Women						
Mean	95			111		
Yng, no yng. kids	−29			−32		
Child under 5	7			2		
Child under 15	9			11		
Oldr, no yng. kids	−2			3		
Full time	−22			−28		
Part time	−0			−1		
Other, non-emp.	22			28		
Country (coefficients suppressed)						
	1960–73	1974–84	1985–	1960–73	1974–84	1985–
Incomplete secondary	19	4	−8	17	4	1
Complete secondary	14	−12	−14	−1	−9	−10
Higher than secondary	−5	−23	−26	−26	−22	−9
R-squared	*0.151*			*0.324*		

the negative status–housework-time gradient over the period. By contrast, while well-educated women might also have used their extra command over financial resources to buy their way out of cooking, on the contrary, the very substantial negative educational attainment–cooking-time gradient at the beginning of the period (with the best-educated women doing 42 minutes per day less cooking than the least educated) has been very substantially diminished (to a 10-minute difference) by the end. (Note that the overall size of the reduction appears rather smaller in Table 7.15 than in Table 7.14: the difference in the estimates relates to the smaller subsample with usable educational data used in the later table.). There are various names we can attach to this phenomenon; some might consider it to be a form of human capital investment within the family by those well-educated women who are presumed to be best endowed (by the advantages of their households of origin) as 'homemakers'. It is certainly only sensible that those with skills within the household should deploy them where their consequences are most overt.

Men at each educational level increase their contribution to both of these activities. But the best-educated increased their contribution slightly faster (perhaps the better-educated respond more readily to emerging notions of 'politically correct' behaviour). As a consequence, what were previously slightly negative gradients relating the two core domestic work activities to educational attainment become slightly positive. Again, this is a refrain repeated throughout this chapter, the better-educated have (in this case just slightly) more work.

Other unpaid work. There are some individual irregularities that interrupt the cross-national patterns of structural effects on the other unpaid work (childcare, shopping, odd jobs) categories (Table 7.16). Most notable is the growth of (particularly men's) childcare time in the UK and the Netherlands (which is part of the reason for the relatively large amounts of time devoted to the general category by part-time and non-employed men in these countries. Otherwise, the demographic variable shows a really rather constant picture across countries, with the younger men, and the younger women doing absolutely the least, and those with young children doing absolutely the most childcare (in one of those tautologous coincidences discussed in Chapter 3 of a structural category and a class of behaviour), and an intermediate level by older men—the English phrase 'pottering about' applied to this sort of use of time makes explicit reference to a gardening activity. Similarly (and with the UK as sole exception in this table) the non-employed (men and women) do by far the most of this activity. For men there is (in all except Hungary, to which we return in a moment), an overall increase in other unpaid work; the picture for women is a little more mixed, but still generally upwards.

As expected the cross-sectional subsample (Table 7.17) shows similar structural patterns; the exceptions being the old communist countries (this is also the case for Hungary) in which in the 1960s, and indeed in the 1980s in Bulgaria, though, because of reforms in Hungary to a lesser degree in the 1980s, queuing for access to goods and services constituted a large part of daily life. (Anecdotes suggest that queuing was often considered part of the working day, which may explain the irregularity in the employment effects here.)

Childcare time shows an entirely expected pattern in the whole-world summary of the more detailed unpaid work categories (Table 7.18). Women show a strong relationship of employment status to this activity category:

Table 7.16. Other unpaid work (longitudinal sample, minutes per day)

	Canada	Denmark	France	Netherlands	Norway	UK	USA	Hungary	Finland
Men									
Mean	99	35	83	84	97	83	97	80	95
Full time	−4	−1	−4	−11	−1	−9	−4	−2	−5
Part time	−7	−8	13	11	−3	50	14	−3	8
Other, non-emp.	20	13	48	54	13	48	25	33	25
Yng, no yng. kids	−37	−9	−21	−21	−31	−27	−16	−27	−27
Child under 5	43	13	15	33	32	28	15	36	32
Child under 15	18	2	3	−1	5	8	5	4	5
Oldr, no yng. kids	−7	−4	−5	−2	−9	−1	−2	−11	−2
1960–73	−6	−25	5		2	−16	−6	21	
1974–84	8		−5	−7	−2	−16	5	−21	−8
85–present	−1	24		12		16	1		8
R-squared	*0.052*	*0.098*	*0.035*	*0.166*	*0.029*	*0.113*	*0.014*	*0.080*	*0.042*
Women									
Mean	131	47	142	124	113	111	142	124	99
Full time	−21	−3	−42	−40	−20	−33	−30	−42	−9
Part time	−4	−1	−3	−10	−12	−2	11	−1	1
Other, non-emp.	18	5	36	15	18	29	25	54	25
Yng, no yng. kids	−51	−19	−45	−16	−58	−37	−30	−41	−43
Child under 5	84	25	86	70	74	64	63	59	89
Child under 15	8	−3	−6	−4	−9	4	−4	5	−19
Oldr, no yng. kids	−33	−7	−40	−34	−34	−19	−32	−25	−28
1960–73	−10	−26	7		−3	−24	5	45	
1974–84	3		−7	−9	3	−27	−4	−46	−9
85–present	3	26		15		26	−1		9
R-squared	*0.167*	*0.133*	*0.375*	*0.301*	*0.207*	*0.306*	*0.149*	*0.443*	*0.246*

Table 7.17. Other unpaid work (cross-sectional sample, minutes per day)

	W.Germany	Poland	Belgium	Bulgaria	Czechoslovakia	E.Germany	Yugoslavia	Italy	Australia	Israel	Sweden
Men											
Mean	84	81	57	124	94	91	117	50	87	69	117
Full time	−20	−4	−3	−6	−2	0	−1	−1	1	−5	−4
Part time	41	10	1	13	16	−11	30		−16	10	36
Other, non-emp.	83	66	42	56	43	6	8	6	−13	21	61
Yng, no yng. kids	−20	−36	−17	−40	−44	−34	−41	−21	−18	−44	−38
Child under 5	26	23	17	12	17	11	8	45	22	33	48
Child under 15	5	7	2	2	6	−9	13	−7	−4	−9	7
Oldr, no yng. kids	−11	−23	−1	10	−10	20	8	−7	−4	−13	−4
R-squared	*0.076*	*0.061*	*0.029*	*0.023*	*0.039*	*0.030*	*0.028*	*0.085*	*0.020*	*0.068*	*0.068*
Women											
Mean	132	154	127	117	158	154	189	97	142	126	146
Full time	−49	−41	−42	−8	−42	−25	−77	−18	−40	−22	−16
Part time	0	19	−24	−5	51	−19	−63		−24	−3	−5
Other, non-emp.	27	71	17	41	55	44	64	14	26	19	89
Yng, no yng. kids	−46	−51	−55	−53	−78	−52	−57	−44	−47	−75	−55
Child under 5	85	63	60	80	16	58	48	78	58	84	97
Child under 15	9	4	8	−27	5	−24	2	2	−14	−28	−10
Oldr, no yng. kids	−28	−42	−25	−13	−1	−35	−29	−22	−44	−47	−44
R-squared	*0.261*	*0.313*	*0.186*	*0.119*	*0.197*	*0.266*	*0.222*	*0.233*	*0.235*	*0.214*	*0.331*

Table 7.18. Other unpaid work categories (longitudinal sample, minutes per day)

	Men			Women		
	Childcare	Shopping	Odd jobs	Childcare	Shopping	Odd jobs
Mean	14	30	42	45	51	33
Full time	−1	−2	−2	−12	−10	−11
Part time	4	6	10	−3	1	0
Other, non-emp.	4	17	11	13	10	12
Yng, no yng. kids	−13	−2	−14	−34	−6	−5
Child under 5	24	2	−1	76	0	−8
Child under 15	−1	−0	5	−8	2	3
Oldr, no yng. kids	−12	−0	8	−37	1	6
Country (coefficients suppressed)						
1960–73	−3	−1	0	−4	−1	2
1974–84	−1	−0	−8	−5	−3	−10
85–present	6	1	7	11	4	6
R-squared	*0.144*	*0.040*	*0.051*	*0.357*	*0.056*	*0.105*

controlling for the other variables full-time employed women spend on average 25 minutes less than non-employed women. The men's employment effect works in the same direction, but is very much weaker, the difference between full-time and non-employed being on average just 6 minutes. But, unsurprisingly, it is the age and family status effects that dominate here. The difference between women with pre-school-age children and those with no children is 110 minutes, and the equivalent for men is greater than half an hour. Over the more recent historical period (i.e. since the early part of the 1970s) childcare time has increased for both sexes, by 15 minutes for women, and by 8 minutes for men. Since only a minority of the respondents spend any time at all in this activity, these changes in average times imply a quite substantial growth in the activity for those with children (clearly this is one of the cases where the use of the OLS regression technique in may produce suspect estimates). We shall consider the reasons for the growth in childcare in the next section.

The whole-world estimates of relationships of employment, family status, and historical period to childcare time are quite neatly reproduced in the estimates for each of the individual countries.

Table 7.19 sets out just the educational level coefficients extracted from the full models including also employment and family status together with country. Men in each category increase their contribution to childcare, though the best-educated increase the most. Well-educated women also increase their contribution to childcare substantially, though the least educated show a small decline. In both cases the best-educated spend the most

Table 7.19. Childcare, shopping, and odd jobs by educational level coefficients (model also includes family circumstances, employment status, and country)

	Men			Women		
	1960–73	1974–84	1985–	1960–73	1974–84	1985–
Childcare						
incomplete secondary	−5	−2	−2	−2	−8	−3
complete secondary	−1	0	5	2	−1	8
higher than secondary	−1	3	6	1	6	10
Shopping						
incomplete secondary	−2	0	−4	−2	−3	−3
complete secondary	2	2	−3	−3	6	4
higher than secondary	5	6	−1	1	4	5
Odd jobs						
incomplete secondary	7	−3	7	12	−5	−0
complete secondary	−1	−5	6	−4	−4	1
higher than secondary	−14	−8	2	−14	−2	4

time in childcare, and this positive gradient increases over time in accordance with the predictions of human capital theorists.

Employment status has a marked effect on the whole-world estimates of time devoted to shopping and other related travel. Here, uniquely among the unpaid work categories, the effects are approximately the same for the two sexes; non-employed men and women both spend around 20 minutes per day more in this activity than do the full-time employed. Age and family status, however, have only a rather limited effect. And in the overall accounts, there is a small increase in shopping time for men, and an only slightly larger one for women, once we control for the effects of the other structural variates. In fact the rather smaller sample of surveys with a standardized education variable shows a small decline in men's shopping time, concentrated among the better-educated, whereas the better-educated women show a 6-minute increase, and the least well-educated women's shopping time marginally decreases.

The shopping time trends for the individual countries are rather less tidy than those for the other unpaid work categories. The employment status relationships are consistent across the countries, at least between the two extreme employment categories. But the age and family status variables show no consistent cross-national relationship with shopping time. Seven out of the nine countries for which we have evidence of historical change show quite consistent and not inconsiderable increases over the period. But two countries, Hungary and the USA, show marked declines. The suggested explanations for the two exceptions are quite different. In the case of Hungary (as already mentioned), the only East European country for which we have cross-time data, the reduction may be related to the economic liberalization through the 1960s and 1970s reducing the time spent queuing. The USA, by contrast, has the highest total of shopping time of all the nine cross-time datasets, and the reduction shown in this figure serves only to reduce its total of time in this activity towards the level of the other Western countries.

Finally we have the odd-jobs category, which includes, in addition to non-routine household maintenance, such activities as servicing cars and gardening. The whole-world table (7.18) shows the same employment gradient as for the other unpaid work categories (non-employed women devote 23 more minutes to this activity than full-time employed women, men, 13 more minutes per day). Older people, both men and women, spend more time in odd jobs than do younger. There is perhaps a slight gender difference detectable in the family status effects: men with children seem to devote a little more time than others to odd jobs, while women spend slightly less. These age and family relationships appear to be quite consistent across countries. And finally the historical trend, which in the whole-world accounts shows, for both men and women, a fall in these non-routine unpaid work activities from the 1960s to the 1970s, and a subsequent increase through to the 1980s, is explained by substantial inter-country variation. In this category, less well-educated men maintained their previously quite high levels of time devoted to odd jobs, where better-educated men have substantially increased their time. And the better-educated women have also substantially increased their time allocation, indicating something of a gender convergence in this area.

Explanations for historical change in unpaid work. The explanation for the reduction in women's time devoted to the core domestic work categories is widely disputed. We have already encountered (Chapter 3) the line of argument proposing that labour-saving technology leaves housework unchanged: the results we have been discussing are so clearly at odds with this well-known position that we should pause briefly to show how they relate to the earlier material.

There were two sorts of evidence for the no-reduction position. The first of these is cross-sectional; we previously quoted the assertion from Szalai *et al.* of the 'counter-intuitive relationship' between domestic technology and domestic work time. The empirical evidence for this was the comparison of domestic work time between the Eastern and Western countries contributing to the 1965 multinational study. Eastern European countries with much less domestic equipment than their Western counterparts, had rather less domestic work time. But the tables on which this comparison was based did not control for either employment or family status. We have seen that having paid work substantially reduces women's unpaid work, and larger or younger families increases it; in 1965, a much larger proportion of women had paid jobs in the Eastern European countries than in the Western, and the mean family sizes were smaller. So, we conjecture, the Szalai result reflected employment and demographic structure rather than domestic technology; this very influential finding was probably a statistical artefact.

The second leg of the argument was the longitudinal observation (reported both by Vanek and in a notably cautious manner by Robinson and Converse) that US time-use surveys of homemakers (i.e. non-employed married women) from the 1920s and 1930s showed if anything slightly less unpaid work than similar surveys in the 1960s. We saw in Chapter 3 that it is also possible to produce rather strikingly similar figures for the UK housewives over approximately the same time span; but the inference we draw is that the near constancy of domestic work over this period for the samples as a whole results from the two contrary class trends—middle-class women increasing their unpaid work time as a result of the loss of domestic servants, working-class women decreasing it as a consequence of the acquisition of domestic equipment. The evidence seems to point strongly towards the proposition that labour-saving technology did in these cases indeed save women's labour; presumably we should adopt a similar explanation for the downwards trend in the more recent multinational data.

What do we conclude for the growth in men's core domestic work? The dual-burden argument (also discussed in Chapter 3) asserts, not just that women maintain their previous domestic responsibilities as they move into paid employment, but also that husbands do not increase their domestic work to compensate for their wives' change in economic activity. The whole-world files as presently constituted are not really a suitable basis for an empirical discussion of this argument. It requires data on the activity patterns of couples, of the sort found in the UK or the Netherlands national data files. But the multinational evidence of growth in men's core domestic work time is consistent with a model of 'lagged adaptation' (developed originally for the UK data). Start with a workforce with few employed married women; wives increasingly enter employment, initially husbands do not substantially change their pattern of contribution to the household, but, subsequently, as the domestic consequent pressures accumulate, some husbands do gradually adjust their practices to take on a few more of the core domestic tasks than previously (Gershuny 1983; Gershuny, Godwin, and Jones 1994). Those households that do not see such an adjustment are presumably more likely than others to break up. Children brought up in households in which both parents have paid jobs and domestic work is shared less unequally will themselves be more likely to share work more equally when they grow up; over time the proportion of all children in the society who come from such households increases. And gradually the male housework time shifts upwards. And as these processes become more visible and talked about, new norms emerge, thus speeding up the process of change.

Lest we be thought too optimistic on gender convergence, we should point to a rather different sort of gender inequality. The dual burden is essentially a quantitative phenomenon: because of the lag in the operation of the processes of adjustment, the total (paid plus unpaid) work hours of employed married women will tend to be higher than their husbands'. But apart from the difference in total work hours, there is also the split of this total between the different sorts of work; even in those households where the total of work is evenly divided, there is still a tendency for women to take responsibility for a larger proportion of the housework (and perhaps more important to feel responsible for it, so that they are more likely then men to spend psychic energy worrying about whether it is done). As a result, formally full-time employed women in each country work substantially fewer hours than full-time employed men, they are more likely than men to take days off work to care for children, and more likely to take extended leave, or to leave their jobs altogether, when their children are small. All this means that married women, in both short term and long, are able to devote less time to their jobs than equivalently placed men and form less human capital as a result; and in turn, *ceteris paribus*, married women perform less well in their careers than men.

Historical change in childcare and shopping time. We have seen a moderate increase in time devoted to childcare. There are really three possible explanations for this. The first relates to the more threatening environment. In Europe the number of cars on the roads has increased continuously through the period covered by our data, with the consequential increasing danger of leaving children to play unattended. And perhaps more important than the actual change in the environment is the perception of increased danger, perhaps as a result of increasing media reportage of road accidents and of other sorts of damage to unsupervised children. So we might expect an increase in particular in child escort activities.

The second relates to child-rearing practices. The American 'new home economics' suggests that better-educated households may spend increasing time in caring for fewer children, as means of maximizing the development of their human capital. The cross-sectional plot of educational levels against childcare time is certainly consistent with this somewhat cold-blooded prediction. Perhaps a more sympathetic statement would refer to changes from traditional authoritarian attitudes, to more child-centred approaches over the period covered by our data.

And there is also a possibility that the change is an artefact of the methodology. The time-use data discussed in this and the foregoing chapters is drawn from the 'main activity' evidence in the time diaries. But there may be other activities going on at the same time. Consider first a mother in an unmechanized household: she may be simultaneously poking clothes in a wash-boiler, stirring food cooking on a stove, and talking to her children. When she writes her account of this passage, even within a well-constructed diary instrument, the childcare activity may quite properly appear as the third item in the hierarchical account—and thus disappear entirely from a 'first activity' summary of the day. Now consider a parent in a mechanized home: the clothes-wash requires a short initial period of intensive work, sorting fabrics, and setting up the automatic washing machine. There is then a period of half an hour or an hour during which the wash requires no attention. The parent is more directly engaged with child during this period, and may as a result be more likely to describe childcare in the diary as the first activity. Childcare activities, previously present but mingled invisibly with other household tasks, may thus be *exposed* by the changed rhythm, the increasing intensity but shorter duration, of domestic tasks in a mechanized household.

There are again conflicting possibilities for explaining the general rise in time devoted to shopping and related activities. On one hand, we might suspect that this reflects changes in the organization of retail distribution. We move (though to very different degrees in the different European countries) from a relatively small, traditional, full-service shopping pattern to what was once thought of as an 'American' pattern with larger, rather more distant self-service supermarkets. With this change comes extra travel time, extra time spent walking within the store to find, compare, and select purchases, extra time spent queuing to pay for purchases. (From the 'chain of provision' perspective which we discuss further in the next chapter, this may be interpreted as a process of externalization of production costs on the part of the distributive industry.) This view is supported by the fact that the European totals of time devoted to this activity appear to be rising historically to the high levels already found in the USA and Canada.

The competing explanation contends that shopping is more akin to leisure consumption than work, and that shopping activities form part of the recreation of a consumer society. It is difficult to evaluate this argument from our data, since we have no general information on our respondents' own views of the work-or-leisure status of their activities. But presumably the leisure explanation relates more to the non-routine shopping activities, those related to the purchase of clothes and consumer durables, rather than to routine purchases of food and other non-durable items. In a number of the individual surveys (though not in the Archive dataset itself) we can distinguish between the non-routine and routine shopping activities: in these cases we see that the non-routine activities account for between one-fifth and one-tenth of overall shopping time. And one of the major subcategories of growth has been the time spent in travel related to shopping, So we are inclined towards the 'organizational change/externalization', rather than the 'shopping as leisure' explanation.

Overall change in unpaid work. We closed our discussion of paid work with the full model adding the effect of the interaction of historical stage and educational level to that of the employment and family status variates. It is appropriate to close the discussion of unpaid work in the same way— particularly as a somewhat similar conclusion emerges.

   The addition to the whole-world story that now emerges from Table 7.20 is a simple one. The growth in men's overall contribution of unpaid work whose components we have been investigating is not an undifferentiated one. The least well-educated men increase their unpaid work by just 13 minutes per week, the best-educated by nearly 40 minutes per week, while the growth of the unpaid work of those with medium levels of education is somewhere between these two figures. The less well-educated women have reduced their overall contribution of unpaid work by just about an hour (remember, this is controlling for changes in employment

Table 7.20. All unpaid work (longitudinal subsample, minutes per day)

	Men			Women		
mean	123			329		
Yng, no yng. kids	−37			−101		
Child under 5	32			87		
Child under 15	6			18		
Oldr, no yng. kids	2			−30		
Full time	−9			−83		
Part time	21			−3		
Other, non-emp.	60			78		
Country (coefficients suppressed)						
	1960–73	1974–84	1985–	1960–73	1974–84	1985–
Incomplete secondary	−6	−4	7	48	−8	−11
Complete secondary	−8	−1	11	14	−17	−6
Higher than secondary	−21	−0	16	−26	−29	−13
R-squared	*0.081*			*0.382*		

and family status) while the best-educated have actually increased their total of unpaid work by 13 minutes per day.

So, some gender convergence, undoubtedly. But once we construct the model appropriately so as to include period–educational interactions, there is also another sort of change, rather similar to what we saw in the case of paid work. The outcome of the various changes we have been discussing is, for men, a complete reversal of the previous negative association between social status (as proxied by educational attainment) and unpaid work, and for women, the virtual disappearance of what was previously a difference of an hour and a quarter per day between the best- and the worst-educated.

Leisure time

Out-of-home leisure. As readers may now be coming to expect, the various different national patterns of out-of-home leisure that emerge from within Tables 7. 21 and 7.22 are not in fact so very different. Once we take account, as we did in Chapter 5, of the differences in survey date, GNP, and political system, the overall means of time are reasonably consistent with each other. And in fact the patterns of effects of the variates also broadly correspond across countries. The non-employed, both men and women, have the most out-of-home leisure time (the only exception among forty observations is that for Hungarian women). Without exception (and also utterly unsurprisingly) we see that the young people without co-resident children have the most time to devote to this. Those with children, generally those with the youngest children, have the most constraints on going out, and hence, the least time spent taking leisure out of the home. The pattern for older people varies a little more across the countries.

And we almost, but not quite, achieve another longitudinal regularity. In eight of the nine countries for which we have cross-time data, out-of-home leisure time increases. The exception, in these results, is the USA. Is this in fact a US exception to a cross-national regularity in patterns of social change? Here, for virtually the only time in the whole book, we have to draw attention to a methodological difference within the surveys included in our dataset. The US data-collection methodology changed, for the 1985 survey, from face-to-face interviewing, to a telephone-based sample. Even with the most stringent requirements for redialling non-respondents, the consequence might be expected to be at the margin, a slight under-response of those who spend the most time out of home—that is, a relatively small bias in terms of respondents, but leading to an under-representation of precisely those who might be expected to make the largest contribution to this particular category of activity. So readers might wish to conclude that the longitudinal generalization stands without significant exception.

Table 7.21. Out-of-home leisure (longitudinal sample, minutes per day)

	Canada	Denmark	France	Netherlands	Norway	UK	USA	Hungary	Finland
Men									
Mean	143	179	97	149	165	122	116	103	138
Full time	-6	-5	-4	-11	-3	-9	-5	-0	-6
Part time	-6	-7	19	20	-6	40	46	-40	-0
Other, non-emp.	26	60	38	43	25	50	28	17	34
Yng, no yng. kids	33	64	45	30	45	42	30	47	31
Child under 5	-26	-34	-9	-12	-3	-30	-5	-18	-19
Child under 15	-12	-31	-9	-11	-18	-12	-7	-6	-8
Oldr, no yng. kids	-11	-12	-11	-18	-29	-9	-29	-14	-14
1960-73	-13	-17		-11	-4	-32	13	-25	-0
1974-84	-18		11	-3	4	6	10	25	
85-present	16	17		6		13	-23		0
R-squared	0.037	0.052	0.041	0.113	0.029	0.107	0.032	0.076	0.028
Women									
Mean	134	176	72	149	166	110	111	68	118
Full time	-16	-13	-5	-3	-13	-13	-9	2	-6
Part time	5	-2	3	-2	-4	-6	-10	-0	8
Other, non-emp.	12	19	4	2	10	14	10	-3	15
Yng, no yng. kids	25	65	36	8	38	39	20	30	42
Child under 5	-17	-36	-15	-5	0	-15	1	-11	-18
Child under 15	-13	-24	-6	-8	-13	-11	-3	-5	-14
Oldr, no yng. kids	6	8	2	7	-1	-9	-16	2	-7
1960-73	-16	-9	-6		-5	-30	13	-21	
1974-84	-13	9	6	-4	5	12	5	22	-9
85-present	13			6		9	-18		9
R-squared	0.020	0.028	0.024	0.013	0.012	0.056	0.019	0.078	0.037

Table 7.22. Out-of-home leisure (cross-sectional sample, minutes per day)

	W.Germany	Poland	Belgium	Bulgaria	Czechoslovakia	E.Germany	Yugoslavia	Italy	Australia	Israel	Sweeden
Men											
Mean	141	92	96	105	82	86	129	161	139	134	111
Full time	−19	−1	−3	−5	−3	0	−6	−6	−2	−13	−2
Part time	50	−24	−6	48	6	−22	−28		48	32	−29
Other, non-emp.	29	37	52	40	63	34	93	57	3	48	45
Yng, no yng. kids	41	69	39	69	58	−2	53	65	64	13	43
Child under 5	−12	−4	−22	−3	−19	9	−13	−26	−26	−16	−30
Child under 15	−6	−15	−5	−2	−5	−15	−21	−14	−2	11	−17
Oldr, no yng. kid	−26	−26	−8	−29	1	12	5	−29	−47	−6	−9
R-squared	*0.047*	*0.064*	*0.030*	*0.059*	*0.046*	*0.009*	*0.057*	*0.059*	*0.049*	*0.027*	*0.037*
Women											
mean	103	66	85	75	54	59	68	133	116	118	92
Full time	−14	−7	−13	−1	−0	1	−8	−7	−9	−8	−6
Part time	−22	13	2	4	−9	−2	−25		8	1	11
Other, non-emp.	15	12	4	5	2	10	7	6	3	6	15
Yng, no yng. kids	50	46	56	58	23	19	39	75	69	28	37
Child under 5	−17	−22	−44	1	4	1	−14	−1	0	−16	−20
Child under 15	−11	−5	−5	−2	−8	−4	−6	−29	−20	5	−2
Oldr, no yng. kids	−9	7	9	−15	9	−3	9	−15	15	−2	−5
R-squared	*0.029*	*0.029*	*0.043*	*0.023*	*0.012*	*0.008*	*0.020*	*0.051*	*0.030*	*0.009*	*0.022*

Table 7.23. Out-of-home leisure categories

	Men				Women			
	Eat, etc.	Active	Events	Visits	Eat, etc.	Active	Events	Visits
Mean	16	18	55	37	7	12	42	42
Full time	−0	−2	−2	−1	1	−2	−1	−6
Part time	3	10	10	−2	0	−1	1	−3
Other, non-emp.	3	12	15	12	−1	2	1	6
Yng, no yng. kids	10	5	18	12	7	4	18	11
Child under 5	−4	−2	−6	−3	−1	−0	−8	−3
Child under 15	−2	−1	−3	−4	−1	−1	−2	−5
Oldr, no yng. kids	−3	−1	−8	−3	−1	−0	−1	2
Country (coefficients suppressed)								
1960–73	−5	−2	−4	−1	−4	−3	−5	2
1974–84	1	1	4	3	0	−0	2	4
85–present	7	3	2	−1	5	4	6	−6
R-squared	0.035	0.037	0.022	0.072	0.028	0.030	0.025	0.101

Table 7.23 sets out the whole-world estimates for the various out-of-home leisure categories. In these whole-world estimates men devote on average 16 minutes per day to eating and drinking out of home, women 7 minutes per day. The whole-world tabulation shows no very substantial employment effect for women, a small negative effect of full-time employment for men, and a more substantial effect of age for both sexes. There are some expected and some unexpected national differences: France and the USA show overall much the most time devoted to this activity. But the tables show that it is in fact mostly French men who eat out, while French women devote rather less than the average of time to this activity. There is a regular historical trend of increase, in this category, over time.

Table 7.24, which breaks down these out-of-home leisure effects by educational level, shows a difference in the education gradient that might be thought to correspond, depending on the reader's tastes, either to the Becker time-use model which has the better-educated, with their higher than average incomes, better able to afford the more expensive eating-out activity, or to the Bourdieu cultural-capital approach in which the

Table 7.24. Out-of-home leisure categories by educational level
(minutes per day)

	Men			Women		
	1960–73	1974–84	1985–	1960–73	1974–84	1985–
Eating out at restaurants, etc.						
Mean	8			5		
Incomplete secondary	−6	2	−0	−3	0	0
Complete secondary	−4	2	1	−3	1	1
Higher than secondary	−1	5	4	−1	3	4
Drinking at pubs, bars						
Mean	8			3		
Incomplete secondary	1	−2	5	−2	−1	4
Complete secondary	0	−4	−0	−2	−1	1
Higher than secondary	−3	−4	2	−2	−2	2
Playing sports, walking						
Mean	18			11		
Incomplete secondary	−3	−0	2	−3	−2	2
Complete secondary	−5	3	2	−2	1	3
Higher than secondary	0	1	3	−0	1	4
Going out to cinema, theatre, or other events						
Mean	56			46		
Incomplete secondary	−6	−8	−6	−6	−10	−7
Complete secondary	1	1	8	4	2	4
Higher than secondary	14	7	8	13	10	16
Visiting (or being visited)						
Mean	38			46		
Incomplete secondary	2	2	−2	3	1	−0
Complete secondary	4	2	−3	1	3	−3
Higher than secondary	4	−1	−9	4	3	−9

Note: Coefficients for age, family status, employment status, and country suppressed.

better-educated are better able to cope with the demanding personal relationships in restaurants. Both in fact must apply. (And a more extensive presentation of the leisure data would allow a more testing evaluation of Bourdieu's approach by crossing the education with the income data that is available in the multinational dataset.) Both the eating and the drinking categories in fact show increases over the period for each of the educational groups. Playing sports and walking occupy 18 minutes for men and 12 for women with employment status having a substantial effect for men, but, puzzlingly, not for women. The older the respondent, the less the time devoted to sports, and the more to taking walks.

Cinema, theatre, attending sports events, together with leisure trips and other leisure travel, occupy 42 minutes of women's average day, 55 minutes of men's. There is a really rather sharply negative life-stage effect; the presence of small children in the household has a particularly depressing effect on this category. And there has been a historical increase in the overall total of time devoted to this activity, of 6 minutes for men and 11 for women, meaning some gender convergence. And the education variable shows a complicated historical evolution, with a small reduction in the best-educated men's time coupled with some growth for this category of women, bringing the totals for well-educated men and women to equality, while the totals for those with the lowest levels of educational attainment remain pretty much unchanged over the period.

Visiting (or being visited) shows a small historical decline over the period, particularly for women (though this difference does not show up in the smaller education sample). Table 7.24 shows that most of this decline has been concentrated among the better-educated (and richer) groups—as indeed both Becker (since this is a time-intensive, income-extensive activity) and Bourdieu (since social visits to friends are less demanding of cultural capital than visits to leisure institutions in the public sphere) would predict.

Passive leisure at home. The patterns of effect of the structural categories are pretty much as we might have expected for the passive leisure category (watching television or video, listening to the radio or recorded music; Tables 7.25 and 7.26). Men, in virtually every case, do more of it than women (the only exception being Belgium in 1965). The non-employed do more of it than others, as do the older adults in our sample. The young do less (thus the activity is pretty much the complement to out-of-home leisure). The historical trend of time spent in this activity is generally an upwards one, but not invariably so: Denmark and also the UK show declines (which might conceivably be related to the role of broadcasting authorities in sponsoring the original surveys used in both of these data-sets).

Table 7.25. Television and radio (longitudinal subsample, minutes per day)

	Canada	Denmark	France	Netherlands	Norway	UK	USA	Hungary	Finland
Men									
Mean	131	134	75	111	111	139	132	77	110
Full time	−12	−2	−1	−5	−5	−7	−6	−1	−6
Part time	−1	−14	−13	−4	−4	−12	−4	23	−1
Other, non-emp.	53	34	23	30	30	59	47	17	31
Yng, no yng. kids	−11	−14	−18	−4	−4	−17	−7	−16	−1
Child under 5	−2	−4	−1	−8	−8	−1	−6	1	−12
Child under 15	3	−2	4	4	4	8	4	4	−3
Oldr, no yng. kids	14	20	9	9	9	11	13	6	17
1960–73	−10	39	−9			11	−19	−18	−13
1974–84	−9		9	−3	−3	−1	9	18	13
85–present	10	−39		5	5	−5	10		
R-squared	0.046	0.086	0.033	0.047	0.047	0.057	0.032	0.063	0.051
Women									
Mean	104	123	65	84	67	126	113	63	84
Full time	−24	−11	−17	−13	−6	−22	−23	−3	−6
Part time	−16		−5	−8	−6	−12	−23	1	7
Other, non-emp.	22	15	15	6	6	25	25	3	15
Yng, no yng. kids	2	11	−7	−0	−12	−2	7	6	1
Child under 5	−11	−13	−10	−13	−8	−14	−4	−6	−11
Child under 15	−5	9	−1	2	4	−0	−7	−2	−3
Oldr, no yng. kids	13	−1	13	7	12	11	9	3	13
1960–73	−12	31	−10		−11	2	−34	−20	−12
1974–84	−5		10	−2	11	−6	13	20	12
85–present	8	−32		3		2	21		
R-squared	0.042	0.089	0.070	0.036	0.036	0.053	0.076	0.079	0.046

Table 7.26. Television and radio (cross-sectional subsample, minutes per day)

	W.Germany	Poland	Belgium	Bulgaria	Czechoslovakia	E. Germany	Yugoslavia	Italy	Australia	Israel	Sweden
Men											
Mean	73	87	91	100	97	89	55	93	113	125	116
Full time	−0	−1	3	−2	3	−2	−0	−2	−3	−2	−3
Part time	1	29	−19	−15	−22	24	51		17	8	7
Other, non-emp.	−3	3	−11	20	−39	150	−8	15	42	8	56
Yng, no yng. kids	−14	−25	−20	−1	0	−23	−15	−27	−32	−8	−3
Child under 5	1	−11	−23	3	6	−4	−10	−1	2	1	−10
Child under 15	4	7	8	6	2	12	10	1	12	−13	1
Oldr, no yng. kids	9	27	16	−1	−5	7	4	26	15	52	10
R-squared	*0.011*	*0.032*	*0.039*	*0.007*	*0.013*	*0.034*	*0.029*	*0.050*	*0.035*	*0.029*	*0.022*
Women											
Mean	67	67	95	73	64	79	41	72	103	117	91
Full time	−19	−1	0	−3	−5	−11	−2	−13	−34	−17	−0
Part time	−6	−17	−17	12	2	12	9		−15	−14	−5
Other, non-emp.	12	19	8	11	7	15	1	10	21	22	7
Yng, no yng. kids	−5	−2	−16	8	−19	−0	−2	−4	−6	−4	13
Child under 5	−12	2	−6	3	6	−10	−8	−12	−19	−15	−13
Child under 15	−1	2	5	3	4	19	2		11	3	−11
Oldr, no yng. kids	10	−6	4	−5	−1	0	7	8	17	25	14
R-squared	*0.044*	*0.032*	*0.030*	*0.007*	*0.018*	*0.048*	*0.007*	*0.039*	*0.083*	*0.044*	*0.025*

Table 7.27. Television and radio (minutes per day)

	Men			Women		
Mean	109			90		
Yng, no yng. kids	−10					
Child under 5	−4			−9		
Child under 15	3			−1		
Oldr, no yng. kids	10			7		
Full time	−5			−14		
Part time	−1			−10		
Other, non-emp.	38			16		
Country (coefficients suppressed)						
	1960–73	1974–84	1985–	1960–73	1974–84	1985–
Incomplete secondary	−13	11	33	−18	13	30
Complete secondary	−16	−5	15	−20	−5	17
Higher than secondary	−26	−24	−10	−31	−20	−8
R-squared	*0.094*			*0.110*		

The educational status model, whose results are given here in Table 7.27, shows the very strong educational differences in consumption of broadcast media that would be predicted by both the Becker and the Bourdieu consumption theories. Indeed, for both men and women the passive leisure time spent by the high- and low-level educational groups has been diverging over the period; while, in this (nearly) whole-world model the time devoted to this activity has been growing overall, much the largest part of the growth, just about three-quarters of an hour per day, has come from those with the lowest levels of educational attainment, men and women alike, while the best-educated group have increased their passive leisure, over this period, by around 20 minutes per day.

Other leisure at home. Once more (weary readers may be reassured that we are very nearly at the end of our systematic tour of the whole-world dataset), the aggregate tables for the other sorts of leisure at home show that the different nations do not really differ. Women (in general, but not invariably) have more of this activity than men, making it in this respect the complement to passive leisure. There is a pretty much monotonic relationship with employment status (this parallels Szalai's finding for this class of activity, of a strong negative elasticity with respect to paid work in his Hungarian natural experiment). And there is also a pretty much monotonic relationship with the different categories of the demographic variable.

Other home leisure, generally but not invariably, is a reducing category over time (Tables 7.28 and 7.29); this is not what one would have expected on the basis of the elasticity-with-respect-to-paid-work argument. Perhaps we should think of this class of leisure as an 'inferior commodity'; it is the least money-intensive of the broad leisure activity categories, perhaps the least expressive of individual distinction, in terms of Bourdieu's arguments, so perhaps we should not be surprised to find it generally declining.

Nevertheless, as we shall see when we look at the more detailed categories of activity of which it is composed, the trends vary (Table 7.30). Time devoted to eating at home declines by 11 or 12 minutes per day for both men and women, which may in part relate to smaller meals, in part to fast food, or to the growth of a 'grazing' pattern, in which meal times become less distinct events, and food is taken, little but often, perhaps simultaneously with passive leisure, in which case it would disappear from these primary-activity-based accounts. Or perhaps we should relate this decline to the previously mentioned growth in eating away from home.

Reading is also a major category, occupying 32 minutes of the women's day, and 42 minutes of men's. There are small negative employment effects for women, and very large ones for men (this is, as in the case of walks, a stereotypical activity of unemployment: non-employed men in general spend three-quarters of an hour more than full-time employed men in this activity, though this varies considerably between countries). There is a moderate U-shaped relationship with the life-stage variable; the presence of small children apparently has a particularly inhibiting effect on reading. There is a moderate historical decline for men but a small increase for women.

Men and women devote 29 and 32 minutes respectively to conversations at home. This is one of the few leisure categories for which the gender means are virtually equal: perhaps the men and women are talking to each other, though the puzzling difference in the historical trend suggests that though the women may be talking more, the men are not listening. The non-employed spend more time in conversation than do the employed. And there is an irregular historical trend. Hobbies and games occupy slightly more time for women (26 minutes for the whole-world sample as a whole) than for men (26 minutes). There is no very determined effect of life-stage on this activity category, nor is there any substantial historical trend.

Table 7.31 summarizes the education–period interaction effects. We see that the decline in eating time is slightly larger among the relatively well educated, while the decline in reading is largest among the better-educated men, as is the decline in time spent in conversations with other household members; by the end of the period covered by these data, the better-educated men spent, in absolute terms, less time talking at home than did those with the lowest level of educational attainment. The better-educated men and women used to devote more time to hobbies, but this gradient disappeared by the end of the period.

Personal care

Finally, we turn to the personal care (sleep, washing, and dressing, plus medical care) category. Reassuringly, for what is basically a biological need,

Table 7.28. Other home leisure (longitudinal sample, minutes per day)

	Canada	Denmark	France	Netherlands	Norway	UK	USA	Hungary	Finland
Men									
Mean	161	174	178	202	163	140	123	131	195
Full time	−14	−2	−9	−20	−14	−11	−9	−2	−16
Part time	17	55	24	58	39	12	44	−10	33
Other, non-emp.	58	14	102	68	118	75	53	45	83
Yng, no yng. kids	−14	−30	−8	−16	−5	−8	−2	12	−10
Child under 5	−14	1	−2	−1	−9	−5	−11	−13	−7
Child under 15	8	12	2	2	6	2	2	−2	6
Oldr, no yng. kids	23	22	4	24	7	10	14	3	15
1960–73	34	−5	−8		−11	18	8	−12	16
1974–84	24		7	15		12	−5	12	
85–present	−30	5		−26	11	−15	−4		−15
R-squared	*0.101*	*0.025*	*0.078*	*0.233*	*0.133*	*0.113*	*0.046*	*0.047*	*0.139*
Women									
Mean	175	193	177	238	167	165	142	120	203
Full time	−32	−25	−41	−42	−41	−41	−36	−17	−23
Part time	−1	−1	−1	−17	−1	−0	−3	25	14
Other, non-emp.	27	34	35	17	25	36	33	21	59
Yng, no yng. kids	−2	−28	17	−9	25	3	6	21	3
Child under 5	−30	−3	−20	−22	−21	−31	−30	−11	−23
Child under 15	1	8	3	6	−1	−3	1	−6	3
Oldr, no yng. kids	26	13	5	20	11	21	25	5	16
1960–73	26	−21	−5		−22	16	1	−12	11
1974–84	25		5	8	23	5	−6	13	
85–present	−23	21		−13		−11	5		−12
R-squared	*0.108*	*0.052*	*0.141*	*0.145*	*0.105*	*0.150*	*0.102*	*0.073*	*0.136*

Table 7.29. Other home leisure (cross-sectional subsample, minutes per day)

	W.Germany	Poland	Belgium	Bulgaria	Czechoslovakia	E.Germany	Yugoslavia	Italy	Australia	Israel	Sweden
Men											
Mean	145	140	182	160	137	134	130	181	138	126	149
Full time	−12	−7	−11	−10	−4	−2	−7	−17	−15	−14	−3
Part time	17	52	31	4	32	39	13		47	37	51
Other, non-emp.	91	84	97	103	71	176	97	159	198	51	43
Yng, no yng. kids	−3	20	−19	−8	−11	21	−2	9	−6	24	−9
Child under 5	1	−10	18	0	0	−2	−4	−4	0	−1	0
Child under 15	2	−4	−8	3	−3	−6	3	−7	0	−5	1
Oldr, no yng. kids	−1	9	19	1	17	2	−0	2	8	13	18
R-squared	*0.058*	*0.072*	*0.069*	*0.091*	*0.036*	*0.032*	*0.075*	*0.164*	*0.224*	*0.072*	*0.029*
Women											
Mean	157	127	196	172	130	131	124	177	166	150	170
Full time	−39	−17	−41	−18	−24	−21	−29	−34	−44	−20	−12
Part time	−6	7	−15	2	0	6	−19	26	−13	5	14
Other, non-emp.	23	30	16	94	34	31	24	26	26	13	40
Yng, no yng. kids	7	27	−3	13	6	16	45	45	15	29	2
Child under 5	−28	−18	−3	−5	−16	5	−10	−24	−23	−31	−22
Child under 15	5	−2	2	−4	2	−2	−6	−10	7	12	−1
Oldr, no yng. kids	6	8	0	1	7	−10	2	−4	17	13	21
R-squared	*0.086*	*0.066*	*0.056*	*0.118*	*0.088*	*0.084*	*0.105*	*0.095*	*0.093*	*0.042*	*0.045*

Table 7.30. Other home leisure categories (minutes per day)

	Men				Women			
	Eating	Reading	Talking	Hobbies	Eating	Reading	Talking	Hobbies
Mean	70	42	29	29	75	32	30	26
Full time	−1	−6	−2	−2	−10	−6	−5	−8
Part time	7	17	5	5	0	3	−0	−1
Other, non-emp.	11	47	18	18	10	5	6	9
Yng, no yng. kids	−10	8	−4	−4	−9	17	2	−1
Child under 5	1	−6	−0	−0	−0	−10	−4	−5
Child under 15	2	−2	1	1	3	−3	1	−0
Oldr, no yng. kids	6	1	3	3	2	2	1	5
Country (coefficients suppressed)								
1960–73	3	3	−4	−4	4	−3	−8	1
1974–84	3	1	8	8	1	3	8	3
85–present	−8	−6	−1	−1	−8	2	4	−5
R-squared	0.089	0.082	0.052	0.052	0.153	0.061	0.065	0.052

Table 7.31. Leisure at home by educational level (minutes per day)

	Men			Women		
	1960–73	1974–84	1985–	1960–73	1974–84	1985–
Eating, meals and snacks						
Mean	69			73		
Incomplete secondary	11	3	−6	9	−0	−4
Complete secondary	10	1	−13	10	−3	−11
Higher than secondary	9	−5	−12	7	0	−9
Reading, reading books, papers or magazines						
Mean	42			35		
Incomplete secondary	−7	−10	−15	−12	−5	−9
Complete secondary	4	7	−10	−1	8	−2
Higher than secondary	31	24	9	22	24	16
Chats,etc., talking, relaxing						
Mean	30			34		
Incomplete secondary	2	8	−6	−1	6	−6
Complete secondary	0	6	−10	−0	8	−5
Higher than secondary	−1	8	−12	0	8	−7
Hobbies, other at-home leisure						
Mean	16			27		
Incomplete secondary	−5	2	−1	−0	−0	−1
Complete secondary	−1	3	1	3	−0	−3
Higher than secondary	2	2	0	6	1	−1

Note: Coefficients for age, family status, employment status, and country suppressed.

Table 7.32. Personal care (longitudinal sample, minutes per day)

	Canada	Denmark	France	Netherlands	Norway	UK	USA	Hungary	Finland
Men									
Mean	523	493	567	537	540	560	532	551	535
Full time	−8	−4	−5	−11	−3	−11	−8	−5	−7
Part time	−12	5	−9	37	6	84	6	34	6
Other, non-emp.	35	45	65	36	26	43	56	73	38
Yng,no yng. kids	10	−3	−1	−2	−6	9	−0	−10	10
Child under 5	−7	−1	−1	−7	−5	−0	−2	−1	−6
Child under 15	−8	5	−8	1	3	−1	−0	−10	−6
Oldr, no yng. kids	2	0	14	9	11	−8	4	22	−1
1960–73	4	8	3		9	−5	−4	−8	3
1974–84	7		−3	0	−9	3	3	8	
85–present	−6	−8		−0		1	1		−3
R-squared	*0.024*	*0.017*	*0.034*	*0.085*	*0.014*	*0.107*	*0.028*	*0.044*	*0.030*
Women									
Mean	551	513	577	563	557	572	562	566	549
Full time	−11	−10	−17	−17	−18	−11	−12	−30	−7
Part time	−3	6	−9	−5	2	1	13	22	9
Other, non-emp.	10	10	16	6	10	9	9	38	16
Yng, no yng. kids	25	8	23	10	24	21	21	22	19
Child under 5	−18	−2	−21	−8	−12	−0	−16	−4	−9
Child under 15	−13	−4	−9	−7	−4	−5	−9	−11	−7
Oldr, no yng. kids	6	0	16	7	7	−11	10	6	−2
1960–73	2	−1	0	9		−14	−7	−16	
1974–84	0		−0	2	−1	9	6	17	−1
85–present	−1	1		−3		2	1		1
R-squared	*0.020*	*0.007*	*0.043*	*0.028*	*0.030*	*0.045*	*0.017*	*0.085*	*0.020*

Table 7.33. Personal care (cross-sectional subsample, minutes per day)

	W.Germany	Poland	Belgium	Bulgaria	Czechoslovakia	E.Germany	Yugoslavia	Italy	Australia	Israel	Sweden
Men											
Mean	566	536	547	546	540	523	551	542	548	555	514
Full time	−23	−7	−10	−7	−9	−2	−6	−4	−5	−22	−3
Part time	44	23	32	−17	98	79	49		19	−70	22
Other, non-emp.	114	107	76	74	113	−29	69	35	67	126	50
Yng, no yng. kids	−18	4	−3	−5	25	29	12	−18	13	14	12
Child under 5	−7	−8	−9	−1	−18	−13	−10	−1	−1	0	−5
Child under 15	17	0	−7	1	1	−1	−3	6	0	10	−10
Oldr, no yng. kids	0	8	21	2	4	21	8	13	−3	−9	0
R-squared	*0.111*	*0.047*	*0.079*	*0.042*	*0.062*	*0.027*	*0.034*	*0.018*	*0.043*	*0.111*	*0.014*
Women											
Mean	575	541	558	544	540	543	543	549	569	574	537
Full time	−25	−26	−23	−11	−16	−17	−29	−12	−14	−31	−1
Part time	−6	32	−2	2	−22	−4	−41		13	−25	3
Other, non-emp.	16	42	8	54	26	28	24	9	4	39	4
Yng, no yng. kids	32	34	27	20	21	48	−19	25	17	55	28
Child under 5	−30	−13	−9	10	−11	−18	−1	−11	−13	−23	−15
Child under 15	−24	−11	−14	−1	0	−6	−3	−5	−2	3	−6
Oldr, no yng. kids	21	22	14	−5	35	19	22	−4	14	−0	0
R-squared	*0.063*	*0.092*	*0.050*	*0.057*	*0.059*	*0.056*	*0.067*	*0.025*	*0.016*	*0.065*	*0.016*

Table 7.34. Personal care

	Men			Women		
Mean	539			557		
Yng, no yng. kids	6			24		
Child under 5	−5			−13		
Child under 15	−3			−8		
Oldr, no yng. kids	4			6		
Full time	7			−16		
Part time	17			−0		
Other, non-emp.	49			15		
Country (coefficient suppressed)						
	1960–73	1974–84	1985–	1960–73	1974–84	1985–
Incomplete secondary	6	6	3	0	7	6
Complete secondary	−4	4	5	−5	−3	5
Higher than secondary	−4	−8	−15	−7	−11	−11
R-squared	*0.043*			*0.040*		

nineteen of the twenty countries' means are quite closely clustered in the range 520–570 minutes per day. I am aware of no reason to suppose that Danes have different physiological needs to the rest of the developed world, so I am reduced to the speculation that there is some feature of the (nationally quite distinctive, fixed, and precoded activity category) data-collection methodology that produces this effect.

Women, in each of the twenty countries except Bulgaria, have by a margin of 10–20 minutes, more personal care time than men (this difference is somewhat smaller when we look at sleep time on its own). Employment has the major sleep-reducing effect predicted by the Szalai experiment (though with the one exception, out of the forty estimates, of East German men). The effects of the demographic variate show less cross-national regularity for men, though for women we find, with some considerable regularity, the trace of broken nights from young children. And, having controlled for the other variates, there is not much, and certainly no consistent, variation over time.

The last table of this chapter gives the whole-world summary for personal care including the period–education interaction. We might not, perhaps, have expected there to be any effect of educational attainment on personal care time. But remember the central principle of the conservation of the day that underlies all the evidence that we have been discussing. We have seen that the best-educated groups in our societies now have more

work than those with lower levels of educational attainment. Szalai's experi-
mental finding, from the rural plains of Hungary in the late 1950s, now finds a
(nearly) global confirmation in the survey evidence. The paid work time of
the best-educated has been increasing, relative to those with lower levels of
attainment, over this period, their unpaid work as well. Sleep time, Szalai told
us all those years ago, is compressible: here we see those with the higher
social positions in our sample, compressing it, by something approaching 20
minutes per day to avoid losing too much of their leisure time.

3. A whole-world summary: the virtuous triangle revisited

The appropriate way to conclude this tour around twenty countries' time-
use trends would seem to be a return to the simple single-picture summary
with which we closed Chapter 5. But the Chapter 5 version plotted each
country's track separately; given that the general conclusion to the lengthy
discussion of the relationship of the individual countries' to the whole-world
aggregate is that the aggregate picture provides a generally quite good
representation of change in at least the broad time-use categories, we can
now simplify it further.

Instead of looking at each country separately, Figure 7.5 presents the
aggregate, broken down now not just by sex, but also by our social

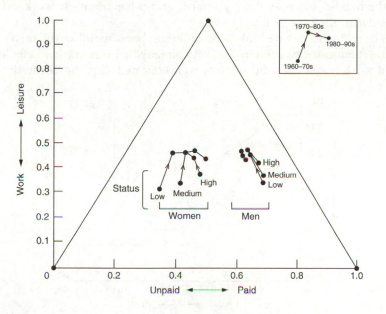

Figure 7.5. Sex and social stratification of time use in twenty countries:
33 years' change

Note: Arrows indicate historical period

stratification indicator, educational attainment. The overall pattern of change that emerges is just the same (as must indeed be the case since what we see on this chart are the great majority of the same 120,000 respondents, with the same locations in historical time—only, now grouped in a slightly different way). We see, as we saw before, the overall gender convergence, towards some point towards the central area of the triangle, that indicates an approximate three-way equality among paid work, unpaid work, and leisure/consumption time. And we also see, as we magnify the central area a little, another phenomenon, which has emerged through the discussion of this chapter. Let us take the men first (Figure 7.6: in this alternative version of part of Figure 7.5 we join up the dots in a different way, so as to show explicitly the status gradient in each year).

We see here clearly the reversal of the old status–work-time gradient. At the beginning of the period covered by our data in the 1960s, those with the highest status had the lowest total of paid and unpaid work, and hence the most leisure. Those with intermediate levels of education, and thus by hypothesis, occupying intermediate positions in the order of social stratification, had intermediate levels of work and leisure. Those lowest in the stratification ordering had the most work and the least leisure time. Over the subsequent third of a century, these positions have been literally reversed, with those with intermediate levels of education and status, still in the middle, but now the high-status group has the most work, and the low status, the least work.

The women's picture looks a bit different, because unlike the men's case, the best-educated women in the 1960s already had very substantially longer paid work hours than did the less well educated. But the domestic work

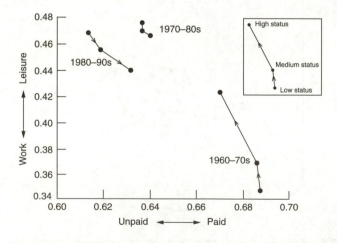

Figure 7.6. Men: a reversed status–work gradient

Note: Arrows indicate status gradient

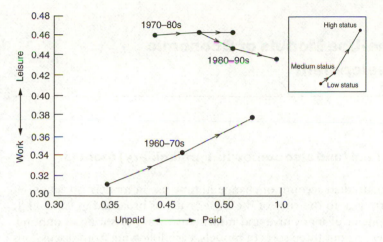

Figure 7.7. Women: a reversed status–work gradient

Note: Arrows indicate status gradient

time of this high-status group, in that era, was very substantially shorter than that of the other groups (presumably they were able to afford to pay for substantial amounts of domestic help), so that, as we see from the figure, they had much the most leisure time, and the total of work time was larger, progressively, down the status ordering. In the latest period we see, just as for men, that the best-educated still have the largest proportion of paid work time of the three education–status groups (i.e. the last data point is placed well to the right of those of the other two groups). But their domestic work time has not fallen nearly so far or so fast as that of the other two groups. As a result, the proportion of their waking time devoted to leisure is now somewhat lower than those of the other groups. In short, another picture, but just the same story: the work–leisure balance among the social groups has been reversed.

Or perhaps, since for both men and women the totals among the three groups are much more similar towards the end of the century than they were in the middle, we might think of what has happened as convergence, with perhaps a little overcompensation at the end. So there, in Figures 5.15 and 7.5, we have it. Three convergences in time-use structure: of nation, of gender, and of status group.

8 Time-Use Models of Economic Development

1. Three final (and also somewhat preliminary) models

Having produced an account of change in time use in modern societies, let us now turn back to the core of the issue that was broached in Chapter 1: the development of innovative and informative ways of social accounting. This chapter sets out three sorts of models, each following from discussions earlier in this book. Though the three models in a way take the place of a conclusion to the foregoing discussions, I would suggest that they also constitute appropriate starting points for further work in this area.

The first of them is the full version of the 'chains-of-provision'-based social account that was introduced in a preliminary fashion in Chapter 2. This shows, albeit in the rather flat, undifferentiated, and aggregated manner of the National Accounts, how the society devotes its time to the satisfaction of different sorts of wants, and what sorts of activities are involved in this. I do not have the means or the expertise to make estimates of this sort in a serious way across the full range of different countries that have occupied our attention so far. So for the first time, in this penultimate—and yet in a different sense, most preliminary—chapter, I retreat to a narrowly British empirical base. I will, however, be able to maintain the longitudinal perspective, considering change in the balance of satisfaction of wants, and in the chains of provision that satisfy them, in Britain from the beginning of the 1960s to the middle of the 1980s.

The second of these models is a pure abstraction. It continues the line of theory, based on the Becker micro model of the individual's time balance, and extended in Chapter 4 to produce a model of the macro balance across the time use of different social groups producing different commodities. What follows here is a further development of that formal statement, so as to allow a discussion of the *welfare benefits* that may be considered to accrue from social change.

And the third takes this abstraction and makes it more concrete in the form of a static macrosimulation, of the most basic kind, of the time-use balance among two social groups, each of which specializes in the market production of a single commodity. I use it to illustrate in a concrete form the propositions about the connections between time use, welfare, and social structure that emerge from this line of theory. And I return once more to my preoccupation with the consequences of time-use regimes for social welfare: what emerges is a lemma to the simple theorem set out in Chapter 4: given that the consumption time and the production time of the various groups in a society are inextricably interconnected, then to be rich a society must specialize in high-value, high-skill paid work.

2. An empirical estimation

Let us now go back to the discussion of Arcadia in Chapter 2, but taking instead the UK data as a model. Table 8.1 gives an aggregated view of change in British time allocation between 1961 and 1985 (including all adults above the age of 17, but excluding children). The rows for each year represent various categories of want, while the columns represent the different sorts of work and consumption time related to each of these. The first seven columns for each year sum to 1,440 minutes, the total population minutes per day divided by the population size, the 'great day' of the society.

These rather simple tables summarize a very extensive and intricate sequence of computations. The first two columns are estimated directly from national time-budget samples. For each year these columns include around 1,200 minutes of the great day of 1,440 minutes, which constitute the society's consumption time. These are the activities carried out by people on their own behalf, or for their own households, and we can infer pretty directly from what we read in their diaries why they are doing these things: we know, in a general way, what sorts of *wants* these activities relate to. In this tabulation I have taken an intermediate level of specificity, adopting just seven categories of want (sleep, shelter, food, home-based services, travel and shopping services, out-of-home leisure, medical and educational services; the original calculations were however based on a twenty-category classification). We know, directly from the time-diary data, how much time is devoted to each of these in the way of consumption and unpaid work. (Notice that there are two further categories here, neither of which involves any direct consumption or unpaid work time from the domestic population, but which nevertheless absorb some of the society's paid work time: 'background services', those services such as police, armed forces, and civil administration, which underlie daily life in an indirect way—corresponding to Adam Smith's category of 'unproductive' state services, 'the fleets and the magistracy', and also exports which go to meet the wants of people outside the society.)

So far, so simple. The major problem is connecting the appropriate proportions of the remaining four hours, which represents the society's paid work time, to the various categories of want. How much paid work goes to satisfy each category of want? Without going through the very

Table 8.1. Change in the distribution of time, 1961–1984 (minutes per day)

	Time outside employment		Time in employment					All paid work in UK	Foreign work from imports
	Leisure consumption	Unpaid work	Managers, scientists, etc.	Other producer services	Consumer service professions	Other consumer services	Other workers		
1961									
Sleep	562								
Shelter, Household ops.	0	293	8	13	1	4	36	61	14
Food, etc.	97	68	5	9	0	1	24	40	10
Home leisure, Childcare	268	12	2	3	0	1	10	16	4
Shopping, Travel	0	41	1	2	1	2	7	13	1
Out-of-home leisure	45	0	1	1	0	6	3	11	2
Medicine, Education	16	0	2	3	10	5	7	27	2
Background services	0	0	4	7	1	4	14	29	1
Exports	0	0	4	7	0	2	25	38	6
All time use	989	215	27	45	14	24	126	236	40
Total minutes								1,440	
1983/4									
Sleep	572								
Shelter, Household ops.	0	73	8	12	2	3	21	46	16
Food, etc.	75	63	3	4	0	1	8	16	6
Home leisure, Childcare	284	17	2	3	1	1	5	12	3
Shopping, Travel	0	70	1	2	0	1	4	9	2
Out-of-home leisure	70	0	1	2	0	6	2	11	2
Medicine, Education	22	0	3	5	15	8	5	36	3

Background services	0	0	5	7	1	4	7	24	1
Exports	0	0	7	9	1	3	21	39	10
All time use	1,023	224	30	43	20	27	73	193	43
Total minutes								1,440	
Change 1961–83/4									
Shelter, Household ops.	0	−21	1	−1	0	0	−15	−15	2
Food, Sleep, etc.	−12	−5	−2	−4	0	−1	−17	−24	−4
Home leisure, Childcare	15	5	0	−1	0	0	−5	−5	0
Shopping, Travel	0	29	0	0	0	−1	−3	−4	0
Out-of-home leisure	24	0	0	0	4	1	−1	0	0
Medicine, Education	6	0	2	2	0	2	−2	8	1
Background services	0	0	1	0	0	1	−7	−5	0
Exports	0	0	3	2	0	1	−5	1	4
All time use	34	9	4	−2	6	3	−53	−43	3

intricate details of all these, it may still be helpful to go through, in a general way, the sequence of calculations necessary to answer this question

We may start by associating each category of want with categories of final output from the economy. The total social final product is the sum of all the goods and services purchased by final consumers, plus all final services provided without charge by government or charities. Each of these commodities has a money value; and most of these categories may be straightforwardly associated with one or other category of want. We can do this on an *a priori* basis (i.e. simply assume that all expenditure on housing relates to the satisfaction of a want for shelter, on cinema tickets to a want for out-of-home entertainment, and so on). Or in principle we might base these attributions on some sort of survey evidence, in which case we might develop an attribution matrix, which would tell us what proportion of each final commodity was connected with each category of want. To keep things simple, I have adopted the *a priori* approach.

Conventionally, investment goods, the construction of plant, and changes in stocks are included in final output, while semi-finished products are treated as intermediate flows. This difference in treatment makes perfectly good sense where the accounts are intended to cover a year or less and accounts for successive years are to be used to investigate short-term variations in economic activity. But these time accounts are intended to investigate relatively long-term phenomena; so in what follows investment activities are treated as intermediate stages of production, and are accounted for in the same way as other intermediate flows of production between industries.

The result of the process of attribution is that *all* the current output of the society can be distributed among the seven categories of domestic wants plus the two residual categories. And we can now use an input–output matrix (slightly modified to distribute investment goods across the sectors of the economy as intermediate products) to find the industrial origin of the value added associated with each category of want (Table 8.1 is based on UK input–output matrices for 1965 and 1983). And then we can multiply the value of each industry's input to each category of want by a labour productivity vector to calculate the total paid labour input. We then multiply the result by industry/occupation coefficients to derive the occupational levels of the paid labour inputs to each want. And finally, the input–output matrix tells the value of the imports embodied in each final commodity, so we can make some sensible estimate of imported labour time associated with each class of want by multiplying by suitable labour productivity coefficients.

This is a very involved and laborious social accounting procedure, which involves in its various steps some rather arbitrary assumptions about the constancy of coefficients across industries (though these assumptions are no more strenuous than those made in conventional input–output analysis). It produces a rather simple table of results. Consider the 1961 table. The first row has just one entry, 562 minutes of sleep (in which following the practice in the rest of the book I have also included personal toilet). I take sleep as an isolated activity without input of any other time—though it could as well be put together with other household activities. The next row refers to shelter and routine household operations; this has no associated consumption time (though it could well be associated with sleep, food, and at-home leisure); it registers 93 minutes of unpaid work (including all non-food-related house-work and household maintenance), 61 minutes of paid work of which just under half comes from various sorts of service workers (the 61 minutes covers all inputs such as construction, manufacturing of household materi-als, provision of purchased household maintenance services, and other household infrastructural and municipal services), and 14 minutes of imported labour (mostly embodied in domestic equipment). The food row contains 97 minutes per day of eating time, 68 minutes of cooking and similar unpaid work, 40 minutes of paid work time (mostly agricultural or food manufacturing), and so on. The total time embodied in exports approximately balances that embodied in imports (though this balance is very dependent on rather arbitrary assumptions about foreign labour productivity rates). Overall we have just under 4 hours of paid work across the adult population, around $9\frac{1}{2}$ hours of sleep and personal care, around 4 hours of unpaid work, and $6\frac{1}{2}$ hours of leisure or consumption time.

We can summarize the changes shown in Table 8.1. in the graphical form introduced in Chapter 2. Figure 8.1 is a more sophisticated version of Figure 2.3. As in that figure, the horizontal division of the box represents the division of the society's day among activities which go to satisfy different categories of want: so the width of the first column represents the propor-tion of the day spent asleep, that of the second column, the proportion of the day constituted by the sum of all the work and consumption activities associated with basic wants, and so on. The height of each column is divided in proportion to the different sorts of activity that meet that want (in 1984 for example 20 per cent of the time related to food and shelter was consumption—mostly eating). The major difference between Figure 8.1 and the simplified Figure 2.3 is in the area above 100 per cent. The box represents the great day of the society. But some of the wants of the society are met in part through work activities of people outside the society: in the figure, imports are expressed in terms of their work-time equivalents (which, for simplicity, we have calculated using UK labour productivity rates). And to balance imported work time a society must export work time; the final column registers (in part) time devoted by the society to production for wants of members of other societies (and in part the 'back-ground services' that cannot be sensibly connected to any specific want in particular).

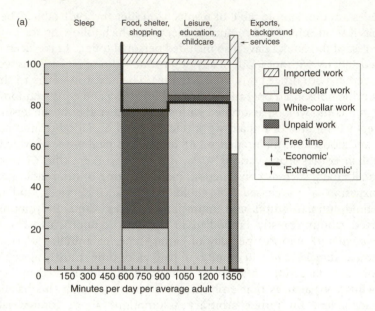

Figure 8.1a. The distribution of activities, UK 1961

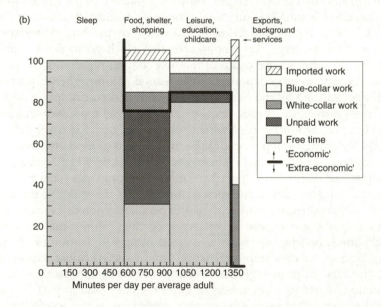

Figure 8.1b. The distribution of activities, UK 1983–4

We can see all the expected features of economic development by comparing the earlier and the later pictures. We see (i) the shift from basic to more sophisticated wants, in the reducing width of the second column and the growth of the third; we see (ii) the declining proportion of time devoted to the money economy, in the upwards shift of the heavy black line; we see perhaps some growth of unpaid work as a proportion of all work (though nothing in what we have found in this book suggests that this a necessary feature of development); and (iii), in the changing ratios between the areas associated with the two categories of paid labour, we see what certainly is to be considered a necessary feature of development, the growth of high-skill relative to low-skill paid labour.

We should also note the correspondence between this account and the conventional National Accounts statistics. The top right-hand side of the picture, everything above the heavy black line that marks the boundary between the 'economic' and the 'extra-economic' (which is indeed the 'production boundary' of the System of National Accounts) is as we have seen apportioned on the basis of the National Accounts statistics, and it will be possible to reconstruct the elements of the money-based National Accounts from the time-use statistics by multiplying by appropriate productivity coefficients. The time accounts simply set the National Accounts within their wider social context.

3. Welfare and change in time allocation: the UK case

In the next section we will think formally about deriving estimates of well-being from time-use evidence. But, first, let us concentrate for a moment on what Table 8.1 tells us about the changing level of welfare in the society. It gives us part but not all of the information we need. We know how much time is devoted to the satisfaction of each category of want. But we do not know how well each category of want is satisfied, and we certainly cannot make any direct inference about this from the time allocations themselves.

We need some quite independent indicator of the state of satisfaction of the various categories of want. One approach for this would be to develop some systems of relatively objective indicators. We might, for example, try to count nutritional intakes (perhaps using data from the National Food Survey) as a basis for estimating levels of provision for nutritional wants. Alternatively we might adopt some rather more subjective approach. Here we might follow the suggestion of counting 'process benefits' (Juster and Stafford 1985), which weight time spent in the consumption activities related to particular wants by the degree of expressed satisfaction with the quality of this consumption time. (The original suggestion involves multiplying the relevant consumption time by the results of an enjoyment scale derived from a questionnaire administered to a sample of time-budget respondents, but perhaps it would in principle be better to use satisfaction data collected within the time-diary format in the manner outlined by Sullivan 1997.)

For the moment however, we must be content with a rather lower standard of evidence. At the level of aggregation of Table 8.1, we can make some tentative progress by assumption. Let us consider those rows towards the bottom of the table which summarize change in time use over the period. We can find in this data evidence suggestive of three rather different processes of change.

Consider the first two rows of the change section, which might be considered to reflect something close to what I previously termed 'basic wants'. We see here, in working-age Britain's great day, a reduction of just under 40 minutes of paid work, a reduction of 26 minutes of unpaid work, and a reduction of 12 minutes over the period from 1961 to 1984. We do not have any direct evidence here about how well these basic wants are satisfied. But would not any impartial observer of Britain over this quarter-century conclude that at the very least, standards of provision of food and shelter have not actually fallen over this period for any substantial part of the society? The inference from the reduction in both sorts of work time must be that technical change has increased the efficiency of this area of provision: less time is needed to provide for a basic want, freeing time to be devoted to the satisfaction of other sorts of want. The number of people involved in providing for basic wants declined dramatically—this is not shown directly in Table 8.1—from about 4 million workers to about 2.5 million from the early 1960s to the mid-1980s.

This is a rather optimistic view of the effect of technical change. A less positive view emerges from the second example. We have listed retail services separately (though they could alternatively have been associated with the two basic categories): we see that the amount of paid work associated with this category has fallen somewhat, but the unpaid work associated with it (shopping, driving) has risen dramatically, from just over 40 minutes per day in 1961, to 70 minutes per day in 1984. Certainly the volume of retail sales must have increased dramatically over this period; presumably the fact that paid work has nevertheless declined while unpaid has increased, has to be interpreted as a proportional substitution of what were previously unpaid activities for paid (i.e. an older system which involved transport of goods for sale to fully serviced small neighbourhood shops is replaced by a newer system of (largely private) transport of people to large, relatively distant self-service stores).

The welfare implications of this depend on the state of satisfaction with retail services. But it is quite possible that a subjective indicator might reveal people to be less satisfied with the present arrangements than with the previous. And if the very considerable increase in unpaid work time—and in the overall proportion of the day—devoted to shopping and domestic travel is not associated with a proportional well-being, then we will have an example of a Hirsch-type economic development process, in which growth of money income is associated with an increase in congestion which reduces welfare. (Or, an alternative interpretation from the same evidence and assumptions: a process in which producers of retail services are able to externalise their costs, passing costs previously borne by retailers in the form of transport from warehouses to retail outlets, and the wages of retail staff, to consumers, in the form of time and expense devoted to travel to supermarkets, followed by time spent selecting goods and queuing at checkouts.)

The third example comes from the rows concerned with luxury services (out-of-home leisure, education, and medicine). Here both consumption time and paid work time have increased: 30 minutes more consumption time, 8 extra minutes, in the great day, of paid work time. Once again, we have no evidence on satisfaction; let us however suppose for the sake of the argument that satisfaction has risen in line with increase in the paid work time. The net extra uncommitted time in the society's great day that comes from the two previous processes is devoted in part to increase the level of satisfaction of this luxury category, and in part to change the manner in which it is taken (i.e. using more time for a given level of consumption). But the overall pattern in Britain over this period seems to have been at least the maintenance of basic provisions with a smaller time input, with the extra uncommitted time devoted in part at least to raising the level of luxury provisions: it would seem to have gained more leisure, and more leisurely leisure.

4. Time use and welfare: the nature of social improvement

This point may be made more formally and generally by taking the theoretical argument of Chapter 4 just one stage further. The model discussed there considered different categories of time as inputs to processes of satisfaction of various categories of want or need, but not the extent to which these wants or needs were *satisfied*. We can now slightly extend the theoretical argument (returning to something similar to, though not ident-ical with, Becker's original formulation of the micro-theory) so as to allow this.

We have said that each particular category of want is satisfied by combin-ing paid work supplied by others with the individual's own unpaid work and consumption. Now, let us think of these two different sorts of time as inputs into the particular processes of provision which serve particular wants. Let us consider these two sorts of time for any individual as being combined by the individual to produce a final state or level of provision for the particular want. These final states are the Z categories in Figure 8.2.

Consider a coefficient Z_i which represents the individual's level of provision for a category of want or need i. The level of provision is determined by the work of other people embodied in the goods used $[T'_i]$ and the individual's own unpaid work or consumption time $[T_i]$.

That is: $\qquad Z_i = f\left(T'_i, T_i\right)$

if we say $\qquad T_i = t_i Z_i$

and $\qquad T'_i = r_i Z_i$

then [with m categories of Z_i] we can write a more general version of equation (3) in Fig 4.4 as:

$$\sum_{i=1}^{m} \left(\frac{w_i}{w} r_i + t_i\right) Z_i = T \qquad (5)$$

The coefficients w, w_i, r_i, t_i, and T are constants at any point in time. So if some Z_a increases, some other Z_b must decrease. But if r_i or t_i decrease over time [technical change], all Z_i could increase. So technical change can lead to Pareto improvements at the level of the individual. Similarly, for the society as a whole:

$$\sum_{j=1}^{n} \sum_{i=1}^{m} \left(\frac{w_i}{w_j} r_i + t_i\right) Z_{(6)} = T_n \qquad (6)$$

where there are n individuals j. Here again, technical change could allow everyone to either maintain or increase their levels of provision of each Z_{ij}. But we are also subject to the macro-constraint that the demand for the labour of a particular class deriving from the society's demand for its product, must equal the supply of labour determined by the consumption pattern of that class:

$$\sum_{k=1}^{p} \sum_{i=1}^{m} \left(\frac{w_i}{w_k} r_i Z_{ik}\right) = \sum_{j=1}^{n} \left(r_i Z_{(7)}\right) \qquad (7)$$

where there are p individuals k involved in the production of commodities used in provision of Z_i.

So the size of the improvement in welfare from an increase in the efficiency of provision for a particular category of want, depends on the consumption patterns of the society as a whole.

Figure 8.2. Time use and welfare

These may be defined either in a subjective or in an objective manner. That is: they may be considered in terms of how each individual evaluates his or her current state of nutrition, domestic comfort, recreational activities, or whatever; or they may be considered in terms of some appropriately weighted count of an individual's nutritional intakes, or use of domestic or leisure facilities; or indeed they may consist of some combination of these two approaches.

The problem here is obvious, but it is exactly the same problem which is routinely faced by economists whenever they attempt to estimate the level of production of any complex good by a branch of the money economy. Consider a motor car. We think loosely of a car as a particular category that can be counted and compared across time. But 'a good is not a good', it is a complex bundle of interlinked potential or latent services. The car now is safer, quieter, better air-conditioned or whatever, than previously. So, if the same number of workers produce the same number of cars now as previously, is their productivity constant or increasing? Economists (at best) deal with this problem by defining a car, not as a car but as a given bundle of latent services, so that the change in labour productivity is evaluated in terms of the combined change in number and quantity.

Becker, who wishes to introduce a separate utility function, describes his Z categories as simple counts of some ultimate commodity. But this serves to obscure the fact that they consist of bundles of actual services provided to given levels of quality—and thus the question of whether these levels of quality can be considered or assessed objectively is, to say the least, open. For our sociological purposes at least, it may be more helpful to think of the Z categories as representing simultaneously both levels of provision for the categories of want, and also states of satisfaction with the levels of provision for particular wants. And in principle at least, the problems of assessing these states are equivalent to those faced by economists in computing the material outputs of industries.

Now just as we have fixed coefficients relating work and other time to quantities of commodities purchased from the money economy, so we have equivalent coefficients relating the different sorts of time to the levels of provision or satisfaction. For any category of want, we will have a coefficient relating a unit change in the level of provision to paid work time, and a second coefficient relating this to unpaid work/consumption time respectively the coefficients r and t in Figure 8.1: note that the meaning of r is now somewhat changed from that in Figure 8.2. We have, for each individual, a set of what are in effect little production processes, chains of provision, each being the means through which a particular category of want is satisfied. Each of these processes involves, in principle, two components: (i) the individual's consumption time, which is the product of the level of provision for the particular want, the Z-score, and the consumption coefficient (t) relating consumption time to these levels; and (ii) the individual's paid work time, which may be computed as the product of the Z-score, the paid work coefficient (r), and the ratio of the individual's wage to the wages of the producers of the purchased commodities used in the satisfaction of that want. Each individual's waking day is the sum of these components for all the categories of want. [This gives us Equation 5, which is a more powerful and general version of Equation 3.]

And this more general version of the micro-accounting constraint allows us to say something quite unequivocal about the individual's welfare. At any point in time, the sets of consumption and paid work coefficients (t and r) for the various categories of want are constants. So, if the individual shifts his or her time from one category or chain of provision to another, the level

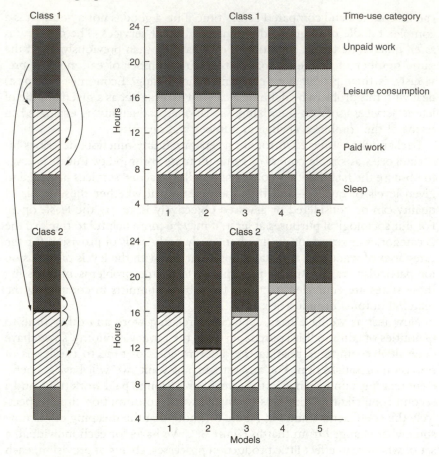

Figure 8.3. A two-class, two-good model

of provision for one category of want must fall, and the level of provision for the other must rise. If the waking day is distributed between activities as we have described, and the t and r coefficients remain the same, there is no way that the level of provision for one sort of want can increase without a corresponding decrease in the level of provision for another.

Economists will at this point be content to argue that, nevertheless, the individual may be able to improve his or her welfare by shifting time at the margin on the assumption that additional satisfaction of some categories of want may be preferred to others (i.e. differences in marginal rates of satisfaction). But this view leads to some problems from a sociological perspective. Can individuals really and in general distinguish the extent of satisfaction deriving from small transfers of time between activities? Do individuals really have fixed utility functions against which their actual activity patterns may be adjusted? (A strong argument might be developed, for example, to the effect that utilities, to the extent that they are detectable at all, may be as well considered a consequence of actual behaviour as a cause of it.) In welfare calculations, there is no equivalent to the 'as if' argument: the logic of the 'marginalist' view of welfare depends on the assumption that people do actually make choices at the margin, and based on utility functions.

While sociologists might reject the marginalist view of individual welfare, we may be happier with the rather weaker assumption that derives from Pareto. A 'Pareto improvement', at the level of the individual, is the circumstance in which the individual maintains the level of provision for all the categories of want and increases the level of provision for at least one of them. Now the microtime accounting constraint tells us that, at any given historical *instant*, Pareto improvements in welfare at the level of the individual are impossible.

But over time, the coefficients of the microconstraint may change. Labour (and capital) productivity in the money economy may increase, with the consequence that particular commodities embody less labour than previously, so that the 'paid work coefficient' (r) is reduced. And the effectiveness of the goods and services used in households might increase, so that less unpaid work is necessary to reach a given level of provision for a category of want, or the quality of purchased services might rise so that a given period of time devoted to a particular category of consumption gives rise to a higher level of provision than it did previously; in either case the consumption coefficient (t) is reduced. If some of the paid work and consumption coefficients do reduce, then clearly it is possible that some of the Z-scores increase without concomitant reductions in others. In short, our model shows that technical change over a historical period (as reflected in the reduction of the r and t coefficients) may result in Pareto improvements in welfare at the level of the individual.

And as for individuals, so for societies. All the individuals in a society must individually face the microtime accounting constraint. But at the level of the society, we are concerned, not just with the balance between different categories of want, but also with the balance between people. A Pareto improvement at the level of the society makes some individual better off without reducing the welfare of any other individual. While, as we have seen, the fixity of the paid work and consumption coefficients at a given historical juncture means that there can be no Pareto improvement at the level of the individual; nevertheless, at the societal level relative (effective, 'take home') wage rates might in principle be changed (e.g. by changing tax rates). As a result, some individual might achieve a Pareto improvement (in the sense of increasing some Z-score without decreasing any other Z-score). But increasing one individual's relative wage must mean decreasing the relative wages of others. So some other individual or individuals must experience a loss of Z-score as a result of the changed relative wages. We conclude therefore that at any given historical juncture, Pareto improvements are also impossible at the societal level. [We can show this formally by manipulating Equation 6.]

Over historical time, however, once we allow technical change in the form of a decrease in the paid work and consumption coefficients, Pareto improvements at the societal level are in principle possible. Technical change means that, for example, scores for some particular Z categories could be maintained for all the members of a society, with less input of time, so freeing time which could be devoted to increasing the levels of provision for some other Z categories. This societal-level Pareto improvement would be manifested as a historical change in the society's overall allocation time between the various production and consumption activities involved in the various Z categories—which is indeed what we have seen in the comparison of the two parts of Figure 8.1.

The scale of the possible improvement resulting from a change in the coefficients is determined by an equivalent to the macrotime constraint that we have previously discussed. The paid work from a particular occupational class goes to provide for some particular category of Z. The paid work time of any occupation/class is a function of all the other classes' desire for the category of Z contributed to by that class's paid work (Equation 7). So, if for example, that particular category of want is satiated at a particular point in history (i.e. the other classes have reached a sufficient level of provision for that category of want), and the paid work coefficient for that particular category subsequently reduces, then, while there may still be some societal Pareto improvement, the improvement will be smaller than would have been the case if that want had not been satiated.

5. Technological innovation and change in a society's time budget: a two-class, two-good demonstration.

We can now demonstrate in a rather general way how a society's time budget may be expected to change over historical time, and in particular why there should be change in the relative sizes of the 'production classes'. The demonstration makes a number of rather strong formal assumptions. These should be interpreted as exaggerations of real tendencies; it should be clear to readers that substituting weaker but more realistic assumptions would leave the main lines of the argument unchanged. What follows should not be interpreted as any sort of historical account, but rather as an exploration of the implications of the theorems outlined previously.

For this demonstration, we can use a simple two-class, two-good version of the model. With two classes, we have just eight categories of time use (i.e., for each class, paid work, consumption or unpaid work time for the two goods, and sleep). Taking sleep as given, we have at any given state of production and consumption technologies (i.e. given r and t for each good) just one unknown. Consider Figure 8.3; suppose the two goods relate respectively to the satisfaction of basic wants (good 2) and luxury wants (good 1). Let us call the consumption or unpaid work time related to good 2 simply unpaid work time and that related to good 1 leisure or consumption time. For the purpose of the following demonstration we shall take class 1's unpaid work time as the unknown variable; we can see that, from our previous arguments, any given value of this will serve to determine class 1's consumption time and its paid work time, and also all the categories of class 2's time.

Model 1 in Table 8.2 provides a set of coefficients for the two-good, two-class model. (The equations defining the relationship among these

Table 8.2.

Model:		1	2	3	4	5
Wage ratio 1:2		5.00	1.67	1.67	1.67	1.67
Hours sleep/day		7.50	7.50	7.50	7.50	7.50
Indir. time/unit cons:	good 1	1.00	1.00	1.00	1.00	1.00
	good 2	1.00	0.33	0.33	0.33	0.33
Direct time/unit cons:	good 1	0.25	0.25	0.25	0.25	1.00
	good 2	1.00	1.00	1.00	0.60	0.60
Hourly wage rate:	class 1	5.00	5.00	5.00	5.00	5.00
	class 2	1.00	3.00	3.00	3.00	3.00
Pop. distribution (%):	class 1	10	10	67	76	69
	class 2	90	90	33	24	31
Welfare, class 1:	good 1 (Z11)	5.71	5.71	5.71	8.21	5.13
	good 2 (Z12)	7.80	7.80	7.80	7.80	7.80
Welfare, class 2:	good 1 (Z12)	0.17	0.17	3.19	4.82	3.46
	good 2 (Z22)	7.80	12.13	7.80	7.80	7.80
Time use, class 1:						
Sleep		7.50	7.50	7.50	7.50	7.50
Paid work		7.27	7.27	7.27	9.77	6.69
Leisure consumption	(good 1)	1.43	1.43	1.43	2.05	5.13
Unpaid work	(good 2)	7.80	7.80	7.80	4.68	4.68
Time use, class 2:						
Sleep		7.50	7.50	7.50	7.50	7.50
Paid work		8.66	4.33	7.91	10.62	8.36
Leisure consumption	(good 1)	0.04	0.04	0.80	1.20	3.46
Unpaid work	(good 2)	7.80	12.13	7.80	4.68	4.68
Income per capita:	class 1	36.4	36.4	36.3	48.8	33.4
	class 2	8.7	13.0	23.7	31.9	25.1
	both	11.4	15.3	32.2	44.7	30.9

coefficients are given in Appendix 2.) Given 10 per cent of the population in class 1 and 90 per cent in class 2, given a 5 : 1 hourly wage ratio between the classes, given the r and t coefficients as set out in the table, then once we know that members of class 1 devote 7.8 hours per day to unpaid work (which since $t2=1$, corresponds to a Z-score of 7.8) all the other categories of time use for the two classes are determined as we see in the lower half of model 1 column 1, and in the left-most pair of histograms in Figure 8.3. And since we know the paid work time and the wage rates, we can also calculate the class and societal per capita money incomes. Model 1 is not of course the only possible social time budget. But the range of possible social time allocations is quite strongly constrained by the principles outlined previously together with the particular historical wage, population, and technological coefficients.

Now, let us further constrain the system by saying (i) that consumption of the basic good is subject to saturation and (ii) that individuals seek to satisfy basic wants before luxury wants (i.e. good 2 is an 'inferior' good). Let us say that at this juncture, 7.8 hours of unpaid work is sufficient to satisfy all basic needs (i.e. a Z-score of 7.8 represents the satiation of basic wants). Now the social time budget is completely determined. At this particular juncture both classes are just able to satisfy their basic wants; class 1 has a little time left over to devote to luxury consumption, class 2 has virtually none.

We can now consider the effect of technological change. Model 2 has just one difference compared to 1. Paid work in production of the basic good is three times more productive (i.e. $r2$ is reduced from 1 to 0.333). Class 2, the producers of the basic good, can now produce three times as much of the basic good in an hour of paid work. But class 1 do not want to consume any more of the basic good.

The precise effect of the change in the efficiency of production of the inferior good depends on the particular assumption we make about the relationship between productivity and the wage rate. We have chosen to assume that wage rates rise in proportion to the increase in productivity (i.e. to the reciprocal of r). (This assumption corresponds to the long-term spirit of the model: it may be interpreted as meaning that there is some combination of institutional mechanisms—monopolies, organized labour—for managing wages and prices, but since its purpose is simply to explore other aspects of the model we shall not seek to justify it further.)

Hourly wage rates for class 2 therefore also rise threefold, with the consequence that the consumption and time-allocation pattern for class 1 are unchanged from model 1 (since the basic goods have exactly the same cost in terms of paid work time). The time-use and consumption patterns for class 2 must now change quite considerably. They cannot consume any more luxuries, since members of class 1 are satisfied with their previous level of provision of basic goods, and hence do not vary their supply of paid labour. Yet production of each unit of basic goods takes less time than previously. The only possible change within the terms of the model is an unsought increase in class 2's consumption of the basic good, with a consequent reduction in paid work time. The overall per capita income for class 2 rises somewhat, as a consequence of the increased hourly wage.

We might be tempted to place some tendentious historical interpretation on this result (for example: that the reduction of overall work hours plus the unsought consumption of inferior commodities represents some sort of technological unemployment). But the point we intend is rather more general and simple. The efficiency of production of the basic good has increased very substantially, but the size of the class producing the basic good remained unchanged, with the consequence that (since an unsought increase of time devoted to the consumption of an inferior good gives no advantage) the technological advance in the system of production has brought no Pareto improvement.

But suppose the relative sizes of the classes changed over the same period in which the productivity of class 2 increased. The only difference between model 2 and model 3 is that, in addition to the increase in the productivity of class 2's paid work, the size of class 2 has been reduced relative to that of class 1. We have adjusted the relative sizes precisely to the point at which both classes are able to satisfy their basic wants, but class 2 is not forced into unsought consumption of the basic commodity: the population ratio between class 1 and class 2 thus changes from 10:90 to 67:33. Class 1's time-use or consumption pattern is still unchanged. But it is much larger. And class 2 now has no unsought inferior consumption, has slightly shorter hours of work than it had in model 1, though these are still slightly longer than those of class 1; and it can now consume some luxuries (since the larger size of class 1 means an increase in the supply of the labour embodied in luxuries).

National income rises substantially from model 1 to model 3. And, most important for our argument, we can see a double Pareto improvement: there are more people in the high-consumption class 1 (so a larger proportion of the population both satisfy their basic wants and have a relatively high consumption of luxuries); and those remaining in class 2 also satisfy their basic wants and have a higher consumption of luxuries than in model 1.

In short, in the restricted circumstances we have defined, growth in productivity of the class involved in the production for basic needs, only translates into improvement for the society if the relative size of the classes also changes. These circumstances are perhaps over-restricted, particularly in relation to the strongly inferior nature of the basic commodity. But we can relax this restriction somewhat. As long as the basic good is relatively inferior, as long as we assume that basic wants are relatively satiable as compared with luxuries which are not (or the rate of decline of marginal utility derived from basic goods is faster than that for luxuries), we can conclude that technological advance in the production of basic commodities gives benefits in part at least by allowing the reduction in the size of the class involved in basic production.

And there is more to technological change than just its impact on the efficiency of paid work. Technology also influences the efficiency of provision for wants through unpaid work. New domestic equipment, for example, or new materials, new sorts of material infrastructure, may reduce the amount of unpaid work necessary for a given level of provision for some sort of want. We can illustrate this directly. Model 4 has similar coefficients to model 3, with one major exception: the coefficient relating unpaid work to the satisfaction of wants ($t2$) is reduced from 1 to 0.6 (i.e. an increase in the productivity of unpaid work); the population proportions are again adjusted so as precisely to satisfy both classes' basic wants. Here we find a further double Pareto improvement: class 1 grows from two-thirds to more than three-quarters of the population; and both classes have more luxury consumption than in model 3.

Per capita incomes also show a striking increase even over model 3. This reflects the longer hours of paid work for both classes, even though wages are unchanged from model 3. But this does not mean that extra luxuries are being purchased at the price of more work. The model 4 effect relies on new technologies increasing the efficiency of unpaid work. Unpaid work is also work, and it has substantially reduced: add the paid and unpaid work together and we find that between model 3 and model 4, class 1's overall work total has reduced from 15.07 hours to 14.45 hours, and class 2's work total reduces from 15.71 hours to 15.30 hours. So improvements in the efficiency of domestic technology may in principle be just as important a part in improving welfare as innovations in what we conventionally think of as production technology.

Finally, we should consider the possibility of what might be termed 'consumption efficiency': changes in time-intensiveness of consumption activities. It has sometimes been assumed (by marginalist time-use theorists, e.g. Linder 1970) that the consumption time per unit of final satisfaction must reduce in step with growth in labour productivity. But the theoretical arguments for this assumption seem rather thin (and the empirical time-use results—showing for example a historical increase in time devoted to such activities as relaxing and casual conversation—certainly do not support it). Model 5 shows the effect of making the contrary assumption, that consumption time per unit of luxury-type satisfaction increases (i.e. $t1$ increases from 0.25 to 1.00). For class 1, hours of paid work and money incomes are slightly lower than in model 3, but for class 2 money incomes, and the level of provision of luxuries, is rather higher than in model 3.

Thus we see various mechanisms through which technical change may improve welfare. We see, in the course of this demonstration, that reduction in the amount of paid work required for a given welfare outcome can lead to improvement; we also see a similar effect from a reduction in the amount of unpaid work required for a given welfare outcome. And we show that, contrary to the pessimistic prognostications of such writers as Linder and Hirsch, intensification of consumption (i.e. the requirement to use an increasing quantity of goods per minute of consumption) is not a necessary concomitant of the development process.

But perhaps the most important part of this demonstration concerns the question of the relative sizes of the classes. In the course of this book we have repeatedly asserted (what may to many readers be self-evident) that progress consists in large part of the growth in the size of the group of high-value-added producers relative to low-value-added producers. Here we demonstrate the proposition directly by showing that, where the low-value-added group is producing relatively inferior commodities (whose consumption may be progressively saturated), technical change on its own produces relatively small welfare benefits (and also some costs, seen in our model by what might be interpreted as a growth in unemployment). By contrast, where the very same sort of technical change is linked to changes in the class or occupational composition of the society, there may be very much more substantial welfare gains, and no growth in unemployment.

The crux is the linkage of the consumption and the production characteristics of the classes. However efficiently the inferior goods are produced, their consumption will not grow substantially. And, without change in the occupational or class structure, consumption of the high-value-added commodities cannot increase because low-value-added producers cannot afford to purchase them. It is only where there is a growing proportion of the society with both high-value-added production skills and high-value-added consumption habits that we really see the benefits of technical change.

9   Humane Modernization

1. Time use and 'progress'

Jobs are created by leisure. Some jobs involve the production of goods which enable the reduction of time spent in undesired menial work activities. Other jobs produce the leisure services used in the extra spare time thus liberated. This is the story of 'progress' that we have told in this book. More people have more of their basic wants satisfied using less of the society's time, which in turn means that more time can be spent satisfying more of people's more sophisticated wants. Both the increasing efficiency of provision for basic wants, and the growth in demand for the satisfaction of sophisticated wants, mean a requirement for more skilled labour. So there are more high-value-added jobs and fewer low value. This is clearly a line of economic growth that improves human living conditions.

We have seen the historical pattern of change in a number of developed countries over the last two or three decades. Not all of the changes that we have seen correspond precisely to the optimistic pattern. Time spent shopping, for example, shows something of an increase over the period, where we might on general principles have expected a decline. And it is clear that societies *can* (and some *do*) choose for at least some term of years to absorb productivity growth in the form of an increase in work time (for at least *some* of their members). But overall, the patterns of change shown in Chapters 5 to 7 do correspond pretty much to the generalization: less work, more out-of-home (hence service-employment-generating) leisure.

What emerges, both from the theoretical arguments and from the empirical evidence, is a picture of economic progress that is by no means exhausted. What we have seen in this book suggests a line of opportunity for the future, a prospect that combines aspects of what are elsewhere described as 'information societies' and 'leisure societies'. Just as the electromechanical technologies did in the 1950s and 1960s, the information technologies may allow us in the future to continue to spend less time in isolated and undesirable unpaid work to provide for basic needs, freeing time which we may devote to satisfying more sophisticated and luxurious tastes in a relaxed and sociable manner.

2. Public policy for humane modernization

We do not have the grounds for assuming that progress, in this sense, is in any way necessary or predetermined. However, the arguments of the foregoing chapters suggest that this pattern of development can be substantially helped by appropriate public policy.

Emerging from the rather theoretical and academic discussions of change in time-use patterns, are some quite clear policy implications. Public regulation promoting a reduction in working hours, through a range of specific mechanisms which we shall discuss in a moment, is likely to have a positive effect on the demand for labour. In such areas as recreation, sports, tourism, education, the effects of reductions in hours of paid work, and particularly the effects of shorter working hours without equivalent reductions in pay (i.e. financed out of general taxation) are likely to be very positive. Reduction in working time provides new opportunities, in the course of the day or week or year, for the consumption of extra services. So it may be appropriate to attempt, through public policy, to reduce paid work. Give people more free time and build more leisure, sports, cultural centres (or equally provide entrepreneurs with tax incentives to do so), and they will spend more time consuming services—and employing service workers.

There are two different aspects of this sort of regulation. There is public policy directly concerned to increase the amount of time available for service consumption. And there are the various policy areas concerned with providing material circumstances and facilities which complement the additional free time.

Time-use policy

Some of the traditional arguments for a public time-use policy are concerned with what is called work-sharing. These arguments are concerned with equity; they assume that there is a given and invariant level of demand for labour (a 'lump' of labour demand), and shorter work-hours are a means to share out what work is available. Such policy proposals must rely ultimately on purely altruistic motives on the part of voters and politicians. And they are therefore vulnerable to the free-rider problem, that each individual member of a mass society, while perhaps accepting in principle that costs should be more evenly shared, may well feel that he or she personally should not bear any of them.

It is, however, not necessary to rely on such pure, altruistic motives. Central to my arguments has been the potential for a dual effect from work-time reduction: alongside the extra free time for consumption (and its direct 'job-sharing' effect) is the extra labour demand which results from the extra consumption. (I refer to this as 'potential' for reasons which I will make explicit in a moment.) The size of the demand for labour is not fixed and given: so the case for these policies is not simply of fairness, but also of potential material benefits to the society as a whole.

The natural question which follows from this concerns quantities. *How much* more consumption of goods and services may be predicted per minute of extra leisure? Careful readers of the foregoing text might perhaps have expected to find some 'elasticity' calculation, showing the leisure consequences of shorter work hours, along the lines of the calculations of the consequences of extra paid work for domestic work discussed in Chapter 8. In fact, for reasons that emerge from the theoretical argument in Chapter 4, the issue is a little more complicated than this.

It is important to understand that there is no simple relationship between extra free time and extra consumption— since, *inter alia*, there are different ways of getting extra free time. The same amount of extra leisure time might come in small lumps as extra minutes per day, or in larger lumps as extra hours per week or days per month or year. And it might come rather rigidly (at strictly prescribed points of the day or the week or month or year) or with more or less discretion on the part of the worker (who might be able to choose when, and in what form, free time is taken). As we saw in Chapter 4, new activities must somehow be fitted in to a pre-existent, quite heavily constrained, and for the most part habitual, sequence of activities. Reducing one of the constraints on the sequence—which is the effect of work-time reduction—still leaves major activity constraints in place. The theory tells us that the precise temporal details of the placing of non-work time, in the day and the week and the year and the life-stage, determine what activities may be undertaken. Let us call that framework of regulations and arrangements determining when and for how long a worker is expected to work the 'work-time regime'. Crucial in determining the consumption effect of extra free time is the nature of this work-time regime, affecting as it does both the individual's availability for consumption and the availability of services to be consumed. The addition of free time might have a substantial effect on consumption patterns, or virtually none, depending on the detail of the particular work-time regime.

These are some of the sorts of questions we must ask before we can forecast the consumption effects of extra leisure time.

- When are service facilities open, and where? (Half an hour of extra free time per day between 5.30 p.m. and 6.00 p.m. provides no more service consumption if all the service facilities now close at 5.30 p.m., or if they are open but located at a distance of more than 15 minutes travel-time.)
- Who is available to join in with prospective activities? (If you take your leisure with your partner and your partner's employer insists on a work-time regime which conflicts with your own, shorter work hours will not mean extra leisure consumption.)

- Must the extra free time be taken each day, or might it be taken in larger lumps on a weekly, monthly, or yearly basis? (12 extra minutes per day might mean more TV; an hour per week might mean an extra restaurant meal; a half-day per month might mean an extra game of golf; five days per year might mean an extra week of holiday.)
- Must it be taken every year? (Parental leave associated with the presence of small children in the household, built up over time or borrowed against future work, might allow a partner to stay in employment who might otherwise have left it—or even encourage couples to have more children. Study leave, similarly accumulated or borrowed, might re-equip the individual as a producer, or, following the trend of these arguments, as a consumer.) And presumably leisure during the working life might be traded against the age of retirement (or against financial circumstances in retirement).

The more constraint that is placed on the temporal location of free time—on the detail of its placing in the day and the month and the lifespan—the less its potential for stimulating consumption. And specific sorts of constraints on time use lead to specific consumption consequences. (So, for example, extra days of statutory leave mean more vacations and more DIY activity; extra public statutory holidays on which leisure facilities are closed, by contrast perhaps produce, depending on the climate, more sunbathing or TV-viewing.)

Time regulation is a major area of public policy: it concerns not just work hours, but also such matters as, on the employment side, statutory family-related leave allowances and employment protection, vacation requirements, retraining and retirement provisions; on the consumption side it concerns the regulation of opening hours and closed periods (e.g. Sunday closing rules), as well as some more indirect measures discussed in the next section. In ways that may not always be obvious to regulatory authorities, this area of policy has important effects for the level and nature of economic activity.

Scheduling constraints (as our example in Chapter 4 demonstrated) keep people (women particularly) out of the workforce, and potential consumers away from services. So public regulation promoting flexi- or glide-time, and the right of employees to vary their weekly work hours, can have positive effects on both labour supply and consumption levels. And there are similar arguments for other areas of public employment regulation: parental leave arrangements, for example, might be extended and made more flexible (so as to be taken by parents of either sex, and at times other than the birth of children); there might be provisions for mid-career 'industrial sabbaticals' for the purpose of continuing education or training—or even leisure; or for more flexible arrangements for retirement, perhaps staggered, or gradual, perhaps allowing for intermittent returns to employment; or for more flexible employment contracts (e.g. 'flexiyear' rather than flexiday, specifying numbers of hours per year, allowing intermittent breaks, perhaps for childcare in school holidays or the care of sick adult members of the household). All of these, in so far as they allow more choice of the temporal positioning of free time, enable more consumption, and more choice over what is consumed.

A general principle emerges from the arguments of this book: the more personal flexibility emerging from these areas of public regulation, the greater the extent to which the potential dual effect of work-time reduction becomes an actuality. The more flexibility people are given to adjust their own activity sequences to fit their work-lives around other circumstances of their lives, the greater the scope for increasing participation in leisure activities and the greater the growth of consumption of services. Work-sharing, on an inflexible daily work-hours basis, is a rather grey and defensive process of continuous redistribution of an ever-reducing number of jobs. Flexible work-time reduction, taking account of the consumption consequences, by contrast, means, to return once more to my theme, more jobs from more leisure.

Other time-related areas of public policy

There are other more general lines of public policy which also contribute to the time-use and consumption programme of our humane modernizing society.

The most important of these is education policy. This has the potential to act on both the supply and the demand side. Education is what initially equips workers to work; the value of the services that are produced is to some extent a function of the education provided for those that produce them. So much is obvious. But specific to the argument of this book is the parallel importance of *education for consumption*. As the range of services provided by a society grows, so its members must develop new consumption skills; many of these may be accumulated in informal ways, through advertisements or examples or through the practice of consumption itself—but there is no reason why the formal educational system should not play an active role in this, both in the education of children, and in continuing education through and after the working life. (And, of course, education is itself an important sector of the economy, both in consumption and in employment terms.)

Also of great potential impact is infrastructural provision. There are arguments for public provision (or direct or indirect subsidy for private provision) of cultural facilities which parallel those for public provision and subsidy of transport facilities. In addition to these is the complementarity with the time-use policy: if there is to be public policy promoting the use of time for leisure consumption, there might equally be public encouragement for the provision of space and facilities for this. And transport policy itself forms a part of these arguments. Since much of leisure service consumption takes place outside of private homes, and private motor transport is inappropriate for many leisure consumers (e.g. children and the elderly), dangerous for tired people, and environmentally questionable, so this line of policy argument may involve promotion of public transport systems.

There are also some important implications for media policy. It has in the past been argued that television-viewing competes with out-of-home leisure consumption activities. Certainly in the more distant past we find some evidence of this sort of competition for time; clearly the demise of mass cinema attendance coincided with and resulted from the mass diffusion of TV. And we may even see some of the last phases of this process in the evidence of historical change in leisure time use presented in Chapter 8. But now there is a quite different potential connection between TV and other sorts of leisure, a relationship of complementarity. One of the chief informal means of acquiring new consumption skills is through broadcast media (e.g. watching opera on TV leads to trips to the opera house). So there may be some new arguments for public subsidy or other regulation of broadcast media to encourage transmission of material that has this sort of educational impact.

And finally, but by no means least significant, are arrangements to promote provisions of services to households which might previously have been provided on an informal unpaid basis by the household itself. In our humane, increasingly high-value-added society, fewer women are prepared to remain as non-employed housewives and few men are willing to take up this role. To facilitate the shift of women into employment, some household services (particularly those which are temporally specific, such as childcare and the care of older or disabled people) must be provided on a paid basis. It becomes a matter of public policy to ensure that these are effectively and efficiently provided in a way that the market *may* not (and to judge by those countries such as the UK which does not have substantial public provision, the market *does* not do so).

3. Liberty, equality—or fraternity

We have the prospect of various alternative patterns for the regulative actions of the State, leading to alternative patterns of daily life, and hence to alternative patterns of economic structure and performance. The particular pattern of public policy that is chosen depends on the nature of the alliance of interests that promotes it. Some alliances are already familiar to us. There is the alliance of the actual or prospective or aspiring (or self-deluding) 'winners' of the political Right, who seek in effect (as in the discussion of the liberal market regime in Chapter 2) the liberty to employ servants. There is also the residual alliance of the vulnerable workers in the traditional manufacturing and public services of the old Left, who seek equality of access to ever-more costly, increasingly shabby, traditional services. The humane modernization described in the previous pages is a third alternative. But where is the political alliance that might promote it?

If there really is no new natural dominant or majority class emerging out of the material conditions of production, and if consumption shows increasingly complex patterns of differentiation, associated as much with such variables as household type, sex, and stage in life as with occupation or relation to the means of production, then we are reduced finally to constructing serious political arguments.

And at the heart of an alliance or coalition supporting the policies that might promote the humane modernization, there are in principle three important arguments, each of which relates in some way or another to the notion of 'fraternity'. First are the arguments for the high-value service economy introduced in Chapter 2: in which trickle down emerges as a less than effective guide for policy since, as chains of production become more complex, increasingly 'the poor employ the rich'. Second are arguments about the life cycle: the better-off eventually become the worse-off—the young and healthy and well paid have a definite and ascertainable probability of becoming old and sick and poor (and if not they themselves, then their children will want educating)—so redistribution to the worse-off or to support medical or educational services is not, in the longest-term sense, really redistribution. Third is simply a moral argument: that irrespective of one's individual interests, it is proper to support the transfer of resources from the better-off to the worse-off.

It is mainly to the first of these arguments that this book is addressed. It contends that the material basis for a society's economic structure is the style of life, the pattern of daily activities, of its members. The mundane acts of eating and drinking and caring and learning and playing constitute the demand that maintains the economy, and thereby provide the jobs in it. A fraternal concern to improve standards of consumption among even the poorest members of society, in part through public regulations and provisions which directly affect the daily pattern of activities, could serve to stimulate the economy in ways that also benefit a substantial proportion of the better-off. And the more the society's consumption consists of services that embody high-value labour, the smaller is the category of 'the poor' to be concerned about.

Appendix 1: Telling the Time: Some Reflections on Time-Diary Methodology

In this Appendix we briefly consider some of the methodological problems in time-diary data collection. It deals with three particular issues: (i) the reason we use diaries to estimate time allocation (briefly, because our temporal experience is of the passage of time, not of its duration); (ii) the consequence of the 'editing' process involved in reducing complex and multiplicitous subjective sense-data into a simple 'primary activity sequence'; and (iii) the implications of high levels of non-response that result from the heavy respondent burden of the diary instrument. None of the conclusions that emerge are final ones, but they may stimulate some readers to pursue these questions further (and they should also provide some reassurance that the author is, to say the least, concerned about these problematical issues).

1. Estimating time use: two experiments

Let us return to the thought experiment introduced in Chapter 4, in which readers were invited to consider how much time, in the past week, they had spent in paid work, watching television, and washing dishes after a meal.

Those whose hours of paid employment vary from week to week, and whose pay is calculated from the number of hours actually worked, will probably have been able to answer the first question immediately, and without any mental arithmetic (because they have already made the appropriate calculations, in the form of a partial work 'diary', for their employers). If there are any readers whose only access to television is through a 'pay as you view', they may be able to work out the answer to the second question quite straightforwardly (if they know how much money they have spent). No one reading these lines (other than an absolute non-participant in this activity) will be able to answer the third question without a rather complicated calculation.

We can demonstrate the reality of the problem suggested by the thought experiment with a real experiment, in which a sample of respondents were first asked questions about their time use (this is sometimes referred to in the literature as the 'stylized-estimate' method: Robinson *et al.* 1989) and then subsequently asked to keep a diary. So it becomes possible to compare people's questionnaire answers with the results of analysis of their narrative accounts of their weeks.

Respondents to a 1986 UK diary study (Ehrlich 1987; Gershuny and Jones 1987) were asked a rather simple question, about how much time was normally spent in the activity on each occasion that the respondent engaged in it. So for example when asked 'How much time do you spend each time you go shopping for food?', about 10 per cent of the sample said that each visit to the shops takes on average 5–15 minutes, 31 per cent said that it takes 60–90 minutes on average. And so on.

Now, compare the answers, to the average duration of the shopping events as revealed by the diaries (Table A1.1). Those women respondents who said that shopping normally takes them 5 to 15 minutes, spend on average 63 minutes per occurrence, and those who claim that shopping normally takes them 30–60 minutes, record in their diaries that they spend on average 66 minutes per occurrence. That is to say, very little of the variance in the diary estimates is explained by the questionnaire answers. We get just the same sorts of results for other sorts of activities.

The two experiments demonstrate something very simple, but quite fundamental, about the nature of the consciousness of time. Everything we do takes place in time. Everything we experience, we experience as a duration, a period of time passed in particular activities or states or circumstances. Yet though (or perhaps because) our experience of our own activities essentially consists *of* time, we do not know *how much* time we spend in our activities.

Our consciousness consists of a continuous sequence of activities, a succession of mental and physical states and circumstances. We can remember, or when challenged we can reconstruct, some salient attributes of some elements of this sequence for the last few days. And where particular points in the sequence can be matched against known times of the day ('clocking-on' times, start times of television programmes, children's bedtimes) then we can calculate the elapsed time spent in activities. Some people in fact have a rudimentary time-sense, and actually know, at any point in the day, how much time has passed. But even that small proportion of readers who normally know the time without reference to a clock or watch, will still have had difficulty in answering our questions, since their time-sense will merely enable them to register the time elapsed since the start of the present activity (e.g. the time spent so far in reading this book), and not to keep a running total of time spent in the same class of activity over a specified period (the time spent reading books or papers during the last week).

Even if we could collect such 'running totals' of time use, for which activities would we calculate them? The categories we use to divide up our time are certainly not 'natural'. Does 'reading papers' include newspapers, or just scientific papers? Does 'paid work time' include time spent

Table A1.1. 'How long do you take...?'

	Questionnaire answers	Mean time per occurrence
Buying food: Men	218	84
< 5 min.	7	51
5–15 min.	19	72
16–30 min.	27	60
30–60 min.	61	75
60–90 min.	72	99
> 90 min.	32	99
Buying food: Women	704	77
< 5 min.	—	—
5–15 min.	72	63
16–30 min.	79	75
30–60 min.	230	66
60–90 min.	221	78
> 90 min.	152	3.1
Preparing meals: Men	339	39
< 5 min.	7	39
5–15 min.	34	33
16–30 min.	110	38
30–60 min.	129	42
60–90 min.	44	48
> 90 min.	15	36
Preparing meals: Women	1,467	45
< 5 min.	—	—
5–15 min.	34	36
16–30 min.	234	45
30–60 min.	626	45
60–90 min.	384	48
> 90 min.	189	48
Clearing/Washing up: Men	458	35
< 5 min.	9	33
5–15 min.	180	39
16–30 min.	184	32
30–60 min.	63	36
60–90 min.	22	35
> 90 min.	—	—
Clearing/Washing up: Women	1,119	35
< 5 min.	18	32
5–15 min.	325	33
16–30 min.	425	34
30–60 min.	293	37
60–90 min.	89	40
> 90 min.	49	39

'scrubbing up' after a dirty job, time spent commuting to the workplace, a period of illicit rest in the middle of working time? And how do we cope with multiple simultaneous activities? People can normally give sequential accounts of their recent activities when challenged to do so. But there is nothing objective in the choice of which aspects of our complex experience are to be considered salient in constructing an account of a past sequence of events. Are you 'watching television' if the TV is switched on in a room in which you are also cooking dinner and calming a crying child? Are you 'washing-up' if your wife has her hands in a bowl of soapy water and you, while talking to her, occasionally dry a plate with a linen towel? Accounts of activity sequences require decisions about such issues; they are constructed rather than natural.

In general, people do not know the answers to these sorts of questions. Answering them involves a number of distinct stages of thought. We must decide what is intended by the terms used to describe the activities—not by any means a trivial problem—and then we must decide which parts of our day correspond to these categories. We must identify the starting and finishing times of each instance of participation in the particular activity, subtract the former from the latter to discover the elapsed time, and then add together the elapsed time for each occurrence of the activity. Most respondents, at least in the context of an interview in which no more than a few seconds are allowed for the entire process of reconstruction, definition, and calculation, will find it impossible to carry it out with any precision—probably for TV, certainly for washing-up, and quite likely for paid work.

By contrast, the process of constructing a diary record is much less demanding, and much less prone to error. After all, we are all quite practised at recalling our sequence of activities over the last day or so, and we can in general identify some particular clock-times for at least a subset of activities in the sequence: we tend to know when in the day we got out of bed, when we started work, what time our television programme started, and so on. One of the main mental mechanisms we use for reconstructing the diary account is asking ourselves 'what did we do next?' so by contrast with the questionnaire method, the diary is less likely to lose particular instances of particular classes of activity. Thus the time-budget diary-based methodology, which asks the respondents simply to recall their sequences (in most cases in their own words) and align them to clock-time, leaving all the subsequent definitional activities and calculations to the analysts, is likely to provide both more accurate aggregate totals of particular time-use categories for any individual respondent (with more systematic recall and fewer lost events, and more explicit and reproducible calculations) and more reliable interpersonal comparisons (since analysts have direct control of the activity definitions and the periodization used in the calculations).

These considerations suggest that, comparing the questionnaire and the diary-based estimates, the diary estimates *should be* more accurate. And if we accept this, then when we find the very weak associations between the questionnaire and the diary estimates seen in Table A1.1, the presumption of accuracy must be in favour of the latter.

The general inability of respondents to provide sensible answers to the sorts of questions with which we started this Appendix is the reason that we must use the complex and cumbersome diary methodology to arrive at time-use estimates. (And the applicability of diary methods is broader than economists may expect: for example, analogous research on questionnaire-based estimates of paid work time suggest that these may produce a progressive net *over*estimate of 10 per cent or more: Hoffmann 1981; Niemi 1995; Robinson and Gershuny 1994.) But many of the factors that explain this inability, also apply to some degree to the process of keeping, or failing to keep, a diary. So we now turn to look in particular at two further experiments designed to throw some light on the meaning and representativeness of the data.

2. Narratives: telling the day

Telling stories is a necessary part of any culture. Stories themselves carry useful information, about how to behave towards others and about the likely consequences of particular courses of action. The act of telling the stories places the narrator in a particular relation, of authority or respect, or friendship, to the listeners.

Telling your own story is a particularly important activity. The way you tell it—the words you use or fail to use, the information encoded in particular phrases—is at once personally revealing, intended to establish intimacy, and at the same time quite impersonal, establishing (and intended to establish) the teller as a member of a particular social category. That you tell your life story to the particular listener establishes complicity between you both, the way you tell the story establishes your own relationship to groups in the wider society (and shows in addition the extent to which you understand what sort of person your listener is).

The telling of the life story relies on a lot of prior knowledge on the part of the listener. You were born at such-and-such a time, went to school at so-and-so, got this job and then that one. In telling this sort of story, you rely on your listener's knowledge of what going to this school and that job means, in terms of the sort of life you actually led at those times, and of the consequences of these past activities for your present life. A life story told in natural language may be rather thin on detail. That is to say, an interested but sociologically naïve Martian would not be able to make very much of this sort of account. The Martian would require a lot more detail about what went on day by day, about what different activities went into a day. (Did you spend all day at school? What did you do at school? What, other than going to school, did you do on a schoolday? How many schooldays in a year? What other sorts of days were interspersed with schooldays? And so on.)

It is not just inquisitive Martians who need this sort of detailed information. Parents ask this sort of detail about the recent lives of their children. Spouse asks spouse, hairdressers ask their customers (though often not vice versa). You woke up early, you showered, you ate, you listened to the radio, you caught a bus. Telling about your day, in some detail, using language that is accessible to people who have not shared that particular day's activity (though they regularly live through similar ones) is a skill that is called upon quite widely, and though it is not an absolute requirement for a successful life it is nevertheless very helpful. People practise this art from childhood, and it is called upon irrespective of social status; rich or poor, well educated or badly, most people have to, or want to, tell their day to someone. Some activities which are special to particular exclusive locations are difficult to tell, because there is no general language to describe them—there need not be any general language for these special activities, since only a few people share in them, and only those who share in them need to know about them. So a child may find it difficult to explain a particular sort of arithmetic or comprehension exercise, for which the class and the teacher have a special word that is meaningless to the parent. And similarly the detail of activities in the workplace, in which perhaps a complicated and continuous sequence of activities takes place for which no vocabulary whatsoever exists, and whose only abstract manifestation lies tacit in the mind of the worker, may defy retelling altogether.

But, with these sorts of exceptions, many people—we might expect these to include a broad cross-section of the population—can conceptualize their recent past in terms of a sequence of discrete activities, and describe this sequence to other people. And, furthermore, people do it, unprompted by Martians or social scientists, as part of their normal lives. It is this ability to 'tell the day' that we exploit in time-budget research.

To 'tell our days' we have of course to select what we consider salient out of the mass of our sense-impressions. Do we mention that the radio was playing in the workshop? We have to establish what activities are, and when one activity finishes and another starts. Do we go to work or walk to the bus stop? Are we working when we stop for lunch? A coffee break? An unscheduled cigarette? In telling about our day, we have to choose language, and the language chosen may or may not be comprehensible to the listener. All of these issues mean that, prior to using accounts of daily life we must try to understand the processes of construction that underlie them.

There are two general methodological criticisms of time-budget analysis using diaries. The first of these problems is a matter of principle: the accounts that people give of their days are *constructed*. We have already discussed the reasons that people can give accounts as a natural part of their social lives. But the diaries we collect as time-budget researchers, are necessarily constrained and standardized. So, are we in effect *inventing* the time-use patterns through our specification of the time-diary instrument? The second problem is a practical one. Time-budget diary instruments are in general quite onerous to complete, and as a result we get high rates of non-response: do the resulting non-response *biases* mean that we have meaningless data?

3. Constructing the diary

There are various approaches to the standardization of activity categories. Precoding, the establishment of a list of standard activities prior to the fieldwork, poses problems of inflexibility of expression. If an interviewer codes the respondent's activities using a dictionary, then the picture of the day is largely a construction of the interviewer. It is also possible to give the respondents quite detailed dictionaries which they use to code their own accounts; this is a very cumbersome procedure, though promising evidence on its performance comes from the Netherlands studies which rely on this technique. Interviewers and respondents can collaborate in the construction of an account; this is a good technique, but costly. Quite the most frequent approach, and that used in the great majority of the studies employed in this book, is to provide an example of a completed diary, and then leave the respondents free to use their own words; this has the disadvantage that it influences respondents to emphasize the precise types of activity found in the example, but it provides a considerable degree of detail for the analyst, and an appropriate degree of respect for the respondent's own narrative skills.

It is possible, through any of these means, to standardize the level of detail of reporting—in effect, these techniques provide a supplementary training and support for the respondents' own narrative skills. But they each leave us still with the essential problem that respondents are *selecting* particular aspects of their own experiences. We cannot eradicate these interpersonal differences, and we should not want to do so. The problem here, of course, is the familiar one of discovering exactly what it is that people leave out of their accounts.

The most straightforward way of dealing with this is by asking people how they construct time-diary accounts. There is interesting qualitative work in this field, interviewing diarists after the survey period about how they used the research instrument. But paradoxically the most powerful evidence about what is left out of accounts comes from material which is, in particular cases, included in time-budget diary instruments themselves.

The main material used in this book, and in time-budget analysis in general, is evidence from the central activity sequence. We ask people 'what were you doing? . . . what did you do next?', and we get the familiar 'telling of the day', as constrained by the matrix of time intervals, and whatever strict or lax guidance is provided as to vocabulary. In a highly structured survey instrument, relying on precoded categories, this central sequence consists of a homogeneous sequence of activities, described in a limited vocabulary—simple to analyse, but more difficult to interpret. Standardization provides a certain level of reliability, in the very limited sense that all the respondents are using the same vocabulary. But, with this sort of evidence alone, we have no way of gauging whether respondents are all using the same vocabulary in the same way. In an unstructured instrument, a respondent might well place 'washed up and drank cup of tea' as one distinct activity. If we tell respondents to use one precoded activity category per activity slot, however, the same respondent might choose one or other of these.

In the more open surveys, where respondents are invited to use their own words to describe their own activities, we find the converse problem. The respondents' central sequences now consist of relatively diffuse accounts which mix, from our point of view, various categories of activity (what?), location (where?), company (who with?), and evaluation (e.g., enjoyable?). The accounts are less homogeneous in language and level of detail, and hence more difficult to analyse; but at the same time they are richer, providing more clues as to how the accounts are constructed by the individual respondents.

And in fact the competing advantages of the 'open' and 'closed' style of survey instrument are not quite as symmetrically balanced as this would suggest. The more modern time-budget diary instruments do more than ask for the 'main activity sequence'. In addition, they prompt explicitly and systematically for the further information which might be sporadically absent, or promiscuously muddled together, in the natural-language accounts. Figure A1.1 shows a page from 1984 UK time-budget diary instrument. In addition to the column provided for recording 'What were you doing?' is a further column 'Were you doing anything else?' The unprompted natural-language account may have included the information that a number of things were happening at the same time: here it is more likely that multiple simultaneous activities will be recorded. Though only two columns are provided in the diary, we frequently find four distinct activities recorded in one time-period, and the slightly differently structured BBC survey we shall discuss in a moment sometimes reveals as many as six. (We should note that the relative coarseness of the time intervals complicates matters further: 'simultaneous' in this context may either indicate events genuinely occurring at the same time, or alternatively, very short events happening in sequence within the 5- or 15-minute time interval.)

Time	What were you doing		Who was involved with you in the main activity? xxxxxx xxxxxx xxxxx xxxxxxxxxxxxxxxx	Where were you during the main activity? xxxxxx xxxxxx xxxxx xxxxx	Time
	Main activity in each quarter hour				
12noon					12noon
.15	Working		people at work	✓	.15
.30					.30
.45					.45
1pm	Ate lunch	read paper		✓	1pm
.15				✓	.15
.30	Working	talked with eman		✓	.30
.45					.45
2pm					2pm
.15					.15
.30					.30
.45	Travelling (car)		✓	✓	.45
3pm	At dentist	chat with receptionist	Dentist etc.	✓	3pm
.15				✓	.15
.30				✓	.30
.45	Picking up child from school		✓	✓	.45
4pm	Relaxing at home	Get children's tea		✓	4pm
.15	Mowing lawn				.15
.30					.30
.45	Mending fence				.45
5pm	Prepared evening meal				5pm
.15					.15
.30					.30
.45	Helped child with homework		✓		.45
6pm	Watched television		✓		6pm
.15	Visiting friends (neighbours)		neighbours	✓	.15
.30				✓	.30
.45	Ate evening meal		✓ ✓	✓	.45
7pm		Cleared away	✓	✓	7pm
.15	Entertained neighbours		✓ neighbours	✓	.15
.30	Travel (bus)			✓	.30
.45	Drink in pub			✓	.45
8pm	Cinema-to watch film	xxxxxx		✓	8pm

Figure A1.1. Diary sample

The explicit request for specific pieces of information which might or might not have appeared in the natural account yields two different sorts of advantages. It serves to structure the account of the main sequence: the fact that answers to questions of 'who are you with?' or 'where?' are explicitly requested elsewhere on the diary page makes it less likely that respondents will include this sort of information in their account of their main activity sequence. Explicitly extending the range of information required, in other words, is a tacit guide for standardization of the structure of the data.

The multiple or subsidiary activity data also yield information about what is missing from accounts of the main activity sequence. But, of course, this conventional hierarchical vocabulary, in which respondents are asked what they were doing, and then if they were doing anything else at the same time, which is necessitated by the narrative frame of telling your day, begs the question of what exactly is happening when people tell their day. The explicit prompt for additional simultaneous activities may elicit extra information that would not have emerged from the unconstrained natural account. It may also have the consequence of systematically suppressing information that might otherwise have appeared in a naturally constructed account of the daily sequence. To make sense of the evidence discussed in this book, we must consider the nature of the editing process through which diary respondents reduce their complex experience into a sequential diary account.

An *ex post* experiment in the construction of time-use accounts

The main drawback of the conventional, structured time-diary technique is its hierarchical nature. Respondents are asked (the language varies but the intent is clear) 'what were you doing?' over a particular time interval (producing a 'primary' activity), and then 'were you doing anything else?' (producing 'secondary' activities). The primary activity is seen by the analyst as being in some sense the most important. The respondent may tend to view the primary activity in this light as well, and therefore may be less meticulous in recording the secondary activities. So the direct use of internal evidence, comparing primary activity patterns with combined primary and secondary patterns as recorded in a conventional diary (e.g. Gershuny and Sullivan 1998), while helpful, does not completely dispose of the problem of estimating the consequences of the editing of experience.

Fortunately we have some evidence that allows us to estimate the consequences of the hierarchical convention. For the UK in 1983–4, in addition to material collected in the conventional hierarchical manner, we also have an unconventional time-budget study (collected by the BBC Audience Research Department) which did not use the hierarchical convention, but simply asked respondents to list all the activities engaged in during a particular period. The survey instrument is illustrated in Figure A1.2; the interviewers actively encouraged respondents to record each of the multiple simultaneous activities. The conventional 1983–4 survey used in the multinational collection employed a very similar activity coding; so comparing the conventional primary activity data with the BBC full dataset does give a picture of the consequences of the editing process.

In real life we are always experiencing more than one thing at a time. We are wearing clothes, standing up, breathing—these things are of necessity so we know that we need not mention them when we give accounts of our days. Other things are obviously of dominating importance: we are at a concert and our whole consciousness is focused on the activities of the musicians on the podium—we are definitely at a concert, an unambiguous primary activity. But on other occasions we are not so sure. The radio is on while these words are being written, and the author, as he writes, becomes aware of a Smetana String Quartet (no. 2: 'From My Life'). He is also

DAILY LIFE TIMESHEET (3)

	QUARTER HOURS					HALF HOURS							
FROM 9.00AM YESTERDAY MORNING TO 1.50PM YESTERDAY AFTERNOON	9.00 am to 9.14	9.15 am to 9.20	9.30 am to 9.44	9.45 am to 9.50		10.00 am to 10.29	10.30 am to 10.59	11.00 am to 11.29	11.30 am to 11.59	12.00 am to 12.29	12.30 am to 12.59	1.00 am to 1.29	1.30 am to 1.59
WAKE/SLEEP	(13)	(19)	(25)	(31)		(37)	(43)	(49)	(55)	(61)	(67)	(73)	(7)
V Sleep	V	V	V	V		V	V	V	V	V	V	V	V
X Wake up	X	X	X	X		X	X	X	X	X	X	X	X
0 In bed not asleep	0	0	0	0		0	0	0	0	0	0	0	0
WHERE WERE YOU?													
1 At Home	1	1	1	1		1	1	1	1	1	1	1	1
2 At Work/School	2	2	2	2		2	2	2	2	2	2	2	2
3 Elsewhere	3	3	3	3		3	3	3	3	3	3	3	3
WHAT WERE YOU DOING? WHAT ELSE? PERSONAL													
4 Washing self, dressing etc.	4	4	4	4		4	4	4	4	4	4	4	4
5 Eat or drink	5	5	5	5		5	5	5	5	5	5	5	5
DOMESTIC	(14)	(20)	(26)	(32)		(38)	(44)	(50)	(56)	(62)	(68)	(74)	(8)
V Prepare food, wash up	V	V	V	V		V	V	V	V	V	V	V	V
X Housework	X	X	X	X		X	X	X	X	X	X	X	X
0 D.I.Y.	0	0	0	0		0	0	0	0	0	0	0	0
1 Gardening	1	1	1	1		1	1	1	1	1	1	1	1
2 Care of children	2	2	2	2		2	2	2	2	2	2	2	2
SHOP & ERRANDS													
3 Shopping	3	3	3	3		3	3	3	3	3	3	3	3
4 Errands, incl. doctor	4	4	4	4		4	4	4	4	4	4	4	4
ADULT CLASSES & CIVIC													
5 Adult classes	5	5	5	5		5	5	5	5	5	5	5	5
6 Prepare for classes	6	6	6	6		6	6	6	6	6	6	6	6
7 Meetings incl. T.U.	7	7	7	7		7	7	7	7	7	7	7	7
8 Religion	8	8	8	8		8	8	8	8	8	8	8	8
ENTERTAINMENT	(15)	(21)	(27)	(33)		(39)	(45)	(51)	(57)	(63)	(69)	(75)	(9)
V Watch sport	V	V	V	V		V	V	V	V	V	V	V	V
X Fairs, Bingo	X	X	X	X		X	X	X	X	X	X	X	X
0 Pubs, Restaurants	0	0	0	0		0	0	0	0	0	0	0	0
1 Theatre, Cinema	1	1	1	1		1	1	1	1	1	1	1	1
2 Entertaining in home	2	2	2	2		2	2	2	2	2	2	2	2
SPORTS & ACTIVE													
3 Doing sports	3	3	3	3		3	3	3	3	3	3	3	3
4 Visit sea or country	4	4	4	4		4	4	4	4	4	4	4	4
5 Museums, art	5	5	5	5		5	5	5	5	5	5	5	5
6 Walks	6	6	6	6		6	6	6	6	6	6	6	6
7 Hobbies, games	7	7	7	7		7	7	7	7	7	7	7	7
8 Pets	8	8	8	8		8	8	8	8	8	8	8	8
9 Moving	9	9	9	9		9	9	9	9	9	9	9	9
LESS ACTIVE	(16)	(22)	(28)	(34)		(40)	(46)	(52)	(58)	(64)	(70)	(76)	(10)
V Relaxing	V	V	V	V		V	V	V	V	V	V	V	V
X Reading, writing	X	X	X	X		X	X	X	X	X	X	X	X
0 Talk incl. phone	0	0	0	0		0	0	0	0	0	0	0	0
1 Records, cassettes	1	1	1	1		1	1	1	1	1	1	1	1
2 Home computer	2	2	2	2		2	2	2	2	2	2	2	2
3 Wandering around	3	3	3	3		3	3	3	3	3	3	3	3
WORK/SCHOOL													
4 Working/studying	4	4	4	4		4	4	4	4	4	4	4	4
5 Breaks at work, school	5	5	5	5		5	5	5	5	5	5	5	5
RADIO													
6 AVAILABLE	6	6	6	6		6	6	6	6	6	6	6	6
7 NOT AVAILABLE	7	7	7	7		7	7	7	7	7	7	7	7
8 LISTENING	8	8	8	8		8	8	8	8	8	8	8	8
TV/VCR	(17)	(23)	(29)	(35)		(41)	(47)	(53)	(59)	(65)	(71)	(77)	(11)
V TV AVAILABLE	V	V	V	V		V	V	V	V	V	V	V	V
X NOT AVAILABLE	X	X	X	X		X	X	X	X	X	X	X	X
0 VCR AVAILABLE	0	0	0	0		0	0	0	0	0	0	0	0
1 WATCH BROADCASTS	1	1	1	1		1	1	1	1	1	1	1	1
2 WATCH VIDEO	2	2	2	2		2	2	2	2	2	2	2	2
WAS ANYONE WITH YOU? YES	3	3	3	3		3	3	3	3	3	3	3	3
TRAVEL: WHY	(18)	(24)	(30)	(36)		(42)	(48)	(54)	(60)	(66)	(72)	(78)	(12)
V Work/school	V	V	V	V		V	V	V	V	V	V	V	V
X Leisure	X	X	X	X		X	X	X	X	X	X	X	X
0 Other	0	0	0	0		0	0	0	0	0	0	0	0
HOW													
1 Walking, on foot	1	1	1	1		1	1	1	1	1	1	1	1
2 Bicycle	2	2	2	2		2	2	2	2	2	2	2	2
3 Motorbike	3	3	3	3		3	3	3	3	3	3	3	3
4 Car/Van/Taxi	4	4	4	4		4	4	4	4	4	4	4	4
5 Bus	5	5	5	5		5	5	5	5	5	5	5	5
6 Train/Tube	6	6	6	6		6	6	6	6	6	6	6	6
7 Boat, plane	7	7	7	7		7	7	7	7	7	7	7	7
	9.00 am to 9.14	9.15 am to 9.20	9.30 am to 9.44	9.45 am to 9.50		10.00 am to 10.29	10.30 am to 10.59	11.00 am to 11.29	11.30 am to 11.59	12.00 am to 12.29	12.30 am to 12.59	1.00 am to 1.29	1.30 am to 1.59

Figure A1.2. A page from the BBC diary

writing. The BBC format would capture 'listening to the radio' and 'working' for this quarter hour. But there is a problem for the conventional hierarchical account: what is the primary activity? (It took at least ten minutes of intermittent worry to identify the piece and the composer.)

The problem is editing a complex and multiplicitous reality, in which many things are happening simultaneously, into a simple sequence of single activities. We know that we can achieve this editing process, we know that we can 'tell the day'. How do we do it? Let us conceptualize the editing process as a procedure for giving (and ceding) priority to one just one particular category of activity in each period.

Different categories of activity will be treated in different ways. At one extreme, the whole of each 15-minute period in which a particular activity is mentioned might be counted as belonging to that activity—in other words, the activity is given an absolute priority, and always appears in the 'first activity' sequence, irrespective of whatever else may be happening over the same period—for example childcare could be taken as the primary activity whenever it occurs. (Only a few activities, none of which coincides with any other, could of course be treated like this.) Or conversely, and at the opposite extreme, a particular activity could be assigned a minimal priority, such that the period is only accounted to the activity if no other activity is going on—so for example, 'listening to the radio' might only appear in the primary activity sequence when there is no other simultaneous activity. Or the mechanism of prioritization might lie somewhere in between these extremes, giving variously high or low priorities to a particular activity depending on the particular circumstances.

We can discover which of these comes closest to the way particular activities are treated in the editing process, by comparing the first activity estimates from the conventional data with alternative treatments of the comprehensive BBC activity listings. Consider Figure A1.3. It gives a number of alternative estimates of minutes per day spent by different sorts of people in various sorts of activities.

The alternative estimates from the BBC activity listings are intended to simulate the alternative extreme versions of the prioritizing mechanism. The BBC maximum estimate corresponds to the 'absolute priority' case: if the activity is mentioned at all during a quarter-hour period, the whole of that quarter hour is ascribed to the activity. The BBC minimum is the converse case, in which the particular activity is considered primary only where nothing else at all is mentioned during the period. The minutes per average day in the various activities, as estimated from the ESRC primary activity data, are plotted together with the two BBC-derived estimates.

Notice first that (with some exceptions to which we shall return in a moment), the ESRC data lies neatly bracketed between the maximum and the minimum values from the BBC data. Of course this is not surprising in the sense that the maxima and minima have been defined as polar extremes,

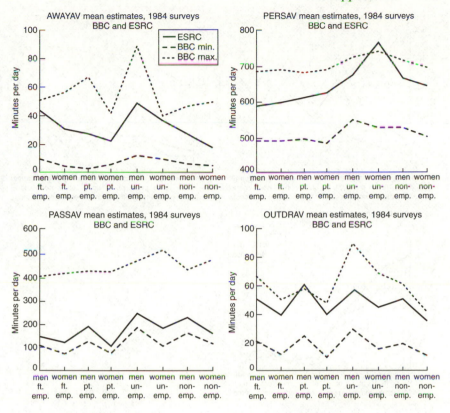

Figure A1.3a. Mean estimates

and any actual process of construction of a primary activity sequence must lie somewhere between them. But consider: the BBC and ESRC data come from completely independent samples, employing radically different methodologies. The BBC diary covered a single day while the ESRC covered a week. The BBC used an interviewer, where the ESRC relied on self-completion. The BBC used precoded categories, where the ESRC permitted natural language recording of the activities. The only methodological connection between the two surveys is that the BBC based their activity-coding scheme on the activity-category scheme developed for the ESRC project. And of course, both were samples from the same population drawn at approximately the same point in history.

The two very different instruments give generally consistent results. The fact the ESRC primary activity data is bracketed by the BBC maximum and minimum constitutes a unique demonstration of the reliability of the methodology.

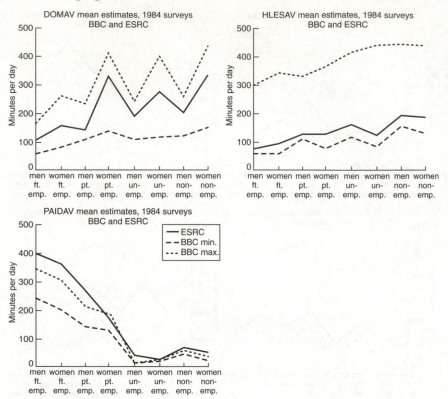

Figure A1.3b. Mean estimates

But the main point of the comparison is the light it throws on the actual process of construction of the ESRC hierarchical account. By looking at exactly where the ESRC estimate is placed between the two BBC-derived estimates, we get a picture of what it is that the primary activity data represents. Take the DOMAV-activity category (aggregated from domestic work, odd jobs, shopping, and childcare). The ESRC data follow exactly the same pattern as the BBC maximum. The relative amounts of time devoted to these activities by men and women, and by people in the various employment categories, are just the same in the two estimates; the BBC maximum is consistently just a little higher. Two clear conclusions emerge: (i) Since the ESRC primary activity is on the whole closer to the BBC maximum than to the minimum, these activities, when they occur, take a high priority in the process of editing the more complex reality into a simplified primary activity sequence; (ii) Different sorts of people seem to construct their accounts in similar sorts of ways—the similarity in the pattern of the ESRC and BBC maximum implies that, at least with respect

to these sorts of unpaid work activities, the same sort of editing of experience is carried out by men and women, and by people in the various
employment categories. Which means in turn that the primary activity
data are a valid basis for comparing the time-use patterns of different sorts
of people.

By way of contrast, look next at the PASSAV (average time watching
television and listening to the radio—'passive' leisure) activities. Here the
primary activity estimate follows quite closely on the pattern of the BBC
minimum. The implication is that these sorts of activities take something
near to an absolute bottom priority in the construction of a primary activity
sequence. If almost anything else whatsoever is going on at the same time,
that other activity, and not radio or television, is registered. (The radio or
television is thus actually switched on, if not necessarily attended to, for
twice or even three times as long as is registered in the primary activity
data.) And again, the fact that the pattern of time use as between the
different sorts of people is very closely similar in the ESRC and the BBC
minimum data suggests the validity of the data for comparative purposes.

The PAIDAV (average minutes of paid work and work-related travel)
category is the main case in which the ESRC estimates lie outside the BBC
limits. There is in fact a quite straightforward explanation for this, arising
out of the differences in the survey instrument. The ESRC's respondents,
completing the diaries themselves, tended to describe the whole of the
period between arriving and leaving the workplace as 'at work' or some
similar phrase. (In fact the example of a completed diary given to respondents unintentionally encouraged this usage.) And a result, the ESRC paid
work data include meals, snacks, and rest-times; the BBC's interviewers, by
contrast, were instructed to exclude such activities from paid work. Once we
have allowed for something like 50 minutes per average day of such breaks at
the workplace (in the case of full-time employees), the primary activity data
come to correspond quite closely to the BBC maximum estimate.

In the case of PERSAV (sleep, washing, dressing: 'personal care') the
primary activity estimate lies approximately midway between the ESRC
limits (though un- or non-employed people seem more likely to give this
priority in their accounts—perhaps because they are likely to have fewer
other things going on simultaneously). For OUTDRAV (outdoor leisure
activities), six of the eight sorts of people give primary activity estimates
very close to the BBC maximum. Unemployed men and women, however,
give primary estimates about midway between the maximum and the
minimum, reflecting the more diffuse nature of their out-of-home activities.
'Going for a walk', for example, a typical leisure activity for unemployed
people, is much more likely to be combined with 'having a chat with a
neighbour', 'window-shopping', 'meeting friends', than is 'going to the
cinema', an activity more representative of employed people's leisure.
AWAYAV ('other away-from-home leisure') lies somewhat irregularly

between the maximum and the minimum. The primary activity-based estimate of the residual 'other home leisure', consisting mostly of 'relaxing', 'talking', 'reading', and so on, corresponds very closely to the BBC minimum, and amounts to less than a quarter of the maximum estimate—understandable since many of these activities are likely to be mentioned as subsidiaries to some other primary household activity. 'Relaxing' and 'talking' in particular are likely to be mentioned as secondary activities accompanying watching television or (in the latter case) meals.

There is certainly evidence that some activities may be attenuated in 'primary sequence-based' diary accounts because they are given low priority in the process of editing the complexity of real experience. And we have also seen that particular sorts of people *may* attenuate particular sort of activity differentially (though in general the patterns are consistent across different social groups). Both of these mean that primary activity distributions are a potentially misleading basis for time-use estimates.

But we can discover where and to what extent activities are being misrepresented by the data. To demonstrate the effectiveness of our knowledge about the processes of construction of time-use accounts for the interpretation of time-budget results, consider the simulation of the ESRC primary activity estimates for the UK in 1984 from the BBC 1984 multiple activity data shown in Figure A1.4.

We know that people asleep cannot be 'doing' anything else. So it is unsurprising that the estimate of 33.5 per cent of the average day devoted to sleep in BBC data corresponds to 33.8 per cent in the ESRC. We have seen that people seldom put TV as a first activity when they are doing anything else; so, in our simulation we have taken the BBC respondents as potential recorders of a primary TV activity only when there is nothing else happening. On this basis we arrive at an estimate of 13.3 per cent of the day spent in the activity, slightly lower than the 15.0 per cent recorded in the ESRC data (i.e. a few activities are being treated by the ESRC respondents as subsidiary to watching television).

The category 'paid work and eating' (the odd grouping necessitated by the presence of meals taken at work within the ESRC's 'at work' category) is one of those which is likely to take priority in diary accounts whenever it occurs; accordingly, in our simulation treatment of the BBC data we take this as the first activity whenever it occurs. On this basis we arrive at an estimate of 27.2 per cent of the day spent 'at work or eating' as opposed to the ESRC's 25.0 per cent. (It is also quite likely that the exception to the 'TV never takes priority over other activities' rule is meals taken while watching television; if this proves to be the case, then the simulation's overestimate of eating time corresponds to its underestimate of TV time.) Domestic and other unpaid work time appears to be neither dominant nor dominated in the first activity accounts. In the simulation we distribute those periods during which unpaid work is mentioned proportionately among all the

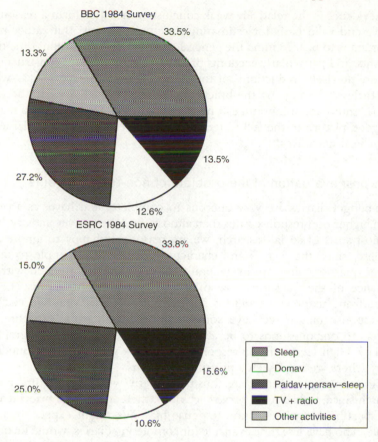

BBC 1984 Survey

33.5%

13.3%

13.5%

27.2%

12.6%

ESRC 1984 Survey

33.8%

15.0%

15.6%

25.0%

10.6%

▨	Sleep
☐	Domav
▨	Paidav+persav−sleep
■	TV + radio
▨	Other activities

Figure A1.4. Comparison of 1984 BBC and ESRC Surveys

activities recorded for the period, and we arrive at an estimate of 12.6 per cent of the day devoted to unpaid work, to be compared with the estimate of 10.6 per cent from the ESRC primary activity data (perhaps suggesting that some of the other categories are somewhat more dominant than is assumed in the simulation). The final residual category in the simulation contains 13.5 per cent of the day, as compared with 15 per cent in the ESRC results.

All in all, when we apply our knowledge of the editing procedures that go to yield a primary activity account to raw multiple activity data, we succeed in producing a reasonably accurate version of the primary activity data. And to look at the result the other way round, this means in turn that we have a reasonably sound basis for interpreting the meaning of the primary activity data. While time-budget data are potentially misleading, we may nevertheless with care avoid being misled. What we may draw from this particular evidence is the relatively weak conclusion that they form a reasonably reliable and valid basis for estimating time-use patterns. But rather more important is to bear in mind the general and obvious conclusion: time-diary accounts, and particularly accounts of primary activities are 'constructions', or more precisely 'reductions' of the sum of conscious experience—which nevertheless (to judge by the bracketing of the first activity data between the maximum and minimum estimates in Figure A1.3) do provide a reasonably good picture of the full range of conscious events which underlie the hierarchical narratives.

An *ex post* evaluation of the problem of non-response bias

Time-budget diaries are very onerous to complete, and have, as a result, much higher non-response rates than almost any other survey activity. Now, for most sorts of social research, we are reasonably happy to ignore non-response, since the factors and characteristics that lead people to fail to answer questionnaires are in general not very closely correlated with the substance of the questions. We may lose a respondent because he has moved from his previous address, for example—but we only worry about non-response bias if we have some a priori grounds for expecting the answers to our questions to be affected by the respondent's geographical mobility. High levels of non-response are only a very serious grounds for worry where we have such a priori expectations.

High non-response rates are thus particularly worrying for time-budget research since, unlike most survey activities, there *are* good a priori reasons for expecting a significant non-response bias. We might expect that busy people, who have less time available for completing diaries, would be under-represented in time-budget samples. Or perhaps, alternatively, the sort of people that do not fill in diaries, are also the sorts of people who are also too lazy to engage in other activities. Either a priori would suggest that the diary sample would be unrepresentative of the activity patterns of the population as a whole—that diarists would exhibit a peculiar pattern of activity, different from that of the non-diarists. (The issue is however admittedly somewhat complicated by the fact that these two a priori expectations operate in many cases in opposite directions and might therefore be expected to cancel each other out.)

Let us go back for a moment to the two experiments discussed in Section 1 of this appendix. The conclusion we drew was that people in general do not know how much time they devote to their various activities. But though we cannot say very reliably how much time we devote to particular activities, clearly we are more likely to be able to answer the more straightforward question of whether or not we have taken part in an activity over a particular period. The next experiment relies on this sort of knowledge. The 1987 UK time-diary study also involved a questionnaire which among other things asked respondents to say how frequently they participate in activities: this questionnaire was used in the initial contact interview, before the respondents were invited to keep a diary. We can use this questionnaire evidence to test the proposition that diarists have different patterns of activity from non-diarists.

The test is really extremely simple. Diaries are rather difficult to complete (the seven-day diaries used in the UK particularly so), and around half of those asked to keep a diary fail to do so. So, of those who answered the activity questions, around half subsequently kept a diary, and half did not. Our the test has a two-step structure. First, we investigate to see if there is a systematic association between questionnaire and diary answers; then (and if there is such an association) we compare the questionnaire answers of those who kept diaries with the questionnaire answers of those who did not keep diaries.

Questionnaire vs. diary estimates of weekly participation rates

Figure A1.5 compares, for the half of the original sample who did successfully complete their diaries, the weekly rates of participation in various leisure activities calculated from two different sources. We have participation rates taken directly from the diaries (so the participation rate is calculated simply as the proportion of diarists who mentioned the particular activity one or more times in the course of the diary week). And we also

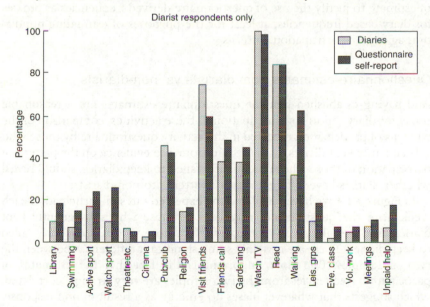

Figure A1.5. Diary activities vs. self-report

have participation rates calculated, for the same group of respondents, but drawing on their questionnaire answers to the battery of 'how frequently do you (go swimming, go the library and so on)?' questions. (In this case we calculate the participation rate as the mean score for each activity, having scored the answer 'once a week' as 1.0, 'once a fortnight' as 0.5, once a month as 0.23, and so on.)

Figure A1.5 does show some differences between the estimates from the two sources. There seem, in particular, to be some 'social desirability' effects (respondents seem to claim to interviewers that they go to the library, for example, slightly more frequently than they report visits to the library in their diaries). But, quite unlike the Table A1.1 comparisons of time-use *duration* data from questionnaires and diaries, which showed very weak associations, the comparisons of participation rates shows, as we expected, rather strong associations. And differences may sometimes reflect, not desirability effects, but interview contamination of respondents' behaviour. (We observed, in a previous study comparing questionnaires and diaries collected for the Scottish Sports Council, that diary reports of swimming and sports were actually rather lower in the questionnaire than in the subsequently completed diary: we concluded that being questioned by the Sports Council about sports participation may be a marginal but nevertheless effective way of stimulating sports participation!)

The point of the demonstration is that the general pattern is more than somewhat similar: there is certainly *enough* similarity between the two sorts of estimate to justify the use of questionnaire-derived frequencies as proxies for diary-based frequencies, at least for the purposes of estimating population aggregate participation patterns

Questionnaire-estimates from diarists vs. non-diarists

And having established that the questionnaire estimates are a reasonable proxy for diary reports of participation in these activities, comparison of the patterns of participation reported in the activity questionnaire by those who subsequently kept diaries, with the questionnaire evidence on the pattern of participation of those who subsequently failed to keep diaries, should reveal whether diarists have different activity patterns to non-diarists.

In Figure A1.6 we have calculated the expected rates of participation each week from the questionnaire responses of those who subsequently kept diaries. And we take similar estimates from those who subsequently failed to keep diaries. There are certainly some significant differences between the two subsamples. But more important is the fact that the estimates of participation frequencies from the two samples are very strongly correlated, which suggests that whatever biases do emerge as a result of non-response, they are not likely to be related to the activity patterns—and in particular the general state of busyness or otherwise—of the sampled individuals.

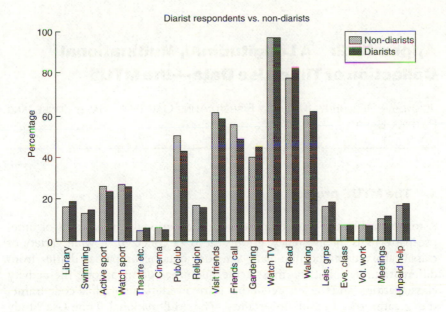

Figure A1.6. Self-reported activities

Appendix 2: A Longitudinal, Multinational Collection of Time-Use Data—the MTUS

Jonathan Gershuny, Kimberly Fisher, Anne Gauthier, Sally Jones, and Patrick Baert

1. The MTUS project

A major problem in intertemporal and international comparisons of time-use patterns is inconsistency among the data collected. A wide variety of classificatory data and non-diary time-use data accompanies diaries from different surveys, but the most acute dilemmas occur among the activity classifications, and the less detail that is involved in the original code frame, the greater the area of uncertainty. The Multinational Time-Use Study (MTUS) started in the mid-1980s, supported by the European Foundation for the Improvement of Living and Working Conditions, as a response to this problem. This project has now expanded and draws on collaborative efforts from teams in the UK, Canada, and Australia. (More detail of the MTUS, access to the survey documentation of original studies now included in the MTUS, access to some time-use data, and listings of technical details of a broad range of time-use studies are available from the MTUS web site: http://www.iser.essex.ac.uk/mtus.)

Its objectives were:

(1) to collect, preserve, document and make available to academic and other users, the original microdata from all extant national-scale time-diary studies.

(2) to produce a single standardized datafile in a common format, both for the time-use data and for other descriptive data about the diary respondents and their households, in a form that is ready to use, and accessible to non-specialists.

The latest version of the common datafile 'WORLD 5.5', contains forty-four surveys from twenty-one countries in all, with surveys at multiple time points from twelve countries. It represents over one-third of the (developed world) national-sample surveys of this type. We are negotiating to obtain access to surveys from Switzerland, as well as the 1981 data from Austria and the more recent surveys from Denmark, France, Norway, Poland, and the USA, raising to fifteen the number of countries in the MTUS with cross-time coverage, and increasing the number of 1990s surveys to a total of

Table A2.1. Current status of the common data file

No. of respondents in WORLD 5.5 (all ages)

	1961–70	1971–7	1978–83	1984–9	1990–4	1995–9
Australia		1,493		1,011	6,879	7,267
Austria					25,233	
Belgium	2,077					
Bulgaria				27,506		
Canada		2,141	2,686	9,946	9,815	
Czechoslovakia	2,193					
Denmark	3,534			3,594		
East Germany	2,152					
Finland			6,057	5,224		
France	3,006	6,641				
Hungary	1,994	6,925				
Israel					3,082	
Italy			3,896	37,722		
Netherlands		1,309	2,730	3,263	3,158	3,227
Norway		3,040	3,307			
Poland	2,759					
Sweden					3,630	
UK	2,363	3,545	1,480	1,996		1,875
USA	2,021	2,046		5,358		
West Germany	2,478				7,200	
Yugoslavia	2,125					

fifteen. (*The reader should note that work on the MTUS is ongoing. This appendix reflects information on the current state of the files as of the printing of this book. The analysis in the main chapters is based on the previous version of the file, WORLD 5.0*).

The WORLD 5.5 dataset

The intention for the WORLD 5.5 dataset is to provide straightforward aggregated totals of time (in minutes) devoted to activities in the course of a single day. These aggregates are calculated from the primary activity fields in the diaries, and take no account of any information about other secondary simultaneous activities (though future versions of the MTUS will include secondary activities). The diaries are recorded continuously through the day, so the aggregate time across all the categories of time use for any diary respondent who has correctly completed the instrument should sum to 1,440 minutes. In two of the countries (UK and the Netherlands) the instrument covers a full week; the aggregates for these two countries are nevertheless expressed in terms of minutes per day in order to maintain comparability. In the cases of USA, Sweden, and Israel, some respondents may have completed multiple (mostly two, but in the Israel case sometimes three) diary days. These are treated as if they were independent respondents.

The oversampling problems that might result from this are dealt with through the weighting procedures discussed below. However any potential 'design effect' consequences of this are ignored.

The age range of the samples in the original studies varies considerably. The previous version of the dataset, WORLD 5.0, adopted a minimal age range, of adults in their 'working-life' stage, aged between 20 and 60. Many of the more recent datasets now cover the full age range (with the Italian surveys including time-use information for infants through to the elderly). The WORLD 5.5 dataset provides the full age range the countries in the datafile.

WORLD 5.5 provides a forty-category activity classification, and a less-detailed twenty-activity categorization (Table A2.4 and A2.5 below). Both are designed to be consistent with the detailed activity list from the Szalai survey, which has greatly influenced subsequent research. Consequently, in most cases recategorization from the original codes to the MTUS codes has been straightforward. The forty-category classification is not fully implementable for some surveys. The earliest Danish surveys, and the 1995 UK survey, where the original survey instruments coded activities into very broad categories, are a particular problem. It has generally proved possible to create activity categories comparable at the twenty-activity level.

However, a reasonably comparable coding-frame may serve to disguise deeper and perhaps more significant differences between surveys. Section 2 of this appendix discusses the methodological variations across the original studies used in WORLD 5.5, and also the availability of demographic and other classificatory variables

2. Methodological choices in time-budget research

The essence of the time-budget technique is the diary method. Respondents produce a sequential account of their time, listing the start and finish time of each distinct event. Within this diary approach, however, there is a very wide range of alternative methodologies. We list here a number of the major variations in the surveys in our collection, with a brief discussion of the rationales underlying the various alternatives.

Population limits and sampling technique

When planning a time-budget survey, we have first to define the population from which the sample is to be drawn. In line with most national sociological studies, time-budget surveys routinely exclude segments of the general population, some of them sizeable: members of the armed forces and security services on active duty, people ill in hospital, in prison, or otherwise institutionalized, the very young and sometimes the very old. Age limits in particular vary considerably from survey to survey and country to country (Table A2.2).

Table A2.2.   Age ranges in the MTUS surveys

Country	Year of study	Minimum age	Maximum age	Age group only
Australia	1974	18	69	No
Australia	1987	15	99+	No
Australia	1992	15	99+	No
Australia	1997	15	99+	No
Austria	1991	10	99+	No
Bulgaria	1988	0	99+	No
Canada	1971	18	99+	Yes
Canada	1981	15	99+	No
Canada	1986	15	99+	No
Canada	1992	15	99+	No
Denmark	1964	15	99+	No
Denmark	1987	16	74	No
Finland	1979	10	64	No
Finland	1987	10	99+	No
France	1966	18	64	Yes
France	1974/5	18	99+	No
Hungary	1965	18	64	Yes
Hungary	1976/7	15	69	No
Israel	1991/2	14	99+	Yes
Italy	1979/80	1	99+	No
Italy	1989	3	99+	No
Netherlands	1975	12	99+	Yes
Netherlands	1980	12	99+	Yes
Netherlands	1985	12	99+	No
Netherlands	1990	12	99+	No
Netherlands	1995	12	99+	No
Norway	1971/2	16	74	No
Norway	1980/1	16	74	No
Sweden	1990/1	20	65	No
UK	1961	15	99+	Yes
UK	1974/5	5	99+	No
UK	1983/4	14	99+	No
UK	1987	16	99+	No
UK	1995	16	99+	No
USA	1965	18	64	No
USA	1975	18	99+	No
USA	1985	12	99+	No
West Germany	1965	18	64	Yes
West Germany	1991/2	12	99+	No
Other Szalai	1965	18	70	Yes

Time of year must also be taken into account. It determines which proportion of the general population will be on holiday and so ignored by sampling procedures, besides crucially affecting the amount of time spent in out-of-doors activities. (Standard sampling methods, using addresses as the primary element in the sample strategy, also ignore individuals of no fixed abode, including the homeless.)

Further difficulties stem from the choice of the basic sampling unit, which may be either a household or an individual diarist. It is difficult to persuade entire households to participate in a time-budget survey. If a household survey is attempted, the survey will suffer a relatively high non-response rate, especially if only complete household data are accepted, but the inclusion of data from incomplete households guarantees problems with bias. Surveys involving diarists selected on a one-respondent-per-address (ORPA) basis generally give rise to a more stable sample of households, but their data will be inevitably be unrepresentative of a general population sample, since members of large households will be seriously under-represented, and require some specific reweighting. The objectives of the sponsor of the particular survey determine which scheme will be chosen. If the analysis is going to concentrate just on population aggregates, then ORPA is probably in balance the most reliable procedure, but then estimates of distributions of within-household phenomena such as the gender divisions of labour and leisure are impossible. If intrahousehold dynamics are of most interest, data must be collected from as many complete households as possible. Fieldwork costs are generally lower following the whole household procedure.

We are forced to conclude that whatever scheme is adopted, time-budget researchers cannot assume the data obtained will be unproblematically random, even within the limits of the sample population. Checking the diary respondents against the general population on all parameters of known importance is vital, and any significant deviations will have to be allowed for in the analysis. Usually, this involves weighting.

The diary period

A similar choice between high non-response rates and maximum utility of the data affects the design of the diary instrument. The length of time the diary covers, which may be anything from a day to a week, is particularly important. Day diaries, which are so much less trouble to complete, will produce much higher response rates and hence the most reliable national estimates of time use, but they prevent detailed analysis of events whose natural cycle stretches over a longer period and may seriously bias estimates of variability. Many domestic tasks and some leisure activities are naturally scheduled on a weekly basis, although people do different things at different times; consequently, there is less variation between weekly activity patterns than among daily patterns, and this is again particularly relevant to studies of the domestic division of labour. The shorter the diary, the greater the chance of overestimating interpersonal variation in behaviour.

Some surveys (e.g. Hungary 1996–7, USA 1975, Sweden 1990–1), while using a one-day diary format, try to obtain more than one diary from their respondents. For instance, in the case of the Hungarian 1996–7 survey,

Table A2.3. Length of diaries

Day-diaries (< 1,440 minutes)	
Canada	1981
Denmark	1964
Day-diaries (1,440 minutes)	
Australia	1974, 1987 (half 1 day, half 2 days)
Austria	1992
Bulgaria	1988
Canada	1971, 1986, 1992
Denmark	1987
France	1966, 1975
Hungary	1965
Italy	1979/80
UK	1995
USA	1965, 1975, 1985
West Germany	1965
Other Szalai surveys	1965
Two, three, or four days	
Australia	1987, 1992, 1997
Finland	1979, 1987
Hungary	1976/7
Israel	1991/2
Italy	1989
Norway	1971/2, 1980/1
Sweden	1990/1
West Germany	1991/2
Week-diaries	
Netherlands	1975, 1980, 1985, 1990, 1995
UK	1961, 1974/5, 1983/4, 1987

diarists were asked to keep four one-day diaries at ninety-day intervals; similarly, the USA 1975 survey asked respondents to provide four diary days, one per quarter, including weekdays and weekends.

Minimum time intervals

Most diary instruments specify standard intervals of 5, 15 or 30 minutes, though some otherwise highly structured surveys (e.g. the Szalai 1972 studies) leave the respondent free to specify the exact start and finish times of activities to the nearest minute. There are serious problems with short intervals: the diaries are very burdensome on respondents and coders. However, longer specified intervals encourage respondents to concatenate activities, and some short-period activities tend to disappear altogether. Conscientious respondents, aware of this tendency, sometimes agonize over their long-interval diaries and wish shorter periods had been provided.

Some surveys have mixed short and long (15-minute and 30-minute) intervals according to the activity-density expected at different times of day. The more recent UK data is based on diaries with 15-minute intervals plus accommodation for multiple activities. Best practice is probably 5 minutes or open-period (1 minute) diaries (Table A2.4).

Interviewer vs. self-completion diaries

Diaries recorded by an interviewer asking the respondent about the previous day's activities—'yesterday diaries'—are more standardized, and far better checked and controlled than 'tomorrow' diaries left behind after an initial contact for the respondent to complete him- or herself on the following day (or days) (though in some countries, like Japan, interviewers return on the day after the diary day to collect the diaries and to discuss any gaps or ambiguities in the diary). Moreover, unlike the 'tomorrow diaries', 'yester-day diaries' carry no inherent bias against respondents who for any reason

Table A2.4.   MTUS surveys: 'Time-slots'

Open-period diaries	
Australia	1974
Bulgaria	1988
Canada	1971, 1981, 1986, 1992
France	1966
Hungary	1965, 1976/7
Italy	1979/80, 1989
USA	1965, 1975, 1985
West Germany	1965
Other Szalai surveys	1965
5-minute time-slots	
Australia	1992, 1997
France	1975
West Germany	1991/2
10–minute slots	
Sweden	1990/1
15-minute time-slots	
Australia	1987
Denmark	1987
Netherlands	1975, 1980, 1985, 1990, 1995
UK	1983/4, 1987, 1995
15/30 minute time-slots	
Austria	1992
Denmark	1964
Israel	1991/2
Norway	1971/2, 1980/1
30-minute time-slots	
UK	1961, 1974/5
30/10 minute time-slots	
Finland	1979, 1987

find writing difficult. Fortunately, newer methods of diary administration have greatly reduced this possibility for bias. Diary techniques including having researchers shadow respondents (particularly illiterate respondents in developing countries (Minge-Klevana 1980)) or giving beepers with audio-recording attachments to respondents and asking them to verbally record their activity at times when they are beeped (Robinson and Godbey 1997). The 'yesterday diaries' are less accurate than a near-contemporaneously recorded diary, and in practical terms they are limited to a one-day diary format. 'Tomorrow diaries' can be of any length, and administering them may be cheaper, especially if the diaries are returned by post. If the interviewer has to make a second visit to collect the diary and check its completeness, the cost differences will be less striking.

The Italian surveys, which deliberately set out to collect diaries across the entire age range, used a complex mix of completion agents. Some diaries were self-completed, some recorded by interviewers, and very young children's diaries are filled in by parents.

Precoded activity categories vs. natural language

In the past, precoded diaries have involved a list of activities or activity codes printed on the diary form for the respondent to tick or circle, rather in the manner of the BBC 1984 diary discussed earlier. This format is inherently limited with respect to the number of categories which can reasonably be fitted into even the best-designed form. An interesting, though perhaps not universally applicable alternative, used by the Netherlands surveys in our collection, is to provide the activity code frame in the form of a look-up dictionary. This type of precoding allows the respondent more flexibility than multiple preprinted activity lists, but it makes far greater demands on the respondent than either the precoded lists or a natural-language diary format, and any truly unusual activities not provided for may be squeezed into inappropriate codes without anyone else being conscious of the problem. Equally, if the diarists record an inappropriate code through confusion or carelessness, or if their handwriting is unclear, there is no possible way for the mistake to be remedied later. Preprinted lists suffer much the same disadvantages. Natural-language diaries may at times be muddied by slang, dialect, or undecipherable local references, but there is a far greater chance of the diary actually being understood.

Natural-language diaries also allow subsequent researchers to search for activities not previously identified as salient, but there is far more variation in the amount of detail recorded in natural-language diaries than in precoded diaries (Table A2.5).

Table A2.5.   MTUS surveys: precoding

Precoded, limited activity check-list	
Denmark	1964, 1987
UK	1995
Pre-coded, detailed activity dictionary	
Austria	1992
Netherlands	1975, 1980, 1985, 1990, 1995

Detailed coding of the time-use variables

Precoding the time-use variables on the diary form tends to limit the number of different codes, although considerable variation can still be found (with the mere twenty-two distinct time-use categories in the Denmark 1964 survey representing probably the smallest useful codeset.) Natural-language diaries permit very detailed coding, sometimes involving several hundred time-use codes, although the bulk of the analytic work on such datasets will normally conflate the detailed codes into more manageable groups. However, coding natural-language time-budgets is a substantial task, which adds problems of ambiguity and legibility to the normal (minimizable) chance of coding error, and with significant costs.

Most of the surveys included in the MTUS use activity code frames derived from the codes used in the Szalai Multinational Survey, with occasional adaptations or enhancements to accommodate their own countries' special peculiarities—mushroom collecting in Norway, for instance, taking a sauna in Finland, or in the Japanese time-budget surveys, flower

Table A2.6.   The 20-category classification in WORLD 5.5

PAIDETC	Paid work, education, etc.	PUBCLUB	At pubs, clubs
HWORK	Routine housework	SPECTAT	Spectator
COOKING	Food preparation, cooking	ASPORTS	Active sporting activity
EATING	Meals and snacks	WALKING	Walking
KIDCARE	Childcare	VISITS	Visiting or entertaining friends
SHOPPING	Shopping (all sorts)	TVRAD	Television, radio, etc.
DTRAVEL	Domestic-related travel	READING	Reading books, papers, magazines
OTRAVEL	Other non-work travel	CHATSETC	Talking, relaxing
PERSCARE	Personal care activities	ODDJOBS	Non-routine domestic work
EATOUT	Eating out	HOBBIES	Other at-home leisure
MEDICAL	Personal medical care	EDUC	Education at school or university

Notes: EDUC also included in PAIDETC
For general analysis, MEDICAL is best combined with PERSCARE (since some studies do not distinguish these). So, excluding EDUC, this constitutes a twenty-activity scheme.

Table A2.7. 40-category classification in WORLD 5.5

AV1	Paid work	AV21	Walks
AV2	Paid work at home	AV22	Religious activities
AV3	Second job	AV23	Civic duties
AV4	School/classes	AV24	Cinema, theatre
AV5	Travel to/from work	AV25	Dances, parties
AV6	Cooking, washing up	AV26	Social club
AV7	Housework	AV27	Pub
AV8	Odd jobs	AV28	Restaurant
AV9	Gardening, pets	AV29	Visiting friends
AV10	Shopping	AV30	Listening to radio
AV11	Childcare	AV31	Television, video
AV12	Domestic travel	AV32	Listening to tapes, etc.
AV13	Dressing/toilet	AV33	Study
AV14	Personal services	AV34	Reading books
AV15	Meals, snacks	AV35	Reading papers, magazines
AV16	Sleep	AV36	Relaxing
AV17	Leisure travel	AV37	Conversation
AV18	Excursions	AV38	Entertaining friends
AV19	Active sport	AV39	Knitting, sewing, etc.
AV20	Passive sport	AV40	Other hobbies and pastimes

arranging. So, collapsing the original survey code frames into the much broader 22-category and 40-category code frames used in the MTUS comparative dataset is relatively straightforward. Occasional difficulties arise even at the 20-category-level, mostly in connection with out-of-home leisure activities such as PUBCLUBS. Similarly, some surveys record mode of travel but not the purpose for which the journey was made. The code frames are briefly outlined in Tables A2.6 and A2.7.

'Simultaneous' activities and other ancillary diary information

Although some diary formats press diarists to record only one activity at a time, the Szalai Multinational Survey and most subsequent formats allow for at least two activities to be recorded as occurring within the same time-slot. Many people often consider themselves to be doing two or more things at once: cooking a meal and talking to the children, driving a car and listening to the radio. Also, within the fixed time-slots of most time-budget diaries, two or more activities may occur sequentially: 'fed the dog then drank a cup of tea', 'tidied myself then walked to the shops'. Respondents doing their best to fit their lives into a standardized diary format may find it difficult to say which of their multiple-occurring activities are to be reported as the main or primary activity for a particular time-slot. One response to this, in conjunction with a precoded activity-list diary format, is to abandon hierarchy altogether, and merely record all activities which took place during the time-slot without any prioritization. Such an approach makes comparisons of time use almost impossible, and completely rules out any aggregate analysis of the diarists' days, although the technique can increase the visibility of some very short-duration or low-priority activities, and the data may still have some utility in sequential analysis, and in estimating participation rates. In the case of research work with the elderly, using diaries with fixed time-slots of one minute have proved most useful, as many significant activities for older people, such as taking medication, last for brief periods (Ujimoto 1990).

Primary-activity diary data are far and away the most analysed element from time-budget diaries, but surveys (especially post-Szalai) often also ask their respondents to record further dimensions of their use of time. Most frequently, the diarists are asked to state where the activity took place, with whom and for whom, as well as to indicate which mode of transport was used while travelling. Less typically, some diarists have been asked to evaluate their activity in one way or another: how enjoyable was it, would they have liked to do more or less of the activity if time pressures were to allow this, or whether they consider the activity to be work or leisure (Table A2.8).

In most surveys, subsidiary activities are coded in the same way as the primary activity, but in a few cases, they are allocated a more limited set of codes (the Finland surveys, for instance). Similarly, code frames for location vary between detailed, 30- or 40-category schemes to a simple at-home–not-at-home dichotomy (BBC 1961). The possible availability of ancillary time-use data for some of the surveys which have been brought into the MTUS as aggregated primary-activity datasets is inadequately documented at present (Netherlands 1975 and 1985, USA 1985).

Table A2.8.   Classificatory 'face-sheet' variables in WORLD 5.5

COUNTRY		HHTYPE	Household type
PERIOD	Survey time-period	EMPSTAT	Employment status
SURVEY	Survey year	WORKHRS	Hours paid work last week
ID	Personal identifier	UNEMP	Whether formally unemployed
DAY	Day of interview	EMP	Whether economically active
SEX		INCOME	Income group
AGE2	Age (estimates where needed)	EDUCA	Educational level intercode
FAMSTAT	Family status/ children's ages	EDTRY	Educational group
CIVSTAT	Civic status		

Classificatory variables

The more that is known about the respondents, the more useful any particular dataset will be. However, researchers concerned to minimize a time-budget survey's generally high non-response rate will not wish to antagonize potential diarists by adding too substantial a questionnaire to their already onerous task. Consequently, the choice and extent of the non-diary data collected vary considerably from survey to survey and reflect the survey's primary analytic aims and available funding. None the less, basic demographic variables are almost universally recorded. Few worthwhile surveys fail to include sex, age, civic status, employment status, an assessment of educational achievement or qualifications, indicators of household composition (especially the presence of children), and some measure of household or individual income. Time-budget datasets organized on a day-case basis also crucially include a day-of-the-week variable.

All these variables are included (for all possible surveys) in the MTUS, together with variables to allow each case to be uniquely identified and rematched with its original survey. Table A2.9 sets out the classificatory variables in WORLD 5.5, and Table A2.10 briefly summarizes the availability of these variables for each survey in WORLD 5.5.

The variables indicating the level of educational achievement and the income variables are the most difficult to coordinate for comparative analysis. Educational systems and examinations vary widely between countries, and not infrequently change from survey to survey within the same country. Incomes expressed in the currency of the country of origin are equally hard to compare. In both cases, the inherent difficulties are compounded by variations in definition and in data collection. Some surveys assess the amount of cultural capital acquired by their respondents through completed years in school, others by qualifications, others still by the type of school or college the respondent last attended. Income variables, superficially more straightforward, at least at the intrasurvey and intracountry levels, sometimes record the individual's own income, sometimes that of the household to which he or she belongs, sometimes refer to earned income only, and sometimes give a total figure. In any event, almost all surveys then group the income figure, more or less broadly. So the possibility of confusion is considerable. However, the most important classificatory criteria are the respondent's levels of income relative to others in that society, and educational attainment relative to completion of the high-school curriculum. In consequence, the education variable in the WORLD 5.5 file follows the format of the OECD ISCED ranking of education standards in different countries. (A discussion of this classification may be found at http://www.oecd.org//els/stats/edu_db/def_uoe2.htm.)

Reweighting to produce comparable national samples

In organizing our data into one large comparative dataset, we had to take into account not only the differences in sample size, but also the very high probability that the carefully designed random samples could have been distorted by the high non-response rates normal among time-budget surveys. The generally accepted methodology for weighting cross-sectional surveys relies on accurate and detailed information about the nature of the original sample, and of the rates and types of response at each sample point. On the basis of adequate *ex ante* information it would be possible to compensate systematically wherever we find that sample points have relatively low response rates, and the achieved interview sample would otherwise under-represent particular geographical areas (and hence under-represent the distinct social mix in those areas). However, in the MTUS we are undertaking a process of historical reconstruction of surveys that were in some cases collected more than four decades ago, where the sample information has not survived, or is unintelligible without the participation of those originally responsible for the sampling, or perhaps the required information was never available.

So we are forced to rely on a technically inferior procedure of *ex post* weighting, which relies merely on knowledge of what the survey's socio-demographic make-up should have looked like, based on knowledge of the population structure gained from other sources. Previous research has shown that the most important categorical factors relevant to explanations of variation in time-use patterns, other than nationality and date, are sex, age, and employment status. Fortunately, national estimates for these factors have been published by the ILO, and these figures were used in the first stage of a complex reweighting process.

A really representative time-use survey would have an equal selection probability for each day of the year. However practical difficulties (e.g. Christmas, reaching people on extended trips away from home) mean that this is unachievable, and surveys tend either to seek merely to give adequate representations of each season of the year, or to represent simply a single season. There is no general attempt to deal with this problem of seasonal representativeness within the weighting system adopted here. (Among the UK surveys, the 1983/4 ESRC (winter) and 1987 (summer) surveys have been combined (to produce the synthetic '1985') and the 1974/5 (summer/winter) two-wave survey has been regarded as a whole. In both instances, this has the advantage of combining cases across seasons, so that these datasets approximate to two-season samples.)

Internal evidence shows really very substantial and systematic differences between the activities of different days of the week, and furthermore we have a priori reasons to expect systematic biases in daily responses (e.g. difficulties in interviewing employed women on Saturdays when they are occupied with domestic chores). So a second stage of weighting was used to ensure that the days of the week would appear to be equally represented in each of the major sex/age/employment categories used in the stage-1 weighing procedure. (Cases in the Netherlands and UK surveys, which used whole-week diaries, are represented in the MTUS by figures for an 'average day of the week', which did not need to be adjusted in this way.)

Thirdly, to adjust for the considerable variation in survey sizes, two further weighting factors were calculated. One, to be used for national analyses, produces a constant 2,000 cases per survey, so preventing a large survey swamping another smaller survey. The other, employed in cross-national analyses, results in approximately 2,000 cases per country, even

Table A2.9.   MTUS surveys: ancillary diary variables

Country	Year of study	Simultaneous activities	Location (where)	With whom
Australia	1974	Yes	Yes	Yes
Australia	1987	Yes	Yes	Yes
Australia	1992	Yes	Yes	Yes
Australia	1997	Yes	Yes	Yes
Austria	1991	Yes	Yes	Yes
Bulgaria	1988	Yes	Yes	Yes
Canada	1971	Yes	Yes	Yes
Canada	1981	Yes	Yes	Yes
Canada	1986	Yes	Yes	Yes
Canada	1992	Yes	Yes	Yes
Denmark	1964	TV/Radio	Yes	No
Denmark	1987	TV/Radio	Yes	No
Finland	1979	Yes	Yes	Yes
Finland	1987	Yes	Yes	Yes
France	1966	Yes	Yes	Yes
France	1974/5	Yes	Yes	Yes
Hungary	1965	Yes	Yes	Yes
Hungary	1976/7	Yes	Yes	Yes
Israel	1991/2	No	Yes	Yes
Italy	1979/80	Yes	Yes	Yes
Italy	1989	Yes	Yes	No
Netherlands	1975	No	Yes	No
Netherlands	1980	No	Yes	No
Netherlands	1985	No	Yes	No
Netherlands	1990	No	Yes	No
Netherlands	1995	No	Yes	No
Norway	1971/2	Yes	Yes	No
Norway	1980/1	Yes	Yes	Yes
Sweden	1990/1	Yes	Yes	Yes
UK	1961	Yes	Yes	No
UK	1974/5	Yes	Yes	No
UK	1983/4	Yes	Yes	Yes
UK	1987	Yes	Yes	Yes
UK	1995	No	No	No
USA	1965	Yes	Yes	Yes
USA	1975	Yes	Yes	Yes
USA	1985	No	No	No
West Germany	1965	Yes	Yes	Yes
West Germany	1991/2	Yes	Yes	Yes
Other Szalai	1965	Yes	Yes	Yes

Table A2.10. Availability of the main classificatory variables in the MTUS comparative dataset (country, survey, day, ID, and sex available in all cases)

Country	Year	civstat	famstat	hhtype	empstat	workhrs	unemp	educat	income
Australia	1974	Yes	Yes	Yes	Yes	Yes	No	Yes	Yes
Australia	1987	Yes	Yes	Yes	Yes	No	Yes	Yes	Yes
Australia	1992	Yes	Yes	Yes	Yes	Yes	Yes	Yes	Yes
Australia	1997	Yes	Yes	Yes	Yes	Yes	Yes	Yes	Yes
Austria	1991	Yes	Yes	Yes	Yes	Yes	Yes	Yes	Yes
Bulgaria	1988	Yes	Yes	Yes	Yes	Yes	No	Yes	Yes
Canada	1971	Yes	Yes	Yes	Yes	Yes	Yes	Yes	No
Canada	1981	Yes	Yes	Yes	Yes	Yes	Yes	Yes	Yes
Canada	1986	Yes	Yes	Yes	Yes	No	Yes	Yes	Yes
Canada	1992	Yes	Yes	Yes	Yes	Yes	Yes	Yes	Yes
Denmark	1964	Yes	Yes	No	Yes	Yes	Yes	Yes	Yes
Denmark	1987	Yes	Yes	No	Yes	Yes	No	Yes	Yes
	1979	Yes	Yes	Yes	Yes	Yes	Yes	Yes	No
Finland	1987	Yes	Yes	Yes	Yes	Yes	Yes	Yes	No
	1966	Yes	Yes	Yes	Yes	Yes	Yes	Yes	No
France	1974/5	Yes	Yes	Yes	Yes	Yes	Yes	Yes	Yes
Hungary	1965	Yes	Yes	Yes	Yes	Yes	Yes	Yes	No
Hungary	1976/7	Yes	Yes	No	Yes	No	No	Yes	No
Israel	1991/2	Yes	Yes	Yes	Yes	Yes	Yes	Yes	Yes
Italy	1979/0	No	Yes	No	Yes	No	Yes	Yes	No
Italy	1989	Yes	Yes	Yes	Yes	No	Yes	Yes	No
Netherlands	1975	Yes	Yes	Yes	Yes	Yes	No	Yes	No
Netherlands	1980	Yes	Yes	Yes	Yes	Yes	No	Yes	No
Netherlands	1985	Yes	Yes	Yes	Yes	Yes	Yes	Yes	Yes
Netherlands	1990	Yes	Yes	Yes	Yes	Yes	Yes	Yes	Yes
Netherlands	1995	Yes	Yes	Yes	Yes	Yes	Yes	Yes	Yes
Norway	1971/2	Yes	Yes	Yes	Yes	Yes	No	Yes	Yes
Norway	1980/1	Yes	Yes	Yes	Yes	Yes	No	Yes	Yes
Sweden	1990/1	Yes	Yes	Yes	Yes	Yes	Yes	Yes	Yes
UK	196	No	Yes	No	Yes	Yes	No	Yes	No
UK	1974/5	Yes	Yes	Yes	Yes	Yes	Yes	Yes	No
UK	1983/4	Yes	Yes	Yes	Yes	Yes	Yes	Yes	No
UK	1987	Yes	Yes	Yes	Yes	Yes	Yes	Yes	Yes
UK	1995	Yes	Yes	Yes	Yes	Yes	Yes	Yes	Yes
USA	1965	Yes	Yes	Yes	Yes	Yes	Yes	Yes	Yes
USA	1975	Yes	Yes	Yes	Yes	Yes	Yes	Yes	Yes
USA	1985	Yes	Yes	Yes	Yes	Yes	Yes	Yes	Yes
W. Germany	1965	Yes	Yes	Yes	Yes	Yes	No	Yes	No
W. Germany	1991/2	Yes	Yes	Yes	Yes	Yes	Yes	Yes	Yes
Other Szalai	1965	Yes	Yes	Yes	Yes	Yes	Yes	Yes	No

Table A2.11.   Weighting variables

SEXEMPWT	Weight: sex, age, employment from ILO data
DAYWT	Weight to adjust sexempwt to give equal days/week
SURVWT	Weight to get 2,000 cases per survey (after sedwt2)
COUNWT	Weight to get 2,000 cases per country (after sedwt3)
SEDWT2	Weight: sexempwt * daywt
SEDWT3	Weight: sexempwt * daywt * survwt
SEDWT4	Weight: sedwt3 * counwt

though the number of surveys per country varies between one and four, so that countries with large surveys are not over-represented wherever WORLD 5.5 is analysed as a whole.

Two thousand cases per survey or per country is not a totally arbitrary figure, it approximates (just slightly larger than) the smallest surveys used in the comparative dataset. None the less, 2,000 is considerably below the median sample size and grossly understates the actual number of cases in the largest surveys. Estimates of the statistical significance of analyses of WORLD 5.5 using SEDWT3 and SEDWT4 are consequently extremely conservative.

The general guidance for these is that SEDWT2 should be used where the analyst looks at individual surveys, SEDWT3 where the focus is on separate countries, and SEDWT4 where the analysis is of WORLD 5.5 as a whole.

Comparing surveys collected using disparate methodologies

Bearing in mind all the methodological variations described above, comparison obviously presents problems. Our primary concerns are change over time and the differences between countries. How can we be certain that our findings show real differences, and real changes, when there are such substantial methodological variations in the surveys? Ultimately, we cannot provide any proof of the validity of our results, but their technical reliability can be tested, at least in part. We suggest three approaches.

First, investigations by ourselves and others have looked at how much impact the research instrument's particular design actually makes on the results. A series of experiments using the full range of methodologies (beeper diaries vs. yesterdays vs. tomorrows vs. observed activities, etc., reported in Robinson and Godbey 1997) has demonstrated the time-budget diary's technical robustness, at least when time use is analysed in broad aggregate measures. So we feel cautiously confident in rejecting instrument design as a significant factor affecting aggregate time use.

Second, sampling differences can be minimized by reweighting. The high non-response rates, and the relatively small samples often used in time-budget surveys as a consequence of budgetary constraints, in any case often leads to unacceptably biased samples, with various population subgroups under- or over-represented. Intrasurvey analysis has been used to test which variables are associated with, and hence can be used to explain, variations in time-use patterns. Where there is no association, sampling differences can simply be ignored. When associations are found, the sample can be reweighted on an a priori basis to simulate the appropriate national population with respect to the relevant factors.

Clearly, this approach is limited to items actually included in the dataset. If a survey has failed to collect the necessary data, no adjustment can be made for that factor: an unsatisfactory situation. However, there are no serious omissions in the surveys in the MTUS. (There are some minor irritants, for example the failure of the UK 1961 and 1974 surveys to determine marital status. More seriously, estimates of education and income vary from the very detailed to the non-existent. Fortunately, analysis shows neither has much effect on time-use patterns once other more significant factors have been taken into account.)

Third, the comparative analysis itself may or may not give rise to systematic patterns. If no such patterns emerge, this does not necessarily confirm or refute the validity of the exercise, but if there are such patterns, regularly obtained—if, with a very large group of surveys, we can show similarities and continuities, shared trends over time between countries, or models of the effects of sociological variables which work consistently across countries, and we cannot produce a priori arguments which suggest that these similarities and continuities are artefacts of differences in the way the data were collected, then we can conclude that the methodological differences among the surveys have failed to hide genuine underlying processes.

This third line of argument is admittedly circular: in effect we justify our methods from our conclusions, and our conclusions from our methods. But, from a certain perspective, the results themselves *must* provide the strongest defence of our work. Much of science—and particularly all science operating at the edge of what is currently known—proceeds in just this manner. We use complex machines to detect elementary particles which cannot be observed except in these machines, and we identify the particles on the basis that they are detected in regular and continuous ways which conform to clearly articulated models of their occurrence; but because of their complexity, in the last analysis, we only have confidence that the machines are operating correctly because they reliably detect the particles in the circumstances that are predicted by the models.

The direct evaluation of the research instruments themselves is in this sense not necessarily the ultimate test of the quality of the data. What are important are the patterns of evidence—the regularities and continuities of time use, and the theories of national differences and intertemporal change—that we can construct out of the data. The ultimate justification for the perhaps somewhat suspect business of comparing disparate datasets is that it produces the often very clear and consistent, cross-sectional and longitudinal patterns of behaviour and change described in the previous chapters.

3. A summary codebook for WORLD 5.5

COUNTRY

1 Canada
2 Denmark
3 France
4 Netherlands
5 Norway
6 UK
7 USA
8 Hungary
9 West Germany
10 Poland
11 Belgium
12 Bulgaria
13 Czechoslovakia
14 East Germany
15 (unassigned)
16 Yugoslavia
17 Finland
18 Italy
19 Australia
20 Israel
21 Sweden

SURVEY: Year when survey took place
          (last two digits only: 1961 is earliest in WORLD 5.5)

ID: Personal identifier
      (unique within any country / survey / day)

DAY: Day of the week

1 Sunday
2 Monday
3 Tuesday
4 Wednesday
5 Thursday
6 Friday
7 Saturday
8 Average day of the week

SEX

1 Men
2 Women

AGE2: Age in years
       (including ages fudged as the midpoint of the grouped age variables used
       by some surveys)

FAMSTAT: Family status

0   Young (age < 40) living without children
1   Living with at least one young child (age < 5 approximately)
2   Living with at least one school-aged child but no younger children
3   Older person without any children of school age or less in the household

CIVSTAT: Civic status

1   Married or living as a couple
2   Single, separated, divorced

HHTYPE: Household type

1   Single person living alone
2   Married couple living without other people
3   Married couple living with other people
4   Other household types

EMPSTAT: Employment status

1   Employed full time
2   Employed part time
3   Unemployed or non-employed (i.e. not counted in the formal labour force)

WORKHRS: Total hours per week normally worked in paid employment

UNEMP: Formally unemployed

INCOME: Income group

1   Lowest 25%
2   Middle 50%
3   Highest 25%

EDUCA: Educational level intercode

1   Incomplete secondary education
2   Complete secondary education
3   Some completed education/training beyond secondary level

Missing values: these vary between countries, so all out-of-range values should be predefined as missing.

References

Adler, Hans J., and Oli Hawrylyshn (1978), 'Estimates of the Value of Household Work, Canada 1961 and 1971', *Review of Income and Wealth* 24(3): 333–55.

Aglietta, Michel (1979), *A Theory of Capitalist Regulation: The US Experience*, trans. David Fernbach, London: NLB.

Andorka, Rudolf, Istvan Harcsa, and Iiris Niemi (1983), *Use of Time in Hungary and in Finland*, Helsinki: Tilastokeskus Statistikcentralen, Tutkimuksia Undersoknin-gar Studies No. 101.

Andrews, F., J. Morgan, and J. Songquist (1967), *Multiple Classification Analysis: A Report on a Computer Program for Multiple Regression Using Categorical Predictors*, Ann Arbor, Mich.: Survey Research Center.

Ås, Dagfinn. (1978), 'Studies of Time Use Problems and Prospects', *Acta Sociologica* 15(2): 125–41.

Asimov, Isaac (1985), *The Naked Sun*, London: Harper Collins.

Becker, Gary (1965), 'A Theory of the Allocation of Time', *Economic Journal* 75: 493–517.

—— (1979), 'Economic Analysis and Human Behaviour', in L. Lévy-Garboua (ed.), *Sociological Economics*, London: Sage Publications: 7–24; with commentary by François Bourricaud: 25–8.

Beitrage zur Osterreichischen Statistik (1995), *Zeitverwendung* (1992/1981), Beitrage zur Osterreichischen Statistik, Herausgegeben vom Osterrechischen Statistischen Zentralamt hfft 1.171.

Berk, Sarah Fenstermaker (1985), *The Gender Factory: The Apportionment of Work in American Households*, New York: Plenum Press.

Blanke, Karen, M. Ehling, and N. Schwarz (1996), *Zeit im Blickfeld. Ergebnisse einer Representativen Zeitbudgeterhebung*, Berlin: Verlag W. Kohlhammer.

Bourdieu, Pierre (1979), *Distinction: A Social Critique of the Judgement of Taste*, trans. Richard Nice, London: Routledge & Kegan Paul.

British Broadcasting Company (1965), *The People's Activities*, London: BBC Audience Research Reports.

Carlstein, Tommy, and Nigel Thrift (1978), 'Afterward: Towards a Time-Space Structured Approach to Society and Environment', in T. Carlstein, D. Parkes, and N. Thrift (eds.), *Human Activity and Time Geography*, ii, London: Edward Arnold: 225–63.

Carroll, Lewis (1889), *Sylvie and Bruno Concluded*, London: Macmillan.

Clark, Colin (1940), *The Conditions of Economic Progress*, London: Macmillan.

Coleman, James S. (1964), *Introduction to Mathematical Sociology*, New York: Free Press.

—— (1990), *Foundations of Social Theory*, Cambridge, Mass: Belknap Press of Harvard University Press.

Converse, Philip E. (1972), 'Country Differences in Time Use', in Alexander Szalai (ed.), *The Use of Time*, The Hague: Mouton: 145–77.

Crichton, Michael (1991), *Jurassic Park*, London: Arrow Books and Random House.

Department of Employment and Productivity (1971), *British Labour Statistics Historical Abstract: 1886–1968*, London: HMSO.

Dow, Greg K., and F. Thomas Juster (1985), 'Goods, Time, and Well-Being: The Joint Dependence Problem', in F. Thomas Juster and Frank P. Stafford (eds.), *Time, Goods, and Well-Being*, Ann Arbor: Survey Research Center, University of Michigan: 397–413.

Dumazadier, Joffre (1967), *Vers un Societe du Loisirs / Towards a Society of Leisure*, trans. Stuart E. McClure, New York: Free Press.

Erlich, Alma (1987), *Time Allocation: Pt.4 Preliminary Analysis–Focus Personal Care*, London: Unilever House: No. 687002.

Esping-Anderson, Gosta (1990), *The Three Worlds of Welfare Capitalism*, Cambridge: Polity Press.

Excel, Jeanet (1993), *A Survey on Time Use in the Netherlands: General Results for 1988*, Netherlands Central Bureau of Statistics, P.O. Box 4481, 6401 CZ HEERLEN The Netherlands, BPA np. H2095-93-S5. 1993.

Fourastie, Jean (1949), *Le Grand Espoir du XXe Siècle, Progrès Technique, Progrès Économique, Progrès Social*, Paris.

—— (1960), *The Causes of Wealth*, trans. T. Caplow, Glencoe, Ill.: Free Press (originally published 1951).

Friedan, Betty (1984), *The Feminine Mystique*, New York: Laurel (first published 1963).

Fukuyama, Francis (1992), *The End of History and the Last Man*, New York: Penguin.

Gershuny, Jonathan I (1978), *After Industrial Society?* London: Macmillan Press.

—— (1983), *Social Innovation and the Division of Labour*, Oxford: Oxford University Press.

—— Michael Bittman, and John Brice (1997), *Exit, Voice and Suffering: Do Couples Adapt to Changing Employment Patterns*, Working Papers of the ESRC Research Centre on Micro-Social Change, No. 97–8.

—— Michael Godwin, and Sally Jones (1994), 'The Domestic Labour Revolution: A Process of Lagged Adaptation?' in Michael Anderson, Frank Bechhofer, and Jonathan Gershuny (eds.), *The Social and Political Economy of the Household*, Oxford: Oxford University Press: 151–97.

—— and Sally Jones (1987), 'Changing Use of Time: Britain 1961 to 1984', *Sociological Review Monographs* 33: 9–50.

—— Iiris Niemi, Zahari Staikov, and Edmund Wnuk-Lipinski (eds.) (1989), *Time Use Studies World Wide*, Sofia: Socioconsult Ltd.

—— and Oriel Sullivan, (1998), 'The Sociological Uses of Time-Use Diary Analysis', *European Sociological Review* 14(1): 69–85.

Giddens, Anthony (1984), *The Constitution of Society: Outline of the Theory of Structuration*, Cambridge: Polity Press.

Giffen, Robert (1904), 'The Recent Rate of Material Progress in England', in R. Giffen, *Economic Inquiries and Studies*, ii, Bell: 99–144.

Goldschmidt-Clermont, Luisella (1982), *Unpaid Work in the Household: A Review of Economic Evaluation Methods*, Geneva: International Labour Office.

—— and Elisabetta Pagnossin-Aligisakis (1995), *Measures of Unrecorded Economic Activities in Fourteen Countries*, Occasional Paper 20, New York: Human Development Report Office, UNDP.

Goldstein, Harvey (1987), *Multilevel Models in Education and Social Research*, New York: Griffin.

Granovetter, M (1985), 'Economic Action and Social Structure: The Problem of Embeddedness', *American Journal of Sociology* 91(3): 481–510.

Gronau, R (1973), 'The Intrafamily Allocation of Time: The Value of the Housewives' Time', *American Economic Review* 63(4): 634–51.

—— (1977), 'Leisure, Home Production, and Work: The Theory of the Allocation of Time Revisited', *Journal of Political Economy* 85(6): 1099–123.

Guttman, L (1968), 'A General Non-Metric Technique for Finding the Smallest Co-ordinate Space for a Configuration of Points', *Psychometrika* 33: 469–506.

Hägerstrand, Torsten (1978), 'A Note on the Quality of Life-Times', in T. Carlstein, D. Parkes, and N. Thrift (eds.), *Human Activity and Time Geography*, ii, London: Edward Arnold: 122–45.

Harvey, Andrew, and Sigmund Gronmo (1984), 'Social Contact and Use of Time: Canada and Norway', paper presented at the meeting on the International Research Group on Time Budgets and Social Activities, Helsinki, Finland, August.

—— Alexander Szalai, David H. Elliot, Philip J. Stone, and Susan M. Clark (1984), *Time Budget Research: An ISSC Workbook in Comparative Analysis*, Frankfurt: Campus Verlag.

Hawrylyshn, Oli (1971), *Estimating the Value of Housework in Canada*, Ottawa: Statistics Canada.

—— (1976), 'The Value of Household Services: A Survey of Empirical Estimates', *Review of Income and Wealth* 22(2): 101–31.

—— (1977), 'Towards a Definition of Non-Market Activities', *Review of Income and Wealth* 23(1): 79–96.

Heckman, J (1979), 'Sample Selection Bias as a Specification Error', *Econometrica* 47: 153–61.

Hirsch, Fred (1977), *Social Limits to Growth*, London: Routledge & Kegan Paul.

Hochschild, Arlie (1989), *The Second Shift: Working Parents and the Revolution at Home*, London: Piatkus.

—— (1997), *The Time Bind: When Work Becomes Home and Home Becomes Work*, New York: Metropolitan Books.

Hoffmann, E. (1981), 'Accounting for Time on Labour Force Surveys', Paper prepared for 1980 meeting as the OECD Working Party on Employment and Unemployment Statistics, *Bulletin of Labour Statistics* 1981(1), Geneva: ILO.

Huizinga, Johan (1966), *Homo Ludens: A Study of the Play-Element in Culture*, Boston Mass.: Beacon Press (originally published 1950).

International Labour Organization (1960–95), *Yearbooks*, Geneva: ILO.

Istituto Nazionale di Statistica (ISTAT) (1993), *Indagine Multiscopo Sulle Famiglie Anni 1987–91: 4 L'Uso del Tempo in Italia*, Roma.

Jahoda, Marie, Paul F. Lazarsfeld and Hans Zeisel (1972), *Marienthal: The Sociology of an Unemployed Community*, London: Tavistock Publications.

Jenkins, S. P., and N. C. O'Leary (1997), 'Gender Differentials in Domestic Work, Market Work and Total Work Time: UK Time Budget Survey Evidence for 1974/5 and 1987', *Scottish Journal of Political Economy* 44(2): 153–64.

Jones, D. Caradog (1934), *The Social Survey of Merseyside*, i, ii, and iii, Liverpool: University of Liverpool Press.

Joyce, James (1982), *Ulysses*, London: Penguin Books (originally published 1921).

Juster, F. Thomas, and Frank P. Stafford (eds.) (1985), *Time, Goods, and Well-Being*, Ann Arbor: University of Michigan.

——— (1991), 'The Allocation of Time: Empirical Findings, Behavioral Models, and Problems of Measurement', *Journal of Economic Literature* 29: 471–522.

Khan, Herman, William Brown, and Leon Martel (1976), *The Next 200 Years: A Scenario for America and the World*, New York: William Morrow & Co.

—— and Anthony J. Wiener (1967), *The Year 2000: A Framework for Speculation on the Next Thirty-Three Years*, New York: Macmillan Press.

Keynes, John Maynard (1936), *The General Theory of Employment, Interest and Money*, London: Macmillan.

—— (1972), 'Economic Prospects for Our Grandchildren', in *Essays in Persuasion: The Collected Writings of John Maynard Keynes*, ix, London: Macmillan Press (originally published 1928): 321–32.

Knudsen, K (1989), 'Shorter Working Hours, Lower Retirement Age or Longer Vacations: Ambivalence in Public Attitudes on Alternative Working-Time Reforms in Norway', *Acta Sociologica* 32(4): 375–87.

Kooreman, P., and A. Kapteyn (1990a), 'On the Empirical Implementation of Some Game Theoretic Models of Household Labour-Supply', *Journal of Human Resources* 24(4): 584–98.

——— (1990b), 'Quantity Rationing and Concavity in a Flexible Household Labour Supply Model', *Review of Economic Statistics* 72(1): 55–62.

——— (1992), 'Household Labour Supply—What Kind of Data Can Tell Us How Many Decision Makers There Are?', *European Economic Review* 36(3–7): 365–71.

Kravis, Irving B., Robert Summers, and Alan Heston, with Alicia R. Civitello (1982), *World Product and Income: International Comparisons of Real Gross Product*, Baltimore: Johns Hopkins University Press for the Statistical Office of the United Nations and the World Bank.

Lévy-Garboua, Louis (ed.) (1979), *Sociological Economics*, London: Sage Publications.

Linder, Steffan (1970), *The Harried Leisure Class*, New York: Columbia University Press.

Lundberg, George A., Mirra Komarovsky, and Alice Mary McInerny (1934), *Leisure: A Suburban Study*, New York: Columbia University Press.

Lynd, Robert S., and Helen Merrell Lynd (1937), *Middletown in Transition*, New York: Harcourt, Brace & World.

Manchester, J., and D. Stapleton (1991), 'On Measuring the Progress of Women's Quest for Economic Equality', *Journal of Human Resources* 26(3): 562–80.

Meissner, M., E. W. Humphries, S. M. Meis, and W. J. Scheu (1975), 'No Exit for Wives: Sexual Division of Labour and the Cumulation of Household Demands', *Canadian Review of Sociology and Anthropology* 12: 424–39.

Minge-Klevana, Wanda (1980), 'Does Labor Time Decrease with Industrialisation?', *Current Anthropology* 21(3): 279–98.

NHK (1971), *How Do People Spend Their Time in Japan,* Tokyo: NHK Public Opinion Research Institute.

—— (1991), *Japanese Time Use,* Tokyo: NHK Public Opinion Research Division.

Niemi, Iiris (1983), *Time Use Study in Finland,* Finland: Central Statistical Office.

—— (ed.) (1995), *Time Use of Women in Europe and North America,* Geneva: United Nations.

OECD (1997), *OECD Framework for the Measurement of Unrecorded Economic Activities in Transition Economies,* OECD/GD/(97): 177, Paris.

Owen, John D. (1988), 'Work-Time Reduction in the U.S. and Western Europe', *Monthly Labour Review* 111: 41–5.

—— (1989), *Reduced Work Hours: Cure for Unemployment or Economic Burden?,* Baltimore: Johns Hopkins University Press.

Pember-Reeves, Maud (1913), *Round About a Pound a Week,* London: Virago (originally published 1913).

Przeworski, Adam, and Henry Teune (1982), *The Logic of Comparative Social Inquiry,* Malabar, Florida: R. E. Krieger (originally published 1970).

Quesnay, François (1798), *Tableau Oeconomique,* republished 1894, London: Royal Economic Society, British Economic Association.

Robinson, John, V. Andreyenkov, and V. Patrushov (1989), *The Rhythm of Everyday Life: How Soviet and American Citizens Spend Time,* Boulder, Colo.: Westview Press.

Robinson, John P., and Philip E. Converse (1972), 'Social Change Reflected in the Use of Time', in A. Campbell and P. Converse (eds.), *The Human Meaning of Social Change,* New York: Russell Sage Foundation: 17–86.

—— and Geoffrey Godbey (1997), *Time for Life: The Surprising Ways Americans Use Their Time,* University Park: Pennsylvania State Press.

Rostow, Walt Whitman (1990), *The Stages of Economic Growth: A Non-Communist Manifesto,* 3rd edn., Cambridge: Cambridge University Press, (1st edn. published 1960).

Rydenstam, Klas, and Anders Wadeskog (1998), *Evaluation of the European Time Use Pilot Survey,* Luxembourg: Eurostat: Doc E2/TUS/5/98.

Sahlins, Marshall (1972), *Stone Age Economics,* Chicago: Aldine-Atherton.

Schmidt, Erik Ib, Eszter Kormendi, Gunnar Vibe Mogensen, and Jon Pedersen (1989), *24 Timer I,* Denmark: Dognet Herning.

Schor, Juliet (1993), *The Overworked American: The Unexpected Decline of Leisure,* New York: Basic Books.

Simon, Herbert (1957), *Models of Man: Social & Rational; Mathematical Essays on Rational Human Behaviour in Social Settings,* New York: Wiley.

Smith, Adam (1910), *An Inquiry into the Nature and Causes of the Wealth of Nations,* London: J. M. Dent & Sons.

Sorokin, Pitrim A., and Clarence Q. Berger (1939), *Time Budgets of Human Behaviour,* Cambridge, Mass.: Harvard University Press.

Sullivan, Oriel (1997), 'Time Waits for No (Wo)man: An Investigation of the Gendered Experience of Domestic Time', *Sociology* 31(2): 221–40.

Summers, Robert, and Alan Heston (1988), 'A New Set of International Comparisons of Real Product and Price Levels: Estimates for 130 Countries 1950–1985', *Review of Income and Wealth* 34(1): 1–25.

Statistisk Sentralbyra (1992), *The Time Budget Surveys 1970–90*, Oslo: Statistisk Sentralbyra.

Szalai, Alexander (ed.) (1972), *The Use of Time*, The Hague: Mouton.

Thompson, Edward Palmer (1967), 'Time, Work-Discipline and Industrial Capitalism: Past and Present', 38: 56–97; repr. in M. W. Flinn and T. C. Smout (eds.) (1974), *Essays in Social History*, Oxford: Clarendon Press: 39–77.

Ujimoto, K. Victor (1990), 'Time-Budget Methodology for Research on Aging', *Social Indicators Research* 23: 381–93.

Vanek, Joanne (1974), 'Time Spent in Housework', *Scientific American* 11: 116–20.

—— (1978), 'Household Technology and Social Status: Rising Living Standards and Status and Residence Differences in Housework', *Technology and Culture* 19: 361–75.

Veblen, Thorstein (1953), *The Theory of the Leisure Class*, New York: New York American Library (originally published 1899).

Ward, Anna, Jeanne Gregory, and Nira Yuval-Davis (eds.) (1992), *Women and Citizenship in Europe: Borders, Rights and Duties*, London: Trentham Books.

Wilensky, Harold L (1961), 'The Uneven Distribution of Leisure: The Impact of Economic Growth on Free Time', *Social Problems* 9 (Summer).

Wrong, Dennis Hume (1961), 'Oversocialized Conception of Man in Modern Sociology', *American Sociological Review* 26: 183–93.

Young, Michael, and Peter Willmott (1973), *The Symmetrical Family*, London: Routledge & Kegan Paul.

Zuzanek, Jiri (1980), *Work and Leisure in the Soviet Union: A Time Budget Analysis*, New York: Praeger.

Index

age, and childcare 193; and domestic work 186; and leisure 202, 207; and paid work time 171, 173; of study participants 272–3; in time-diary surveys 109; and time-use 148–9
aggregate day 81–2
Aglietta, M., *Theory of Capitalist Regulation* 39, 82
agricultural work 51–2, 108–9
altruism, and work-sharing 243
Andorka, Rudolf, Istvan Harcsa, and Iiris Niemi 108
Andrews, F., J. Morgan, and J. Sonquist 160
Arcadia, time allocation on 22–7
As, Dagfinn 142
attribution process 226
Australia, core domestic work 188; educational variance 149; income variables 150; leisure patterns 204, 213; paid work time 174; personal care patterns 217; television and radio use 209; time-use 163; unpaid work 195
Austria, time-diary surveys 278

background services 223, 227
BBC Audience Research Department, time-budget study 14–15, 258–66
Becker, G. 52, 73, 79, 82, 93, 94, 95, 206, 210, 222, 231, 233
behavioural change, and structural change 117–31
Belgium, core domestic work 188; educational variance 149; leisure patterns 204, 213; paid work time 174; personal care patterns 217; television and radio use 209; time-use 163; unpaid work 195

benefits, non-monetary 9
Berk, Sarah 183, 190
Bourdieu, Pierre 50, 82, 84, 145, 207, 210
Bulgaria, core domestic work 188; educational variance 149; income variables 150; leisure patterns 204, 213; paid work time 162, 163, 174; personal care patterns 217, 218; television and radio use 209; time-use 163; unpaid work 192, 195

Canada, cross-time comparisons of change 108; domestic work 131, 187; educational variance 149, 177; income variables 150; interactive effects 157; leisure patterns 203, 212; paid work time 63, 122, 172, 173; personal care patterns 216; television and radio use 208; time-use 143, 163; unpaid work 194
capital, cultural 50, 85, 86–7, 119; defined 85, 87–8; educational 85, 86–7; social and material 85, 87, 145; *see also* human capital
car maintenance 197
Carlstein, Tommy and Nigel Thrift 82
census findings 1
chains of provision 11, 17–18, 21, 35–6, 190, 222; individual 233; innovations in 27; and shopping patterns 200
childcare 114, 180, 192–6; age effects 193; and education level 193, 196; and employment status 192–3; and family status 193; historical change 199–200; increased time 126, 129; public provision 247

children, effect on time-use 148–9; *see also* childcare; family status
Clark, Colin 2
class, changing patterns 72–5; and consumption 30–2; and education 32; relative size of 239–40, 241; and unpaid work 65–8
class convergence 5, 7, 30–2
Coleman, James 78; *Introduction to Mathematical Sociology* 161
congestion, growth in money income and 231
'consequential' events 118–19
conservation of the day 164
consumption, and accumulation of human capital 36; balance with work time 80–1; as category of time use 1; common model of 10; distinction from work 28–9; and economic development 21, 83; and employment 4; high-value-added 29; increased 73; interaction between individuals 99–100; labour required for 96–7; marginal propensity 39; 'potlatch' model 70–1; and production 27; ratio of labour to 34; regulation of 39–40; and social differentiation 31–2, 47; social relations of 30; time requirements 8
consumption efficiency 240
consumption zones 233
conversations, as leisure 211
Converse, Philip 137
cooking 180, 189–90
correlation, spurious 138
Crichton, Michael, *Jurassic Park* 65
cultural capital 50, 85, 86–7, 119
cultural facilities, public provision 246–7
Czechoslovakia, core domestic work 188; educational variance 149; leisure patterns 169–70, 204, 213; paid work time 174; personal care patterns 217; television and

radio use 209; time-use 163; unpaid work 195

Denmark, domestic work 131, 187; income variables 150; interactive effects 157; intertemporal time-use comparisons 108; leisure patterns 203, 207, 212; paid work time 172; personal care patterns 216, 218; television and radio use 208; time-diaries 278; time-use 143, 163; unpaid work 194
deskilling 37
diary surveys, *see* time-diary surveys
domestic work, age effects 186; attitudes to 56; by men 8, 69; changes in time allocation 112–17; changing standards 54–5; definition 108–9, 180; and education level 190–2; elasticity 55–6, 128–31, 186–92; gender differences 3, 55, 165–7, 170, 186–7; gender role convergence 128–9; and historical change 54–7, 65–9; increase in 8, 51; negative elasticity 182, 184; reduction in 51, 68–9; simultaneous activities 200; women's responsibility for, *see* dual burden
dual burden 9, 31, 51, 180; diminishing effect 68–9; and historical change 54–7; and 'lagged adaptation' 198–9; research 148
Dumazedier, Joffre, *Towards a Society of Leisure* 60

Eastern Europe, domestic work in 198; men's unpaid work 114–16; political model 43; women's employment 111, 144, 169
eating and drinking, at home 211; as leisure 206–7
economic development, and changes in occupational groupings 83; and changes in work and leisure time 109–17; and consumption 21; feudal model 70; horizontal and

vertical shifts 26; and hours of work 51–3; and leisure preference 61–4; reliance on leisure 134–6; and social differentiation 72; social and economic regulation 39; and technological change 19; and time-scarcity 12; 'trickle down' model 38–9, 40–1, 57; and unpaid work 65–9

economic tables 83

education 147, 281; and childcare 193, 196; and class 32; and consumption 145, 246; and domestic work 190–2; and leisure 210, 215; and paid work 7, 175–80; and personal care 218–19; problems in classifying levels 149–50; and social stratification 175–80; and unpaid work 7

education system, and development of human capital 39

educational capital 85, 86–7

effect parameter analysis 161

Ehrlich, Alma 250

elasticity, estimates of 182–4; leisure 181, 244; sleep 181; of time-use 164, 169; unpaid work 181–6

employment, and consumption patterns 4; and leisure 210

employment contracts, flexible 245–6

employment status, and childcare 192–3; and gender effects 165–7; and shopping 196–7; and time-use 147–8

enjoyment scales 229–30

environmental change, and childcare 199; costs 59

Esping-Anderson, Gosta, *Three Worlds of Welfare Capitalism* 35

estimation of time use, difficulties of 250–2; stylized-estimate method 249–50; thought experiment 249

European Union, social policy 10

Eurostat, time-use survey 108

exports 26, 223, 227

factor analysis 137

'family friendly' policies 56

family status, and childcare 193; and out-of-home leisure 202; and paid work time 171, 173; and time-use 148–9; and women's time-use 169

feminism, influence of 129

Ferguson, Adam 47

Finland, core domestic work 187; cross-time comparisons of change 108; educational variance 149, 177; elasticity of domestic work 184; gender convergence 37; interactive effects 157; leisure patterns 203, 212; paid work 162, 163, 172; personal care patterns 216; reduction in gender differentiation 157; television and radio use 208; time-use 143, 144, 163; unpaid work 106, 194

flexi-time 245

food, exports and imports 227; as want 223, 227

Fourastie, J. 2

France, coefficient of variation 143; core domestic work 187; education and paid work time 176–7; educational variance 149; income variables 150; interactive effects 157; leisure patterns 203, 206, 212; paid work time 172; personal care patterns 216; television and radio use 208; time-use 163; unpaid work 194

fraternity, concept of 248

gardening 108, 180, 192, 197

gender differentiation 31; and attitudes to domestic work 181; changing patterns 72–5; compositional changes in women's employment 178, 180; education and paid work time 178–80; effect of employment and family status 122; and employment status 165–7; estimates of time-use 168; Finland 157; leisure 206–7; paid

gender differentiation (*cont.*)
    work time 172, 174; personal care
    218; and social differentiation
    47; unpaid work 148, 158; work
    elasticity 182, 184–6
gender equality, pressures for 8–9
gender ideologies 56, 120; and
    domestic work 190; in liberal
    market regimes 37; in social
    democratic regimes 36–7;
    traditional 183
gender role convergence 5–6, 31, 73–4,
    117, 199, 220–1; leisure
    activities 207; unpaid work
    201–2; work–leisure balance 133
gender symmetry 148
Germany, core domestic work 188;
    leisure patterns 169, 204, 213;
    paid work time 174; personal care
    patterns 217; political model 43;
    television and radio use 209;
    time-use 163; unpaid work 195;
    work hours 63
Gershuny, Jonathan 54, 71, 198, 258
Gershuny, Jonathan, Iliris Niemi,
    Zahari Staikov, and Edmund
    Wnuk-Lipinski 182
Gershuny, Jonathan, Michael Godwin,
    and Sally Jones 198–9
Gershuny, Jonathan and Oriel
    Sullivan 258
Gershuny, Jonathan and Sally
    Jones 108, 250
Giddens, Anthony 82, 84
Giffen, Robert 1–2
glide-time 245
globalization, as cultural diffusion 10;
    economic 10; technological 9–10
GNP (Gross National Product), and
    time-use 146
Goldschmidt-Clermont, Luisella 106
Goldschmidt-Clermont, Luisella and
    Elisabetta Pagnossin-Aligisakis
    106
gradients, negative 177; reversed
    179–80
Granovetter, M. 92

'great day' of society 24–6, 80, 81
Gronau, R. 82
Guttman, L. 137

habit 79; and activity patterns 90–1
Hadza people (Africa) 52
Hagerstrand, Torsten 82, 84
Harvey, A., A. Szalai, D. Elliott, P.
    Stone, and S. Clark 137
Harvey, A. and S. Gronmo 108, 162
Hawrylyshn, Oil 106, 131
Heckman, J. 161
Hirsch, Fred, *The Social Limits to
    Growth* 50, 57–8, 59, 231, 241
historical change, and behavioural
    change 117–31; in childcare
    199–200; and 'consequential'
    events 118–19; decomposition
    of 121; and dual burden 54–7;
    education and paid work time
    176–7; and elasticity of domestic
    work 54–7, 65–9, 185–6, 189;
    hours of work 51–3; and national
    differences 140; period effects
    146–7, 153; regression analysis
    171; and time-pressure 74–5;
    unpaid work 197–9
hobbies and games 211
Hochschild, Arlie, *The Time Bind* 56,
    183, 190
Hoffmann, E. 253
holidays, number of 178–9
home-based services, as want 223
household panel data 182
household surveys 18, 274
housekeeper paradox 2
housework, *see* domestic work
Huizinga, Johan 61
human capital, aggregate totals 78; and
    microsequential theory 84–7; and
    routine 87
Hungary, coefficient of variation 143,
    144; core domestic work 187;
    educational variance 149;
    interactive effects 157; leisure
    patterns 202, 203, 210, 212; paid
    work time 122, 123, 125–6,

145–6, 162, 163, 172; personal care patterns 216; shopping time 129, 197; study of time-compressibility 181–2; television and radio use 208; time-diaries 274–5; time-use 163; unpaid work 192, 194

'imbeddedness' of social change 92
imports 26, 227
income, as consequence of human capital 175; and consumption patterns 145; in Eastern European countries 43–4; levels 281; in liberal market regimes 43; marginal utility 8, 61; in social democratic regimes 43–4; and social stratification 150, 175–6; and status 150; and technological change 240; and time allocation 110–12; and time-use 150
information technology 242; home use 3
International Labour Organization (ILO), *Yearbooks* 64, 105, 109
International Standard Classification of Occupations 18
Israel, core domestic work 188; educational variance 149; leisure patterns 204, 213; paid work time 174; personal care patterns 217; television and radio use 209; time-use 163; unpaid work 195
Italy, core domestic work 188; educational variance 149; leisure patterns 204, 213; paid work time 174; personal care patterns 217; television and radio use 209; time-diaries 277; time-use 163; unpaid work 195

Jahoda, Marie, Paul Lazarsfeld, and Hans Zeisel 59
Japan, attitudes to domestic work 56; intertemporal time-use comparisons 108; 'time affluence' 57; time-diaries 276

Jenkins, S. P. and N. C. O'Leary 121, 162
Jones, D. Caradog, *Social Survey of Merseyside* (1930) 106
Joyce, James, *Ulysses* 16–17, 45
Juster, F. Thomas and Frank Stafford 52, 106, 229

Kahn, Herman 61
Keynes, J. M., General Theory 39; 'The Future Possibilities for Our Grandchildren' 58–9
'knowledge workers' 73
Kooreman, P. and A. Kapteyn 82

leisure, age effects 202, 207; balance with work 131–6; categories 205–7, 207, 211, 214; and citizenship 60; congestion of 51, 57–8; and economic development 134–6, 242; and educational level 210, 215; elasticity 181; and employment status 210; and family status 202; future of 135–6; at home 207–11; and liberty 60; as non-productive use of time 48; out-of-home 202–7, 223, 242; preferences 8; progress increasing 46–7; recorded in time-diaries 262–3; as social construct 49; and social differentiation 9, 12, 60, 69–70, 72; subjective value 49; time limits 73; in traditional societies 57; and transport policy 246–7
liberal market regimes 12, 20, 35, 37–45, 247–8
life-stage effects 12
Linder, Staffan, *The Harried Leisure Class* 57, 134, 240, 241
logic of progress, *see* modernization
Lundberg, George, Mirra Komarovsky, and Alice McInerny 106
luxury services 231
Lynd, Robert and Helen Lynd, Middletown survey 60, 67

macro-theory 77, 79–80, 100, 102–4; balancing time 97–100; social constraints 100–2

macroconstraints 12–13

macrotime budgeting constraint 27

Manchester, J. and D. Stapleton 162

manufacturing activities 33

manufacturing industry, work hours 64

mapping, time-use 142

marginal utility of income 8

Mass Observation Archive 54

material economy 83–4

media policy, public regulation 247

Meissner, M., E. Humphries, S. Meis, and W. Scheu 55

micro-aggregate theory 77, 78–9; time allocation 93–7

microconstraints 12, 27, 235

microsequential theory 77, 81, 82, 100–2; choice as scheduling 90–1; and human capital 84–7; role of habit 90–1; 'routine' and social change 91–3; sequential events 85–6; time geography 88–90

military activities 70

Minge-Klevana, Wanda 51–2, 72, 215

models of variance, additive 155, 156, 157–9, 167; fully-saturated 155, 156; interactive effects 152–7; linear regression 152–4; macrovariables 159; microvariables 159; P-T effects 150–2, 154–5; semi-saturated 153, 155–6, 158–9; undersaturated 162

modernization 28–32, 42–5; definition 33; increasing work and leisure 46–7; and public policy 243–7; and time use 242

money, waste of 49

money economy, less time to 229

Multinational Longitudinal Time-Budget Archive 108

Multinational Time-Use Study (MTUS) 270–2

multiples classification analysis (MCA) 151, 160–1, 162, 167

narratives, 'telling the day' 80, 253–5

National Accounts 2, 13, 222, 229; extensions to 4

national convergence 5, 220–1; work-leisure balance 133

national differences 137–40; additive category 139; composition of population 138–9; and historical change 140; interactions with other variables 139–40; and national factors 138–9; paid work time 172, 174

national effects 151

National Food Survey 229

national representativeness, techniques for 141

national samples, variation in size 141

necessary time, *see* personal care

negative gradient hypothesis 177

Netherlands, childcare by men 192; coefficient of variation 143–4; core domestic work 187; educational variance 149, 177; elasticity of domestic work 182; income variables 150; interactive effects 157; leisure patterns 203, 212; paid work time 63, 123, 145–6, 172; personal care patterns 216; television and radio use 208; time-diary surveys 161, 255, 277, 278, 280, 282; time-use 163; unpaid work 106, 194

Niemi, Iiris 108, 252

norms, behaviour attached to 120; changes in 92; development of 81

Norway, core domestic work 187; cross-time comparisons of change 108; educational variance 149; interactive effects 157; intertemporal time-use comparisons 108; leisure patterns 203, 212; paid work time 63–4, 172; personal care patterns 216; television and radio use 208; time-use 143, 163; unpaid work 194

nutrition 24, 229

obligatory time, *see* unpaid work time
odd jobs 180, 197
Owen, John 53

paid work 142; age and 171, 173; as
    category of time use 1; changes in
    time allocation 110–12, 116–17;
    differentiation of trends 149; and
    educational level 7; and elasticity
    of time-use 164; empirical
    evidence 105; and family status
    171, 173; gender differences
    170, 172, 174; increase in
    high-skill 229, 242; individual
    233; length of working day 179;
    national effects 172, 174; ratio
    to commodity price 79; recorded
    in time-diaries 263; reduction
    in hours 61–4; and social
    differentiation 175–80; structural
    and behavioural change 122–6;
    variables 162–3; women's rates
    of 123–5
parental leave 245
Pareto improvements 232, 235–6, 239
Peking Declaration of the World
    Congress of Women (1995) 4
Pember-Reeves, M. 106
personal care 116, 142, 211–19,
    compression of sleep time 219;
    and education level 218–19;
    gender differences 218; recorded
    in time-diaries 263; *see also* sleep
pets, care of 180
physiocratic model of time allocation
    82–4
Poland, core domestic work 188;
    educational variance 149; leisure
    patterns 170, 204, 213; paid work
    162, 163, 174; personal care
    patterns 217; television and radio
    use 209; time-use 163; unpaid
    work 195
politics of progress 42–5
pre-industrial societies 23
primitive societies 47, 51–2, 61
process benefits 229

production, and consumption 27;
    increasing efficiency of 236–41;
    regulation of 39
productivity, increased efficiency 24;
    measurement of 233
progress, *see* modernization
projects 92–3; and routine 87
Przeworski, Adam and Henry
    Teune 138–40, 141, 150–2,
    154–5
public policy, broadcast media 247;
    care of children and elderly 247;
    cultural provision 246–7; and
    humane modernization 243–7;
    regulation of working hours
    245–6

Quesnay, Francois 82–3
questionnaires, and diary reports
    267–8; limitations 250–3
queuing 129, 192, 197

rational choice, and time-allocation
    78–9
reading, as leisure 211
recursiveness 76, 77, 81–2, 101
redistribution 248
regulation, of consumption 39–40;
    distinguished from central
    planning 40; of production 39;
    significance of 40
retirement, flexible arrangements
    for 245
Robinson, John and Geoffrey
    Godbey 108, 277, 285
Robinson, John and Jonathan Gershuny
    253
Robinson, John and Philip Converse
    108, 142, 198
Robinson, John, V. Andreyenkov, and V.
    Patrushov 108, 142, 249
Rostow, Walt 2, 4
routine, and human capital 87; and
    projects 87; and social change
    91–3
Russia, cross-time comparisons of
    change 108

Sahlin, Marshall, *Stone Age Economics* 52
sampling differences 285–6
satisfaction, levels of 229; luxury services 231; marginal rates 234–5; time necessary for 79
scheduling, constraints on 90–1, 244–6
Schmidt, Erik, Eszter Kormendi, Gunnar Vibe Morgensen, and Jon Pedersen 108
Schor, Juliet 53
'self-servicing' 30, 33, 71
sequences 244; adjustments to 80–1; recall of 252; *see also* microsequential theory
sequential accounts 81–2
servants 36, 66–7, 103, 198, 247–8
service class 20, 41
service sector 1–2, 20, 41
services, alternative service economies 35–42; background 223, 227; high-value-added 34–5, 248; household 247; low-value-added 34, 37, 72; luxury 231; role in modern societies 33; traditional 34, 248
shelter, modes of provision 103–4; as want 223, 227
shift-share analysis 120–2, 171
shopping 180, 196–7; 'American' patterns 200–1; by Internet 3; estimation of time use 250; externalization of costs 231; increase in time 126, 129, 242; as leisure 200–1; and queuing time 129, 197; substitution of unpaid services for paid 230–1; as want 223
Simon, Herbert, *Models of Man* 138, 139
simultaneous activities 200, 256–8, 279–80
sleep 116, 227; compression of 219; constancy of 5; elasticity 181; variations in 144–5; as want 223, 227; *see also* personal care
smallest space analysis 137

Smith, Adam 2, 223; *The Wealth of Nations* 83
social accounting 226–9
social capital 85, 87, 145
social democratic regimes 12, 20, 35–7, 38–45, gender roles 36–7; virtuous circle of income 36
social differentiation, *see* education; income; social status
social final product 226
social innovation, and changes in time-allocation 103–4
social policy, and development of human capital 39; and free market 10; and time-use 10–11
social status, and consumption 31–2, 47; convergence 73; and gender 47; and leisure 12, 60, 69–70; and occupation 32; stratification and differentiation 29–32
Sorokin, Pitirim and Clarence Berger 106
Spain, work hours 63
Standard Industrial Classification 18
status convergence 220–1
structural change 117; *see also* historical change
study leave 245
Sullivan, Oriel 230
Summers, Robert and Alan Heston 110
surplus, determined by technology 72–3; methods of distribution 70–2
Sweden, core domestic work 188; educational variance 149; elasticity of domestic work 184; income variables 150; leisure patterns 204, 213; paid work 162, 163, 174; personal care patterns 217; television and radio use 209; 'time affluence' 57; time-use 163; unpaid work 195
Szalai, Alexander, Multinational Comparative Time-Budget Research Project 108, 197–8, 278,

279; *The Use of Time* 14, 137, 169, 181, 210, 218, 275

technological change, determining surplus 72–3; and economic development 19; and efficiency of paid work 230, 236–40, 241; globalization 9–10; and income 240; influence of 27; labour-saving 3, 30, 54–6, 66–8, 103, 128, 181, 190, 197–8, 240; and patterns of time-allocation 103–4; and unpaid work 240–1

television and radio, high-value-added skills 34–5; recorded in time-diaries 263, 264

Third Way 44

Thompson, E.P. 52

'time affluence' 57

time allocation, micro-aggregate theory 93–7; physiocratic model 82–4

'time famine' 57

time geography, and microsequential theory 88–90

time-budget constraint 79

time-diary surveys, advantages 18, 251; age restrictions 109; classificatory variables 280–1; comparison of different methodologies 285–6; construction 255–69; development of 106; diary period 274–5; *ex post* weighting 281–5; Finland 280; interviewers and self-completion 276–7; and literacy levels 276–7; material omitted 255–8; methodology 249–69; minimum time intervals 275–6; Netherlands 280, 282; non-response bias 255, 266–8, 281–2; 'open' and 'closed' styles 255–7; over- and under-estimation 148; population limits 272–4; practical difficulties 107–8; precoded categories 277–9; primary and secondary activities 258–66, 279–80; reliability

106–7; single day 143–4, 161; USA 280; use of natural language 277–8; use of 14–15; whole-week 143–4, 161

time-pressure 3; and historical change 74–5; personal experiences 74

time-scarcity, and economic development 12

time-use, estimation of 78, 80

time-use regimes 11–12; liberal market 12, 20, 35, 37–45, 247–8; social democratic 12, 20, 35–7, 38–45

transport policy 2–3; and leisure consumption 246–7; and time geography 88

travel, as want 223

trickle-down theory 38–9, 40–1, 57

two-good, two-class model 236–8

Ujimoto, K. Victor 280

UK, changes in time-use 143–4, 163, 223–41; childcare by men 192; domestic work hours 131, 198; educational variance 149, 176–7; elasticity of domestic work 182, 184, 187; income variables 150; interactive effects 157; intertemporal time-use comparisons 108; leisure patterns 203, 207, 212; paid work time 53, 63, 122, 123, 172; personal care patterns 216; political model 43; television and radio use 208; time-diary surveys 161, 192, 223, 278, 282; unpaid work 194

unemployment 118, 147, 178, 179; psychological effects 59

unpaid work 142, 180–202; attitudes to 181; by men 73; as category of time use 1; changes in time allocation 112–17; and class 65–8; definition 105–6, 108–9; and economic development 65–9; and educational level 7; elasticity 181–6; and employment status 147; gender convergence 201–2;

unpaid work (*cont.*)
    gender differentiation 158, 171;
    historical change 197–9; increase
    in 8, 229; inelasticity 68–9;
    'lagged adaptation' model 198–9;
    overall changes 201–2; recorded
    in time-diaries 261–2, 263–4;
    reduction in 73–4; in social
    democratic regimes 36–7;
    structural and behavioural
    change 126–31; women's
    concentration in 9; *see also*
    childcare; cooking; domestic
    work; odd jobs; shopping
USA, coefficient of variation 143;
    cross-time comparisons of
    change 108, 163; domestic work
    hours 54–5, 187, 198; educational
    variance 149, 177; elasticity of
    domestic work 184; hours of
    work 53; income variables 150;
    interactive effects 157;
    intertemporal time-use
    comparisons 108; leisure patterns
    202, 203, 206, 212; methodology
    202; paid work time 63, 122, 123,
    172, 173; personal care patterns
    216; shopping in 197; television
    and radio use 208; 'time famine'
    57; time-diaries 275; unpaid work
    194
utility, marginal 239
utility functions 95, 233, 234–5

Vanek, Joanne 54–5, 65, 67, 180, 198
variables, country effects 151–2, 154–7;
    macro-characteristics 145–7;
    microlevel 145, 147–9; national
    145–6
variance, decomposition of 141, 150–9;
    models of 137–40
variation, coefficients of 143–5; in
    leisure categories 149

Veblen, Thorsten 57, 60, 69–70, 72, 73,
    76, 107, 176; *Theory of the Leisure
    Class* 47–50
visiting, as leisure 207

wage rates 235–6
wants, basic 11, 73, 230, 238–9;
    categories of 223; and final output
    categories 226; increasing
    sophistication 229; luxury 11,
    73, 238–9; relationship with
    paid work 223, 226–9;
    satisfaction levels 229; saturation
    of 238–9
waste, of money 49; of time 49–50
welfare, reduced by growth in money
    income 231; and social change
    222; and time-use 231–6
Wilensky, Harold 52, 53
women's employment, Eastern Europe
    144
work, definition of 131; providing
    access to leisure class 50; as
    social construct 49; *see also*
    domestic work; paid work;
    unpaid work
work-sharing 243–4
work-time regime 244–6
working day, length of 179
Wrong, Dennis 92

Young, Michael and Peter Willmott,
    The Symmetrical Family 53, 55–6,
    107, 180
Yugoslavia, core domestic work 188;
    educational variance 149; leisure
    patterns 169–70, 204, 213; paid
    work time 174; personal care
    patterns 217; time-use 163;
    unpaid work 195

Zuzanek, Jiri 106

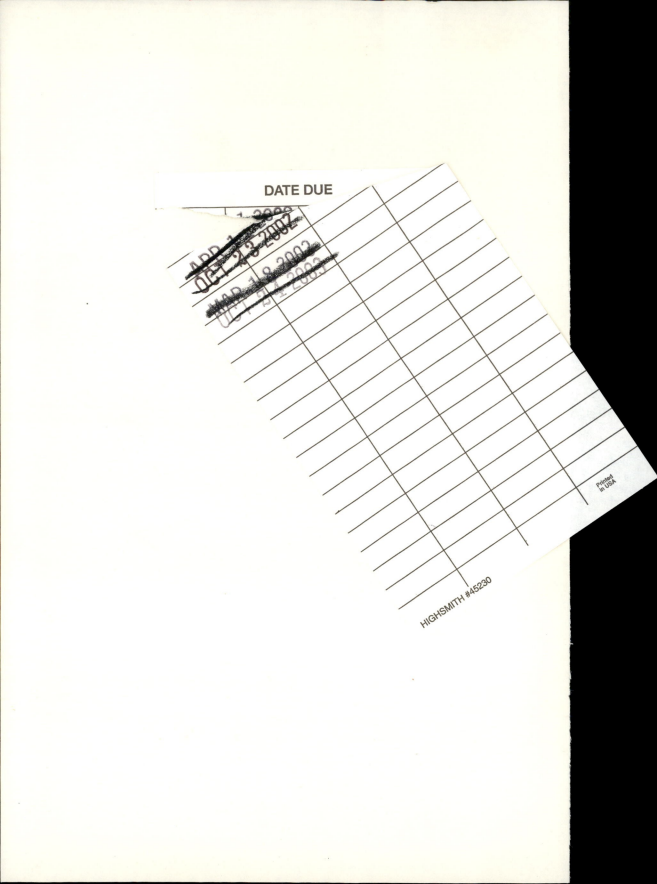

DATE DUE

APR 1 8 2002
OCT 1 8 2002
MAR 1 8 2002
OCT 1 8 2002

Printed
in USA